MUSIC FOR A LONG WHILE

MUSIC FOR A LONG WHILE

FRANCIS JACKSON

Published by Francis Alan Jackson

A CIP catalogue record for this book is available from the British Library.

ISBN 978-0-9576722-0-8

Book and cover design by Clare Brayshaw
Cover photo © Graham Hermon

Prepared and printed by:

York Publishing Services Ltd
64 Hallfield Road
Layerthorpe
York YO31 7ZQ

Tel: 01904 431213

Website: www.yps-publishing.co.uk

For Priscilla

CONTENTS

FOREWORD

Every Christmas Eve since I can remember Christmas started with the service of nine lessons and carols in York Minster. Even the tree was hidden behind locked doors until we returned home – excited and looking forward to what lay ahead!

Thus the Minster and its music – in particular the Organ – has always been a significant part of my life.

Little did I know as a child just how significant that was to be. That it was to be part of a life changing experience.

I had often seen Francis Jackson leading the choir or heard him playing the organ. Little did I realise how we were to meet or how momentous our friendship was to become!

As each year passes – for me music endures as a life consuming passion with the Organ remaining the focus of that emotion.

My thanks go to Francis for making a memorable day perfect for thousands of people – for the Widor Toccata and last but not least for the time and effort that he put into the preparation necessary for staging a ceremony never to be forgotten. Particularly in Yorkshire!

Katharine Kent

PREFACE

The idea of writing this book took serious form in 1974 having been in my mind for several years. The inspiration to bring it to fruition arose from my involvement with Sir Edward Bairstow's biography, *Blessed City*. My sources have been a mixture of diary entries, letters home from the war and recital tours, notes and accounts of special events and press reports, together with my own recollections. The aim has been to set down a record of a long and active life, graced with many blessings, which I hope may be of some interest to the readers of the wonders that I have undergone.

As to finding a title, there were many suggestions one of which was 'Perfectly Frank'. Though in a way applicable this was quite properly thought not entirely suitable. Then at length there came to mind the 78rpm recording by Alfred Deller of Purcell's *Music for a while* (... shall all my cares beguile). Considering a lifelong occupation with music – something like 85 years – perhaps a slight adaptation of Purcell's title is permissible. My long while cannot be a record, but it has certainly been a complete joy and privilege.

FAJ
East Acklam
2013

FIRST DECADE

My musical gifts were discovered early, and to whoever's house I was taken, I was sure to be asked to play the piano. I didn't always enjoy this, and very often the company talked throughout my efforts. I don't remember my very first lessons – the unprofessional ones which Mother must have given me, though they were probably merely answers to my questions, or showing me which note to start on and which finger. Our big upright piano, in medium walnut with several medals portrayed as proof of its excellence, was in the front room of our house at 8 Belmont Terrace, later re-christened 26 Horsemarket Road, in Malton, North Yorkshire. This piano had been Grandfather Suddaby's, at the Crown Hotel in the town. It had the name 'Smith Holey, Gillygate, York' on it, but he was the agent: the piano was made in Germany.

There was a mahogany whatnot at the treble end containing the music and, on the top shelf, the gramophone. This was the more or less portable Decca that my father had won in the raffle when his mess in France was disbanded at the armistice. It was cubical, in two equal halves, and the horn was a bowl in the upper. The noise from the soundbox was transmitted along an arm, and then this became gradually wider until it curved over and ended within an inch or two of the centre of the bowl. The sound was magnified finally by the copper-coloured bowl. The tone-arm with the soundbox on the end was held up by a clip inside the lid when not in use.

There were a number of records that came with the gramophone, mostly HMV (His Master's Voice) black label entitled 'Disque pour Gramophone' and they were mostly piano solos by Wilhelm Backhouse (or Backhaus more likely). The one I remember best was *La Campanella* of Liszt, and there were times when the top notes ran quite out of the hearing area – not so much the hearing as the recording area. All that came through was the impact of the hammers, not the pitch of the notes. Another, with a light blue Columbia label, had the minuet from Beethoven's *Septet*, the start of which I was very mystified to find later in another key in one of his piano sonatas. There was also one that I liked very much called *Opium Smoke* which I have never come across since. The march *Blaze Away* was a great favourite, and *The Great Little Army* too.

From my uncles Willy and Bobby and Aunt Adelaide at my Grandfather Suddaby's hotel, the Crown in Wheelgate, we borrowed some popular items like *Shufflin' Along* and *The Shores of Minnetonka* which were attractive at the time. They also had Cousin Elsie Suddaby's first recording, a ten-inch, dark-green label HMV recording of Purcell's *Hark the echoing air* and *When I am laid in earth*. She and my mother were related since their respective fathers (both named William Suddaby) were first cousins. By this means I learned the meaning of 'once removed' as applied to cousins. There was great pride as we gathered round their more imposing cabinet gramophone (which stood on the floor) to hear her. Elsie later said that I could distinguish the different records by the amount of dirt on the label; which was just about true. The colour, of course, helped as well. Anyway, I had many happy hours listening to music in this way, before radio came along, and enjoyed winding it up and putting on the records.

8 Belmont Terrace was a great big Victorian house, next to my grandfather's garage in which he kept the buses that he hired out as a sideline. The house overlooked the cattle market, but had no garden attached. My parents had the use of one of the gardens further down the terrace in which we kept hens. I went there by myself one day and let the hens out, which was not a popular move. I remember being coaxed into the house at bedtime with the promise of washing – at the kitchen sink – in warm water, standing on a stool; the formula which I always fell for was 'Stooly wash, warm water!' But there was a bathroom. We

soon moved to 4 East Mount which had considerable garden that was a great pleasure to us all. It contained a very tall Robinia tree (or pseudo-acacia) and a great many loganberries growing round the walls.

The musical talent I had been born with was accepted quite naturally and talked about sensibly. I think one or two people, including Paul my brother, were afraid I would become 'swelled-headed' as the expression went; he was determined I shouldn't and always took the opportunity to take me down a peg. It must have appeared to him that I was showing-off sometimes when I really didn't mean to! So I think I became very sensitive to this and tried my best to appear as unremarkable as possible. One of my teachers at the National School, Bertie Leaver (whose brother Noel H Leaver did the meticulous water colour of the Minster and Bootham Bar given to us by Aunt Sybil – and now in Edward's possession (1985) since we left Minster Court) did not mince matters during class and called me 'fancy man' on one occasion which I didn't like. If it was not the music part of me he took exception to, then he must have thought I was giving myself airs. He was musical, playing the piano and singing in a very loud alto, but he was not very popular with us. And at that period soon after the first war with all its grimness and austerity, short back and sides, and with the slump coming on, anything fancy or effeminate was not to be tolerated. Music, to some, was a feminine pursuit, Bach and Beethoven notwithstanding. Not that these two composers held much sway in the world I inhabited then. Church music, our drawing room sessions, and my music lessons, first with Maud Wilson and then with Arthur Ayres ARAM, were my only sources of music, not forgetting the afore-mentioned gramophone of course.

The musical tradition at Malton church was a lively one. It was in a healthy state under Canon AJ Walker who was vicar in my time as a chorister there, in the mid-1920s. He was a vigorous, dynamic, kindly man, greatly loved, who did untold good in the parish and gave us a Christian example to follow. He was musical and trained the choir, leaving Arthur Ayres to play the accompaniments. This worked admirably because Mr Ayres though a fine musician was incapable of taking a rehearsal or of keeping discipline. *Songs of Praise* and *The Psalter Newly Pointed* were new at that time and were introduced, the *Psalter* to both churches and the hymn book to Saint Leonard's where we had services on the second and fourth Sundays of the month. *Ancient and Modern* persisted at Saint Michael's, so the hymns were an interesting mixture. Such were the finances, real or imaginary, that the chant books and psalters had to be taken from one church to the other since no second set was even thought of, and a boy, fairly brawny, was detailed to carry the somewhat weighty suitcase back and forth, which never brought forth a single complaint.

Canon Walker's presence was always stimulating, and his choir practices were quite an event, conducted in the chancel with Mr Ayres at the organ and Eddie Atkinson pumping the bellows when we were at Saint Leonard's. We enjoyed the little Parry in D *Mag* and *Nunc* with the cadential trill just before one of the glorias. Walmisley in D minor was a favourite and we entered into the newly-formed Diocesan Musical Festival in the Minster at its beginnings in 1928 directed by the redoutable Doctor Bairstow ('The rudest man in Yorkshire' according to Canon Walker). I remember spotting a B natural in Byrd's *Faux Bourdon* evening service when we were all gaily singing a B flat. This made quite an impression but to me it meant nothing. It was just there and plain for anyone to see.

My parents had taken part in the concert version of *Merrie England* and other things under Doctor Thomas Ely's direction. He lived fairly locally and had published a composition called the *Spanish Jew's Tale* as I remember – a copy of it (or perhaps two) resided in the ottoman with *Messiah* and a few other like works in which they had taken part. What must have been their first encounter with symphonic music took place at the hands of Canon Walker and his vicarage gramophone. Two favourite pieces were Beethoven's seventh and César Franck's symphony though, now I come to think of it, the former may have been heard a little later when the Cardales succeeded the Walkers in the Vicarage. The allegretto made an impression. I am sure it was the Walkers who had the Franck, and I well remember how thrilled Mum and Dad were with it, particularly the faith motif. About the same time my schoolboy friendship with the rather dashing devil-may-care Jameson Boyd (Jim) Buckley, whose father had been on one of Scott's expeditions, brought me into contact with Schubert's *Unfinished*. This was *his* family's symphony, as Franck's was the Walkers', and I was much affected by its poignancy which I thought had something to do with its incompleteness.

The wireless was beginning, and provided us with various kinds of music. We always used to listen to the London Radio Dance Band under Sidney Firman, Jack Payne, then later, Henry Hall. At first this was the limit of our understanding, but our experience broadened later.

The enjoyment of these early years was, however, always overshadowed by the threat of war and military service. We heard from my father some things about *his* war. There were, in fact, two photographs, framed in passe-partout on either side of the dining room mantelpiece mirror, one of Hill 60 and the other of Hill 62. Both had been laid waste by bombardment, with stumps and skeletons of trees and very little else. It seems strange that such macabre things were given us, rather than things of beauty, to live with. But we regarded them with interest, and I don't think we were aware of the more horrific side of them or of the war in general. For Dad it was a great adventure I think. He was not away for long. He was in a reserved occupation until things became really tough, so I think he saw not much more than a year of active service, and he rose no higher than Second Lieutenant. We had his photograph on the wall, too, in uniform, as well as that of his elder brother Francis, known as Uncle Frank, who died of dysentery during the campaign.

My father was Borough Engineer and Sanitary Inspector as the painted glass upper half of his office door in the Town Hall conveyed. He had been in that line all his life and was, in fact, never employed anywhere else. He was born on 8 April 1888 at Ebberston Vicarage, not far from Scarborough, where my grandfather Francis William was vicar along with the next village of Allerston. He was born in 1835 in Bradford, at Great Horton, the son of a carpenter, I think, called Thomas Jackson. He, my grandfather, was described in a testimonial as 'gentlemanly', and he became an MA of Trinity College Dublin. His wife Sybil Bliss was Irish, which must have accounted for the black hair my father and at any rate one of his sisters possessed. This was Evelyn, the second daughter. Sybil was the eldest, then after Evelyn came Frank (Francis Bliss Altham), Margaret and then William Altham, my father. They were all christened Altham. There was also another son, the eldest of all, who died in infancy.

Grandfather was chaplain on the Madras railway in India during its construction, I believe from 1868 to 1872. According to the silver salver presented by his brother officers, he was married in 1872. On returning to England he was curate at Bolton Percy to Bishop Crosthwaite. The transcription of the registers in his beautiful handwriting is now in the care of York University Borthwick Institute for Archives. Leaving Bolton Percy he took the living of Ebberston near Scarborough, remaining there until his death in 1904. My father was then aged 16 and was at Saint John's School, Leatherhead, of which he always spoke with great affection. One of the masters was Ted Marsh, who was evidently a good friend, and the Head's name was Rutty. From Dad's descriptions and imitations of him, he appeared not to be the most appealing of God's creatures, speaking with a somewhat sarcastic sneer, though this was probably a caricature. Dad's great friend from school days was Alan Coleman, after whom I take my second name. He and his wife Edith came to stay with us often, and I with them at 34 Sandhurst Avenue, Withington, Manchester, during my early teens. It is an odd coincidence that Allan Wicks' father was at Leatherhead at the same time as Dad. I found this out when Allan became my assistant in 1947, and that Dad was known as Black Jack. Allan's father was 90 in the spring of 1977. My father would have been 89.

Aunt Sybil we came to know the best of the three Jackson aunts. She was always coming to see us and we felt we were very much under scrutiny for behaviour and, particularly, for speaking. She held that one could always tell a person's social status by the way he or she spoke, and our vowels were corrected for northern errors: 'rain' had not to have the same vowel sound as 'rare', etc. Our parents appeared to support Aunt Sybil in this, or perhaps it is nearer the truth to say that they didn't seem to disagree. I suppose that Dad had been brought up to do as his eldest sister bade him; though no doubt there was the usual arguing of siblings. Small wonder it was that she never married and, as far as I know, never had any suitors.

So we were brought up to do the right thing and I did my best to please everyone as I became conscious of the refinements I had not previously been aware of. I think this made me self-conscious and set me to worry about things like speaking 'correctly' and being a credit and so forth. Aunt Evelyn (the younger sister of Sybil) of the black hair, was known as Pat because of her Irishness. I knew her the next best after Sybil because I often went to stay at Cranwell village in their old stone house where she lived with uncle Arthur H Lowe. He was the local doctor and Medical Officer of Health. He wore thick glasses and was always rather preoccupied and hard to come to know. He was said not to like children, and did not have any of his own. I must have been the only child to invade the even tenor of their life together. I looked forward to my visits tremendously. Once the buttercups were in full spate in the fields and that was probably at Whitsuntide. I also remember playing about with lavender, honesty and southernwood, which would be in the summer holiday period. I was allowed to do whatever I wanted – which included nothing outrageous – and busied myself around the garden or, when it was wet (which I cannot remember it ever being) in the house, doing I cannot remember what, although the gramophone was a great attraction with its own repertoire of records that was quite a mixture with light pieces cheek by jowl with the odd Wagner item. But I was so happy being given a free rein with no restrictions. Auntie Pat was always quiet and gentle, very erect, and with a twinkle and a quaint tilt of the chin and throw back of the head to denote surprise and interest. Once I upset an ashtray, which at home would have caused somewhat of a scolding. Auntie Pat was upstairs at the time so I called upstairs to tell her about it. Her reply was quite unconcerned. It was suggested that I just 'flick it around the room', and my heart warmed to her.

During one of my stays there, aged about ten years, trouble erupted over a tooth, so I was taken to Grantham to have it extracted. The memorable features of that visit were first, the freezing of the affected part by a jet of some kind from a syringe held some inches away and, second (presumably the kindly dentist having been warned of my musical proclivities), being taken to see his pianola. On this he pedalled away at Chaminade's *Automne* to my delight, initiating my lasting fondness for a piece that probably did not pass muster with my austere and judgmental mentor, Doctor Bairstow.

Even in those days (1929) they had two cars, one an Austin 7 convertible which was supposed to be Auntie Pat's but which I only saw driven by Uncle Arthur. Talking of garden things, it was at Cranwell that I first encountered buddleia, with countless butterflies ecstatically fluttering around, and the strong heady scent that always takes me back to those happy days. Nowadays it seems odd that the sanitary arrangements to do with the attractive old stone house were of the kind necessitating a walk into the garden to a small building of a contemporary date – well shielded among the bushes – which had accommodation for two and was hardly suitable for someone of my uncle's medical standing... Also, Uncle Arthur installed his own electricity generator. It was a Kohler, and it started up when any light switch was turned on in the house or an outhouse. After a few seconds the light would appear and the little machine would be heard from over the yard doing its bit to make life in the country easier and less primitive.

I used to go unaccompanied by train from Malton to Grantham. I was always picked up at Grantham where we would make any calls that were necessary, which included shopping of course since Cranwell, fourteen miles away, was a tiny hamlet with no vans that I knew of to visit, selling things. I now begin to remember the kind of system whereby travelling difficulties were overcome. Mother and Dad would be *au fait* with the habits of various people, and it is quite likely that they knew someone who travelled by train each day to York. Thus it was a simple matter for them to be asked to see me on to the Grantham train at York. Mother herself would not wish to come to York with me for several reasons: money was not plentiful; she was fully occupied looking after the house; and going to York was quite an expedition, by whatever means. Society had not yet become mobile, in fact many years were to elapse before it did – well after the second world war. And we never possessed a family car. The trains were pretty reliable and between York and Malton there were slow ones that took an hour, stopping at all six stations, and expresses that did the twenty-one miles in half that time.

There was also a bus service of a kind, not yet well organised and not completely reliable. It was a tedious and lengthy process until the road was widened and straightened. It is salutary nowadays to see what remains of the old road, near Whitwell, and to gain an idea of conditions for driving when the road was little more than a country lane, when cars were a comparative rarity, and the bus journey was two shillings (10p) return between York and Malton, and one-and-twopence single (6.5p).

Dad was a voracious reader and spent his evenings mostly with books, long evenings from directly after tea (high tea at 5.10 or so) until bedtime. He never succeeded in infecting me with his pleasure in reading, but I remember his reading *Alice in Wonderland* to me. His council meetings and his committees, which on certain evenings prevented his own private reading, were not popular on that account. He was also a freemason. This, however, lapsed latterly, as did his evening visits to the Crown, meeting his friends of the Camalodunum lodge (the Roman name for Malton – as well as for Colchester).

Mother seemed always to be a cheerful person like her mother, attracting similar people in our direction. She and Dad were great supporters of the tennis and cricket clubs, which seemed to be peopled by these enthusiasts. We had long Saturday afternoons 'down at the cricket field', drenched in sunshine while the white-clad figures disported themselves and the periodic applause would break out and tea would be served, Mother being a leading light in the catering. I remember the smell of the sandwiches and the hot tea and the paraffin cooker that boiled the water. Sometimes I was alone and wandered into the wood behind the cricket field, beyond the curling pond, all done in asphalt with a raised path somewhere down the middle. Here through the wood the river ran, the Derwent, on its rather sluggish way, which induced a certain awe in me and made me prefer company. My brother Paul did not seem to be there very much, and I was thrown back on any friend I might have taken with me, or any other child who happened to be there similarly at a loose end. We would borrow a racquet and ball and fool about in the long grass behind the pavilions, annoying those inside the wooden hut which served for the tennis players with banging the ball against it. There was Mrs Hudson, Sadie Taylor, Marie and Nancy Goldie, Miley I'anson, his brother Charlie, Jack Lott who one afternoon hit so many sixes he eventually cracked his bat and had to be given another; and many others whose names I forget. I can remember the smell of the green grass and of the grass decaying in the heap of clippings. These smells always taken me back to 'down the cricket field' and its carefree days.

Sometimes we had musical evenings with Mother doing what seemed a very competent job at the piano, as well as being a soprano with a strong voice. She had learned Grieg, some Chopin, a few pieces popular during her teenage and early twenties, and certainly the first Beethoven Sonata (as the copious tell-tale pencil markings testify) in d'Albert's three-volume edition which I later inherited and used, then handing on to our grandson Sam when he went up to Cambridge in 2005: he, and I suppose all the music students, were required to play through all thirty-two of them 'however badly' since they were considered in many quarters as being the musician's New Testament, the Bach *Forty-Eight* being The Old.

For the musical evenings Dad would put down his book and render *My Old Shako* or the *Floral Dance*. He then got hold of *The Crocodile* which the Vicar had sung at some parish do. There was also *Gretna Green* and I cannot remember whether it was his song or Mother's. Certain other people would come in, too, fellow choir members Ida and Geof Read, Mr and Mrs Ben Hall and their daughter Dorothy. Ben's great piece was *The Windmill*, which we thought appropriate since he was tall and the first words were 'Behold, a giant am I, aloft here in my tower' – Longfellow's words. Then other non-musical evenings took place. We were bidden to go to bed and be good, best clothes were put on – very much the 1920s style to be sure, short skirts and low waists – the silver entrée dishes were taken out, pressed into service, and the best silver coffee pot polished up. Then we would hear the doorbell ring and the greetings would take place and, thereafter, the muffled voices underneath us as cards were played until we fell asleep.

It was a great pleasure to talk before going to sleep, and Paul and I usually found something to talk about. Later in our teens we had little, if anything, in common and went our separate ways, he to the mechanical and motoring fields, I to the musical and sociable. For the moment, however, we got along during our times together at home satisfactorily. One of our pre-sleeping games was guessing people's names from initials. Much later, each seemed to find the other more companionable, with a greater forbearance and wish to share the other's interest and point of view. Each of us took after one of our parents: Paul was born a Suddaby, I a Jackson. Angela, who arrived when I was six, became more of a Suddaby as she grew older. Paul and I would never be taken for brothers, he with his sandy hair, me with my mousey and our completely different looks. Neither did Angela do much in the way of leisure pursuits with her brothers but depended on her female friends for companionship.

Mother's relatives were all about us in Malton. I can only vaguely remember her mother, in her long, black bombazine at the Crown. She was born Susan Jane Yates, daughter of the founder of R Yates & Sons, the agricultural merchants, still in Railway Street. Her certificate of marriage (30 April 1887 at Saint Leonards' Church) to my grandfather William Matthew Suddaby (1857-1929), gives her name as Susan Jane Yates Wardell and her father's as Ralph Yates, iron founder. It would seem that her mother's maiden name (Margaret Wardell) was being perpetuated since her untimely death, to distinguish her four children from the five of her father's second wife Eleanor Humphreys (died 1906). She was cosy, cheerful, and gregarious. Being a landlord's wife would bring out that side of her nature. However, I heard as late as 2006 from my cousin Christopher Suddaby (son of Willy and grandson of said Susan Jane, my grandmother) that she was not liked by her daughters and that, having a spell in hospital, she was visited by only one of them. I never heard a whisper of this from my mother, her eldest daughter. Naturally one casts around for a reason for such a state of affairs and, looking at her photographs, one might perhaps discern a somewhat domineering personality. Certainly I remember an incident at the Crown which would bear this out. I was with her in the billiards room where a folding screen was receiving a coat of white paint. Not satisfied, evidently, with the way it was being done, she seized the brush from the painter and energetically continued the operation in her own way. Her piano-playing was of a similar nature: the *War March of the Priests* was arresting and authoritative. It was also – my impression of almost ninety years ago remains – accurate as far as I could judge at that tender age. I was seven years old when she died, and I remember frequent visits to the cemetery at Malton to see to the flowers on her grave, as was the custom at that time.

After she died my grandfather was looked after by Auntie Adelaide, the only unmarried one. Something had gone wrong in this direction, and her suitor (who I remember coming sometimes to see her) would not get on with the job. She had a rather sad, unfulfilled life, moving out when her father died and the place and business was taken over by Bobby her brother. (Bobby junior, his son, was the next landlord, then his widow Madge with her sons (Robert) Neil and John, keeping the Crown in the family for another generation. Neil then took over completely.) Adelaide lived as a companion to a Mrs Peacock and died of cancer shortly before the war, aged 44.

The other aunts were similar to Adelaide and my mother, though each had individual characteristics of which we came to be aware. Mother was the eldest to survive, being preceded by Samuel who died in infancy. Adelaide came next, then Marcia, Olive Octavia and, last of the daughters, Susan Victoria. The two boys Bobby and Willy completed the family, the elder of the two whose advent must have occasioned some rejoicing. The last survivor of the eight children, Susie, became a widow of 40-odd years; her husband Len Kirby, of the Helmsley firm of auctioneers known as Seth Kirby & Sons, died young from being gassed during the war. We saw her on her eightieth birthday at Helmsley, April 16 1977. She died in 1979 and I played her beloved *Evensong* by Easthope Martin at her funeral, on the organ on which she used to enjoy hearing me play it. Their only child was Mary Cynthia. I went often to stay with the three of them in their house at Helmsley across the market place from the Black Swan, later to become a café. Mary and the Parkers next door provided playmates. The stream caused much pleasure as it picturesquely babbled its pebbly way down the village or smoothed out to a somewhat more dignified pace at the lower end in the park. Up on the higher ground behind the village we took ourselves to explore Beckdale and the wood where lilies of the valley grew in profusion. Then once a week the cinema came to the hall on the west side of the market place for which a noisy generator in a van or lorry provided electricity. This was quite an event and the sound was companionable as one lay in bed before sleep. One thing I found hard to take was being forbidden to play anything but hymns on Sundays. Such an embargo seems strange and unreasonable a couple of generations later. My aunt cannot have realised that the classical composers were surely respectable enough for Sabbath use, but played safe in her efforts to prevent works such as *Kitten on the Keys* and *Ain't she sweet* sullying the sacred atmosphere.

My Victorian aunt Sybil Altham Jackson, was born in Pothanore, India on 15 October 1873 and died in Southbourne on 2 March 1966. After nearly half a century of having her, like an institution, ever present, always the same, at Christmas and birthdays and occasionally in between, it was strange without her. I say always the same, and so she was until towards the end when her 92 years began to take their toll, her sight and hearing having suffered and her writing lost its firmness. Not that this in the least prevented her from writing and, latterly, from merely signing her letters. For she was of the same vintage as Churchill, and had the same undauntable, indomitable character, for all her tiny frame and apparent frailness. Always the same she was, even to the last time I saw her a few months before her death. Despite her poor sight she would be liable to see the very things we didn't want her to see. Anything we said that we wanted to be kept secret was quite certain to be heard, fastened on, and an explanation demanded. The television was a boon to her, and she had to sit about a foot away from the screen to see it. Her younger sister and I, feeling once in need of resuscitation, produced the sherry, which was immediately noticed, and a glass had to be poured for the older sister, despite the doubts about its advisability that had been cast on it by her doctor. Needless to say, there were no ill effects.

I telephoned her on her eighty-eighth birthday and asked her how old she was. She told me but immediately got her own back and asked me my age. As it happened, I was exactly half her age then, which neither of us had realized till that moment. I suppose she was slightly outraged as well as flattered to have her age under review.

From my very earliest years, she was the Jackson relative who made the most impact; on my brother and sister as on me. She had, like her two sisters, migrated to the south of England where she was companion to elderly ladies in turn. Each year, I suppose in the summer, she came and spent quite a time with us – it may have been a fortnight – and was the only person who did this. We enjoyed having someone visiting the house as children do, but Auntie, though providing us with this enjoyment, brought with her a certain austerity and discipline on which we looked with some uncertainty. We would not have had her keep away for anything and I suppose we secretly hoped, each time, that we would get away without being pulled up for mispronouncing a word, broadening an 'a' vowel, or holding our fork wrongly. We never did. Always, it seemed, there was something needing correction, probably only one thing each visit, perhaps, but it had to be done, and was done. Not that our parents had failed in bringing us up as average nice children. Even the best brought up are not perfect, and it was the small chink in the armour that Auntie detected and fastened on, usually as we were politely taking her round the garden after lunch. Naturally we found it exasperating, but we dared not say so, and promised to do better in future, rehearsed the offending syllable and continued the garden round.

There was never any let-up where manners and politeness were concerned. But her use of the word 'gentleman' had a slightly different connotation from the one I was used to for she related how one day during the war a nicely spoken young man had delivered some commodity at the back door and she was 'sure that that young man was a gentleman'. She was right, because he was found later to be a member of an aristocratic family who was deputizing at the store concerned: an unusual situation at the time perhaps, but more common later. I think she did also accept that gentlemanliness was to be found in the lower strata of society, but her interest lay mainly in the higher ones. She was very well informed about heredity, as about the world situation and, as befits a Victorian clergyman's daughter, about the Bible. Nothing could catch her out when it came to the good book, and this reputation was gained quite early amongst her brothers and sisters, giving rise to the outrageous rhyme 'Anything in the Bibble, ask Sybil'. She, the eldest of the five, was the only one able to pass on from memory who her forebears were and where they came from, and I am glad to have persuaded her to write some of this down, albeit in rather shaky writing, before it was too late.

My father, the youngest of the five, was fourteen years her junior, and so would come under her nursemaidship. No nonsense would be stood, though I have a feeling that pranks were played, and taken in good part. In our youth there was never any sign of lack of understanding between them, so I suppose they had reached long since a working arrangement; or it may have been that the Irish in the rest of the family, which seemed to have passed Auntie by, caused them to shrug off such slings and arrows as came their way. Not that she was unreasonable, merely what is sometimes called a stickler; and sticklers can be slightly irritating at times, however reasonable.

She had her violent prejudices, not least concerning religion. Her brother-in-law became a Roman Catholic and, after his death, great care had to be taken not to let his copy of the Bible fall into her hands. The three sisters then lived together but she, the eldest, was the undoubted boss, even though the house and furniture belonged to her widowed younger sister. Friction there was at times, but eighty years of conditioning had made the ménage workable, and we, seven hours away from them in a train, were thankful they were able to look after each other.

When Aunt Sybil had migrated from the north (not her native north, for she was born in India and 'had a black nurse' as she used to tell us to our astonishment – and once even produced a snapshot in substantiation) she went to the district where retired service chiefs and their wives lived to inordinate old age. Nothing happened there in Southbourne but church on Sunday and sherry parties; we heard all about who attended both these, in her fairly frequent letters. People interested her intensely, and, when she visited us, we were told what things they had said and done, and how they lived, in minute detail.

But when I first became conscious of her and her movements I suppose in the late 1920s, she had recently left Stalybridge and moved to Switzerland, there to live in a hotel at Vevey to be companionable with her lady, whose name was Seymour, she being descended from the family of Jane, Henry the Eighth's third wife. She had enough French to get along, but always carefully rehearsed her piece before going out shopping. We used to take a great interest in the stamps with 'Helvetia' printed on them and I well remember my mother's being asked to be sure always to put tuppence-ha'penny on her letter and not a penny-ha'penny: otherwise it seemed to cause great inconvenience at The Hôtel des Alpes.

Auntie was always extremely careful with money. I don't suppose she ever had very much, or earned a great deal, and I don't remember ever being tipped on her visits to us, though I may have forgotten. If we were, it was not a large amount, and we were duly appreciative because I think we understood the circumstances. Our birthday presents were carefully thought out and usually wrapped up somewhat flimsily, but they always arrived just about intact. Latterly, and for some years her treasured possessions were gradually passed on to us, some of them not of much use, but always interesting because they mostly were of some significance to her and their history was given along with them. It pleased her, too, to give them where she thought they would be appreciated, rather than to keep them to be thrown out after she was dead. For instance, a pair of silver cufflinks in need of repair was sent to me. They had belonged to her brother, my namesake, the third surviving child of the five, who died during the First World War. Belonging to him also was a beautiful set of buttons, each with a minute sporting picture, which my uncle must have worn, along with many an Edwardian dandy. These duly graced my yellow waistcoat and afforded pleasure to my own children in their earlier days.

She kept only her small possessions with her. What furniture she inherited from my grandfather's vicarage at Ebberston she deposited in a cottage she bought years ago and let furnished. This was within three or four miles of the vicarage, and we used to have it for our family holidays during the summer. From it we took an infrequent bus four miles or so to the coast. These were great days and we revelled in the freedom and the country sounds that we came to connect with holidays.

I have left the cottage till last because in many ways it epitomises my aunt's life and thought more than anything else. Several times I heard her relate how she had bought the cottage with her savings. Once, indeed, she caught an errand boy smoking a cigarette and told him, characteristically, that if he saved his money instead of buying cigarettes he would be, as she had been, able to buy a cottage or something just as useful one day. What effect her words had we shall never know but, delivered in her quietly authoritative tone, they could not have been completely ignored, for I can remember most of the admonitions that came my way. My mother, living in Malton, closer to the cottage than the owner who was domiciled south of Winchester, had the job of looking after lettings, coping with tenants, collecting the rent, and other details. This she seemed to enjoy. For some time there was living there a Mrs Griffiths, an aunt, as I remember, of Doctor CH Kitson (1874–1944) who was at that time Professor of Music in the University of Dublin. He was famous as author of several books on Harmony and Counterpoint, Fugue and Canon (eleven according to

Grove). When, at her death, it became known that it was he who was to see to the winding up of her affairs and that mother was to meet him at the cottage, there was nothing else I could do but ask her to take along my autograph book. He duly and kindly signed it, on 24 July 1931, telling mother that he spent his life correcting octaves and fifths, and illustrating the fact in my book with an example of what he was so constantly up against. Mother's reward for those years of effort came when the property was left to my sister Angela, married to the vicar of Saint Neots, Stanley Griffiths, later to become canon of Peterborough: no relation; a mere coincidence.

CHORISTER

Childhood life at Malton was always happy. For me, things have come my way without any trouble. For a start, music was no effort. I was born with a natural talent, and working at it and developing it was pretty well unalloyed pleasure. There were, it is true, times when practising was irksome, but when I'd got the hang of it and found what a benefit it can be – and what a necessity – that made all the difference.

It was not until I came to Doctor Edward Cuthbert Bairstow (ECB) that my horizons widened and I learned that music was not an exercise merely to be got through but rather a natural expression of one's very being. I can never be too grateful for his attitude and his example. It seemed as if this was the only right course, and it brought me true satisfaction. As a result, one was provided with a yard-stick for the rest of one's life, making one intolerant of compositions and performances which lack the true spirit and stuff of music.

Then there was my chorister training. To be singing almost daily in York Minster, with its marvellous organ played by Bairstow with whom we were in such close contact, was the best possible thing for me. It all began at the end of 1928 when my father received a card from Doctor Bairstow saying 'I can hear your son play any Saturday in January except the 19th at 5.0. Please let me know when you will be bringing him'. I went, and played. I also sang: thus was established the contact which without doubt set my career on the road to a cathedral organ loft, though I never once thought it would be my lot to succeed the great man in his prestigious post. No doubt one hoped vaguely, subconsciously, and then dismissed the idea as impossible.

I was put straight into the Minster Choir and was excused the usual probationary period in which the choristers learned their job. This was not looked on with favour by the other boys and took some time to live down. I never rose to the heights of head chorister and my voice was not strong. Doctor Bairstow tried to get me to sing solos but I found it difficult to conquer my nerves sufficiently to avoid mishaps. I was shy of singing solo and took a long time to find enough confidence to do it properly. I thought my voice was going to play tricks and crack, so sure enough it did. My apprehension used to cast quite a big shadow over things, as I knew ECB could be intolerant and say cutting things which made me miserable. Once I knew I would have to sing a solo with a top A flat, and I worried about it for two days and in the end pretended I had a headache and was excused from the choir that day. It did not occur to me to practise it for two days instead of worrying about it. However nothing was said and I got away with it, but the incident is not one I recall with much satisfaction. He was also devastating at times in his comments. Once I muffed a solo, perhaps because as usual I was scared, and this drew from him the remark ' ... he's got a white liver ...'. My record as a chorister must have fallen short of his expectations, though he never said so. But I am pretty sure I was all right as a chorus boy: indeed once I was the only one to come in at the start of the Maurice Greene anthem *Lord let me know mine end.* The Assistant was playing from a figured bass and the top part differed from what was in our copies. But I was listening to the bass so I knew where to come in.

There was, however, one rather notable exception to my rather dismal solo career, and that was at the last evensong of 1931. *The Seven Joys of Mary* was the final carol, and all the best soloists were absent, smitten with illness. Thus the seven solo verses were perforce given to me at short notice – and it was broadcast. My greatest fear with that carol, as I still remember, was that I should sing the wrong verse, so I took particular care to count each one firmly on my fingers. Perhaps it was this fear that did away with any other, for I know that for once I enjoyed singing a solo, and there were some quite complimentary comments from listeners. Evensong was at that time broadcast every Tuesday, and this, as ill-luck would have it, was one that my mother who was a faithful listener did not hear. She and my father were attending the coming-of-age celebrations of Viscount Milton. Malton was part of the estate of Earl Fitzwilliam, Lord Milton's father.

Malton is eighteen miles from York by road and twenty-one by rail, and the Minster Song School was, and still is, a day school. So I had to travel to York every day by the 7.24am train, arriving home again at 6.12pm with still an hour or more of homework to do. It was hard work but was no hardship when I loved the choir work so much. I put on weight, and was rarely absent even when the Sunday bus services were erratic; I usually got there. I used even then to think it a privilege to be in daily contact with such a great man as Bairstow, and I have never ceased to be grateful for the opportunity. One could learn a tremendous amount from him, on all aspects of music, little bits of philosophy and other things.

We all held him in great awe, but not all the choristers liked him as much as I did. He was terrifying when we did not do our job properly, but on looking back I think he was possibly kinder to me except, of course, when I 'funked' a solo (how often he seemed to use that word) but I knew I deserved all he gave me. Survival was not easy, but most of us managed to get through. There were, of course, varying degrees of method of accepting all this. Some shrugged it off while others hated him for it and went on harbouring a grudge for the rest of their lives. I didn't like it at all, but there was no way of escaping it all the time. My admiration of the man kept me going, and I was very much aware of the privilege of being in such close contact with someone so great and so well known and famous. But there were times when Bairstow would relax and tell us about his adventures on his travels; his stories were wonderful. His way of taking choir practice, too, galvanised us, and his sense of humour kept cropping up in odd remarks.

One day in 1932 during my choristership at York, John Ireland had come to our morning choir practice with ECB who quite often would bring anyone who happened to be staying with him at Minster Court, so we always had our autograph books at the ready. It was a thrill for us to actually see and be in contact with the person we knew of as somebody famous or who had actually composed the music we sang. On this occasion Ireland was receiving an honorary doctorate of music from Durham University during Bairstow's professorship.

I began lessons with Doctor Bairstow soon after starting as a chorister, and continued till the war came and I joined the army. I was astonished from the first at his attitude to music. He regarded it as something different from what I had imagined before – something free and natural; it must express one's feelings or else it was insincere. Of inhibitions there must be none. Before this, music had been a rather serious business entailing hours of dreary practising (though not by me ...) and not very enjoyable even employing the facility I had been born with. It was Bairstow who made it real to me, made music alive and, above all, enjoyable and fulfilling. It was something not apart from everyday things, but a natural expression of them. And music had to be beautiful. That word, with his own characteristic way of pronouncing it, was often on his lips. I have a pretty good idea what his opinion would have been of some of today's music where beauty is not allowed. It would have been almost impossible for him – born as he was some twenty-six years before the end of Victoria's reign, and at the height of his powers in the Edwardian era and the Romantic Movement – to adjust his tastes to such an extent. Not that he was obdurate, hidebound or inflexible, for he appreciated the modern composers of his own day. He enjoyed Walton for one, when he was still considered the most advanced of composers. But Walton has beauty – and I think Bairstow was right, and would still be right today.

His teaching was always inspiring, even when he said very little. To me he was always encouraging, and it was invariably with a light step and a feeling of well-being and having done well that I came away from lessons. I say 'invariably' but there were three times (in ten years) when I had wiggings from him for being slack – and I shall never forget them... Indeed I shall not forget as long as I live the many sessions I had with him, at the Minster organ or in his music room. I can still remember clearly things he told me about most of the pieces I studied with him. His remarks were always succinct and to the point and were thus easy to remember. And it seemed that he would always say whatever was in his mind without fear or favour. This was his most characteristic trait I think, and earned him the respect we all bore him. He in turn respected those who did their job properly, but woe betide any impostor or poseur. He himself was always himself and so had we to be, or we heard about it in full measure.

As an organist he was one of the finest of his day in the Romantic tradition. In this as in all things he was a perfectionist, and I never once heard him play a wrong note. True, I did once hear him start a soft Nunc Dimittis on the Tuba Mirabilis, to our intense delight as choristers, but a wrong note never. Evensong was in the nave that day, so we had the full benefit of that great reed stop whose horizontal pipes pointed directly at us, and the five-second reverberation seemed to take for ever to die away.

Our day began with choir practice at 8.45am, every day except Wednesday. This lasted an hour, and on Tuesday and Saturday was full choir for all but the first fifteen minutes. On Tuesday, Thursday, Friday and Saturday, Matins followed at 10 o'clock, but on Monday we went into school for two and a half hours that used to drag. We much preferred the matins days. Evensong was sung daily, always at four o'clock, and only Wednesday was 'plain'. That was our day off, our 'weekend', since we were on duty on Saturday and Sunday. We even had school on Saturday morning and, in addition, an hour's practice before evensong, so it was a full schedule, and we really felt we earned our Wednesday and certainly appreciated the relaxation it provided.

But Wednesday was not always the plain or 'dry' day. If a saint, or the eve, fell on it, another day was allocated, usually Tuesday or Friday, occasionally Monday. Ascension Day, of course, always caused the change; and when we came to Holy Week, when sung matins and evensong were required every day, our plain day was postponed to Easter Week when we had the great luxury of two days' holiday in succession. Then, after Low Sunday, our real Easter holiday began – six whole days. The Christmas break, likewise, was of the same length, but here a great problem arose. Our holidays, as at Easter, consisted of the six days between two of the Sundays after Christmas. As it was necessary to sing the Eucharist on the red letter days after Christmas it was sometimes difficult to find a clear space for our meagre break, and we might have had to wait for it for as much as two weeks until Saints Stephen and John, Holy Innocents, the Circumcision and the Epiphany were out of the way: it all depended on which day of the week Christmas Day fell. But our well-earned respite came at last, and we were ready for it. I don't doubt that, by reason of the constancy and the application we all needed to bring to it, something went into our characters which otherwise would not have done. I do not remember that there was grumbling about it, nor fatigue, or staleness, but there may well have been. I did not object to it myself in any way, so complete was my enjoyment of it all.

If Advent was on the solemn side we knew what would inevitably come at the end of it, but its beginnings were just as striking. As the days were becoming shorter, Evensong (at four o'clock) started as daylight was fading and ended as darkness had quite fallen. Advent Sunday's great musical treat was *Sleepers Wake*, first chorus only, accompanied by Sir Edward in his inimitable fashion, full of wonderful rhythm and vitality. We did not know then, without our Hi-Fi's, how Bach's orchestration sounded, so were more than happy to manage with just the organ. As soon as we began rehearsing this (two or three days before we were to perform it), Christmas was on the way. The same thought still comes to mind on hearing this music.

Christmas, at that period, was different from what it has since become. To begin with, it did not start in September. Advent Sunday was soon enough for us to begin thinking about the joys to come: four weeks was long enough to anticipate it all and to look forward to the abrupt transition to the festive, joyful Christmas pieces after so long a time with music of a more austere nature.

The Minster choir observed the Advent services in their subdued cassocks of blue, refraining from donning their festive ones of scarlet. Suddenly on Christmas Day all was happiness, brightness and jollity. *For unto us* and more of *Messiah* constituted the anthem at Evensong. For the service music there was Stanford in C or one of the more florid, expansive settings, which were a vivid contrast to the sober ones of Tallis, Palestrina, Byrd and Caustun, all sung without accompaniment. Now the organ was let loose, the Tuba Mirabilis blared forth in its splendour and we opened our throats as wide as possible and enjoyed it all to the full. Everybody wished everyone else a happy Christmas and the Chapter's present to each chorister of a shilling was much appreciated. There might also have been an additional offering from a satisfied member of the congregation.

Christmas having arrived, a small number of the best boys would, for a Sunday anthem, sing *Slumber Beloved* or *Prepare thyself, Sion* from Bach's *Christmas Oratorio*, regardless of the fact that we were not contraltos.

The full choir topped this off with the marathon slog of *Glory to God*, so different from Handel's conception of it. Then on the days following Christmas and in our scarlet cassocks (with surplices over them, of course) for a fortnight at least we added a carol to the end of Evensong, most of them from the *Oxford Book of Carols*, newly published only a year or two previously in 1928. George Wither's *Rocking Hymn* in its new setting by Vaughan Williams we found particularly attractive and affecting, and we liked the atmosphere of *In the bleak midwinter* set by Holst who was still alive, and his *Personent Hodie* with its militant rhythms and, of course, *Lullay my liking*. Warlock's *Balulalow* was also a favourite, affording a solo boy a chance to shine. And there were more carols, most of which have stood the test of time. One of Bairstow's favourites was the aforementioned *Seven joys of Mary*, sung to him as a child by his mother. But perhaps the most popular of all was his own carol, *The Blessed Virgin's cradle song* published in 1900 when he was 25, for treble voices and again with a solo, short but significant.

Our summer holiday consisted of 20 days – Monday to Saturday – with two Sundays free. Thus we sang on 50 Sundays out of 52 each year. When we returned to our singing on the Sunday after whichever holiday it was, the boys came for an hour's practice at 9.15am, to be joined by the men in the latter half-hour. The music chosen was well known, probably Stanford in B flat, not necessarily something we had sung in the days leading up to the holidays. Repeats were avoided as much as possible.

At York there were the Musical Society concerts. As choristers we were usually needed to sell programmes in either the Exhibition Building or the Rialto ballroom or skating-rink. Thus one heard people like Heddle Nash, Keith Falkner, Muriel Brunskill and, of course, Elsie Suddaby who appeared frequently. Not that I very often bothered to listen to the music. As a member of the Minster choir I took part in the Bairstow concert in 1930, in the Rialto. The *Saint Matthew Passion* in its reduced form was a hardy annual and we had to attend the Tuesday rehearsals leading up to it. In my chorister days, when we all together sang the duet *Behold my Saviour now is taken* (no soprano being engaged), once or twice I sat exactly behind Leon Goossens, oboist, of whose fame I was not then aware and who did an enchanting job of the obbligato in *I would beside my Lord*. I found the constant string accompaniments to Christus a bit tiresome but enjoyed the *ripieno* in the first chorus and the duet before the thunder and lightning chorus that was left to the boys, tutti, thus saving a soprano's fee. Sybil Eaton doing her obbligato to number 47 was always elegant and impressive, but Steuart Wilson often sang flat as evangelist.

What was not always so pleasant was school under Mr Scaife. He was doing a splendid job with one assistant and had built up a formidable record of exam results. We were not to let it down, and the tension was on pretty well all the time. There was little we could do but get on with the job or risk otherwise his full wrath on our heads. There was quite a lot of this, which I didn't enjoy. The cane played a regular rôle in it. Anyone who got below G, that is FG (fairly good) or less for homework automatically had a stroke or two on the hand, which today seems a barbarous custom. We always seemed to be on a knife-edge, and the firm discipline was never relaxed, unlike choir practice. Here there was discipline to be sure, and Bairstow did not have to bother about imposing it for one would never dream of taking liberties with him. Scaife, as we called the headmaster, was great in his way, but in a smaller way and only locally. This is what we would have thought if we had tried to analyse the situation at the time, I suppose. There was not the compensation of the talent that Bairstow possessed, and the sense of fun and of humour was limited.

The only times when school became more fun were the dark December days at the end of Christmas term. Lessons would finish half an hour earlier so that he could read us *A Christmas Carol* in abridged instalments. Scaife knew it very well and kept our attention. It was very graphic and full of atmosphere. The schoolroom at the time was one-storey, open to the roof and had a gallery for access to the choir room all along the northwest front. So its rather gaunt Victorian aspect and the only just adequate lighting helped to create the right kind of feeling as the short days were coming to their end. I think this introduction to Dickens began my liking of his writings. I was given *David Copperfield* for a prize and I doggedly read my way through it, not missing a word and thoroughly entering into it. The book was constantly with me during my journeys between Malton and York, particularly during school holidays when there was time to be put in between matins and evensong and nothing else to do but mooch around York. I did eventually finish the book, but it took me months.

It was soon after I joined the Minster choir that there appeared one whose presence would make a difference to our lives by his interest in and support for our efforts. Cecil Hilton Wybergh had been retired for some years from teaching and had come to live near York. We noticed him at once at a Sunday morning nave Eucharist as he untied the rope across the centre aisle which was intended to bar those seated in the nave from going to take Communion (those wishing to do so were meant to use the chairs placed between the choir and the sanctuary) and hurled it out of the way, his face bearing a determined expression. As we found later, this was a characteristic action – no nonsense was to be stood, nor liberties taken: his route was to be absolutely straight, above-board and correct in all things.

So he made himself known to us and gave us treats of various kinds, most chiefly outings in his bull-nose Morris – four or five of us at a time – to interesting places like Brimham Rocks, Flamborough Head, Fountains Abbey and – on a certain 15 May, probably 1931 – to Durham Cathedral, during Arnold Culley's time as organist. (It was the long psalm that caused me to remember the date.) The tone of the organ was noticeably brighter than we were used to at York, due most likely to its Willis origins. As we were leaving after evensong (in our red blazers) we were caught up by a breathless cleric wishing to greet us. This was the Reverend HY Ganderton, head master of the Chorister School who also precented the service in his melodious voice. I came to know him well in due course, being accommodated as his guest in the school when sitting the various examinations for my degree: these were usually in March when the cathedral close (known as the College) was liberally supplied with crocuses, providing the somewhat anxious time with something pleasurable. On these occasions I used to meet John Dykes Bower, recently arrived at Durham from Truro.

Plenty of interest was there for us to enjoy and to profit from, all done for our pleasure as well as for Mr Wybergh who had been obliged to give up his chosen profession during the Great War on account of his hearing deficiency. His family roots were in what is now Cumbria, so he was conveniently placed to take on the role of acting organist of Carlisle Cathedral in the early 1900s, one of several including

Sydney Nicholson who covered the eight years from 1902 when Doctor Ford retired, until the appointment of Doctor Wadely. His hearing problem was apparent thus early (he was then in his thirties) yet he was able to discharge the necessary duties. It also gave the choristers the opportunity to work their wicked will. Having discovered that Mr Wybergh's cue for starting up the canticle after the reading of a lesson was seeing them close their books and return them to the shelf under the music desk, they arranged to do this at a point during the lesson, with an effect that can only be imagined. This was told me by Doctor Wadely.

Mr Wybergh installed himself into his bachelor flat in the hall at Escrick (formerly the seat of Lord Wenlock), five miles or so south of York, and became organist in an honorary capacity at the church there for some years despite his considerable deafness. He was a very competent player, spending the mornings in practising, Rheinberger being one of his favourites. Another of his pieces was the Saint-Saëns *Fantaisie* in E flat. During the school holidays when the choir was still functioning, between matins and evensong I boarded a bus and joined Mr Wybergh in the church where I became acquainted with the organ repertoire, supplementing what was to be heard in the Minster. It would have been at one of those sessions that, having played the *Saint Anne Fugue,* he quoted the picturesque pronouncement made (probably) by Doctor Crotch – according to Harvey Grace and HH Statham – that it sounded 'as if it ought to be fired off with cannon' whenever the final pedal entry of the subject was played: I have never forgotten that – and agree wholeheartedly that it is one of the supreme moments in organ music.

Lunch in the splendid dining room would be followed by Beethoven symphonies and other duets on his upright Broadwood; or there might have been a stroll in the extensive grounds. On one of these I was taken to a rose bush, shown a bud, and told that the full-blown flower was much more worthwhile; this referring to his preference for the music of his time over that of the Tudors and other early composers. Any music that he rated as inferior was branded 'bumble-puppy'.

He had been at school at Saint Michael's College, Tenbury, in the latter days of the founder, the Reverend Sir Frederick Arthur Gore Ouseley, Bart., M.A., Mus. Doc. Oxon, Precentor of Hereford

Cathedral, and Professor of Music in the University of Oxford. The College had existed since 1856 to provide a model for the performance of Anglican church music. Thus Mr Wybergh was well versed in the cathedral tradition, and used to give us titbits of information about 'Sir Frederick', such as that he always used the orchestral oboe for 'grin like a dog' when Psalm 59 was sung. Also, how in his undergraduate days, being caught out without transport he chartered a special train and, hoping this fact would impress the authority who had demanded an explanation for his delinquency, merely had the reply 'You did well, Sir Frederick'. We sang some of Ouseley's music: the morning and evening canticles known to us as 'Eezly in Oo' and – a great favourite – the anthem *It came even to pass*, also in E.

It was probably not surprising that Sir Edward and certain of the Chapter, mindful of their responsibilities for the York choristers, should have been uneasy about who they consorted with. Choirboys can hold a kind of attraction for a 'certain type' of person, of which they were well aware. In the case of Mr Wybergh, nothing could have been further from the truth: his interest as a dedicated teacher was in the mind of the boy, as well as in the music of the church. This placed us in an awkward situation, pulled in opposite directions between our Minster situation and a friendship that we enjoyed. One day, when there was the question of my accepting an invitation of his that might be disapproved of, he wondered quizzically if I would be prepared to bow myself down in the house of Rimmon. (A reference to II Kings v.18, explained by Brewer in his *Dictionary of Phrase and Fable* as 'to palter with one's conscience; to do that which one knows to be wrong so as to save one's face'.) Mr Wybergh, with his dogged determination, and with obviously nothing to fear, persisted in the relationship, while we were always aware of the disapproval that cast somewhat of a shadow over it. Whether he had ever tried to meet any of the Minster authorities in a normal, friendly manner to gain their confidence is doubtful, though any approach he might have made could have foundered: indeed, a brush-off by Doctor Bairstow could have been a distinct possibility. Once, at a lesson, the subject was raised by Doctor Bairstow and my defence (aged 13 or so) that Mr Wybergh was all right because he was a Master of Arts and a Bachelor of Music of – yes – Oxford, drew the rebuff that that was nothing to do with the matter.

At the age of sixteen I was taken to see Saint Michael's College, Tenbury by Mr Wybergh. This was during our visit to the Three Choirs Festival at Hereford, the last one attended by Elgar who conducted both *Gerontius* and *The Kingdom* as well as the viola version of his cello concerto played by Lionel Tertis. We also had CB Rootham's setting of Milton's *Ode on the morning of Christ's Nativity* which was not very well received but appeared the following year at Gloucester where we heard it again under the composer's direction. Also present was one of the foremost sopranos of the day, Elsie Suddaby, along with other soloists of like category. At the next Three Choirs Festival *Gerontius* and *The Kingdom* were to be heard as well as Elgar's *Second Symphony* but without the composer's presence: he had become ill soon after the previous gathering and died on 23 February 1934. The following festival was therefore a memorial to him and his long connexion with the organisation.

I last saw Mr Wybergh when I played a recital in Exeter Cathedral, he having gone to live in Exmouth at the Grand Hotel ('Grand in name only' was his assessment), where I had a meal with him during which he was able, despite his failing eyesight, to pour white wine accurately into our glasses. He came to the recital complete with his hearing aid, but probably heard very little.

MALTON ORGANIST

It always seemed likely that another conflagration would break out. This was one thing that clouded the otherwise ideal situation. There were, to be sure, other things not so pleasant that did not impinge on us: unemployment and other hardships that we hardly heard of. The general strike of 1926 was only a few years before. However, nearly four years were to elapse before war was declared, and fully five before I was drawn into it. In the meantime the halcyon days continued.

Having become aware, as a chorister, of the sound of organs and the thrill of the crisp upperwork and the suppressed energy of the full Swell at York, I was thrilled to discern these same attributes on a smaller scale at Helmsley where I used to stay with my Aunt Susie Kirby. The Contra Oboe was particularly interesting, with its special piston and octave coupler, and taught me the value of a double reed in a Swell chorus. The other stops were very strongly characterised and, along with the beautifully made console, convinced me that Arthur Harrison was the only organ builder worthy of notice – an attitude fostered in no uncertain manner by Sir Edward. The church organist was CE Buckley, a pupil of Bairstow, whose right leg was stiff, for which reason the (balanced) Swell pedal was placed on the extreme right of the pedal board and remained so long after his death. The organ was rebuilt by Harrison around 1930 and was a source of great happiness to me.

A few years later, having left school at the age of fifteen, and being appointed to Malton church as organist aged sixteen, I found an organ of a similar character in Saint Leonard's. It was built in 1907, but with tracker action (Helmsley has pneumatic) and only an 8' Swell of six stops, with Harmonic Flute 4' for variety. This was moved to Saint Michael's soon after the 1939-45 war and later still in 1975 received a pedal reed in place of the Open Wood. This was done in order to encourage the tone to go into the church, as it had been prevented by the wall formed by the big wooden pipes. Many years later it seemed that this might not have been a good move, especially in the light of strict conservation which became important, but there was the undeniable fact that reed tone in the bass gave the appearance of a larger organ, as was evident when hearing it in the nave or listening to recordings.

Malton used to have two parishes, Saint Michael and Saint Leonard, which became joined. The churches were used alternately, until Saint Leonard's was handed over to the Catholic Church. The acoustics of Saint Michael's were less resonant than Saint Leonard's. The choir preferred the latter to sing in, and the organ was quite adequate. On being moved, however, it was found to be less effective, but the 1867 Thomas Harrison (then of Rochdale) was deemed to have served its time and was taken out and dispersed, some pipes to the McClure organ at Edinburgh University. This was a pity as even with its 25-note pedal board it was a viable instrument for service use and provided me with many hours of practising time, supplemented by the odd hour on the other organ with its complete pedal board when I could find someone to pump the bellows, and where I could practise the five top notes. (Years later Boris Ord made the point that 'You should get up there twice a week'.)

Saint Michael's had an electric blower quite early, perched up on the inside porch of the vestry doors – a noisy arrangement and what Arthur Harrison called 'rough and ready' when he came to inspect it and the Saint Leonard's organ. Having to find someone to pump was a nuisance, but for some time I was able to have the services of an ex-chorister, Ernie Large, who did it in exchange for piano lessons. He was very faithful, his only failing being to keep letting the wind run out as he engaged in conversation with someone through the churchyard railings. The church professed to be unable to afford an electric blower, the cost of £100 at that time being found too daunting. The student of today can count him/herself fortunate to have all the necessary wind at the press of a switch.

Limited though the old organ was for practice, with its short compass pedal-board, straight stop-jambs and a hitch-down swell pedal, it afforded good experience in controlling an instrument with a mere three composition pedals to the Great. And in later years, organs of a similar vintage held no terrors when one occasionally came across them (as in Denmark 1955). The Swell tremulant was useless, being far too rapid, putting one in mind of the shiverings that assailed one in the icy temperatures that were pretty much the rule in churches during wintertime.

As to the disappearance of the old Saint Michael's organ, I wish now it had been possible to keep and restore it. But at that time it was old-fashioned and had no pistons, its pedal board and manuals were deficient in notes, the stop jambs were straight, the Choir was buried under the Swell and lacked bottom octaves to its Gamba and Clarinet. Its mixture, also on the Great was rather flutey and strident. Nevertheless, today it would be regarded as a treasure by conservationists and could have been impressive if restored. Its successor remains despite attempts to oust it when in the early 1970s the soundboards were split by an over-efficient heating arrangement. I was able to point out that this splendid organ was the heritage of the church and town, and made of top grade materials by the best builder of the time. Did this generation relish the idea of going down to posterity as the destroyers of their heritage (both theirs and that of generations to come) to replace a fine traditional organ with a mass-produced electronic imitation, one which was obsolescent as soon as it was made? Mercifully, sense prevailed and I hope it always will, both there and elsewhere.

I moved on to be a full-time music student with Bairstow, having left the choir in 1933 and successfully negotiated the Durham matriculation that was the essential qualification for the taking of the (external) degree and was the highest of the exams attempted at the Song School. Only selected pupils attempted it, and we were left to study on our own, while the class, taken by Scaife, went on alongside. This took quite a deal of concentration, and a lot of time must have been wasted as our minds wandered. The relief of pulling it off was intense, heightened of course by the gloomy expectancy leading up to it and the thought of the horror that would ensue and the ridicule that would fall on our heads were one to be ploughed. But now the way was clear for me to 'go to Doctor Bairstow; straight up to the organ loft' which was the phraseology used by Mr Scaife in dangling the much wished-for carrot under my nose. It was a most wonderful feeling, on opening the envelope containing the result, to know that here was an end to schoolwork and a green light for the start of a musical career. Of course I could have re-sat it, but the fact that this was not going to be necessary gave an unimaginable boost to my self-confidence. Such successes were, as ever afterwards in similar circumstances, received with pleasure by friends and those 'interested in me' or in my progress, as Mother used to put it.

The gramophone that in 1933 I bought with some of my choir money on leaving the Minster had at first only organ records. But soon Ravel got hold of me and I bought the quartet (played by the Galimir, directed by the composer), only the first record to start with, but followed closely by the remaining two. The family must have been driven to distraction by my unceasing playing of it in the evenings at 4 East Mount when we were all together. But I couldn't have enough of it, and what I considered the weird, spooky harmonies gripped and fascinated me. They were, of course, something utterly new and outside my experience. And to be able to have it all in one's own sitting room was wonderful – one can only wonder at and be thankful for the benefits that the 'mechanization of music' (one of Bairstow's concerns and fears at this time) has bestowed on us. A generation that has grown up since then and takes it all for granted can have no idea how much more fortunate it is, and how infinitely easier for study life can be. If only this greater ease brings a greater happiness. It is more often the harder path that brings about such a state. One can, however, hope that fuller lives will be the lot of those music students who, undoubtedly, are saved a great deal of drudgery in such activities as reading scores at the keyboard or having to imagine the sounds. It is to be hoped that the imagination is given enough exercise to fit it for such pursuits as orchestration, which depend entirely on this facility.

As my chorister days at the Minster came to an end I became friendly with Dennis Laughton, who was a keen lover of music and an ardent admirer of ECB. He involved himself in music in York and was one of the founders of the British Music Society branch in the 1920s, which still flourishes and of which I eventually became president. Dennis Laughton lived with his parents at The Elms, 104 Heworth Green, where I used to stay for odd nights when, after a function, or concert, there was no way of returning to Malton. We had holidays together in 1933 and the following year, 'doing' cathedrals and plaguing their organists. He had gramophone records, and more than once took me to the Spa at Scarborough to hear the orchestra under Alick Maclean. I was introduced to him in the green room directly after he had conducted Beethoven's *Pastoral Symphony* and was impressed by his feelings for the work: '... Oh, the depth of that music', he said as he mopped his freely perspiring brow. Thus under Alick Maclean I was introduced to Beethoven's Sixth, Quilter's *Children's Overture*, the Venusburg music, *The Mastersingers* overture and others of his favourites which had been included in the programme at Dennis's request.

Dennis Laughton encouraged me in my piano playing and once, when I gave a recital in the Tempest Anderson Hall in the Museum Gardens, he went so far as to hire a huge grand from Leeds especially for the occasion. This cost him £12! He also saw that I was included in the BMS members' concerts that happened annually when we, the members, played our party pieces. My pianistic efforts included Beethoven's *Sonata* opus 109 in E minor, Rachmaninoff's arrangement of the Mendelssohn *Scherzo* from the *Midsummer Night's Dream* and the Ravel *Toccata*. Ted Holman and I also did duets for two pianos and once persuaded Doctor Bairstow to come and hear us do his *Variations*. Esther Groves of the well-known York musical family played the cello, and Miss Cass the piano. Sir Benjamin Dawson used to sing to Lady Dawson's accompaniment, Dorothy Lane-Fox played the violin, Cyril Jackson (later vicar of Aldborough and Precentor of Salisbury, but at that time minor canon at the Minster) played a duet with me and once in 1935 with Dean Bate. He was a good pianist and had me at Almery Garth, his York house, for two-piano duets. He had given occasional broadcast piano recitals from Leeds: one of his programmes included the first movements of both the Ravel *Sonatina* and Benjamin Dale's *Sonata* in D minor, a capital piece on a big scale which is never heard. The same can be said of a work of his for viola and piano – a suite I think, in which I once accompanied Bernard Shore in the Minster, on piano. Looking back it seems strange that a cleric who was an amateur pianist (but a good performer) should have been thought fit to play on the air: one reason possibly is that broadcasting was as yet under suspicion and beneath the dignity of the big guns. However, a little later I did hear Bartôk himself in recital and, incidentally, was nonplussed by his own compositions.

In his days as curate in Malton, John Bacchus Dykes served at Saint Michael's before becoming the well-known composer of hymn tunes, of which *Hymns Ancient and Modern* contains so many. I was appointed organist in 1933 by the vicar, on the recommendation of Sir Edward, and took up duties at both Saint Leonard's and Saint Michael's in September or October. My predecessor was Thomas Hallford, of Sheffield, who had succeeded Arthur Ayres a year previously and was moving to Alnwick parish church. He was a formidable musician and a rock solid personality with no frills; he obtained a DMus at Durham. His Sheffield accent was quite marked though gradually he tried to reduce it, at Bairstow's suggestion. ECB thought he should try and polish up his image and not, for example, answer 'I don't mind if I do' when asked by Lady Bairstow to have a piece of cake at teatime. But it did not suit him as well as his natural manner: he became somewhat self-conscious. In the end, however, he landed a cathedral organistship – Llandaff – having in the meantime held the post at Brighton parish church. It was during a bombing attack on Brighton that his wife and small daughter were killed, he himself being away from home, in the forces I believe. I met him again at a Cathedral Organists' Conference. He told me the shattering fact that his second wife, whom he had brought back from Italy, had died in childbirth. This was too much for him, for he himself died not long afterwards. He was a great loss in every way. He must have been some ten years older than I. He helped me with my playing and we also played jazz duets. His choir training at Malton was inspired and produced splendid results with firm discipline and hard work.

Thus, when I took over the church music at Malton from him, things were in a healthy state, and I did my best to keep up the standard. It was not thought to be an easy job for someone just turned sixteen years of age to control adults, two of whom had been my school teachers, headmasters of the National School. But it was the younger end that caused me problems at first, though not sufficiently to spoil the end result. I eventually got the hang of discipline and enjoyed working with the choir. We also had six or eight ladies, of varying usefulness, Mother included: she was very useful and as keen as mustard, enjoying the singing immensely and attending most regularly, as did Dad. He was a frequent lector too and a great friend of the vicar, Roger Franklen Cardale, the successor to Canon Walker. Little did I imagine at that time that I would one day be addressing his wife as Aunt Elizabeth. This came about through my marriage to Priscilla, whose brother John and sister Betty both married children of the Cardales. After the Friday choir practice when it was at Saint Michael's we would all go to the vicarage for a cup of tea; when it was at Saint Leonard's we met at our house, four or five minutes' walk away, on East Mount – number 4, then number 6 when in 1937 we moved to the bigger house next door which had more garden and also more sunshine.

Churchgoing was taken seriously. There was full matins and evensong that everyone was expected to attend. There was also the 'Quarter to Ten', always at Saint Leonard's, sung by a voluntary choir to Merbecke or Martin Shaw's *Folk Mass* alternately. There were fewer, if any, distractions then: cars were rarities and days out for pleasure happened infrequently, so attendance was good and you knew pretty well who was going to be there. The choir's repertoire consisted mainly of hymns and psalms. We rehearsed them faithfully week by week without finding them boring. But we usually had an anthem to get our teeth into, to which we looked forward: it took us long enough to learn it and to polish it up for performance. The biggest challenge was sung evensong on Lenten Wednesday evenings which we did mostly unaccompanied. There was always an anthem, *Lord for Thy Tender, Call to Remembrance* (Farrant), *Let Thy Merciful Ears*. In the last, the basses found great difficulty in finding the C natural after the first E in the initial E major chord and always wanted to go down a minor third to C#; very naturally, because the sopranos and tenors had sung G# and F# making it sound as if it is in E major. I hankered after canticle settings, and only very occasionally were we allowed to sing them, Walmisley in D minor being the favoured one: the little Parry in D that I had sung here as a boy was forgotten.

I experienced a great deal of pleasure and fulfilment by organizing short recitals once a month after a shortened evensong. They lasted half an hour and had a soloist for two groups. Dick Birdsall played the clarinet and saxophone, Katherine Marshall-Jones sang Bach, and Helen Cardale, the vicar's daughter (studying cello at the Royal College of Music) joined in. Frank Green and Edmund Meadows (Minster songmen), occasional Minster choir boys, and Ida Read, an excellent alto from the choir, all took part. Once we brought in an upright piano for a Mozart trio (in G) with Kathleen Procter, a violinist and my future wife's aunt, and Helen Cardale. This trio combination was a regular weekly event. It was organized by Kathleen in the first instance and continued for some years. We met regularly at the vicarage and worked hard and in detail at Brahms (C minor and C major), Beethoven in D (Ghost), the Mozart already mentioned, Haydn, one by Jean Huré on Breton folk songs, Ireland's third and others. We also brought in a viola, Myfanwy Jones from Ebberston vicarage (daughter of one of my grandfather's successors) or Irene Hawkins (mother of Brian and aunt of John, Susan and Charles Tunnell, who all contributed to music in the Minster in the years ahead), to have great fun with Walton's quartet, and no little difficulty too. The trio proved fruitful not only music-wise: both Helen and I were fortunate enough to meet our life's partners in Kathleen's nephew and niece. If she had not been hooked on chamber music the course of one's life could have been very different.

It was not until I was 18 or 19 that the gramophone as a serious purveyor of music was brought to my attention by Walter Douglas, son of the vicar of Salton, who became a great friend. He was primarily an artist but had a love for Beethoven and Bach, and was up at Oxford. We listened also to the Proms on the wireless and enjoyed Brahms' symphonies and Walton's *Viola Concerto* which was fairly new then, as also was Vaughan Williams' Fourth, which was more than I could cope with. It was of immense value to be able to discuss these pieces as soon as we had heard them. Those few years immediately before the war were ones on which I look back with pleasure as being stable and full of promise. People's sense of values seemed to be right and money was worth something. All seemed to take a pride in their work and got on with it.

We also had the amateur theatricals in which to join: *Tilly of Bloomsbury* and *The Rivals*. The former was successful but the latter flopped because Edward VIII chose the day of the performance to abdicate. A wireless was brought in so that the audience could hear the King's speech, but there was an interminable delay before it started and at the end of it neither audience nor players had much stomach for what remained of Sheridan's comedy. Mabel Douglas, wife of the vicar of Salton, did a fine job of producing and welded us into a well-knit and happy bunch, encouraging us all to go dancing, swimming or walking together and getting to know each other, which helped greatly where self-consciousness was apt (with some of us) to make difficulties with our acting. Not that I was ever anything but pretty hopeless as Mr Rylands the curate or, still more so, as Falkland. But I enjoyed it all, the sociability mainly, sometimes driving home after a dance at 3 o'clock as the summer dawn was breaking.

And then it happened. On the very day I became eligible for military service in 1935 – my eighteenth birthday – Mussolini invaded Abyssinia. This was indeed a blow, and it gave one a nasty feeling that one might be called up at once and sent out there till the matter was cleared up. Sometimes I wonder whether some determined move of that sort might not have been a good thing and have shown Mussolini – and his pal Hitler – that things like that were not appreciated.

And all the time my studying continued and my weekly visits to York for lessons with Doctor Bairstow. These were the important and serious parts of my life, the goal being the Mus. Bac. and the RCO diplomas. I cannot deny that the exercises were tough going, but Bairstow's book aimed to humanize what had, perhaps up until then, been a dry-as-dust academic process requiring strict rectitude and little else. Bairstow was writing his book at the suggestion of Stanford with the object of teaching counterpoint alongside harmony rather than after harmony had been presumed to be learnt – a very logical notion and difficult to imagine why it had not always been the case. Thus instead of the usual phrase 'Harmony and Counterpoint', the book's title reversed the two disciplines. Also dealt with were modal harmony and counterpoint. The book's sole aim and object is to develop musicianship and imagination rather than mere following of rules and avoiding consecutives and such academic considerations. The book was still in typescript, and we

38

were lent a chapter at a time and trusted to take care of it and return it in good order, although there was no warning to this effect. Before the days of easy copying he was extremely relaxed about letting the precious, unique manuscript out of his sight and, as far as I remember, having no trouble. When eventually the book was published it was well received and probably helped to earn his honorary Oxford Mus. Doc.

As mentioned previously, his main concern all his life was that music should be beautiful, as can readily be seen in his compositions, especially the violin variations. Anything ugly was not to be allowed at any price. My efforts in this direction under his strong influence were pervaded by the same quest, even the exercises. The result might have been improved if I had in fact left out that part of it and paid more attention to the nuts and bolts. What constituted beauty could be learned from listening, but this is, I suppose, a matter of opinion on which agreement may not always be possible. The Bairstow violin variations might be thought by some to be over-emotional, and emotion in an examination is questionable and of less value than efficiency. The compositions I produced, insignificant and worthless, were too full of chords of the seventh (caught from Ravel's *Quartet*) and other coloured sounds, producing a synthetic emotion, and resulting in meaningless mawkish meanderings.

It is perhaps not widely realised that the universities used to regard music as a Cinderella subject, and only comparatively recently allowed it to attain the standard of a tripos. Vaughan Williams, at Cambridge in the 1890s read history as his main endeavour, and graduated in music only as a secondary matter – on sufferance as it were. It was Mr Wybergh's contention that I would be much better going to Oxford, even after I had taken the BMus at Durham, and persuaded me to try for the organ scholarship at Keble. This I did, though it was a very unwise step to take. Whether Sir Edward knew about it I never found out; it was never mentioned. Mercifully my ignorance of Latin ruled me out – and probably other things too – and Meredith Davies beat me to it. Perhaps it was on that visit that Doctor HK Andrews took me to meet Sir Hugh Allen up in his eyrie above a gateway in New College; he was Professor of Music then. On entering his study we found him engaged in writing at his desk. We waited until he had finished, when he looked up and said, quite sharply, 'Are you Jackson?' I admitted that

I was. 'You're a tot', came the valued information. He had clearly been expecting me, but was not prepared for someone several inches shorter than Doctor Andrews, though I was of average height.

After dinner that evening in the senior common room, as Doctor Andrews' guest, I witnessed the remarkable post-prandial event as part of the semicircle seated round the fire. Much conversation took place, led by the vigorous Sir Hugh, while I could follow the progress of the port in its decanter, set off by him (on the left) down the sloping runway in front of the fire to whoever was at the right hand side of the fireplace, avoiding any disturbance. My previous encounter with Sir Hugh, on 15 May 1932 or 33 was in the Salvation Army citadel in York where he was adjudicating the Yorkshire Choral Competitions and I had been accompanying a soprano soloist. I asked for his autograph and, as he wrote, he remarked 'Long psalm today'. The significance of that will be known to any cathedral chorister. Also present at the New College dinner was RO Morris, famous for his book on sixteenth century counterpoint which Herbert Howells thought so highly of, so much so that he had read it more than once for sheer pleasure. RO Morris was to swim into my ken a year or two later, in a different context.

Another influence that played a large part in my life happened by accident. In the Minster some time in the mid-1930s I happened to meet an enthusiast for the church, its music and organs who was from Scotland. He was acquainted with a good many cathedral organists (among them in previous years a fellow Scot named Charles Macpherson, organist of Saint Paul's Cathedral until 1927) being interesting, articulate and full of facts and information about all manner of subjects, including eastern religions, Tibet, orthodox, as well as those nearer home. He was a Catholic Apostolic but attended the Scottish Episcopal Church. His name was Norman Doran Macdonald and he must have been aged around seventy. He had trained as an advocate but never practised. Coming from a legal family his father was a much-respected judge who refused a peerage, to the disgust of his grandson Don who became Sheriff of Greenock.

We enjoyed our meeting and I was promised a visit to Edinburgh and many of its organs. This duly took place, as well as a short stay in his large baronial-style house at Auchterarder near Gleneagles where I found his wife most sympathetic and greatly interested in music. A great feature of the drawing room was a huge black Bechstein grand with elaborate carving the like of which one could hardly have imagined. If I remember correctly, two pianos of this design were made, the other for the Empress Frederick. Mrs Macdonald was a competent pianist with a repertoire which included the Chopin *Fantasie Impromptu*, Grieg's *Ich liebe dich* and a *Coronach* by Edgar Barratt, published by Elkin in 1917 and also in an organ arrangement by Eaglefield Hull; an emotional piece in the key of D flat which created quite an impression. She had composed a few short pieces, one being a song in praise of *Men of the Dandy Ninth* to her own words – a patriotic wartime gesture towards the Ninth Highlanders, 'The Royal Scots', with which her family were concerned.

The visit was enjoyed and appreciated on all sides – which included a fellow guest Admiral Sir Edward Headlam, a relative of the then bishop of Gloucester. From it sprang a few short years of friendship during which I was to Mrs Macdonald (as I look back) something like what Debussy had been to Nadejda von Meck, though only in the holidays and in a very different category. Music was the main preoccupation, with the formation of a library of 78 rpm records which were constantly played causing great satisfaction. As the collection grew, the two cases in which it resided gained quite a weight as they were lugged between Coll-Earn and Malton thrice annually which is rather different from the modern way where an unbelievable number of items can go easily into a pocket.

I brought as much of Ravel's music as could be had on recordings and Mrs Macdonald became as enthusiastic about it as I was. During the Christmas holiday, together we wished to express our great regard for his music and composed a letter that, with her knowledge of the language, she put into French. But almost at once, to our disappointment and grief, we read of his death in, I think, the Daily Mail under the headline 'Ravel, Genius who looked a jockey' and it was in the obituaries that we learned that he had written a piano concerto for the left hand. The other one (the 'Double-Fisted' according to David Swale) had been a favourite in its recording by Marguerite Long, declared on the label to have been conducted by the composer but later disclosed as done by Pietro de Freitas Branco. I came to know the work very well and as a party piece would play the solo part on the big Bechstein along with the gramophone in a somewhat unequal balance. This happened once rather late one evening when Doctor Wilfrid Greenhouse Allt called in. He was then organist of Saint Giles' Cathedral, Edinburgh, and later moved to London as Principal of Trinity College of Music, a very cheery, friendly, loquacious soul. I came to know him well after the war in connexion with the RCO where we were both on the council, and with the Saint Cecilia Festival service when I wrote the anthem in 1963: he was very much concerned with the organisation. He was also a regular attender at the annual congress of the Incorporated Association of Organists. He enjoyed relating how, in conversation with Queen Elizabeth (later Queen Mother) and Princess Margaret, the question arose as to the correct pronunciation of 'acoustic'. Asked by the Queen to pronounce, Doctor Allt replied 'In England we say cow and in Scotland coo' to the great amusement of all. 'Remember that, Margaret' said the Queen, 'coo in Scotland, cow in England'.

One of the notable features of Coll-Earn was the considerable acreage covered by the grounds – all kept in order by one full-time gardener named Anderson, and with a fine collection of trees of great variety. This formed a very good antidote to too much physical inactivity listening to music, and the view of the blue hills near and far was appealing as seen from the study with its two turrets at the top of the house where the EMG gramophone resided.

Sometimes Mr Macdonald had his own original way of organising events. There were excursions too, mostly to organs but also to local places of interest such as Drummond Castle with its spectacular gardens, or Saint Andrews, which was chosen chiefly for the Willis organ in Saint Salvator's (the university) chapel. Mr Macdonald apparently had the entry to whatever organ he wished. We went to Glasgow, to both cathedrals, Park Parish Church, Hillhead Parish Church with its three-manual Willis where the organist was Vernon O. Wright whose son became the Queen's private chaplain. The big Rushworth organ in the Church of the Holy Rude at Stirling was a target, as were most of those in Edinburgh, the products of the local firm of Ingram being much in evidence, our visits evidently taken seriously since the head of the firm himself, Mr Gray, turned out to do the honours more than once. At the time I was not greatly impressed with their products, finding the voicing somewhat ordinary and the diapasons breathy. On Sundays I played one of their organs (a two-manual) in Saint Kessog's church, Auchterarder, complete in my newly acquired BMus hood whose Palatinate Purple colour was the object of some admiration, the whole ceremony under the command of Mr Macdonald as it seemed, in his cotta.

I was taken to the Reid Memorial Church and to Saint John's, Prince's Street (both with Rushworth organs), to the McEwan and Usher Halls. At the latter, as Mr Macdonald related, many years before, Widor was to give a recital, but the UK system of stop control was unknown to him and a cause of great frustration, eliciting from him in his anguish 'Pas de système, pas de système'. He was being looked after by Mr Macdonald whose role would then be to calm him down and suggest remedies.

At the McEwan Hall, still with its Hope-Jones console up in its gallery on the left hand side, I was upset by the blue sparks emitted by the electric pistons (or stop-keys) though they were quite harmless. I wish I could remember the sounds of the organ, many of which must still exist since the Willis rebuild. The console had been brought down to floor level when later I played a recital which, again, is too long ago to bring up any tonal recollections.

The two most significant happenings, however, were not far from each other at the west end of Princes Street. Alfred Hollins had been at Saint George's West Church since 1897, and he very kindly and willingly obeyed Mr Macdonald's command to show off his (Rushworth) three-manual to this tiresome and importunate pupil of Bairstow, the latter's name, no doubt, providing a handle to achieve the desired request. Hollins was a Yorkshire man, born in Hull and with strong York connexions, which could have had some effect on the situation. My memory of him was of a kindly, placid, humble person, content to do what was asked of him, and I can only regret that I have no recollection of any conversation with him. I do remember that he asked me what I would like him to play, and the only piece of his that I knew was the *Concert Overture* in C minor so I asked for that. It had been played at Malton by Thomas Hallford, though slightly 'under the counter' as it were, being regarded as rather inferior in some quarters (Bairstow's notably) or 'bumble-puppy' according to Mr Wybergh. My hope is that I showed adequate appreciation for the honour he did me, which now is very real and precious in my memory.

Saint Mary's Cathedral, round the corner from Doctor Hollins' church, had interested me through the occasional recitals of Robert Head's which I was able to tune into on the Scottish Regional network, usually late in the evening. The tone of the fine Father Willis coupled with what was to me its far-off romantic location and a wireless reception which was not perfect – fading from time to time – and chiefly the brilliant and commanding Tuba, provided a great deal of wonder and enjoyment in those teenage years. So it was with great anticipation that I approached Saint Mary's. In my early teens I had written to Arthur Harrison (who had rebuilt the organ and supplied a new detached console) asking for a specification and expressing my puzzlement as to the necessity for two cathedrals in one city. He replied, patiently telling me that Saint Mary's was the equivalent of the Church of England in Scotland. I was introduced to Robert Head, the organist, who allowed me whatever length of time I wished on the organ. I was always welcome, on subsequent visits, to play again, usually with Mrs Macdonald close by drinking it all in, and her husband controlling the situation. He liked the Franck *Pièce Héroïque* which he called 'Pedal Moanings at the bar' being unaware that it was not the pedals but manual sixteen-foot stops. On learning that, he dropped 'pedal' from his sobriquet. In former times there had been an organ in Coll-Earn of which all that remained was a row of diapered pipes on the wall of the study – a room high up in the house, where the record sessions took place.

I did my studies with Bairstow, taking the ARCO (January 1936) and the Durham BMus exams, first part, second part, and the final part that was the exercise. This was a string quartet which I submitted in March 1937 and which satisfied the examiners, though I can't think how. I had a strong wish to compose things, but no knowledge of how to go about it. Except for the slow movement (which had a good tune that Sir Edward liked) it was very much a prentice piece. I don't think even ECB told me very much: he said I should jot down themes when they occurred to me, as such things were often reluctant to appear at bidding. Apart from the technique of harmony and counterpoint that he taught me so thoroughly, about the only other bit of composition mechanics I can remember was the necessity for providing plenty of themes and motifs for development in the course of a movement. So many academic works were submitted, he said, which contained a first subject then, in due course, a second subject, and nothing else; not a group of each, such as he showed me Brahms used in his fourth symphony that ECB produced as an illustration (Sir Edward had recently given a lecture on it at the RCO).

At the RCO I won the Limpus Prize for the highest marks in organ playing. And life continued, enjoyably, though tinged with uncertainty as Hitler increased his power, disturbing the whole of Europe and beyond.

SOLDIER

The Sunday morning service in Saint Michael's church, Malton, at 11am on 3 September 1939, starting at precisely the same hour as the deadline set for war to be declared was, to say the least, uncomfortable; no-one knew what lay ahead, our lives disrupted completely, turned upside down. As to the matter of my calling-up, there was quite some anxiety about my studies, resulting in an application for postponement of army service. This appeared to have the approval of everyone – family, church, Sir Edward – so went ahead. The tribunal panels, or whatever they were called, were respectful, calling me Mr Jackson; they saw my point of view and awarded me some deferment. My second appearance before them some months later was different; the form of address was omitted and my surname sufficed, a somewhat more acerbic tonality. That period of civilian life in a wartime situation was not the most comfortable, and there was the odd mark of disapproval very occasionally to contend with. The experience of blackout, shortages, travel difficulties and the uncertainty of things over all was new and something to be faced with firm resolution. Life carried on as best it was able until I was a civilian no longer.

The day I joined the army, 15 October 1940, was the same date on which brother Paul had enlisted in the Royal Air Force five years earlier. It was Auntie Sybil's sixty-fifth birthday. Mother was heartbroken and broke down as I looked back from the garden gate on leaving the house on East Mount. But I was ready for a bit of adventure and rather glad to be away from parental influence. I had also become uncomfortable about staying out of the forces, having been given postponement, so it was with some relief that I boarded the train on 14 October and came to the Olde Bell Hotel at Warminster (a different kind of Minster from the one I had been used to), so as to report punctually next morning. On doing so I was taken in a lorry to the camp and given a very greasy fry-up. It was kindly meant, and we conscripts were somewhat respectfully treated by the regulars. I think they were even a little sorry for us. Later on, when giving vent to frustration of some sort and roundly cursing the army for sucking you into it, you would be offered the sound advice: 'Shouldn't 've joined'. Many of the others called up with me turned up very late in the day, most of them having travelled from Yorkshire, starting that morning, fully aware that they could not arrive by the time stated. That was an early taste of the very different mode of behaving, one quite new to a sheltered civilian. The general philosophy was that if you could get away with something all was well. This included appropriating anyone else's property, which meant that it was wise to leave nothing where it could be lifted.

We conscripts had the good fortune to be together during the initial training period, so friendships were formed and one began to learn about other people's circumstances and background. It was the character of a person that mattered, not his social status. Later, we were inevitably mixed in with the regulars and usually happily so.

But for the moment we had to be made into soldiers. Our training began at Headley, near Bordon in Hampshire, and we were billeted in empty houses in the village, mine being the Church Gate stores, next to the churchyard. There were six of us in one room, with just enough room to spread our straw palliasses. Other rooms in the same house were similarly filled, and there were washing problems with the single bathroom. These seemed to solve themselves as a tacit kind of staggering system evolved. The soldier needed plenty of ingenuity, never knowing into what situation he might at any time be plunged. He was continually adjured to 'improvise' which was certainly something I could do though in another connotation.

I wrote home regularly throughout my army service and Mother kept my letters. In recent years Donald Webster made selections from these letters in preparation for this account, and put in comments that I quote, with much gratitude to him.

15 October: 'I am enjoying myself tremendously. The companionship is all one could wish. ... I think I shall like it after all. The village of Headley where we are now is very pretty and off the beaten track. We are to learn about tanks – elaborate course and I shall come out a fully qualified mechanic. A jolly lot of good I should do as one – it'll be a bore having to learn about it.'

26 October: 'I spend about a bob [a shilling or 5p] – a day on eats such as a cup of tea (1d.) and a bun at 11.00 am (breakfast is at 7.00 so we're hungry by then), tuppenny bars of chocolate for the odd five minutes between sessions and a cup of tea in the evening. We get only bread and cheese or jam or meat roll for tea, and nothing after that... Just having a big mend. Buttons keep flying off at all sorts of odd and inconvenient times so I'm securing against it.'

30 October: 'Well here we are at last after a fortnight of it. I am feeling very fit as a result of PT [physical training] every day as well as two drill periods daily ...'

Having given my occupation unequivocally, I was at once pounced on by the Padré, Christopher Perowne, to play the organ for church parades. This was splendid as it gave me access to an instrument. I was also invited to use Mrs Blanford's bathroom, and that of the Squires in a beautiful modern house called Benifold up on the hill. I had meals at the rectory and, later, the use of its attic for billets. Tudor Davies was the Rector's name and he had a wife and three daughters.

The most significant event at Headley was my visit to Vaughan Williams. In September 1939 I had attended a lecture he gave in York for which he had braved the blackout. There is a very good photograph of him with EC Bairstow in the latter's biography: he must have been taking the chair. I spoke briefly to him and obtained his autograph. Now, I had lost no time in writing to Sir Edward Bairstow telling him about my new life. I was stationed at Headley, but the address of the regiment was Dorking. In his turn, Sir Edward speedily replied 'I enclose a little letter to RVW, whose address is The White Gates, Westcott Road, Dorking. I am sure he will be kind to you. Go and see him'.

I sent the 'little letter' and received a reply dated 8 November. It was written by Mrs Vaughan Williams and signed by her husband. It ran:

Dear Mr Jackson, I shall like to meet you again very much – and will not make a definite appointment because I do not know what your free times are. But I am in most days, and could always make some free time for you any time you like to come in. The only time I know that I am not free at present are tomorrow, Saturday and Sunday afternoon – but anyway it might be safer to ring up as I do sometimes go out.

Yours sincerely, R Vaughan Williams.

I had rung up and spoken to VW on a terribly inaudible line from the canteen, and fixed up when I was to go and see him. Dorking was getting on for forty miles away, beyond Guildford, and transport was not by any means easy at that time. There were a number of buses but they were all full, so I got a lift from Aldershot to Dorking direct with a wild Canadian driving an army car. He got me there, and deposited me almost on the doorstep by 3.45pm. The door was answered by a coloured lady who was almost immediately followed by an energetic VW who took my groundsheet into the kitchen to dry: it was a pouring wet day. There were also two maids and three cats.

I was a chorister when his *Te Deum* was first sung in the Minster – in 1929, the year after it had been written for the enthronement of the Archbishop of Canterbury. It appeared very modern indeed to an eleven-year-old. We also used the *Evening Service* in C for village choirs – an excellent piece: also we did *O Clap your Hands, Lord thou hast been our refuge* and, most notably, the *Mass* in G minor. This was a very rare and courageous thing for choirs of that period to undertake: one remembers Holst's non-plussed reaction regarding its standard of difficulty on receiving the manuscript. We also had the *Oxford Book of Carols* (edited by VW) very soon after its publication. One of VW's first remarks on settling down at the White Gates that day was an enquiry about Sir Edward Bairstow: 'Well, how is the great man?' Iris Lemare always referred to him as Uncle Ralph, which I believe most or all of his female pupils did.

My account of the visit, written the following day, 17 November 1940, begins:

'He really is a dear, the most lovable soul you could meet. He is so young in spirit and most entertaining in his quiet way. He talks very quickly but distinctly and quietly and laughs heartily when amused, which is often. He insisted on helping me to butter as people always took such tiny helpings he said, and he went out half way through tea to wash the marmalade off his fingers, and his wife told me that he usually managed to get marmalade not only all over the table but on the floor as well. He is very much in possession of all his faculties and almost childlike in his simplicity. I loved the way he sat puffing at his pipe after tea, enjoying it thoroughly, the picture of contentment as we discussed music, choral and otherwise, but not his, alas. He seemed as though he did not want to talk about his own things, as I would have liked to do. There were heaps of things I wanted to talk about but there was no opportunity. He asked me what I had composed, and I got as far as mentioning an overture, giving its history, its beginnings as a violin piece (which Sybil Eaton once played in Bairstow's house at York).'

'I said I was no composer really, in fact that I had dried up since May. He replied "I think that's a good sign", and that it was preferable to having a wealth of ideas of questionable value – quality rather than quantity in fact… encouraging if true! I think it is true, though, that ideas will come all in good time. I believe he found it hard going at first, but look what he has produced. I ventured to ask his wife what he was working on, and she said it was difficult to say as he always had more than one thing on the way and it was hard to know what would emerge. "So let us hold tight. Something will be coming soon."'

'I then said I was stuck for a libretto for the Mus. Doc. Exercise, and he said why not one of the psalms – which was what I wanted to do at first – or Ezekiel, or Job, or – oh the bible is full of likely things, he said. He loves it. He produced a copy of *The Bible as Literature* and read a long passage from the beginning of Ezekiel most beautifully and said it was definitely Aeroplanes. Wonderful stuff but bewildering.'

He used this passage later for his *Vision of Aeroplanes* in 1955 – an extraordinary work unlike anything else he wrote. At teatime he had two large cups of tea poured out for him at the same time, breakfast size and of pleasing pattern.

'He has a massive frame and a huge square face: his hair is thick and tousled, only just turning grey, at 68, not a scrap bald: an open necked shirt, odd waistcoat, jacket and trousers, with carpet slippers in which he shuffles about the house, covering his very large feet…. I cannot think he would ever forget anything; he was never at a loss for a name and, as I came away, remembered about my gas mask, which I had forgotten about and had left in the little cloakroom. The house was very interesting, full of character and atmosphere. It seemed somehow untidy, though you could not put your finger on anything that was out of place. There were some lovely things, and the room was big, square and lofty, open to the roof, with a balcony round where the first floor would have been. The woodwork was all dark and the walls white, and there was a big grand piano and a radiogram. His wife is extremely nice but, alas, an invalid. Her face shows clearly that she has had much suffering, and her hair is silvery, straight and shiny, cut level all the way round. Dressed in black, and on a high chair, her slim figure was quite arresting. She is genuinely fond of music, especially Ralph's. Her sister was there, with her husband Doctor RO Morris, whom I had met at New College when I was there at dinner with HK Andrews. He remembered the occasion and admitted that he had not connected the two Jacksons. They all knew Sir Marmaduke Strickland-Constable [who I knew at Malton early in the war] who was in fact RVW's pupil for a time. He said that Marmaduke was a very good musician. They also knew Guy Warrack and Howells and others I know the names of.'

'AND – RVW talked of Ravel. He has the greatest respect and love for him – his wife too. She asked me if I played "those three" of which *Le Gibet* was one, and I said I did. He said that Ravel was the most lovable of men, had tremendous vitality and was interested in everything, liking particularly the green-grocers' shops in London where he stayed with them more than once: he loved the colour and the set-out of the fruits and said there was nothing like them in Paris. He also wanted to see all the picture galleries. After being shown the National Gallery and the Tate he asked to see the *Vallasse*. "What?", asked VW: he meant the Wallace collection. He was in Paris in 1909 working with Ravel.'

'I asked him about an article in the previous Sunday Times by Ernest Newman on *Serenade to Music*, wondering what he thought of it. (Newman tries to work out why 'the peculiar sweetness of the *Serenade* comes about, and says that the principle is that of the simultaneous sounding of chords that are normally opposed to each other' resulting in 'a soft clashing, and effect of gentle cross-purposes.... Two harmonic dimensions telescoped into one.') But VW said he hardly ever read Newman as he took the Observer, but he said he thought he had read it – some pupil had brought it along. Funny he didn't remember much about it, or set any store by it. He said that Newman and he were 'enemies', but only in the press I think. I mentioned the recording of *The Lark Ascending* and asked him what he thought of the performance. He said they were very good and that Grinke had taken them there the other day to play to them. … He is a dear man. It is difficult to think that *London Symphony, Tallis, Lark, Wenlock Edge, Rhosymedre* and all the other joys I don't know have come from him. It was an indescribable thrill for me and so stimulating after being isolated from music for a time. I had plenty of ideas as I came back in the bus and *Serenade* and other pieces running through my brain.'

I visited the house again briefly some twenty-five or thirty years later when William Cole had it and had changed its character by cleaning it up and having less furniture. The next time I looked for it when I was doing an opening recital in Dorking parish church for Martin Ellis in 1987, it could not be found. Dry rot had caused it to be pulled down and the grounds had been built on. One of the houses kept the name though, and it had white gates of course, but it was rather sad since the former was a house of character and with interesting associations. It could have become a VW museum, like Ravel's.

||O||

I found the south country attractive, with its blander climate and atmosphere. I had seen little of it up till then, and the more opulent houses and the higher standard of living were different from what I was used to in Yorkshire. Places like Selborne and the Ogbournes were of great interest by reason of their beauty and antiquity, heightened by the peacefulness brought about by minimal traffic in wartime. When, later, we were moved to Pennings Camp at Tidworth and were at the foot of Sidbury Hill, WH Hudson's *Shepherd's Life* became required reading. His description of the springy turf was very true. The view from the hilltop was stunning, and put me in mind of Houseman's 'coloured counties' in Shropshire. I tried to sketch it in watercolour.

My wish for adventure, and relief to be breaking free from restrictions of home and a narrow country town existence was very soon rudely shattered when, one day, I realised that I was in the army for as long as the war lasted. And nobody knew how long that was to be. This had not dawned on me before and now came as a pretty devastating revelation. Apart from my fellows, who were all in the same predicament, there was the uniform, the army food, the routine: lights out, last post, reveille; the training: gunnery, radio, driving-and-maintenance, map-reading, drill, gym, cross-country runs, the polishing of brasses and boots, the blanco-ing (in glorious khaki technicolour) of our equipment and webbing, the room inspections with our beds all tidily set out; all these and the expectation of nemesis in the shape of being 'put on a charge' should the required standard be not attained. All this, of course, in a completely different atmosphere from that we were used to, with no-one to go home to tell about it and to receive comforting words from.

There was, however, leave to look forward to every so often, permission applied for, travel warrants to be claimed, then train times to be worked out and the weary trek to the station and a seat if you were lucky. It was something like a couple of hours to London. To York from Kings Cross was four hours, not a minute under, then York to Malton; all this starting from Headley at 12 noon, arriving at journey's end long after blackout in the winter months. What bliss it was, to have a bed with sheets, ironed and sweet-smelling, to wake up to the old familiar sounds, with no brusque command to 'show a leg' but with the prospect of a long day of doing anything to be wished, or nothing. It was sometime during this period that I happened to meet an RAF pilot who told me that he usually managed to take his leave when one of his fighter planes needed to be flown northwards. His home, as I remember, was not far from the plane's destination in Lancashire, and his flying time was about a quarter of an hour. I could not help noting his nonchalance as I compared his lot with mine, and my eight-hour trudge to cover a similar distance. But it was worth it, even though it might be short.

Gradually we settled in as we became used to the new life, and formed our own way of organising our days, doing what interested us in our spare time, reading, writing home, listening to a rare broadcast symphony concert on a crackly portable set, an evening in the NAAFI, an occasional home-made concert. My room-mates were considerate when they knew I wished to listen seriously, and it was an event when a series of all the Sibelius symphonies came along.

We soon found friends of similar tastes and were able to exchange ideas and learn from each other. Two were literary enthusiasts, Alfred Ewan and Derrick Hodgson, the former a good artist and art teacher in Hull. I was introduced to poetry, Aldous Huxley, Eliot, Auden, Spender, Isherwood, and I discovered Wordsworth, Shelley, Keats and much else, having bought cheap paperback anthologies and been given Herbert Read's *Knapsack*, a kind of Weekend Book of poetry and prose designed for the serving soldier.

I have since given great thanks for this. So far poetry had not come into my life, except for a small book called *Modern Poetry* used at school, selected and edited in 1920 by Quiller-Couch that was a set book for matric. It had Whitman, Bliss Carman, R Hodgson, Bunyan, Kipling, Yeats, even de la Mare, but they did not enthuse me. I did, however, set as a solo song John Davidson's *In Romney Marsh*, the main attraction being the concluding lines 'The beach with all its organ stops/ Pealing again prolonged the roar'. Bairstow was kind about it, observing that there was a lot of poetry in it! (I think he meant in the music ...) I was to meet Herbert Read at a friend's house after the war, briefly, but found him somewhat hard to come to know. Perhaps he was as shy as I. He made no effort, and appeared, in fact, to be bored by the proceedings. His wife, Margaret, was a good viola player and entered into musical activity at Hovingham festivals and around the Ryedale district in which was her home at Stonegrave, between Hovingham and Helmsley.

From Headley we could get ourselves by some means to Alton or even Winchester where it was a pleasure to see something different, to poke about the shops – mostly book shops were our interest – and call in somewhere for tea and a cake. Aunt Sybil was then living at Shawford, south of Winchester, so I was able to pay her a call or two. Alton was within our radius where, in happier years afterwards, I played several recitals in the church.

I spent Christmas 1940 learning all the delights of Rummy and lived it up at the Regent Palace Hotel: bed and breakfast 8/6d (42.5p) per night.

27 January 1941: 'Our new sergeant is the foulest little squirt with a temper to match. He looks like he is, hunch-backed, small red screwed-up face – quite mad of course.'

2 February: 'Four chaps interviewed for commission, but I couldn't summon enthusiasm for the army, and that's what they're looking for.'

6 April: 'Visited London and saw a hole in the roof of Saint Paul's. Amen Court, the home of Dykes Bower the organist, quite flat. Heard a concert conducted by Basil Cameron. Very good indeed. He gets fine results with apparently little effort. The programme included the first performance of Britten's Violin Concerto. It was queer, but probably (!) good.'

22 April: 'I am losing one of my pyjamas rapidly. It tears as fast as I sew it, so I had better tear it up and use it for rags. Meanwhile will you send me a fresh supply, please?'

Easter: 'Magnificent billet. It is on a hillside covered in trees, mostly Scots firs but with two magnificent oaks, and a fine Wellingtonia fir, tall and well proportioned, also some cherries on the bank opposite to our window that bid fair to bloom within a fortnight. The rooms, 2 for 5 of us, are furnished and have carpets, curtains and ash trays – in fact everything civilised ... The maid comes round with the vacuum cleaner every morning so there's no cleaning to do ... Sent a letter to Scaife [Headmaster of the Song School]. Can picture him reading it to the boys.'

During a short stay in hospital I had to 'eat with a nail file and a pocket knife, in the absence of more civilised cutlery. Hardly conducive to recovery from Pharyngitis. The padre gave me news of Dykes Bower and Boris Ord, of King's College, both of whom he knew at Cambridge. I had to miss Moura Lympany – I wanted to know whether it was male or female – and what it looked like. So much rubbish on radio – jazz, jazz and more jazz... We get postal deliveries on Sundays. At the Queen's Hall, Sunday afternoon concert, I heard Rachmaninoff's second *Piano Concerto* which Eileen Joyce played beautifully, and looked lovely in blue velvet.' Naturally this brought to mind the occasion when she had played Beethoven's first *Piano Concerto* at a concert by the York Musical Society, conducted by Sir Edward and I turned her pages. Food tended to loom large in letters at this time, and in a period of strict rationing it was wonderful how my parents were able to send substantial amounts to supplement army fare.

8 May: 'Had a pretty ghastly two days on divisional exercises on Thurs. and Fri. We set off at 4am in our trucks. The tanks went on

ahead. We stopped every ten yards, and, with a pause in a wayside barn for breakfast which lasted about two hours (the pause), we eventually reached a place somewhere near Brighton at 8.00 pm the same evening. Then we sloshed around in the mud inches deep filling the tanks with petrol after stew and tea in the open. The next day was equally unprofitable.'

14 May: 'We went up to Aldershot this afternoon. The guns on the pellet range weren't working, so we just had a Horlicks and went into two shops. The wasted time is simply incredible... Took part in a talent competition in the village hall. I played the Chopin A Flat *Ballade* and Ravel's *Bolero* with side drum accompaniment, and received first prize – 100 cigarettes. It proved that they do enjoy a bit of good stuff sandwiched in occasionally.'

22 May: 'Singing in a concert – only part songs though, and played *Sonatine, Jeux d'eau,* and *Valse Noble* No.1 by Ravel.... It's nice playing to people who like something a bit more modern than Chopin.'

24 May: 'A Heinkel of some sort was brought down. I heard a burst of gunfire above me, a sort of muffled one, then a good dollop of anti-aircraft shells and a bomb flash. No explosion though. It was too far away – just a few tracer bullets.'

26 May: 'Had athlete's foot – it's rather an amusing name, for me at any rate!'

30 May: 'Letter from Melville Cook. Had been to Bach Passion at the Minster. News of article in Yorkshire Evening Press about the Minster Choir School and a reference to me. Had hoped to see Vaughan Williams again, but had to be on guard duty.'

3 June: 'Heard the Franck Symphony. It is a lovely work, but you can tell an organist wrote it. The orchestration is thick in parts but it all sounds good.'

Radio batteries and their replacement were a constant theme in my letters. It shows how fortunate folk are nowadays in what they can get so easily – in reception, quality of sound and performance, and the sheer abundance of music. I wonder if they appreciate it.

4 June: 'Bairstow wrote to say that Iris Lemare was full of beans and takes on too many things... They have altered a lot of the Dean's [Herbert Newell Bate] petty alterations in ritual at the Minster, on the day after the funeral.'

5 July: 'My tank has been changed ... and is now a Mark 6 with an auxiliary turret, which later I suppose will be my place. It means I have an extra gun to look after.'

12 August: 'Looked in on a choir practice at Winchester Cathedral. Doctor Rhodes plays like an angel and is very nice and quiet. The choir is excellent, especially the boys, and the new Harrison organ is lovely.'

13 August: 'Our new sergeant knocked a tree down with a runaway tank this morning – lucky for him it was only a tree – a fairly substantial one – and not another tank – or a soldier! His comment was "No tiller bars wouldn't work and no brakes wouldn't 'old."'

'I took myself to Salisbury Cathedral for Evensong and Sir Walter Alcock – now aged eighty – asked me up to the loft with him. He was very chatty and nice. He had a great grudge against parsons (a familiar theme) and poured out his heart about them and their narrow stupidity. He evidently is too gentle with them, and is a charming old man. Told me to go when I can. On my next visit I heard Stanford's D Minor *Postlude*, and after it Sir Walter showed me a few stops and was awfully pleased with his organ. He was bucked that I am a Bairstovian, as he taught Bairstow at the Abbey. Makes me his musical grandson, as he said. I've got a marvellous book called the *Musical Companion* edited by one Bacharach – about 750 pages, and has a lot of grand stuff in it.'

On those warm summer days the scent of the lime trees in the cathedral close was wonderful. I have seldom smelt them anywhere as strongly since, even at Salisbury, which I came to know better in the days of David Willcocks who had taken over from Alcock and lived in the same house, 5 The Close, from 1947.

||◆||

It was necessary to establish a system of codes with my family so that they would know where I was sent in the event of an overseas posting. Wartime censorship was very strict. Double Summer Time was a controversial wartime experiment (the clocks went forward by two hours), which the farmers didn't like, but it was something I found very congenial.

One learnt such ploys as squaring the sergeant when one wanted leave, so that he would mark one present when in fact one was away. We had so many hopes of leave that were dashed at the last minute, but I did manage a travel warrant from Tidmouth to Gleneagles to visit the Macdonalds that was much appreciated. It was sad to read of the recordings of Walton's *Violin Concerto*, and a copy with Heifetz's bowing marks being sunk in mid-Atlantic, even before the composer had had the chance to hear and see them.

During 1941 I became quite good on the accordion which was very useful for accompanying songs, psalms, hymns, popular songs and ballads. This resulted in my becoming 'more and more dissipated' – I went to three smoking and drinking evenings in about five days. My best piece was *Under the Double Eagle* (which I used to play with Mother in a four-hand piano arrangement), being pleased with myself for playing the bass tune on the left hand buttons of the squeezebox. The composer's name was Wagne.

It was always expected that the regiment would be sent abroad. Of course we were never told anything about future plans, and speculation and rumour were rife in the eleven months of our training. Then we were fitted out with tropical kit and sent to the River Clyde where, on the *HT Strathaird* we loitered for some time in the estuary awaiting the formation of our convoy.

I wrote home on Monday 29 September 1941, C/o A.P.O. 1515 [Army Post Office]: 'After two sweltering nights in the bowels of this ship berthed at Glasgow, and a third which I spent on the deck, we pulled out seawards at last. It was at 5.15pm yesterday whilst we were having evensong that we first moved, and it was thrilling to see the countryside and the docks and shipyards all slipping silently by. Greenock and Gourock passed and Milton House on the hillside at Bowling where I had lunch once with Mrs Mcdonald in the garden of a friend of hers with the roses out (looking over at the Clyde and with the sun shining on it). As darkness fell we anchored off Gourock on the South and the Holy Loch and Loch Long on the north. Dear old Scotland again, the mountains changing always, and the ship turning slowly round, giving us a change of view without ourselves moving. The sunset last night was as if we were being consoled by it, departing from home. The colour lingered long, till darkness at last prevailed. I played to the officers in the mess afterwards, Ravel's *Valse Noble* No. 1, and Chopin's C sharp minor and D flat waltzes. On Saturday night I had played Chopin's A flat *Ballade* and *Bolero* with drums. Today opened miserably with rain and mist but became a perfect afternoon with such colour on the hills and in the September sky, just as I used to see at Auchterarder. After 4 o'clock tea I stood and watched the tongue of land jutting out into the deep blue silvery water – the point between the Long and Holy Lochs with a few houses and a church steeple on it, silhouetted strongly with the fainter hills behind. The sun was shining almost straight at me, and I began to think it was an Italian lake I was on. But as the sun went down the ocean took on a darker tone, almost severe but really Scottish, the little sharp steeple standing out still strongly. We went round to the port side and there was the moon, half full. Large and yellow, in the pale blue sky, its long reflection stretching from us to the further shore (to Gourock that is) like millions of electric bulbs flashing in and out in an electric sign in Piccadilly Circus, the sea itself like jet black velvet.'

Friday 3 October: 'We moved out on Tuesday about 8.30pm – I didn't know we were going till we passed the submarine nets across the Clyde Estuary. I went up to the mess and played Chopin's *Prelude No 1*, Brahms's A flat waltz and the *Bee's Wedding*. When I came down again it was a beautifully clear night with a white moon, so I stayed wandering about the ship till 11.00, watching the islands and headlands as we passed them. Everything beautifully calm. Next morning I awoke feeling the ship rolling about, and began to be sick. I didn't eat a thing all day, except for a bit of bread and butter at teatime, which did not remain. Every time I moved I was sick, but was moderately well lying and keeping quiet. I was ill on boat drill practice and had to go to the side. Three others followed suit. My birthday was the plainest I have ever spent; it was like the previous day only worse. I staggered up to see the doctor, unshaven and miserable and got a powder to take, and a chit to say I was ATTEND C (excused all parades) and could have my bed, which I did, and never stirred from it all day.'

'Today was calmer and I felt better – I had two slices of bread and marmalade up on the deck, and a shave during which the air raid alarm went. Nothing happened by 2 o'clock. The food is excellent. I had a little delicious vegetable soup, pork, turnip, roast potato, stewed fruit and custard and felt much better for it. We have brown bread only and South African butter, which are both as good as possible. Also plenty of jam or marmalade. Next day I felt worse again (Sat.) as the sea was rougher, and hardly ate anything at all. I managed to finish most of the scoring of the hymns for the Sunday service, with one yet to be finished before 10.30, the time for service. I felt better on Sunday and we had glorious sunshine for the first time, which put a different complexion on things. I rehearsed the band at 9.30 with the hymns (O God our help, Blest are the pure, Eternal Father and The King) and my scoring sounded quite well in spite of the absence of the second saxophone. The ship heaved a good deal and I had to hold on to a table whilst conducting. All the players are good, and specially so the trumpets (3). Evensong at 5.00 for which I played the piano. The moon rose over the water at twilight, a big orange ball – I played at a concert in the officers' Mess – very badly as I had felt rocky all day and could not get a piano to practise on. I did *Minstrels*, Brahms A flat waltz again and Falla's *Fire Dance*, with Chopin's D flat waltz for encore. Everyone got merry.'

It fell to my lot to provide the music for church parade. It was remarkable that a fairly healthy gathering of players could be found among all those soldiers who embraced three trumpets, a tenor trombone, two altos and a tenor saxophone, two violins, one cello and a pizzicato bass. We lacked a firm bass and I made a note to bring in a piano next time. I wanted us to play an opening voluntary, and the only piece I could think of was Mozart's *Ave Verum*. We rehearsed it and it came off successfully. The following Sunday we essayed the same procedure but without trying it through again beforehand – such was my inexperience. The result was rather a shambles, due perhaps to the players' being not of professional standard. Whether or not there was an outgoing voluntary on either occasion is not recorded.

Tuesday 8 October: 'Yesterday I went on PT which was nice and we had a very good lecture by Mr Montgomery on the commandos, who did the Lofoten Islands raid. Boat still decidedly unsteady, and it was difficult balancing in PT. I was not too well. Today the sea is a deep rich blue and the other ships in the convoy a misty blue. The sun is higher and stronger – we cannot bear it to shine on our books as we read. PT was washed out by a boat drill practice. The boat is quite steady and the sea calm.'

Eventually we moved, striking out westwards sufficiently to be out of range of the German U-boats, then south and eventually into Freetown for supplies and refuelling where we anchored for four or five days in the mouth of the Sierra Leone river. The local people came around selling bananas, coconuts and lemons (small green ones which were probably not lemons but limes) by means of a basket let down the side of the ship. They also dived for pennies with great skill and never missed one: they also kept asking for a 'Glasgow tanner' to be thrown to them. Writing home I mentioned flying fish which looked like swallows skimming over the surface of the water, glistening in the sunshine like silver bullets – this was out in the open sea where a huge school of porpoises one day were gracefully leaping up out of the water and suddenly turning all together and careering in the opposite direction.

19 October: 'Things to do have cropped up and rather curtailed writing. I have been reading *Pickwick* with intense enjoyment. I have started *The Quest for Corvo*, a very interesting account of AJA Symons' researches of Fr. Rolphe, alias Baron Corvo, writer of *Hadrian The Seventh*. We moved out of Freetown after lunch, where we had been for 4 or 5 days, anchored in the harbour. It was incredible to be within sight of Africa, and for so long – and a nice, clean and colourful place it *looks*. We had quinine doses to keep our pulses low and prevent malaria – we also applied mosquito ointment, but there was no need really. The great thing about being in harbour was that there was no blackout [in force in the UK at the time], and there was smoking on deck at night. It was lovely to see the lights of the town and the other ships in the convoy – something I had not seen for 2 years at least. We slept with the portholes open, which made it considerably cooler; that is, when we didn't sleep on deck. We were driven indoors 2 out of the 4 nights, by rain, and one night I just let it rain on me, and was none the worse. A remarkable phenomenon was the lightning each night, and sometimes to be seen in the day also. Sometimes there were 5 or 6 storms going on at once, giving an almost continuous flickering. There was no thunder to hear unless the storm was nearer. Last night was an amazing display – the lightning was pinky-blue and was almost overhead once, followed by a colossal thunder-clap, which sent the chaps hurtling away from the portholes as though the ship had tipped over. We could see the other ships and the town and the hills behind almost the whole time by the light of the flashes. It started during the concert at which I played *The Minute Waltz* and *Shepherd's Hey*, with *Country Gardens* for

an encore. There were prizes, but I, having won £1 (first prize) the previous Saturday with *Bolero* and the *Bee's Wedding*, didn't get one. A young airman played Liszt's *Concert Study*, but it didn't go down. He has a good technique.'

'There have been concerts of classical music on gramophone records, and much enjoyed they were, as a change from the noise and constant jazz, thumped out the day long. The Padré asked me if I would like to try the records by myself, which I did today, with great pleasure. It reminded me of home too – a thing that had not bothered me at all till then. It was a brand new HMV portable – there are more than one on board – and the records are brand new too – some of the newest recordings. *Petrouchka* (sides 5 & 6 only) were new to me and a great treat – a virile work. *Brigg Fair*, *The Cuckoo*, Tallis *Fantasia* (Boult), *Water Music* (Stokowski), *Carneval Overture* (Czech Phil), and a lovely *Slavonic Dance* – No 10 (or 2, as on the Menuhin record of the same piece) in E minor. The Tallis is a superior one to the Boyd Neel's Decca version – a more elastic reading. The *Carneval* is a very spirited rendering. For church, my scoring of Mozart's *Ave Verum*, carefully rehearsed, sounded nice, out on the top deck. The hymns were As with Gladness, Conquering Kings, and Jesus calls us. The first and third were done by someone else and had a lot of bad part writing (doubling of the bass an octave higher, etc) which made the rehearsal difficult – altering of parts etc. The music has put on a new complexion to this life – better even than Headley or anywhere else – strange that it should come on board a troop-ship. Last Sunday night in the Officers' Mess I played the *Minuet* and *Toccata* of Ravel (*Le Tombeau de Couperin*) and got thunderous applause, much to my surprise; so I played the little Poulenc, which they didn't like quite so much.'

Tuesday 21 October: 'On Sunday (the day I wrote the above) I went to bed about 8, feeling quite "done up", but I was hauled out at 9.00 to play in the Mess again – I thought I had eluded the Sergeant who came calling for me out on the deck; I kept quiet, but he sent someone to find me. Anyway, I went, and played *Alborada del Gracioso* without any previous practice, and feeling none too well, and sticky about the hands, to boot. I played it very well though; almost better than ever. It is curious how I do play better at concerts – I must forget all my fears of technique in my anxiety to get the piece across. I know *Alborada*

[Ravel: *Miroirs*] well, so there really is nothing to fear anyway. Before that I played Poulenc's *Pastourelle*, and for an encore, the *Minuet* from *Sonatine*, both of which they liked; but *Alborada* got enthusiastic applause.'

It was a good thing that I had a memorized store of pieces to draw on, not being able to carry sheet music about. The only printed piece I had was a miniature full score of Ravel's *Rhapsodie Espagnole* with its fascinating orchestration. It had been easy at that young age to memorize, especially difficult pieces. Usually by the time I had thoroughly learnt something I knew it by heart.

'Bed at 11.30. I awoke next morning with a cold and sore throat, so saw the MO about it, who gave me tablets either to suck or pound up and dissolve for a gargle. It took me two hours and ten minutes of waiting in a queue to see him – a good job I wasn't expiring or had acute appendicitis – the whole army is stupid like this – our entire time on the ship is spent in waiting and queuing, if not for food, parades, then for apples and biscuits at the canteen. I had injunctions to lie down and keep warm, which I gladly did, not feeling too good, both yesterday and today.'

'A most excellent violinist turned up in the band, name of Davis or Davies, who knows Dykes-Bower well and was reading law at Durham. So today after tea I wrote out *Pavane pour une Infante défunte* & *Pièce en forme d'Habanera* which he played nicely. He likes Ravel, in fact calls himself a Ravel fan. Hope to do lots of music with him, but he didn't bring any with him; same with me. Sleeping up on deck last night, I was driven in at 9.30 by a sharp shower, and got drenched in my green pyjamas waiting in the crush to get indoors. Not too good, for one with a cold, but I was no worse this morning, and not much better. Being under the weather makes you fed up with life on a troop ship; also the continuous talking and shouting and fooling of the louts, and the jostling; all of which don't bother the healthy soldier – not even me. ... We saw a huge school of dolphins (or I think they might have been porpoises) diving in and out of the water in most graceful fashion. Yesterday the alarm went for "Boat stations" and depth charges were dropped, but we were all clear in less than ten minutes.'

Thursday 23 October: 'The MO told me to take it easy for another couple of days yesterday and to do no PT. Being on sick parade precluded my attendance at any lectures before dinner. I wrote hard at *Overture* [my orchestral piece which began as a violin piece and was played by Sybil Eaton] for Davies to play, which he did jolly well, also the 2 little Ravels. Slept out, but so windy I had to come in at 3.15 feeling very disgusted and full of cold. Finished *Overture* on Friday and Davies played it magnificently. He is dead in tune and has a fine technique. The piece sounds a great deal fuller than on the piano alone. He gets the double harmonies at the end of *Habanera* without any trouble. The hymns arrived for Sunday, so Mr Thomas continued to excuse me duties in the morning to score them. Young B, in spite of being such a good pianist (or probably because he is) is quite simple and a bore. A most surprising sunset after a grey day. Just before the sun went down it appeared below the clouds for 2 or 3 minutes and tinted everything golden-red. Then when it disappeared it edged the clouds through the rift just along the horizon with gold, and tinged them with red, and sent up rose-coloured rays – all of it in such a small space, taking up no more than six inches of sky above the horizon; and it wasn't more than 3 feet long. Because we have been crossing the Equator some time now, the weather has been almost winterly, with a cold wind, and I have got more cold. I'm glad, because it must have been unbearable if any hotter than a few days ago. The sun is 6 degrees south of the Equator so I believe.'

We next called at Capetown, South Africa, where we could hardly believe what we saw in the shops – a complete contrast to what we had left behind in England, particularly large bars of chocolate piled high in the sweet shops. There was a concert in a largish concert hall in which I played the *Minute Waltz* and was informed by the compère who introduced me that my friends called me Maestro. That was news to me; but it stuck to some extent for a while and was in fact metamorphosed into Mousetrap by one colleague.

But what stays most with me is the reception accorded me by the cathedral organist, Doctor Alban Hamer, who called for me at noon on the four days we were docked in Capetown, and drove me to his home where each day Mrs Hamer spared no pains to feed me. How fortunate I was to have found this wonderful friendly family. I wrote home on Monday 3 November 1941 on Doctor Hamer's notepaper headed 'Linton, Queen's Road, Sea Point, Capetown':

My dear Dad,

I have been having an uproarious time at the hands of Dr. Hamer, the Cathedral organist since arrival here on Thursday night. I have spent all my spare time at his house, having meals of the most luxurious kind – even better than Mrs J's wartime efforts!

We are to be aboard at 10 tonight. This break has made all the difference to us – we all got rather grumpy after a month all together, but this should just set us right for the rest of the journey. I played a bit on the City Hall organ yesterday, a good Norman & Beard, and also played the last hymn, The King (which they always sing pianissimo in wartime, and very effective too) and Bach's A minor prelude and fugue for the voluntary after the evening service at the Cathedral last night. The organ is a very good Hill, from Saint Margaret's, Westminster, and has a magnificent Tuba.

Doctor Hamer took me to meet the Archbishop of Capetown, Archbishop Darbishire, at his palace on Saturday – a lovely white Dutch-looking house – and the garden was full of honeysuckle, roses, violets, foxgloves, Watsonia lilies, a whole pergola of bright red passion flowers, jacaranda etc., water lilies and a tangled mass of every conceivable kind of low growing flower by a stream. The vegetation is most intriguing – we went to the botanical gardens today and saw all sorts of lovely things. All this in November. There was wood-sorrel in the Archbishop's garden, in the shade, and jolly nice and cool it was. It is pretty hot when the sun's out. It would be nice to live here, but not for more than 3 or 4 years. Sorry but I'm going to be whisked off to a Brahms's Requiem rehearsal now. Lots of love – see you soon I hope – Frank.'

Our next port of call was Durban, but we did not go ashore. Then northwards, keeping Madagascar to starboard and into the Red Sea reaching Port Tewfik (Bûr Taufiq) in Egypt which was our destination.

8 February: 'We are continually on the move, halting for a few days at a time, but there is no rest, and every day is like the last. We have no time to think or fret. (Letter took 8 weeks less a day to reach Mrs Macdonald in Scotland).'

16 February: 'We were in a lovely little valley within sight of the sea a few nights ago but unfortunately had to leave. It was full of flowers of all kinds. The prevailing colour was pinky-mauve ...'

Soon after we arrived in Egypt the advent of General Montgomery was a tremendous morale-booster. Our progress westwards (and our regress at times) was nevertheless a thing of mystery, doubt and boredom, among the unending scene of nothing but sand, without a single green leaf or blade of grass by way of relief from the monotony. Our living quarters were either in trucks, lean-tos to one side of them made out of canvas stretched over some kind of supporting frame, and our food, mostly bully beef and biscuits (which was on our Christmas dinner menu that year; although, to be fair, what was our more usual fare came a few days later), and sometimes we had yams instead of potatoes. Our one-pint-a-day of water came to be supplemented by a water cart that sought out oases wherever we encamped, bringing us water of varying quality.

Without a complete record of our movements along the north coast of Africa it is not possible to say what happened or where: censorship was strict and our family code was not a great deal of use. The name of our dog at home, Topsy, came in useful for Tripoli and Tunis (the correct Tripoli, one hoped, whose authentic name is Tarábulus) and no doubt there was the occasional odd subterfuge besides.

There was one location that is indelibly fixed in my mind, however, and is probably the grimmest episode of all. We were for some time leaguered some dozen or so miles inland from Tobruk (Tubruq), doing nothing and noting how that port kept changing hands between our own and Rommel's forces with all the concomitant *son et lumière*.

Time hung heavily, but I was at last able to put down on to paper what I had been wanting to do for close on twelve months. The urge to compose had been, to say the least, pretty dormant, but my wish to set Robert Frost's *Tree at my window* as a song – I had in mind Elsie Suddaby – came to fruition. Alone in my DIY tent, at bedtime, the moment came. I wrote until the small hours, never looking back. My illumination was from diesel oil served by a wick of rope through a hole in the lid of a round cigarette tin. Having finished, I blew it out and slept soundly despite the half gale still blowing that had accompanied my outpourings. It was an indescribable pleasure to behold, on waking, the final result of so much thought, all complete (but for the addition of one insignificant bar) and in need of no further attention.

[*Historical note*: Elsie did sing it and I accompanied her in a broadcast from Leeds when she was appearing in the festival in the late 1940s. Also included was Shelley's *Widow Bird*, one of three songs I wrote on as many days in early May at Fort Capuzzo, a place not far from the regiment's location, where we had been sent as a relief from so much uninteresting sameness, where we found the most wonderful bathing in crystal clear water, deep blue, in a small cove. We took full advantage and were the better for it. This was at, or near, Sollum.]

Before long, however, things changed dramatically and we were in the thick of one of the fiercest battles of the campaign. A few miles west of us, at the intersection of two tracks in the four points of the compass was the place that had assumed the name of Knightsbridge. It was here, as May was coming to an end with the sun beating down mercilessly, that the wind blew the fine loose sand into a veritable pea-soup situation: that wind, known as the Khamsin, blew for a period around that time of year. The sand got into your hair, your eyes and ears, everywhere, and thirst was the worst that could be imagined. We 'brewed up' tea, drank it, and immediately had to do it again, though our supplies were limited. And all the time the noise of the engagement, each side trying to blow the other to bits – and to what purpose? – continued unabated: we could not tell how things were going nor where supplies would be needed. Were the enemy advancing and would we have to pick ourselves up and retreat eastwardly in double-quick time?

All we knew was that we had been preserved, miraculously, to fit ourselves for further activity of the same kind. The result and the full details are to be found, no doubt, in histories and accounts that may have been written. My own overwhelming feeling, getting on for seventy years after, and coming upon a map which showed Knightsbridge and other places we knew about but had little idea of their location, is of the unbelievable futility, the waste, of humans and resources, the suffering, sadness both with us and at home and the disruption of the lives of countless numbers: and all for nothing. Having put it all into the back of the mind and then to come upon it again so long afterwards, having been preserved to be able to look back to remember and re-live that appalling episode after forgetting it completely and utterly, brings on a feeling almost impossible to describe: how could we have stood its rigours, and horrors, the very antithesis of the things we hold dearest?

2 June: 'I don't think I shall ever grouse about having to wash up again after this – even in cold water. I sometimes think I'm another person. The lack of music doesn't bother me so very much. There isn't really time to think about it. There is no change in the scenery. All is a flat interminable waste – the North African desert.'

12 June: 'We have a pint of water a day to wash in (actually for all purposes), and some of it is very salty, so we are not too clean. We live in the back of a lorry, and the mess is a lean-to. Food is tinned, except for biscuits which we get in lieu of bread.'

After Knightsbridge I wrote home on 16 June 1942: 'I really didn't know what to do about letting you know I was all right after the battles, as I know you hate the sight of a telegram. Furthermore had I sent one I would most assuredly have been hit the next day. As it happened, we cleared out of the danger zone and spent five or six days at the seaside. Now they have gone up again, leaving our lorry behind, not at the sea-side unfortunately, but out of danger for the moment. I hope you are not very worried – I did write a letter card as soon as I could, but without boasting that I was all right. Anyway, you would gather that I was all right, which was all that was necessary. I heard the BBC news one night at 9.0 (your 8.0), which I expect was the same as yours, and heard a very lurid account of the fighting here. That was a pity I thought; and then a night or two later they mentioned us by name I'm told. We certainly did well. The holiday by the sea was lovely, so blue it was, and with quite a broad green strip along the edge, for 200 yds or so, which was difficult to explain. The sand also was very white and tropical-looking. And the water was so warm – I had 4 bathes on 2 days, 3 on all the rest – always one at 7.0 am; that was a parade, but we did more or less as we liked for the rest of the day. I borrowed an accordion, which was whole, fortunately. I did tell you about the v. old one I had, didn't I, with hardly any black notes and leaking bellows and some notes that only worked when you sucked and others only when you blew. Well, this one was heaven – I could play in the extremest keys – even did *Poet & Peasant* in its proper key of D. I had it for two nights and we sat up quite late singing – it was good fun.'

19 June: 'Managed to hear Walton's Violin Concerto and his Bach orchestrations for the ballet *The Wise Virgins*, including *Sheep may Safely Graze*.'

28 June: '12 days since I wrote, but it seems longer. A lot has happened since then and we have been tearing about in this lorry hectically, backwards and forwards, and all the time you will be wondering about me. This slowness in the mail is a curse at such times, but I hope you aren't too worried. This life is awful and my old car-sickness comes up when we hare along over the bumpy desert trying to keep up with the convoy. Anyway, that's nothing. The worst thing is that poor old John Hodgson was killed in action on the 17th, and with him Norman Jackson, two of the nicest chaps in the Squadron. They both came up with me. You know how much I thought of John and I shall feel his loss very much once we are back to normal again. He wrote some poems out here, and one of them ends – 'God, release me from this lean, lethargic land'. ... We were within 20 miles of civilization 3 or 4 days ago but only for a night as it turned out, and up we had to go again to deal with Rommel. He's a clever devil – the whole Nazi organisation is the devil's own handiwork, else how could such wickedness prosper. That sounds like a bit of a psalm. ... I have seen some RAAF trucks and looked out for Paul but haven't seen him, nor heard where his squad is or anything. I had a letter from Sir Edward by the same post and he seemed very pleased to have heard from me. Also 2 fine ones from Dennis, full of news, telling me Sir E. had told them at the prize giving all about my letter to him and the competition on the ship when I won £1 with *Bolero* and *Bee's Wedding*. It's amazing how popular *Bolero* is – they all like it quite as well as the lower jazz things.'

It happened that for a while my brother's Royal Air Force unit was not far from our regiment at Castel Benito, and when I was in Tripoli with a theatrical venture he was near enough to attend a performance. Being a sergeant he had more freedom to move around than I, and our first meeting was a big surprise. He had located our regiment and began enquiring where he could find me, trying for various appellations – Jackson – Francis – Frank – and so on, with no success. 'He plays the piano' ... and at once all became clear: 'Oh, you mean FINGERS!' Such was my fame. And I had a feeling that I rose a little in their estimation, having a brother with the exalted rank of sergeant, albeit in a junior service.

I also wrote to say that 'I found absolutely nothing in Jane Austen's *Emma* – people having colds etc and some of the characters are quite exasperating in the stupid, petty things they talk about and do. Stephen Leacock's *Literary Lapses* I found very amusing'.

8 July: 'I received news about the film *49th Parallel* which has music by Vaughan Williams. Iris Lemare had queued up for two hours in the snow to see it. I can't imagine what it's about with a title like that. Nothing like *39 Steps* [a novel by John Buchan that had been filmed recently in an Alfred Hitchcock production] I take it? Fancy the Malton Picture House getting it anyway. We *are* coming on.'

In a letter to my father on 12 July I enthused over White's *Natural History of Selborne.*

15 July: 'I see my name with full list of degrees among the famous old boys of the Minster School. I think they deserve a sub from me, so will you send old Scaifey half a crown and some lovely sloppy greetings from me, which he loves. Say I've seen the magazine and think it's the cat's whiskers.'

19 July: After reading the score of the Firebird I wrote, '*The Danse Infernale* is a most astonishing thing for rhythm and fire. I don't suppose anyone but a Russian or the devil could have written it. I remember your listening to it by yourself in the old house when we were all out and saying how marvellous it was. Doctor Forsyth and Peter [at Malton] heard it also one night and said they'd never heard such tripe in their lives… The glare from the sun is awful, and I'm so thankful for my dark specs. The university chap from Yorkshire reminded me yesterday that it's hay-time in England now. I wonder how the garden looks. I would like to get on a piano again. Except for a quarter of an hour recently I've gone eight months without touching an instrument. The muscles were out of practice and soon tired. But honestly, I think I played every bit as well as I used to, including the *Hungarian* and *Blue Rhapsodies* – by request.'

Amidst all the waste and frustrations of war, it was good to exchange news about horticulture in Malton, as a reminder that the workings of providence still continue in wartime. This was appreciated particularly during the years in the North African desert.

25 July: 'Heard favourable comment about a broadcast of Vaughan Williams' *Hugh the Drover*. ... My accordion playing is much better now, especially the left hand buttons. My repertory now includes *Blaze Away*, *Stardust* and *The Skaters' Waltz*.'

11 August: 'Went to some gramophone concerts near Alexandria, and was very impressed by Walter Gieseking's playing of Cesar Franck's *Symphonic Variations*.'

22 August: 'Played some two piano music in Rawicz and Landauer style. Bob Lees of Scarborough is knowledgeable and wants to talk about music. He seems to fill Melville Cook's place for me.'

My friend Mrs Norman Macdonald wrote to Doctor Vaughan Williams on 18 September 1942 (when I was in Egypt) thanking him for his 'glorious music' for Coastal Command and 'the deep impression' his 'glorious harmonies and marvellous variety of effects' made on her. His reply, in his own hand – addresses and all – ran

Dear Mrs Macdonald.

Thank you very much for your letter – I like to think that through the wireless I have made friends I may never meet in the flesh – though perhaps we shall actually meet one day!

Yours sincerely

R Vaughan Williams

The writing is almost illegible, but the address on the envelope, with its economy label and its two-and-a-half-penny stamp arrived safely on 24 September.

Writing home, I mentioned the development of my cooking skills: boiled puddings featuring dried apple rings. It happened occasionally that one met someone who had a connexion with home, which gave a boost to our morale. On 24 October 1942 I told my parents about a new arrival among us, name of Wood who when stationed at Whitby had been on an exercise in Castle Howard park when the tank broke down. He and his companion had found Doctor Forsyth and his wife close by, wood-cutting – a hobby of theirs. (Doctor Forsyth was our family doctor, and ushered my brother Paul, sister Angela, and me into the world.) The doctor fetched the soldiers food and butter (a rare commodity at that time) and they had got on famously together and planned to meet again. But in a letter home not many days later (6 November) I had to pass on the sad news that Wood had been killed in action, adding that he was 'such a nice quiet man'. We had to become case-hardened to such incidents.

30 October: My sister Angela had been to London for the first time. I wrote: 'A grand place. Doesn't Malton seem quiet and easy going when you get back?' and I recalled visits to the Lyons Corner House in Piccadilly.

In November 1942 Rommel's retreat began in North Africa.

5 November: Sir Edward Bairstow was a frequent correspondent. He said that the slow movement of Purcell's *Trumpet Sonata*, recently discovered in York Minster library, was more moving than any other he knew.

7 November: 'Scoring hymns for incongruous ensembles in church parades.'

16 November: 'There was a card from John Hodgson's widow. Poor lass, she feels empty without her husband. He was a great friend, and now life has become, to say the least, pretty dry.'

One unfortunate period in the desert nearly drove me to distraction when an insecure quartermaster sergeant, whose clerk I had become, bullied me with unbelievable lack of nous. He must have been of the opinion that, to be on top and in command, it was necessary to lash me with his tongue at every opportunity and to find fault with me whatever I did.

I wrote a letter to my parents from Tmimi on 25 November 1942, which was delivered on 20 February 1943: 'The quarter-master is away so his staff is playing. The job is quite a good one for me, given to me to preserve my hands, as was the Mess job. But why should there be a snag in good jobs – the Q is competent enough but oh so *difficile*. He is away for 5 days on a court martial as a witness and life is liveable once more. I'm not one to smooth things over and turn a deaf ear on everything unpleasant that's said, so there is bound to be friction. The driver and I have adopted the course of "silence whatever is said". I don't know whether we get more tellings off through this, or less, but we still get enough. The poor fellow is undeveloped and quite childish, not fit to wield such authority. He hurls his crown at you whenever you try to talk to him as a man, with the result that you have to pipe down. This "time basis" for promotion is all wrong – a man should be chosen for his capabilities rather than the time he has served. Don't think it's getting me down – I know he feels inferior to me and that is a comfort. He was in the band, so knows quite a bit about music – ie military music. It gives us something to talk about and I can see he tries to make an impression. But I can always go one better on that subject if I want to quieten him. I'm afraid I don't respect him – no-one does anyway – he doesn't merit it. Everyone hates him like poison and I suppose, comparatively speaking, we get on well. I have been sacked twice but am still here! Nothing came of it either time. I call him by his Christian name and he calls me Jacko, so it really looks quite a matey outfit to any outsider. I'm doing my best to do my best for him, and so he can't legitimately complain of anything I don't do or do badly. It's good training for the memory and he's quite indulgent when I forget something. I am his storeman-clerk, which means that I write any letters for him, help with the men's pay-outs, and look after and issue clothing and kit of all kinds. It's like shop-keeping really.'

As time went on I became quite desperate, having stuck the quartermaster's behaviour for a long time, and eventually sought an interview with the squadron leader only to be told that there was a war to be fought. Later in the day, however, I was sent for and some form of solution was worked out. I was moved to another squadron.

'I will send you the snap which a friend took in earlyish September while we were in camp. The lorry is the one I'm in now with chaps playing cards by candle-light, and of course a very strict blackout. There is a canopy over the framework now and it's quite cosy. The chap leaning on the mudguard is my predecessor as storeman (I was clerk only, at the time), the other standing is the former driver who was sacked for not making a cup of tea one night for the Q. His friend the storeman went with him as a protest. The one above me is of Swiss extraction, called Gaeschlin – a religious, parsimonious soul, though rather nice. I might as well tell you that I also was sacked, the second time, for not giving him (the Q) a biscuit and jam, as he was dodging up and down the column when we stopped for a few minutes one day! I'm getting a post-card for you, so when you get it will you send this snap to Sir Edward to let him see how all his carefully-instilled ideals have gone for six!'

73

'At present, Eric Roe, my Yorkshire friend I told you about a bit since, is on the lorry, by a bit of unforeseen good fortune. He lives at Addingham near Ilkley, and knows Appletreewick and Sir W. [William Milner] like the back of his hand. He speaks broad Yorkshire but is a most lovable fellow – jolly and very interesting, with a fund of glorious stories which keep me chuckling all day. He was a farmer and later a fish and chip frier, and was a batman till his boss was wounded out here. He can twist the Q round his little finger, by telling him exactly what he thinks of him, but in the form of a joke so that it doesn't get his back up. The new driver, from Derby, is only 20, and tall but stupid with no sense of humour. He can talk a donkey's hind leg off on any subject, including music; has a prodigious memory for statistics. ... Saw porpoises and flying fishes.'

Seeing what I wrote on 25 November reminds me how more than once I was informed that my method of speaking was not of the standard expected of a Yorkshireman: not that my delivery was anything remarkable; certainly nothing which approached what, at that period, was referred to as the Oxford Accent. Perhaps it was this that was troubling them, among other things. 'It's curious when one considers how one is living with people one wouldn't look at twice in civilian life and is with them the whole day and night – seeing, in fact, more of them than of one's own people in one's life at home. We don't even go out to business or anything else to relieve the monotony. And yet there are few upsets. I do believe a large percentage of soldiers like being away from home, especially from their wives... Not so much with civilian soldiers as with the regulars.'

Earlier that year I had written, 'I am still very much in wonderment at these chaps. I just cannot make them out. There are two regulars in particular .... The thing is that you must think the worst of anybody – the facts must be twisted to show the chap a wrong'un. It's most disturbing; and I wonder if it is merely a question of judging others by oneself? You make a casual remark by way of making yourself agreeable only to find yourself deep in a mire of abuse and blame'.

'I heard Jack Payne's dance band for half an hour and some classical pieces. It was all lovely after so much silence, even though the reception wasn't very good ... After delays in the post, ten items came on one day.'

7 December: 'I can toss pancakes with accuracy and great sureness now, though not without a few casualties at first. ... I'm realising more and more the truth of your maxim "Trust no mortal" – and finding out what a high percentage of rotters there are, and am wondering if it's the army's influence that makes them so. It's very amusing making a list of deadly people. I thank heaven for my honest upbringing.'

31 December: 'I have become very fond of Doris Arnold's radio record programme "These you have loved", but less fond of the *Warsaw Concerto*. What's the point of listening to pseudo-Rachmaninoff when you can get the real thing? I am joining a concert party and singing first bass in a vocal quartet and making their arrangements. I think it will be great fun, and I think that my voice is better now that I don't have to sing alto or treble to fill in! ... Alas the accordion ciphered at the service on Christmas Day. At a regimental concert I performed two poems by my namesake Thomas Jackson.'

2 January 1943: 'I heard Elsie Suddaby's broadcast of songs of Purcell, Armstrong Gibbs and Parry. It was lovely. My recent listening has included the third movement of Dvorak's *Fourth Symphony* (now numbered 8), the slow movement of Beethoven's *Fourth Piano Concerto* and the third movement of Tchaikovsky's *Pathétique* played by the Boston Symphony Orchestra – terrific. However I was less keen on Schumann's *Overture, Scherzo and Finale.*'

The books I'd read recently 'with much pleasure included Mottram's *Spanish Farm*, Gertrude Bell's *Letters*, H.G. Wells' *Short History of the World* and Dickens' *Edwin Drood*. The opening of the latter I thought was magnificent, but the ending, by a woman, was unconvincing'.

15 February: 'The rehearsal is tonight, and crisis number 1 has occurred – I'm on guard! Isn't it amusing – they send for me specially to start the band then whip me on guard at the first rehearsal.'

21 March: 'I'd just turned round to sort the mail which had just come in when a voice behind me said "Is there a bloke called Jackson here?" And whose voice was it, do you think? Paul's! He is quite close and came over in an old buggy with an Australian.'

30 March: 'I think I've said before that it isn't a bad thing that I've had to come into this outfit – one learns real comradeship. In fact I've made some very good friends, among who is Willie England, the Archdeacon's nephew as well as Eric Roe.'

4 April: 'I laid on an incredible dinner – quite a record, for everything came right – fishcakes from tinned salmon and dehydrated spuds with a little flour and pepper, all rolled in thin oatmeal and they came out like Fortnum's best – lovely and crisp on the outside, and moist in the middle and just the right flavour. I ought to say that one of the party was sick during the night – but that was a mere detail.'

10 May: 'Willie England is arranging a concert for which I have to write music. I have no paper to write it on. I don't fancy ruling the staves at all. My task is a march. Wouldn't it be awful if I turned out to be another Eric Coates? Anyway why shouldn't a chap be able to write any kind of music ...'

14 May: 'Played a Cavaillé-Coll Cathedral organ in Tunis – 3 or 4 days after liberation. My three friends had to pump a kind of treadmill affair. Cavaillé-Coll manufactures the best diapasons in the world, but lots of gadgets on the instrument seemed to make no difference to the sound. The sacristan came and requested the *Chanson de Georges* several times, ie the British National Anthem. He dragged Willie England to see devout worshippers loyally bobbing up and down like Jack-in-the-boxes, disturbed in their devotions. A letter from Bairstow contained much encouragement, following his receiving some compositions of mine. I have been busy making some jazz orchestrations which is good practice, and I've added *Kitten on the Keys* and the *Ritual Fire Dance* to my piano repertory.'

20 July: 'We were visited by three famous stage personalities. Leslie Henson told Willie England that he liked my stage manner and that I could make a career of it (which I don't believe....). I also met Beatrice Lillie and Vivien Leigh, who was perfectly sweet and looked lovely. [Known in her circle as 'B Lillie', Beatrice was famous as an actress. Vivien Leigh, married to Laurence Olivier, was very well known for her films. I gave her a light from my cigarette.] I'm excited about Vaughan Williams' new symphony and wonder what kind of style it is in. You remember his last perhaps – I have the records – No 4, discordant, almost brutal. He seems to change his style with every work. There was some doubt as to what key it was in, and they rang him up to enquire. He replied that he didn't know.'

16 August, Tripoli: 'My new billet is only fifty yards from the Mediterranean. Lots of swimming and diving between writing for a

new revue. Learnt a lot about orchestration from doing the previous one. I have a much bigger band for this one: 3 saxophones, 2 pianos, 4 violins, guitar, clarinet, 2 trumpets, cello and double bass. A gorgeous theatre and a lovely conductor's rostrum for me.'

25 August: 'Six shows in seven days in palatial country houses taken over by the army. Acoustically superb, and we've been reinforced by three expert musicians.' ...

'I think I shall run an anti-army campaign when the war is over and write a red hot book on its colossal mismanagement.... The army does make you catty. We have just been picking holes in some of the other people, and thoroughly enjoying it. ... I feel very excited about the orchestrations for the band. Played the Cathedral organ (in Tunis), this time *avec electricité*, including Bach's *Prelude and Fugue in D*, the one I played for the Red Cross recital in the Minster with Melville.'

14 September: 'The stands the band use have my initials on them. Think of your son following in Harry Roy's footsteps. ... Have met some charming folk who feed me and a friend. Even spent the night there two nights ago on a spring mattress. My goodness was it a treat ... Bought copies of *Chants d'Auvergne* by Canteloube – very cheaply in Tunis ... perfectly charming...'

At that time I met a fine violinist Mme Gazon-Kanter who had known Ravel and 'she told me things about him you would never read in books of his life' but I can't remember them. We played Faure's *Sonata*, 'which is a peach ... There are twelve in the band, including a clarinet, 3 saxes, trombone, violin, guitar, accordion, piano, trumpet. ... Except for the pianist all can double on a second instrument ... [I] stand up there wagging my hand'.

21 September: '*Chatanooga Choo Choo* and *How Green was my Valley* are some of our current numbers, and I actually sang! Nothing but rudeness has come from the band, but I can take it. Frank Jackson and his Leadswingers. I wonder what you think of your son – isn't it awful, and after his cathedral training too! At any rate it's sampling another of the many facets of this life which I think is necessary.'

9 October: 'Solomon was here for a live [piano] recital. Wonderful... My saxophone proficiency is improving. Only four practices on it since the end of August. Hope soon to be able to stand up in front of band

and knock out an occasional swing chorus. We played to over 2000 in the open air, and had a party afterwards in the corporals' mess.'

4 November: 'Met Roger Cortet the leading French flautist. He often played with Ravel, and talked of him and other notabilities as though they were quite ordinary people. He recorded *Brandenburg Concerto No 4* with Thibaut, and *No 5* with Cortot. He also played the flute in *Daphnis and Chloe* when Ravel was in the audience, a mere fourteen days before he died.'

11 November: 'I had a temporary commission as Captain Jackson because of my involvement with ENSA (the Department of National Service Entertainment). At a concert I played a medley of the Grieg and Tchaikovsky concerti, the *Waltz of the Flowers*, Delibes' *Naila Waltz* and *Liebestraum*, with four swing numbers as an encore. After one of my piano recitals someone wrote "Mr Jackson is by no means a conventional cathedral organist, for he is a brilliant executant on the piano" – implying that the others aren't?'

22 November: 'I so dislike officers' parties and drinks. They're such a waste of time, making conversation about something you're not interested in.'

27 November: 'Being in the Army is an education in human nature – almost the only good thing in it.'

As one goes over these war-time letters, contrary sentiments are sometimes expressed, sometimes because of a temporary improvement in one's fortunes, and sometimes because one felt more able to make the best of things at one time than at another. This is a condition we all experience throughout life, but in the armed forces and its peculiar living circumstances one encounters it in extreme form.

'Heard Ravel's *Mother Goose* at a concert for the first time. The orchestration is so refined and gossamer-like. They couldn't get a double bassoon for *Beauty and the Beast*, but all the odd instruments for *Bolero* were there, including the E flat clarinet and the Soprano and Tenor Saxes. I haven't got "hot" playing off to a fine art yet. This you can get only by instinct, and by listening to other people. I have got over the difficulty to some extent by playing duets with the padre's batman, who is very good in the right hand, whilst I romp away in the bass. My musicianship revolts against the continual sameness of the left hand. Duke Ellington's blues fail to move me. Sometimes I prefer good swing to some serious composers... I enjoy playing the Sax and am swotting on the Clarinet.'

10 November: 'Band has been dissolved by John Gabriel, the Divisional Entertainments Officer, who wanted to create a rival show. So many really nice people and thoroughly talented musicians in my band want to come to "Jackson Towers" one day.' Gabriel was in the York Repertory Company before the war.

17 November: 'Betty (legs) Grable certainly is lovely, and I liked her singing in *Coney Island*... After the end of the band I'm keeping very quiet.'

We were at Boufarik, Algeria, on 15/16 December 1943, when I set *Stopping by woods on a snowy evening*, Robert Frost's poem.

5 January 1944: '53rd Training Regiment Band is billeted here [Boufarik] for a month. It includes members of the BBC and London Symphony Orchestras. I orchestrated Humphrey Bourne's *Eighth Army March* for them. A Quartet from the band played some movements I wrote ages ago. I accompanied a Xylophonist who was "discovered" by Carrol Levis on radio.' Levis was a show biz personality who toured the music halls in search of local talent, which he then invited to his show.

22 January: 'Took part in a jam session in a cattle truck on a train journey ... Am orchestrating the Warsaw Concerto, a work I hate.' Spike Milligan is just as critical in his book *Adolf Hitler. My part in his downfall.* I think I thought it necessary at that time to be critical of such music, an attitude picked up from Bairstow.

23 January: 'Played in a concert with a Welsh choir... I don't like the sound of the Sax except when you're playing hot stuff. It seems so easy to get a noise like a cow on it.'

31 January: 'I received 41 letters today. Maurice Jacobson of Curwens made encouraging noises about my song *Widow Bird* .... Melville [Cook] writes to say he has given three well appreciated piano recitals. He slams jazz, which tickled me. Perhaps he has not had the same temptations as myself, or else it's his serious nature against my innate frivolity. I can't help thinking, though, how my music will be broader for knowing it and enjoying it. The great thing is that there is now one more pleasure and one less annoyance in my life. And it doesn't affect my serious music one atom.'

4 March: 'I have done well to learn the accordion and the sax out here. Another "straight" instrument would be useful.'

9 March: 'Have taken *Dark Town Strutters' Ball* as the band's signature tune.'

Band activities faded out in due course, to be revived back in England on reaching Catterick for my final military months.

I promised to write a wedding march for my sister Lal (Angela) who throughout my period of overseas service was a most faithful and affectionate correspondent. Alas, the muse was not willing so poor Angela had to make do with something else – I hope not Mendelssohn.

3 April: 'I met Marlene Dietrich at an officers' dance. They fell over one another in wanting to dance with her. After one dance with me she turned to me and said, "tank you. Dat vas wonderful" or was it her complimenting the band's playing? No! Of course not. She is certainly very attractive, and doesn't look a day over thirty – though she must be more [she was then 43]. I've never seen her on the flicks, so I've booked myself a seat for her *Flame of New Orleans*.'

11 April: 'I'm now back as Technical Clerk and playing 2nd Sax in the band. The Sergeant Major is first trumpet, so rank isn't observed unless there are folk around. I'm getting more used to the Clarinet Boehm system; after playing the Sax it's much easier.'

16 April 'My duties are … monotonous. Set the table, clear it, see each sergeant has a meal and a cup of tea. It's not much better than feeding pigs… I'm heartily sick of foreign countries and share Browning's sentiments. What apparently matters in the Army is the power to lead and control men, no matter how unlettered or uncultured. It doesn't occur to them that the two might go together, culture and leadership. Perhaps in the Colonel class you will almost always find it, in the Major class about 10%. Then less as you descend, till the culture is almost non-existent. When you reach the Troopers it becomes a little less than the Majors.'

19 April: 'I'm still entertaining hopes of playing Brahms' and Mozart's *Clarinet Quintets* and perhaps Ireland's new Sonata.' [This did not happen.]

29 April: 'I am laden with full pack and all the rest of the Boutique Fantasque for having a tiny speck of dust on my boots.'

15 May: 'I had a letter from Sir Edward, on receipt of my Trio... He was very encouraging, and said "It was very kind of you to copy out your trio. It must have been a long and arduous proceeding, especially as you have to manufacture your own music paper. I was very interested in the trio. It has your fresh, youthful style, as of old. The war has not robbed you of that. You have not become old or pessimistic. You seem to speak musically in a present day idiom without effort or self-consciousness. I hope you always will".'

This eventually became part of the trio for violin, cello and piano, opus 128 of 2001. Originally for flute and viola with piano, I got Roger Cortet to try it through, with a violist friend and me while I was near Algiers where the Cortets were living in a somewhat cramped attic conditions with their small child.

13 June: 'Bob Lees (from Scarborough) proposed that we formed a two piano duo like Ethel Bartlett and Rae Robertson or Rawicz and Landauer. I don't want to go back to Malton Church and teaching, especially urchins. I would like the Minster job (Assistant) and the two piano could fit in... I was bored by the Mozart *Clarinet Concerto* [changing my mind 'to some tune' later on] but found in Haydn's *Oxford Symphony* some lovely tunes.'

16 June: 'I think Verdi's *Aida* over-rated.' I wrote to Mother that we had 'sailed on your birthday [25 May; from North Africa] and arrived [in Italy] on the Saturday morning. No alarums and excursions but as usual you couldn't move on the ship'.

19 June, at San Vito, near Bari, Italy: 'I find myself generally fonder of Mozart than hitherto.'

It was at San Vito, a short way north of Bari that, finding it was to be Sir Edward Bairstow's seventieth birthday in less than a month, the only present I could offer would be a composition. So I got to work and in three days produced the *Impromptu* already mentioned, which arrived in time: this was the first piece I was to have published. Soon after returning to York I was able to go to the Minster organ with him one evening and play it to him.

23 June: 'My dear Dad, It was a real pleasure to get your detailed description of life in the garden yesterday. The roses seem to have turned up trumps: they must be very lovely – how I wish I could see them... There is a wireless in the tent ... which has a persistently loud

grind and hum, but mercifully purveys the "better" kind of music, due as much to the new General Forces Programme as to the Serg.-Major whose wireless it is... We suffer from one of the ten plagues here, that of grasshoppers – huge things an inch long who crawl over everything and into your bed if you're not careful. We have mosquito nets to keep them out.'

31 July: 'I can't understand the craze for Delius. The *Walk to the Paradise Garden* is insipid like film music, and Scriabin's *Poem of Ecstasy* a nine days' wonder, like the Delius, I suppose.' [Another *volte-face.*]

18 August: 'I have had such a pleasant 4 or 5 days in which I've seen a good bit of the country and driven a good many miles. The scenery was stupendous, riding over huge mountains, almost along the summits, with the road following the line of each little spur, twisting and turning every few yards, and a drop of many hundreds of feet below and a view of miles and miles through the clear air. ... Sometimes you get a conical hill with the village spiked on top and part way down the sides like icing on a queencake... Then the absolute silence in a valley when I switched off and could only hear the stream over the stones, no louder than breathing; and not even a sheep bell tinkling.'

This was the journey I drove from Naples north-east to Vasto, during which I failed to turn a sharp bend going uphill, and spilt most of the peaches I was carrying for the chaps' ration.

1 Sept 1944: 22 Gen. Hospital, CMF [Central Mediterranean Forces] '... I find myself with an attack of jaundice miles and miles away from the regiment [then seeing action at San Savino] so you can rest assured I am all right and lapping it up.'

For a couple of weeks I was in hospital at Taranto with fellow patients from many different countries. The situation and attitudes have changed somewhat since then. There was 'a very nice Scots Sergeant in the next bed to me... He nearly burst when I asked him if he really did take salt and not sugar with his porridge... Then there is a Madagascan, ... [who] swears he is 51 and was in the first war, but looks no more than 30 at most. He chants parts of the Mass – Tantum ergo etc. etc – quite correctly, to everybody's chagrin, with all the actions, kneeling, crossing himself, wailing; and then switches to some secular piece, something nostalgic which entails more mock-weeping, interpolating quick darting comments... in explanation. Then when you call him Sam or Sambo he sulks and pretends to cry and goes out in a huff. He came to me crying one day and said "*Ils m'apellent Sambo, et je m'apelle David ...*" He does it all with complete unselfconsciousness, just like a child.'

'How precious is broadcast music. *Till Eulenspiegel* converted me to Richard Strauss. Began Winifred Holtby's *South Riding* and enjoyed it greatly.'

14 September, no. 1 Convalescent Depot, CMF: 'The Educational Corps ... provides all kinds of lectures and debates, also language classes, of which I am indulging in French of the top grade (conversational) with gramophone records... At the French class was a sergeant ... [who] made it known I could play the piano ... I worked out a medley, with the introduction to Grieg's concerto, the *Valse des Fleurs*, middle of Tchai's quartet popularly known as *Isle of May* [sic], the tune from his piano concerto. Then into swing with *Don't get around much any more, I'll get by*, and *Honeysuckle Rose*. I think it worked. The swing dispelled the gloom cast by the "classics".'

21 September: 'I'm giving a piano recital, all on my own ... you'd laugh to see the poster they've put up: "A Master of Music" in flaming colours... My hands ached the day after playing through my programme, and I've not practised since.'

23 September: 'Tomorrow and Monday I am giving a gramophone programme ... with what suitable records are available, and giving my views on the pieces... The first recital is to be classics, and the second the Romantics.'

30 September: 'I am working in the pay office ... Paul is at Brindisi.'

During my convalescence a series of weekly piano recitals strained my memorised piano repertory, and there was no hope of getting any printed music. 'Have formed a friendship with Captain William Devlin, Dame Sybil Thorndike's son-in-law, and Raymond Raikes of the BBC, who is a colleague of the announcer Alvar Liddell.'

1 October: My broadcast from British Forces' Station at Bari included records of music by Vaughan Williams, Falla, Rimsky-Korsakov, Ravel, Walton and Debussy.

I continued to send home items for the scrap book.

8 October: 'Here's a bit more lumber [such as programmes] that may amuse you. ... one day I hope to come and edit & docket all of it

and hand it down to posterity in usable form. I'm sure posterity will be grateful ...'

'Last Sunday I had a letter from Captain Devlin (...who was in our revues at Tunis & Tripoli ...) asking me to go and broadcast a programme of my favourite records.'

18 October: 'Devlin had enquired fully at HQ, very keen to have me, but they gave him no encouragement whatever. ... I'd been trying for ENSA a year previously, and ... I'd been offered the job of director of a Music for All in Tripoli which was stamped on hard... The hazards of broadcasting include hitch hiking, and the risk of not getting to the studio on time.'

27 October: 'Did a broadcast recital which included Ravel's *Valses Nobles et Sentimentales* (No. 1), A Debussy *Arabesque*, Jackson's *Soliloquy*, and have decided to use the words of Spenser's *Epithalamium* for my MusD exercise.' [For the exercise I wrote a symphony instead, thirteen years later.]

On 30 October news reached me of my father's death, aged only 56. In a recent letter he wrote, 'we know how to get the best out of life and to take the rough with the smooth'. Even so, it was a body blow, all the more acute because so long had elapsed since I was last at home. The telegram conveying the news gave the cause of death as brain fever which I later learned was brought on by the excessive amount of extra work he had to take on in the wartime situation. A letter of condolence from the vicar in Malton spoke of his reading of the lessons latterly as lacking any expression or vitality. Of course one could not avoid feelings of extreme anxiety and utter helplessness at my mother's plight, in the midst of those uncertain times, suddenly to be left on her own. My sister Angela who was nursing nearby was a solid comfort and support, though, had it been necessary, Mother's strong character would have enabled her to manage on her own.

7 November: '... I am to be lent to ENSA for a week.' This week became three. 'There are 5 girls and 2 chaps in the show ... a good Welsh bass-baritone; the producer Sefton Yates ... 2 ballet girls, a contralto, an accordionist and a violinist called Kitty. ... We played at the Con. Depot on Tuesday, 2 shows with 1,400 at each.'

My letter dated 12 December 1944 mentions a poster advertising my musical activities: 'Jive with Jackson – everything from Delius to the Duke'. However 'everyone shudders when I play *White Christmas*. Also played, by request, the *Warsaw Concerto* and Dvorak's *Humoresque*. The Sergeant Major sits for hours listening'.

There followed a spell in the transit camp at Bari where I took part in concerts in the Merrydrome along with Harry Secombe and any others who had anything to contribute towards the alleviation of boredom.

12 January 1945, Rome: 'Made my first encounter with Berlioz' *Symphonie Fantastique*, and visited Saint Peter's Rome and the fountains. My penny trick worked – in the fountain – for at the next port of call who should I find there but an officer from the regiment whom I know very well, who volunteered to give me 4 unofficial days' leave. I have been to the opera three times, and seen *Tosca, Traviata* and *Bohème*. It was all superb, and in the first two was the darling of Italy, a magnificent soprano called Maria Caniglia. The production was terrific and so were the singing and the orchestra. I think I must be coming round to opera again. Tomorrow we return to be ready to start out with the regiment on Sunday – Angela's birthday, the fourteenth! What a thing to have to do on such a day. But to think of going back after more than four months away and having been offered so many nice suitable jobs is a bit hard.'

'Yesterday I went to St Peter's – a long walk which took 45 minutes. It is of course a magnificent building but I couldn't get the full significance in such a short time – I think you need to be there for some days just contemplating it before you get it. The colouring and mosaic work are superb, and it is so simple in design, just a simple cross with a dome in the middle and all this wonderful carving over all the walls. I was relieved when the Sistine Chapel was closed, as I could not have appreciated Michaelangelo then. Today I played the organ at the American church, a weird contraption. I tried what the awkward beast would allow me to, including the *Impromptu* I wrote for Sir Edward's 70th birthday – this for the first time, and it sounded nice.'

'There is a young chap who frequents the piano rooms of the Forces' Club here and who plays the Grieg and Tchaikovsky concerti. He is another of those people who have a phenomenal technique and can get around the keyboard like nobody's business, but have no musicianship. It's such a pity, but then, I suppose, were it otherwise there would be hundreds of top-notchers. However, we are going to do both these concertos tonight on two pianos – I doing the orchestra. Would you believe it as well – he cannot read music! It must be a painful process learning anything. He is a nice lad anyway, but it is a pity he doesn't do the thing properly. I have just read Hardy's *Under the Greenwood Tree* and thoroughly enjoyed it. It's so nice and peaceful.'

19 January: '… it is appallingly dull writing figures all day & dealing with forms etc. … I'm getting used to it, what with my previous clerking, & the experience at the Con. Depot job of writing names, numbers & regiments all day at full tilt …'

15 February: 'The Christmas parcel has arrived! … intact except for the hair oil which smashed unfortunately and cut the socks slightly. But the sweets and biscuits are lovely … though they are a bit soft… The "Listeners" make good reading… I have ordered 3 scores from Banks [York's music shop], also asked them to try & get me the "Gramophone".'

In my letter of 18 February I commiserated with my mother in her inability to go to church any more because of the frightful music. Perhaps her words strengthened my resolve not to return to Malton Parish Church as organist and choirmaster. Something of life's incongruities was revealed in my letter of 5 March, which mentioned McNaught's essay on Bax and the *Garden of Fand*, and my orchestrating *Canteen Bounce*. That month the band was playing most evenings.

10 March: 'What a musical snob I used to be. There is something about swing and playing a sax that fascinates me. It will give place to the serious music I really love once I'm out of the army, though it may remain an occasional treat… I seem to make friends easily and it is difficult to say good-bye. I could accumulate an enormous correspondence, especially when moving about. I would like to keep the best musicians and form a dance band in civvy street.'

12 March: 'After a journey lasting from 10.0 till 5.0 yesterday over a bumpy road with the air in the back of the lorry filled with dust … we came through the place of my name saint.' [Assisi, of course.] 'Arthur Sainter, the Ilkley organist, lent me a copy of *The Organ* which I read without the consuming interest I used to have in it. I am now all for the *Gramophone* and want to be able to make records myself.'

25 March: 'Sir Edward says he doesn't play voluntaries any more because of the noisy congregations. He made cursory reference to

my *Impromptu* but hasn't noticed my quotation from his Communion Service, or hasn't remarked on it in any way. I don't think he can have looked at it very thoroughly. Perhaps it's no good. Heard Schabel's recording of the *Emperor* on the radio ... and *In the Mood* – much to my delight.'

20 April: 'I get incredibly envious when I hear the glowing accounts of Vaughan Williams' new symphony (the fifth) and can hardly wait to hear it. His Testament of Beauty someone called it, "in his best countryside mood – like the *Lark Ascending*".'

21 April: ' I hate being aroused in the early morning to go out on patrol for 2 hours. I usually take some music and think it right through. A symphony twice through usually fills in the time nicely... Churchill says "The long night is ending". I admire him a lot, in spite of what everyone says against him.' Perhaps we should have been better prepared for the electoral upheaval that took place a few weeks later. Churchill lost, to a Labour landslide.

29 April: 'I have a billet where there is a very nice upright piano, which I bashed all last night and this morning; also lots of Chopin, some Beethoven Sonatas, and lots of opera of course. Everyone loves Grieg's *Spring*, Ravel's *Bolero*, opera arrangements, *Ave Marias*, Liebestraum and *Poet and Peasant*.'

On 2 May I wrote to my sister Angela. 'There is a climber on one of the farm buildings here for all the world like wistaria in flower, but in leaf like white jasmine, with both flowers and leaves out at once. I found seeds of it, so it may be persuaded to grow with us. It has no smell unfortunately, but is still a lovely colour. The Robinias (pseudo-acacia) are in full profuse blossom, like white laburnums, also white spireas, solid long branches of white. We are still in the farm I told Mum about, and no-one knows for how long, but I think we may not move yet awhile. It's the most comfortable billet yet – kind people and a good upright piano with loads of Chopin and Beethoven Sonatas. All conversation is conducted in Italian so a bit of a strain as I don't know the tongue; but it's like French, so you put an o on the end of a French – or English – word and there you are. Today we had dinner with them – two of us. We had a speciality of this neighbourhood – very oily but good, and finished off with strawberries! We went 2½ *chilometri* in a small cart this morning to pick strawberries – a field of them, but there were a lot of unripe ones; soldiers had robbed the only ripe ones last night. The cuckoo was shouting close by; and for the last two nights two nightingales were likewise giving tongue in no uncertain manner, both at once. ... There is a cuckoo clock in the room where we sleep – the big living room – which gives us much amusement. It goes clang-cuckoo, clang-cuckoo and at the half hour clang-cuckoo-bang, the bird disappears, the door shuts and you've had it. (Read this part quickly: it's the speed with which the bird performs these gyrations that makes us laugh.) ... It's funny to think the war in Italy is finished – at any rate we have finished and I am thankful. We don't rejoice, not knowing where they'll put us next; but everyone is pleased and expecting to go into occupying the cuckoo-clock land (Austria) but heaven knows we are due for England.'

VE Day 1945:'It is a different story being out of battle once more and being in a peace-time army. The relief is great – I have not fully realized it yet ...'

My letter to my mother describes our position for the first time: 'We are about 200 yards from the banks of the Po, south of it, north of Ferrara by 3 or 4 miles. I have been into the town once or twice and quite enjoyed it. The cathedral is very fine – a smaller edition of St Peter's and mellower. The town reminded me of Salisbury. The country here is flat as flat, with lots of corn and meadow land. A man was scything in a field close by yesterday, and beyond, the trees looked as if they belonged to England. The cuckoo is hard at it, and the martins and swifts and swallows (I don't know t'other frae which) are here in strength, and nightingales at night.'

17 May: 'Sir Edward would like to go to Southern Africa to see his son. This would necessitate three months' absence. Franklin (his pre-war deputy) is somewhere in the Far East. He would like me to deputise for him. After some discussion, the Padré was encouraging, and said he would mention it to the Assistant Chaplain General, who would in turn talk to the 8th Army Commander. He was my Brigadier when I joined up. However, it was said that a favourable response was more likely if something were done from the York end. Wouldn't it be lovely to be Minster organist for three months, monarch of all I surveyed in the organist's domain AND to be home as well? I have been away from home for three years and seven months.'

We passed through Assisi again, Mestre (where we could barely see Venice in the distance), and paid a visit to Florence (in search of a clarinet) and from Palmanova took a trip to Trieste along a spectacular road high above the intensely blue clear sea. I wrote home on 20 May 1945: 'I saw in Padua yesterday two glorious saxophones – an alto for £55 and a tenor for £62/10/0 [£62.50] – both brand new. Hitherto the trouble has been finding instruments. Now that we find them they don't want us to have them, the regiment can well afford them, and they really need them if they want a band. However, this is most uninteresting, so I'll tell you about my latest flirtation. I told you about the Ferrara lady whose sister's piano I played, and how she sought me out at my billet – fully 5 or 6 miles away – on her bicycle. She had remembered my regiment and must have noted the number on the wagon…. The first time she brought me a bottle of alcohol (pure!), a writing pad, views of Ferrara, pencils and rubbers. Two nights later she arrived with two *more* writing pads, quires of paper, pencils, rubbers, five eggs and a flat tyre. We got the tyre off with spoons, mended the puncture after having first mended the pump, and set her on her way just as it was growing dark, she promising us some cognac for our trouble. Two nights, three nights went by and no Maria, and so we moved. But she found one of our chaps in the town a few days later and gave him a typewritten letter illustrated by pictures in case I didn't understand the Italian. She had seen one Jon from London … with our signs on his lorry and had given him a *fiasco* (flask) of wine to bring to me and my *amicos*. Jon had already told me that he had drunk it himself. In the envelope she scrawled that she had meant to send me some music, but will do so another day. So there we are.'

'… At the saxophone shop I met Signor Zanibon, the proprietor, who is also a publisher. And he asked me if I played the piano, and I said yes, and the organ (he spoke good English), so he said "I will give you some music". He led me to the shelves and picked out one of his publications saying "Are you a high organist?" I said I wasn't sure. "Are you a deeficult organist?" and I replied "Well, yes" (but could have said that my vicar probably held that opinion, which would have been lost on him, for sure). I got him to write on it, which he did with many flourishes and an air of importance as a souvenir of the victory.'

The piece of music was by Oreste Ravanello. Its title is *Mystica – Suite di tre pezzi di concerto – per Grand'Organo*, published in 1939 in Padova. I have been unable to discover any information about the composer, but when some years later I asked Fernando Germani, Italy's most famous organist, he replied that he was old-fashioned. At all events there are thirty-six items by him noted on the back of the copy, some of which appear substantial. The welcome inscription Signor Zanibon wrote on the copy reads 'Remembering the Victory, souvenir of Padova, with the best wishes of the Publisher G. Zanibon 8.5.45'.

1 June: 'Fancy the august Oxonians recognising a provincial organist (Sir Edward) by giving him an honorary Doctorate.'

8 June: 'Sad about Dennis's death (Dennis Laughton). Fancy how many of our friends who would not have died but for the war… I did think about a commission in the Education Corps, because there wouldn't be the same huntin' and fishin' clowns in an Ed. Mess – they would have other interests. Then it might mean I could conduct an orchestra or do chamber music or something like that… I think that jive will gradually recede from me. However, the band's drummer told me I could make between £20 and £40 a week if I got in a big band and became known, as he considers that I've "got something".'

Oh dear, how uncertain it all was.

19 June: 'I received a letter from Melville Cook, serving in the Far East, in which he says how he "likes the colouring and the moonlight", but still says he would swap it all for Vaughan Williams' *Silent Noon*.'

'I have just filled in a form re the army educational scheme … I put that I wished to take the Mus. Doc. Exam in October 1945!, and need time and opportunity to write a large-scale choral and orchestral work for this exam! That will shake 'em I hope …'

8 July: 'I have been doing orchestrations specially for our 4 wind instruments … It is excellent practice for me – finding out what comes off and what doesn't.'

27 July: 'I feel out of patience with the Church… Have done ever since I joined the Army… And feel there are more ways of getting a living at music than burying yourself in a church or playing hymns all the year round. There are the BBC and ENSA, and all kinds of jobs that take you around and bring you into contact with real music. No really great musician has been organist for long. Stanford was heartily

glad to descend the stairs of Trinity for the last time, and Britten, Walton, Bax and Vaughan Williams I'll bet didn't touch an organ much after they got into long trousers. Pupils always annoyed me because they were so stupid and would not see... I thank God I came out of my rut to join this awful army. What does it matter what one does so long as one is happy? Vaughan Williams had a church organist's post for a short time at St Barnabas, South Lambeth, but was glad when it came to an end by reason of his atheistic or agnostic tendencies.'

29 July: 'A letter from the regimental chaplain to the Chaplain General has been sent in the hope that I may be given a posting to the York area, so that I can help at the Minster. Things are in a bad way there, I hear.'

7 August: 'Though I have done nothing but travel during the past five years I don't feel I could settle down to some drab job like I used to have – seven years at Malton – musically I mean. I'm dreadfully afraid of getting sucked into an ordinary organist's job, and remaining in it for the rest of my life. The organ is a noble instrument and thrilling – I love it still, but it is limited, and with only Bach's fugues in its repertoire in the line of really great music, one gets stunted, morally and musically with too much of it... I don't want you to worry about my future because something is bound to present itself. I feel obliged to do the Minster job so as not to let ECB down in his declining years... But it would not be for long. The army ... has given me the chance to see life, past and future in proportion, and I am scared at the thought of once again dropping back into what I used to be, when life has so much to offer.'

At this stage it was impossible to guess what life had to offer – something far better than I could ever have hoped for, and not something that called for changes in my aesthetic, professional and religious outlook. Looking back on one's thoughts of so long ago, in unreal, disturbed and distasteful conditions, one cannot help but find confusion, illogical and contradictory expression – sometimes to cause a blush of embarrassment perhaps – but probably interesting as charting one's development leading to an eventual settled existence.

For a few weeks before the regiment returned home we were close by Palmanova, a few miles south of Udine, which had an unusual layout of stone buildings – houses most likely – around a huge octagonal 'square' making it difficult to find the right road to take when leaving, each façade of the octagon being identical. Here I was smitten with an unusual condition that caused me to be unable to eat, no matter how hungry I felt. There is probably a medical name for it, and it is likely to be of psychological or nervous cause, in my case not surprising perhaps, after almost four years of a strange and unwelcome mode of living. But it eventually cleared up naturally, aided by slippery elm, which was one of several sovereign remedies in which Ron Cosgrove (from Preston), the band's drummer, had implicit faith.

From the transit camp my progress was slow, but as hostilities were winding down there was no urgency, and a more relaxed life style could be enjoyed.

20 August: '... just to tell you not to write any more, because I am coming home! The date is ... between the 24th and 30th that we start, and we are coming over land.'

Wednesday 29 August, Naples: '... I've got this far ... we missed the boat which goes tomorrow and it is perhaps better as we ought to get a plane on either Saturday or Sunday.'

Post Office Telegram, 1 September 1945: 'Arrived safely home perhaps Sunday.'

LIFE'S WORK BEGINS

The flight home was easy, following the west coast northwards from Rome, keeping over the sea, which afforded an excellent view of the coastline. It was of course a wonderful moment to set foot once again on our native soil after so long away. Home leave was unbelievably wonderful, with sheets between which to sleep and food that was eatable and pleasurable, to say nothing of the family reunions and old friendships.

There followed some nine months at Catterick camp as clerk in the orderly room. Richmond being close by I was able to see a good deal of Doctor AJ Bull, organist of the parish church, to play for Sunday evensong and afterwards to enjoy supper and a pleasant evening at his house. I was also much involved with a band, which was enjoyable, but I could not avoid slight feelings that it was something I ought not to be involved with. That did not really matter; it was all recreation, which we could not be blamed for taking part in during those unsettled times. I became the owner of a Francis Barnett two-stroke motor-cycle which facilitated not only the three or four miles between Catterick camp and Richmond but also home leaves during which I visited the Minster and Sir Edward as often as I could. He had introduced me to the Dean very soon after I returned from service abroad.

It was not long after my return to England from Italy that my first significant recital took place. I was not yet demobbed when Dean Milner-White asked me to take part in one of his series of 'An Hour of Music in the Cathedral'. This was on the Wednesday afternoon of 24 October 1945 and included the first performance of the *Impromptu* I had composed for Sir Edward's seventieth birthday in August of the previous year. I shared the programme with Joan Vernon who played piano solos and the Bach D minor concerto, with the organ providing the orchestral part. Reginald Rose, music critic of the Evening Press, York's local paper, wrote of the *Impromptu*: 'This is a work of great merit; though modern in style its modernity is of inspiration and not for mere effect'. Reggie, as he was known to us all, had been organist of Saint Olave's church since his arrival in York on the day of Queen Victoria's funeral. He was a popular figure and much respected in the city and among the musical fraternity. He came often to sit in the organ loft for evensong.

It was Dean Milner-White who sent my fee for the recital; not a financial boffin, for there was none at that time: the whole concern was run by a few staff in quite a different way from what it became half a century later. I was addressed as 'Dear Mr Jackson' and the letter was very appreciative, though the Dean had to miss it, being occupied in Blackburn. Sir Edward commented to David Hird on 3 January: 'Owen Franklin is back and Frank Jackson is just hanging around at Catterick. His playing is still as good as ever though he has done practically nothing all these years', presumably referring to playing only... Four months later another letter came from Dean Milner-White, dated 15 March; this time 'Dear Jackson', and continued:

> Today Franklin has been formally appointed to the Organistship of Doncaster Parish Church and leaves here after Easter. Everybody, the Chapter, Sir Edward and myself, are most anxious that you should succeed him. The Assistant Organist's stipend is small, too small – no more than a songman's. I am sure that the Chapter will be ready to raise it at least to £200 per annum (though I am speaking at the moment for myself). In view of Sir Edward's illness, however well it may turn out, the Sub-organist will undoubtedly have more serious responsibilities and fuller work. You who love Sir Edward and know his ways are, of course, exactly the right person to come to the aid of the Minster at this moment. But we all want you very much for

yourself! Although I cannot yet state the financial conditions, this is a formal and official offer of the post. I want to send it at the first possible moment in view of your coming demobilisation. It may even be that we could hasten it if necessary in order for you to take on, if you will, as soon after Easter as may be.

May I say finally with what eagerness I hope for an affirmative answer and your return to the Minster family?

Very sincerely yours

Eric Milner-White, Dean

What more could I have wished for? Receiving such a letter – and without the slightest effort on my part – was unbelievable, with its promise of the wonderful things I had continually dreamed of and never thought possible.

My doubts about an organist future and the strictures I had placed on the church and the organ world were all put aside in an instant. I hastened to send my telegram of acceptance and later learned that the Dean had burst round to the Bairstows' with the news in his usual enthusiastic manner. Any disappointment I may have felt at being rejected for Doncaster (for which I as well as Owen Franklin had applied and was interviewed) was more than made up for by the thoughts of the prospect that was opening up before me. I took up my duties in mid-April, by which time Bairstow was in the nursing home and failing in health. Thus the entire load of the Minster music fell on me from the start and, though I was technically his assistant, I never worked with him after becoming such – but had had plenty of experience with him in previous years.

In another letter the Dean spoke of asking for special leave for the first fortnight after Easter since I had to return to Catterick until the end of my army service in July. It seemed a little strange that one could not have all the leave one wished for; why in fact did we need to be kept treading water, as it were, in the army when we were no longer needed and could have been doing something useful back home? Perhaps there was a fear of another war. No doubt there were other good reasons, and by this time we were more than used to toeing the line and knuckling under.

There were treats, apart from the dance band and the Richmond church. In May, on two successive evenings I played the piano with the band of the Royal Mounted Artillery in the César Franck *Symphonic Variations*, in a concert conducted by Mary Brownrigg and David McBain respectively, in Leyburn Town Hall. The latter drew a kindly and appreciative letter of thanks from Lieutenant R J Audrey, wishing me well in my appointment at York.

Sir Edward had suffered greatly from lung trouble that laid him low in the Purey-Cust Nursing Home close by the Minster for some weeks. As I arrived each morning by train, on the way to the choristers' 8.45am daily practice I looked up at his window and saw his profile, which became lower day after day until he became too weak even to be propped up on pillows. On May Day, the first of the month, Lady Bairstow telephoned to tell me he had died. It was the 'plain day' with no choral activity and I was at my mother's in Malton.

So now the daily service music of the Minster was entirely in my hands: it had been so for the two previous weeks since I began my work as assistant. But with Sir Edward there, however immobile, we knew he was still the ultimate authority. Now suddenly, the whole scene was changed: the Minster without him was a different place and we were uncertain what would happen. My leave that had made possible my presence at his funeral came to an end, and two months more of army service – with short spells of leave now and again – brought me back again to civilian status with nothing to detract from my enviable new job.

I had conducted the choir for his funeral on 4 May and saw to the musical arrangements. This was quite an ordeal considering the immense congregation that filled the nave and included a very large number of distinguished colleagues, friends, pupils and admirers of him who travelled to York for the service. Sir Ernest Bullock, one of his earliest pupils, then Professor of Music at Glasgow University and previously organist of Westminster Abbey played the organ. The Croft Burial Sentences were sung at the start, Sir Edward's best known anthem *Save us O Lord* and his arrangement of Gibbons' *Jesu, grant me This, I pray* were sung, and at the conclusion Sir Ernest played what was the most favourite of Sir Edward's Bach works, the 'Great B minor'.

There was another major event, again putting me in at the deep end, which was conducting the annual Diocesan Choirs Festival on the second Saturday of July. The secretary was Benjamin Summerton, organist at Tadcaster Parish Church, who for many years (until his death in 1971) ran the Festival with complete efficiency and great success. This year, 1946, brought in 711 singers, ten choirs from Hull, three from Teesside and many others. The press report states that my hymn tune christened 'Malton' written some ten years earlier was included – by coincidence, or perhaps as the committee's compliment to the festival's new conductor. Wood in D was the setting of the canticles and Handel's *For all these mercies Lord we sing* and Batten's *O praise the Lord* were the anthems. I had sung at these events, first in 1928 with Malton Church choir when the movement was started and then as a Minster chorister in 1929. In later years I had played the piano, placed half way down the nave, to assist Sir Edward (who conducted) in keeping it all together. And now I was at the helm, not without misgivings, to be sure, but rewarded afterwards with the encouraging press review by Reginald Rose who mentioned 'clear direction' and 'careful and inspiring work at rehearsal'.

Within a day or two of this was the annual meeting of the British Music Society of York, a body which was founded in the early 1920s for chamber music and to encourage British music. I became a member in the thirties and used to take part in the concert given each year by members up to the start of the war. And it seemed that I lost no time in joining in once more, with Ravel's *Jeux d'Eau* and the Poulenc *Toccata*. There were songs too, as well as cello solos by Helen Procter, my future wife Priscilla Procter's sister-in-law. Apart from this the Minster engaged my complete attention and energies.

The summer holidays came for the choir – all twenty days, Monday to Saturday with two Sundays sandwiched in – then September, and October with its Full Chapter meeting on the eighth. Little did I anticipate what this would bring. The Dean wished me to be available to answer some questions about maintenance of the organ. So I waited to be summoned to the Chapter House where all the canons were seated robed in their best canonicals. I was shown where to sit, wondering what the questions were to be. The Dean spoke up – not about the organ, but the chap who played it. Would I like to be that person? Well, of course I would. But surely, stepping into the shoes of the mighty Sir Edward Bairstow was not my role: they had got the wrong man. So confused and bewildered was I that I found it impossible to utter a word. The Dean then stepped in with the notion that perhaps I would like to think it over, and I left the unimaginable scene.

So my time as acting organist – and Master of the Music, as the statutes have it – the time from 1 May was what turned out to be a five-month-long audition, which evidently had been satisfactory, and I now had to come to terms with the consequences. The senior vicar choral and sub-chanter Hugh Frazer had continually urged me to use bright colours on the organ which is really what I had been brought up by Bairstow to do: he himself provided a shining example. So I tried to comply, and what I did must have found favour, though I am sure there would have been at that time some who would have found it showy and vulgar. (Opinions differ so: I heard from somewhere that *Blessed City* was never sung at Christchurch, Oxford, during Sir Thomas Armstrong's time there [1933-55] for the same reason.)

Naturally there had been much speculation all along as to who would be appointed, and I was continually being informed that I was the right person – from many quarters – and I steadfastly set my face against any thoughts of having the job or being competent to do it. I was twenty-nine years old and it required someone older and with far more experience to fill the post adequately. I had even expressed the hope that Melville Cook might do as Bairstow had done thirty-three years earlier, leaving Leeds Parish Church. It could have been pleasant to work with someone who had been a friend for some twelve years, and I would have welcomed a spell as an assistant and been quite content until something else came along. I constantly speculated as to what it might be. One cathedral organist with whom I discussed the succession had ventured the opinion that he would have to think very carefully if the offer were made to him.

Nonentity that I was, I had some feelings of trepidation about my appointment to the Minster. But I need not have feared: any contrary feelings there may have been were not in evidence. Not until after my retirement (in 1982) did I become aware of what was described to me as a furore over the choice of a 29-year-old nobody to succeed the towering Bairstow. There had been some dissatisfaction, though nothing specific, and hardly to be wondered at considering the immense status of the job and the many would-be contenders for it. But at the time I was fortunate not to be troubled with that aspect of it. Of ripples I was certainly conscious and it appeared that more than one of the top musicians in the land had offered to lend a hand in one way or another in order to ensure the appointment of the right person. I noticed a certain coolness in only a couple of instances, but at my first conference of cathedral organists the atmosphere was friendly and kind, particularly so with Stanley Roper whose welcome was very warm and genuine. I was also already fairly well acquainted with several established members of the conference, two of whom (George Gray of Leicester and Gordon Slater of Lincoln) were Bairstow's pupils. HA Bennett of Rochester had been his assistant before going to Doncaster parish church. In addition I had come to know John Dykes Bower, then at Saint Paul's, on my pre-war exam visits to Durham when he was there.

I have certainly been most fortunate in so many ways, having achieved more than I could have thought possible; not, I hasten to add, through any virtue of mine. Things seem just to have come my way – fallen into my lap. How could I ever have thought, for instance, that the chief of these, my appointment to the Minster, could have happened, even at twice my twenty-nine years of age? I did not even have to apply: it was offered to me to my utter stupefaction. To follow the great Bairstow character, world-famed and prodigiously musical, presented a challenge I felt hardly able to meet. Having worked as Sir Edward's assistant for the last ten days of his life, and then for the next five months shouldered the entire burden of Minster music, I knew the ropes pretty well. What was intimidating was the idea of following his extra-cathedral activities nationally and globally. He was regarded as a kind of monarch of the north but exerting strong influences southwards, and one wondered how much of what he was concerned with would have to be undertaken.

Yet here was I, saddled with an onerous situation: the obvious course to take was a nervous breakdown; not a serious one though, from which I soon recovered. I had to come to grips with so many things – first of all how to train the choir to its best efforts; what of the repertoire, the Psalter, chorister discipline, and a thousand other matters. The one thing that posed no problem was the organ, which I loved to play for services – the psalms in particular, though I relished the elaborate anthem and service accompaniments such as Stanford (in A particularly), Bairstow (in D, especially the communion) and many others, which I had been doing since coming back from the army. I reversed Sir Edward's policy of playing no voluntaries after evensong, and enjoyed letting the organ be heard by the undoubted organ-loving fraternity who came primarily for that purpose – and for others who enjoyed the *sound* of the organ rather than the intricate knowledge of its repertoire. I was showered with letters expressing pleasure and encouragement, all of which I have kept: it took quite a while for the euphoria to abate.

On being appointed I was paid £400 per year with the promise of a further hundred when I obtained a doctorate. As it happened eleven years were to pass before I achieved this but my salary was increased before then. It was not important to me: my great joy and fulfilment was producing the music for the glorious building already mentioned. I was able to live somewhat frugally, with Mabel Taylor to keep house, until I began to earn a little more by teaching privately. Recitals soon became frequent though they were not well paid at that juncture. But I managed without undue difficulty to subsist in that large organist's house in Minster Court, with its elegant rooms and staircase, furnishing it by degrees, helped by loans of furniture. Eventually when Mr Wybergh's flats were given up and the hall at Escrick became a school he lent and then gave us some pieces. Other loans included a boudoir grand which made two-piano duets possible. I was already the proud possessor of the Bechstein grand on which I had had my piano lessons, and had bought from Lady Bairstow. The dining room and drawing room windows, five of them, each needed seven yards of material for curtains, so gifts of elderly pre-war ones (including two pairs of brown ones from Lady Bairstow) were most welcome.

Every penny had to be counted. When it came to indoor decorating there was no question but that one must do it oneself. When I took up residence in 1947 a coat of inferior dark green paint had been applied to the stairs (each step of which had three balusters), paint that did not dry completely and remained always tacky. The completion of the huge task of covering it all with cream paint, including fifteen doors in hall and landing was the cause of an enormous psychological boost even when it began to wrinkle by reason of the wartime quality dark green paint underneath it. Dark paints had been in use for the ground floor, that for the dining room being brown – two large windows, two massive doors with Georgian overmantels, an ornate fireplace, a picture moulding and a three-foot-high dado round the entire room. This was a daunting prospect, which did not take into account the colour-washing of the walls and ceiling. I do not remember how the latter were done but two coats of Adam Green (no relation to Jesse Green, the Clerk of Works) were painstakingly placed over the brown at considerable cost in time and patience.

At one stage, my appointment having been accomplished and the settling-in process started, Boris Ord appeared on the scene as Milner's guest for a few days, his close connexion with the Dean having been forged at King's College, Cambridge. He came to the services and choir practices and was sociable and companionable in his characteristic manner. It seems clear to me now, looking back, that he had been summoned to observe how the new organist was progressing. At one juncture there had been consternation that all was not well, and that the boys were producing bad tone. One of the judges who had attended Sunday matins on what was then called 'Assize Sunday' ('There's no such Sunday in the church's calendar', Milner declared later) ventured his opinion that he could make them sing properly in no time at all given the chance, and Milner passed on this information to me. Whether this was what sparked off Milner's appeal to Boris (if that is what it was) I do not know, but at all events Boris was exceedingly tactful with me. His only suggestion, as I recall, was to dispense with an alto who spoiled the blend – which I had wanted to do but did not relish the idea of taking the necessary action. He may also have dropped hints that I took without being aware: I probably sought his advice, too. The visit was enjoyable from my point of view and certainly left nothing but pleasant memories.

For a time, Boris and the King's College choir had their detractors who thought them precious. Doctor Moody (of Ripon) made no secret of his antagonism and was rude to Boris at a meeting of the Cathedral Organists at Durham, and Boris was clearly upset, telling me about it.

For the chorister boys in the second half of the twentieth century (as well as before and, it is to be hoped, after) the choir provided a wonderful foundation for a career in music as well as in other walks of life. The repertoire embraced works from the sixteenth century to recent compositions, providing a variety of styles as well as enjoyment and education for the boys. Lenten items were solemn, testing our patience perhaps, but as Easter arrived we revelled in uninhibited pieces and almost sang ourselves hoarse by the end of evensong with the big Wood anthem and Bairstow's *Te Deum*, unaccompanied and in its manuscript double choir version. There were plenty of anthems to give us enjoyment – many canticle settings too. Crotch's *Sing we merrily* was a favourite with the boys who delighted in vocalising (if that's the right word) the two bars *tasto solo* introduction on the organ to the words 'Eggs and bacon must be taken every morning when we awaken' – only in rehearsal though. Similarly a prompt entry to the Mendelssohn extract from *Elijah* was assured by singing 'Hey diddle diddle the cat and the fiddle and He watching over Israel'. One thing the boys hugely enjoyed was the beginning of the first Tchaikovsky piano concerto which they often let forth with huge gusto at the end of a choir practice after my few bars' introduction on the piano.

Some of the numbers in the Brahms Requiem gave us plenty to think about, and the final section of Bairstow's *Of the Father's love begotten* was enormous fun, giving us great satisfaction, in rehearsal as well as in performance. That last word was not the one Milner favoured with regard to our efforts in church: they were to the glory of God and not a show-off, as he would express it in his characteristic rather unctuous tones.

Providing music for the daily sung service was seldom or never easy; every service was a challenge and had to be the best we could manage – which is after all every choirmaster's aim. The Dean was intensely interested, always encouraging as well as intelligently and wisely critical. Having been Dean of King's College, Cambridge, he was well versed in the repertoire, and always knew exactly the right anthem for any occasion and for even the most obscure of saints.

Having been brought up in this field by Bairstow – to whom music meant so much, and who taught us choristers and anyone else with whom he was concerned in producing music – we were well aware and accepted the fact that we must understand the music we were performing so that we could pass the message on to those who were listening. Thus it was my constant aim to bring out the full meaning of what we were singing and not to bother too much about the kind of imperfection that will creep into most performances (and which nowadays are ironed out in the search for perfection in recording, disallowing the tiniest imperfection and giving a false impression).

Many years later, in fact long after I had retired, the tape recordings which were regularly and persistently taken by alto songman John Rothera – on his Ferrograph tape recorder from the 1950s until he (and I) retired in 1982 (both on the same day) – were transferred to more permanent systems and found to be an almost inexhaustible mine of what the choir had been up to. Not all of it was perfect – mistakes could happen, extraneous noises would appear – but the over-riding conclusion one arrives at is of a bunch of dedicated singers giving of their utmost to put across the message that they were charged to give.

In those early years in the appointment it was natural, I suppose, for those whose interest lay in organ and church music to wish to have a look at the new organist of York Minster after the long reign of Sir Edward; though I did not realise it at the time. In any case 'York Minster' was the draw rather than the name of the player. There were also invitations to Organist Association dinners for the same purpose, necessitating a speech, which was something completely new, needing a knowledge of how to go about the task, both in the preparation and the delivery of it. In the early years this caused a great deal of anxiety, and I don't doubt that those prentice efforts were capable of much improvement. Gradually, however, one seemed to find a way of finding how to come up with something not utterly boring, so much so that what at first was an ordeal became fun to do. A combination of playing and after-dinner speaking took place at Hull, the organ being the four-manual Compton in the church of Holy Trinity: this in October 1947.

Before this there were recitals in the Minster during July 1946 (a series which I opened with Bach BWV 564) to be followed by Melville Cook, Susi Jeans, John Dykes Bower and, a very welcome and unusual scoop, T Tertius Noble. He, his wife and son Philip had taken an early opportunity to visit England after the end of hostilities and he gave two recitals, a week apart, which drew very large audiences. It was some thirty-five years since he had left the Minster for Saint Thomas New York, but there were many people who remembered him from his York days as well as those who knew his reputation.

After both recitals he was besieged by crowds of people, who had known him so many years before and wished to shake his hand, and I had to pilot him through the crush to see him safely into calm waters on account of his sight problem. This was not yet a serious difficulty so far as his playing was concerned: he could manage in a good light to see the printed music, and life in general was as normal; indeed one morning he came by himself from his hotel on the other side of the Minster to have breakfast with me, walking in his usual energetic manner. His visit was of the greatest delight to us all with his friendly charm of manner. We sang his B minor *Magnificat* and *Nunc Dimittis* in his honour: it was written almost half a century earlier in, I presume, the house where he used to live – and Bairstow next – then myself. This was, apart from five excellent chants, the only composition of Noble's that Bairstow had kept in the repertoire, I suspect on sufferance; his standards being so very high, and Victorian music being largely anathema to him. That it has kept its place in cathedral music lists is testimony to its vigour, and with the passage of time its rich harmonic colouring has taken on a welcome period charm.

During their stay over here the Nobles made what cannot have been an easy journey to the west coast of Scotland opposite the islands of Rhum, Eigg and Muck, a somewhat daunting undertaking even for those of a much younger age. Their object was to meet once more the leader of the York Symphony Orchestra that Doctor Noble had conducted with such notable success. Editha Knocker, who lived in York in the early 1900s, had been a favourite pupil of Joachim and became a fine teacher, to the advantage of Doctor Noble and the orchestra. A letter she wrote to my wife's aunt Kathleen Procter (who had played in the orchestra in her younger days) tells how 'it hurt me to see him physically so aged, though he is still his dear old cheery self. We were terrified for him while here, as he is so nearly blind and we have no roads – only very rough tracks. Neither he nor Mrs Noble could manage them … He is quite unchanged, bless him. Doctor Noble spoke most warmly of F Jackson and seemed to think he was just the right man in the right place', which naturally pleased me, coming from one so legendary and which, dear reader, I am conceited enough to pass on to you.

Soon after my 1946 appointment to York, and spending some time in London, I attended some Promenade Concert rehearsals in the Albert Hall through the good offices of Basil Cameron, the well-known conductor at that annual event. In one of these was *Legend* by John Ireland, composed in 1933, and he was there to hear it rehearsed. I was fortunate to spend some time with him and to hear about the piece (played then by Kyla Greenbaum) a composition of a very special character – for piano and orchestra – imbued with a mystical atmosphere and, I am sure, quite rightly of great significance to him. It was new to me and when I asked him if it was often to be heard, with a slightly hopeless gesture he said perhaps once in five years. Then, to my everlasting regret, I volunteered that that was more than many composers had, to which he meekly agreed. Certainly it deserves to be heard frequently. I was sorry, then, to find that he was not satisfied with its performance that evening. What was wrong with it I do not know, but as soon as it had ended I went round to the green room to find him in a disturbed state, pacing about and turning the pages of the score back and forth in his distress. He was alone, and on seeing me, burst out with 'That's the worst performance of any piece of mine that I've ever heard and I don't mind putting it on record'. Expressing my sympathy I soon left – though I often wish I had stayed to learn where the trouble lay. I believe that he often was likely to take the line that his compositions were not having the attention he felt should be given them, and it is more than probably true that this is the case. For some years during his lifetime his lovely piano concerto was regularly done at the Proms, and other works appeared more or less frequently. One cannot but sympathise with his wish for more performances; his music is of a quality that stands up so very well among those of his contemporaries and is certainly not such as to be treated in any way as second rate or less than worthy.

‖O‖

Back at the Minster, an event which we had enjoyed taking part in was the recording of church music for the British Council along with six other choirs. I have three letters from EH Fellowes; that of 4 January 1949 says

> 'as the Council have put upon me this rather grave responsibility I should like to come up to York and hear the anthems about a week before the recordings. I can manage it quite well in a day from here, if trains run as they used to'.

He wrote the letters himself – by candlelight so it is believed, as Merbecke would have done in the same house at Windsor in the shadow of Saint George's chapel four centuries earlier. In his clear, neat calligraphy on a small sheet of notepaper he gives all the information about the pieces, with accurate timings: of *What are these,*

> 'Gray's anthem will have to take two sides of a 12-inch record. I expect you are familiar with the anthem for I heard it in the Minster in Bairstow's time. The turn-over should come on page 8: but I doubt whether there would be room on the record (4.35 is the extreme limit of time) to get as far as the word 'utter' and it might be advisable to change over some where [sic] earlier on p.8 ...'

It was fascinating to find this authority on earlier music, then aged 78, whose many editions we used regularly, dealing in a twentieth-century method of sound reproduction. We also recorded Wood's *Hail gladdening light,* which Doctor HK Andrews criticized (privately to a mutual friend) for the slower tempo we adopted for the middle section.

There were further sessions in the next two years: the series was welcome encouragement and was well received. We read the reviews with interest. A broadcaster intimated that we sang *What are these* with great verve or gusto. But we could hardly agree with a writer who dealt with SS Wesley's anthem (not our recording) which he averred was *aptly* called *The wilderness.* Perhaps he had not been a chorister and brought up with the standard repertoire.

Here I recall the Reverend John McMullen, for many years Vicar Choral, minor canon, a sensitive musician, quite a pianist, and a most valued member of the Minster community, who used to engage one at length on meeting somewhere in the precincts, to one's great profit and amusement. There are a host of recollections over a period of a good half-century which remain firmly in the memory to gladden the heart, the most frequent perhaps being the possibility of a meeting in the cobbled lane by Dean's Park and being regaled with a lengthy, amusing and always perceptive account of some musical event he had encountered. Once he shared his delight with me concerning Artur Schnabel's dental visit for filling replacement. On learning that the cost of the operation was to be two pounds and ten shillings, he commented 'Fifty shillings for shifty fillings'.

John's knowledge of pianists (as of all music) and his critiques were acute and wide, from Myra Hess on; and to have known her and others (notably Howard Ferguson) was a huge joy to him as to us, who were treated to his impressions of them; impressions too of a different kind, humorously done at the piano with much subtlety. I know, too, that he was appreciative of the music and the choir during my time alongside and am grateful for his trusty support of one's efforts, with his inside knowledge of the workings and problems involved. Just as for reliable advice on any aspect, including repertoire which, as Sub-Chanter, was his especial care under the eagle eye of Dean Milner-White at our weekly music meetings.

His chanting of the offices with his sense of pitch and his clear enunciation was as perfect as could be found, an attribute which informed his readings and his too infrequent preachings, that revealed his deep knowledge and spirituality couched in phraseology of a rare quality. One remembers how more than once John seemed to lose his way and to omit something, perhaps one of the versicles, to the choir's consternation, or announced the psalms prematurely instead of singing 'Praise ye the Lord'. We always had to be ready for such contingencies.

MILNER AND MINSTER MUSIC

Over time the thought has occurred to me that Dean Milner-White's warm interest in and understanding of the younger male of the species could have been a factor in his choice of me as organist. Also he saw me (or any other who might have been in the running) as clay to mould to his own wishes. Indeed, he kept me very securely in his sights and guided and nurtured me along the way he wished me and the Minster's music to go. My first meeting with him was at the hands of Bairstow and was in the south choir aisle of the Minster as choir and clergy were assembling for evensong. It must have been a Friday, Bairstow being robed to conduct the unaccompanied choir, in the aisle and not up in the organ loft. He seemed keen to effect the introduction even though there was hardly time before the vestry prayer. Milner (as he was usually referred to or, as an irreverent member of the Minster works team had it, 'Chalky' White) glowed in characteristic style and, with his mind on higher things, was lost for words and could only utter 'very nice' through his cheerful enthusiastic smile.

I suppose Milner had kept hearing of me from ECB, and this first *rencontre* was probably of significance to both of them since they must have had in mind the vacancy for an assistant organist that must soon occur. Bairstow had dropped a few broad hints to me in letters that he wanted me to fill it when the day arrived. I was on leave from the army, having recently returned from four years in the Middle East and Italy, during which time Bairstow and I had exchanged letters regularly. I returned to Catterick to complete my army service, where one day a letter from Milner arrived offering me the post of Assistant. I replied by telegram in what might be construed as slightly Milneresque phraseology ('Accept gladly and gratefully'), this before I had had any chance to soak up any of his mannerisms, which were not at all hard to copy or to memorise: eg. 'The GLASSSS; thiss Minsstah ...'.

It was then that Milner began trying with the commanding officer to have me demobbed before time, on the grounds that there were several important services to be thought about and which one man on his own, and now rather ailing, could not manage. Not yet being conversant with Milner's methods it occurred to me that he was perhaps laying it on a bit thick with the CO. Later, one came to expect this kind of thing and to take it as a matter of course. Not that there was anything really wrong in doing so: it was merely, at that stage of my acquaintance with him, a little surprising. But it usually worked; Milner got his way and no-one was any the worse for it, apparently.

My appointment as successor to Bairstow was no doubt consistent with Milner's general policy, but I was known to the Precentor, CC Bell, and to Freddie Harrison, librarian and chancellor, since my chorister days. There seemed no hurry to choose a new man and I do not doubt that it had crossed the minds of more than the one who confessed to me that York would be nice preferment. And here was Milner scuppering any such ambitions at a stroke. He would of course be well aware of the effect of such an (almost) unprecedented move – Nares was aged 19 when appointed to York in 1735: an all-time record probably – but Milner was quite equal to dealing with any reservations that might reach his ears. It would seem that a pattern for younger cathedral organists was being set, although this was not the first instance in modern times; Gerald Knight went to Canterbury at the age of twenty-eight.

Pursuing his policy Milner had already brought in a fourth bass songman, bringing the men's strength up to ten. As to repertoire, he wanted the best of all periods and the use of the Tudor Church Music editions for Tudor music. We could have as many Latin anthems as we liked, but in the 1950s long before Vatican 2, the eucharist ('Sung' then, 'Solemn' later) had to be in English. Once, the Byrd three-part was undertaken in Latin by the assistant organist around that time during the summer holidays without my knowledge – or the Dean's – and, as John McMullen put it, Milner had to do quite a lot of batting as a result, dealing with complainants.

Milner was very particular over the choice of music and was always infallible in his selection of anthems. His knowledge of the repertoire was wide, after his many years at King's with Boris Ord and 'Daddy' Mann, and he would pounce upon exactly the right piece without a moment's hesitation. I observed this time after time. Milner had very definite ideas of the music he wanted, and it was as well that his taste was so impeccable: had it been less so Bairstow would have been sorely tried. Milner told me that Bairstow was at first suspicious of his suggestion of a clear-out of the repertoire, but soon was able to accept it. This speaks of Milner's tact – some might say willingness to gain his own ends – which allowed *give* as well as *take* in such negotiations. Although he held strong opinions and had distinct likes and dislikes, he was always ready to consider opposing views and could be persuaded to change his own. In fact I did on one occasion overcome his abhorrence of Henry Smart's *Magnificat* and *Nunc Dimittis* in B flat, that extrovert setting with its trumpet fanfares, so alien to the sentiments expressed by the Blessed Virgin. It seemed not inappropriate for a nave service on a bank holiday, and he agreed that we could do it. Over the years I was able to persuade him to allow us to restore pieces like Garrett in D (by a Cantabrigian of whose compositions Milner did not think a great deal), Stainer in E flat and some others he did not like, including Bairstow's own big communion service in D which was too flamboyant for his more ascetic taste. The previous dean, Herbert Newell Bate, preferred Wood to Stanford and found Bairstow's ebullience hard to bear. Milner not only allowed Stanford but admired and enjoyed it. All of his complete day's services were in the repertoire, except the unison one in D, which had been tried and rejected during my time as chorister.

At Cambridge Milner had been very friendly with Charles Wood, than whom there can have been no more delightful person, according to his expressed opinion. Thus he was very much in favour of his compositions, of which few were in the York repertoire, and he lost no time in bringing them in, rather to my annoyance. Wood was constantly being held up as a paragon, which was rather counter-productive as far as I was concerned. However, as usual Milner had his way and I eventually came to agree with him. The double-choir anthem *'Tis the day of resurrection* I always thought manufactured rather than spontaneous, but it could not be dislodged and came later to have pride of place on Easter Day at evensong. This was despite the solemn *Te Deum* at the end of the service, making two unaccompanied pieces of a similar nature in close proximity, with the lengthy *O Filii et Filiae* processional hymn between them. The *Te Deum* was invariably Bairstow's, in D, in its manuscript unaccompanied version. Milner was inordinately fond of *Father all-holy* and chose it for most consecrations of bishops, for which occasions it vied for popularity with Wesley's *Thou wilt keep him in perfect peace*. The Sternhold and Hopkins metrical *Magnificat* and *Nunc Dimittis* was an imaginative choice of his for BVM festivals, and I believe they were composed by Wood at Milner's suggestion. He would not countenance a Latin canticle at evensong, nor at matins, though perhaps a German or French anthem would have been approved. His standard was that it should be 'understanded of the people', who are at this stage better educated than ever before. He would expect the Church of England office to be in English: the anthem is a different matter. The psalms were sung to the English Psalter which was compiled by Bairstow, Buck and Macpherson. As a chorister, I had been brought up on it so was for many years totally in favour of it; but at length I came to see its weaknesses and was supported by Milner in transferring to another system (*The Psalter Newly Pointed*). However, this was greatly to the chagrin of Canon Freddie Harrison who did not wish Bairstow's work to be thrown out and had almost certainly not been consulted at Chapter level nor heard a word about any proposed change.

Milner had instituted the weekly meeting with his organist (then ECB) to choose the music for the following week. This was on Mondays after the evening meal and it provided a chance for the two of them (and probably Lady Bairstow as well) to chat in a relaxed way about a variety of topics. The 'Scheme' as the service list was called, was taken across the road to the printer next morning; a proof was provided, and the finished article arrived faithfully in quantity on Saturday for distribution. Thus Milner secured Bairstow's confidence, and a happy though short period of some four years' co-operation ensued. More than one of Bairstow's letters to me during the war bore the news that 'the new dean is a dear; he knows all the boys by their Christian names', and one can understand Bairstow's relief to have a sympathetic spirit to work with after the antagonism of the previous regime. Later, when I had taken over the duties of Master of the Music, my involvement with the local orchestra necessitated changing the Monday evening meeting to 5.30pm. The Succentor, John McMullen, brought along the music list he had prepared and it was passed round for comment. The music was discussed and any amendments to the schedule were made. Any other relevant subject was brought up, such as choir deportment, chorister parents and songman vacancies, ensuring that everyone was in the picture concerning the music and musicians. The services were very near to Milner's heart and he wanted them to be as perfect as possible. He attended them very frequently, being rarely absent.

In the late 1940s the choir gradually improved and reached a steady standard which held for some years, this despite the problem of songman recruitment which resulted in frequent changes and shortages. At one time there was only one bass. Undoubtedly money was at the bottom of the trouble, but there was never any question of raising salaries. Milner's attitude appeared to be that sufficient reward was to be found in the daily singing of beautiful music in a glorious building dedicated to the worship of God, and – if the thought so much as entered his head – that the gas bill would take care of itself. The decani bass, Ted Woodhouse, on retiring after countless years of faithful service received a visit from the Dean across the park and was informed that he would be having a pension of a pound a week. This was around 1950.

Things must soon have begun to go more as Milner wished, for he was always ready to praise as well as to offer kindly criticism. He usually thanked the choir after service as the clergy walked between their ranks in the aisle on the way to the vestry. When I was there on unaccompanied days he would say 'Thank you, mister organist', sometimes so faintly that only the final two consonants were audible, but usually with his beaming smile. Thus in lighter moments the choir came to regard '…ssst' as high praise.

The pattern of choir holidays that existed during my time as a chorister persisted until well after my appointment but with one change. Milner thought that more rehearsal would be beneficial and so his suggestion was that matins on Thursday and Saturday should give way to full rehearsals. This gave us plenty of time and, eventually, too much. But when we wanted to have matins reinstated there were difficulties and objections.

The next change to take place was the release of the songmen from all morning duties on weekdays. Full practices were held in the afternoon before evensong, and matins was sung by the boys on their own. This gave us the opportunity to sing, among other things, the *Te Deum* and *Jubilate* by Walmisley for two trebles, the manuscript of which had been obtained by EMW from among AH Mann's effects and which was later published by the Church Music Society. Incidentally, from the same source the Minster library became the repository of the score of Stanford's orchestration of his *Te Deum* in B flat. So matins continued for a few years until the start, in 1967, of the great restoration of the Minster which was to last five years. But it became clear that to have the work interrupted, even on two days of the week, was uneconomic and thus not possible. Sung matins, therefore, came to an end, except of course on Sundays.

For a dean to put his oar in to musical matters to such an extent was probably fairly uncommon among the cathedrals. Other deans were perhaps not so concerned or so sensitive to music and were content to leave the choice to their organist. But Milner knew what he wanted and his way of having it was to keep in close touch with his musicians and to use his powers of persuasion, which were considerable.

By these means a dictatorship became a democracy and it worked happily enough. True, there could be frustrations. There was never any thought of unilateral action by the organist. The Dean's permission must be sought before any new music was brought in, however tiny a piece – a hymn even – but the process was a fair one and depended on a flexible attitude on both sides. On one occasion there was a scene after a Sunday evensong concerning *How sweet the name of Jesus sounds* which had been chosen by Canon Tardrew. Milner was furious and aggrieved to have a fine service let down by a weak final hymn. He took quite a time to becalm himself, and I found him clipping a hedge to relieve his frustration as he proceeded to give me a full account of the incident and his feelings about it. One piece I introduced without asking was the *Lord's Prayer* by Stone, but this delighted him; I knew he was fond of it.

As far as I know, this was the way every department was handled. The father figure was there, keeping a benign hold on the whole concern, and problems were ironed out with minimum difficulty. One suspected that the same held good with his canons on the administrative Chapter, and that Milner's will triumphed. When in 1960 I persuaded him that a nave console should be added to the organ, I happened to mention to the Canon Treasurer, George Addleshaw, that the Dean had approved it. But he knew nothing about it and was extremely annoyed at the lack of consultation. It appeared to be a decision made by the Dean on his own and one that would be nodded through at the next meeting. One might wonder whether in fact Milner intended paying the bill himself, which I think could have been possible since he showed similar munificence on more than this occasion.

It happened that one day some years later, while Priscilla and I were painting the inside of the open dining-room windows, Milner came into the Court with someone else and stopped for a word. He was very pleasant, making jocular remarks such as 'Do you realise that every drop of paint that is put on represents one note of music lost to the world?' To this there was a perfectly good answer, but if it came into either Priscilla's mind or mine at that moment it did not pass our lips ... His relationship with those around him could, as this account shows, be cordial and friendly. He was, however, sometimes capable of ignoring you, his mind being probably on some important matter, or on his way to the eight o'clock communion before which he did not wish to speak. Francis Woolley, organist of Newark parish church until his death in the 1950s, was at Cambridge where he knew Milner. He told me that one day along the King's Parade he saw Milner approaching. They had not met for a while and Woolley expected somewhat of a welcome. Milner at first did not recognise him and was walking past him. Recognition, however, dawned and Milner half turned towards him and said 'Oh, it's you', and walked on.

Another Cambridge visitor to York in those early days was Patrick (Paddy) Hadley, the Professor of Music who put up at the Station Hotel. An idiosyncratic character rather addicted to the bottle, he announced to the Dean that he was going to call him Eric, somewhat to the Dean's surprise. It was very nearly Christmas and the Dean was keen that the choristers should sing Hadley's *I sing of a maiden* before he departed on 24 December. The only problem was that the twenty-third was still darkest Advent during which season not a note of Christmas music must be heard. Milner was very strict on this point, but in his usual manner he was able to get round it by dubbing the day before Christmas Eve 'the eve of the Eve'. This was entirely characteristic; no doubt it was tongue in cheek, but it provided Milner with what he wanted even if it meant flouting the rules he himself had set. So all was in order and Paddy thought the boys were good. On being asked – in our front hall – to write an evening service for us, he said that he would begin well enough but would stall when he came to the socialist sentiments – putting down the mighty and exalting the humble and meek. So we have to content ourselves with but two of his compositions, the other of course being *My beloved spake* which, Boris Ord declared in my hearing, Paddy wrote for the marriage of one of his girlfriends to one of his boyfriends.

Milner was very keen always to encourage his organist to compose music, and had persuaded Bairstow to produce the *Lamentation*, to the infinite credit of both of them, and *Six Songs of the Spirit* (Milner seemed to like sibilants). He told me that for these he had suggested something like a hundred poems for Bairstow to choose from. He was also usually thinking of new ways to do services, and one of these concerned the *Benedicite*. He thought its length could be reduced if one side of the choir sang the first half of each verse while the other simultaneously did 'Praise him and magnify him for ever'. He had suggested this to Harold Darke when he was at King's during the war, without any result, so it was tried on me and I produced the almost finished piece in two hours, though in a slightly different but still truncated form. He also would have liked to replace the *Gloria Patri* with 'Let us bless the Father and the Son with the Holy Ghost: let us praise and exalt him above all for ever'. Thinking it was on the short side, I had it pointed out by Canon George Addleshaw that there was more of it to be found in the liturgy of the Scottish Episcopal Church, and this is what I used. It continues 'Blessed art thou O Lord in the firmament of heaven, praised and exalted above all for ever'. I dedicated the *Benedicite* to Milner and think he was pleased. He did, however, comment that I had rather dwelt on the lightnings and clouds, and repeated them, when the whole object was to cut down and save time. However, it seemed to me that I had taken a right course and felt unable to alter it without injuring the balance. Another piece for which he chose words was the anthem for the unveiling of the astronomical clock, the Royal Air Force memorial, by the Duke of Edinburgh in 1957. An excerpt from the words appears on the clock. He said that he had 'arranged' the words rather than composed them and had tapped various sources in so doing. Its title: *Remember for Good, O Father*.

His sensitivity to music usually brought forth informed comment. On hearing for the first time Kenneth Leighton's *Magdalen Service* he declared it to be like a tragic ballet. He was also appreciative, and probably slightly envious, of one's ability to hear music mentally while reading it silently. This was quite often needed at the Monday music meetings and he once commented kindly on it and expressed a wish that he could do it himself.

Mr. Scaife, Master of the Song School from its founding (or refounding) in 1903, had run the school in his own way and provided an education for the choristers which served them well in its day. Eventually he would retire and the matter of a new colleague with whom I was to work happily was of especial concern to me. This I am sure Milner understood. When Scaife did retire there was an interregnum, and this was filled by the amiable HWB Camidge until the new man's arrival.

Milner was, as always, troubled by the Minster's finance problems and bethought himself long and hard how to save as much money as possible. A kind of solution was to appoint as Master of the Song School a priest who could act as vicar choral on occasion. The price of the Burnham scale of pay for teachers could not be afforded so the good candidates were ruled out. The priest who was appointed came from an industrial parish in south Yorkshire, was not a qualified teacher and as it turned out was not a success, was most unpopular and completely out of sympathy with the aims of the choir. This for me was a situation of the utmost gravity and seriousness, and one which would, I could foresee, adversely affect my work with the choir. His presence at all the services had an inhibiting effect on the boys, who stood in fear of him as he 'glared' at them, as directed by Milner: a malign influence indeed. There was no possibility of any change in his attitude: every attempt to come to some agreement ended in stalemate and quarrelling, only making matters worse. My desperate appeals to Milner to curb his influence fell, after an initial approach that was reasonable and encouraging to me, on deaf ears. Thereafter I was made out to be in the wrong; my discipline was too lax and I was unfit to be in charge of boys. Discipline therefore had to be in the master's province; in fact everything apart from their singing was to be under his jurisdiction. In addition boys were not to be allowed to speak to the songmen at any time, on or off duty in school or Minster.

It appeared, from all this, that Milner had been listening to his views and had fallen in with them, realising that his chosen man had given up working in a thriving parish to come and teach twenty-five small boys, and that if things did not go as he wished he would return to a parish. This was said to me more than once by the man concerned, so I am quite sure that the same threat was uttered to Milner to the latter's discomfiture. This man had to be placated at any cost so other considerations had to be swept away; and as it was most unlikely that the organist would resign such a prestigious position, his feelings in the matter could be disregarded, flouted and ridden over rough-shod. There was a marked contrast with his predecessors, George Arthur Scaife and HWB Camidge, who had at all times been most careful to encourage in the boys the right attitude towards the music and to stress its importance: never was any attempt made by the next man to do the same thing. Though the boys remained loyal to me, a slow wearing down of enthusiasm eventually became apparent, and my inspiration gradually drained away. This probably did not reveal itself to Milner as listener to the choir's performances, for he did not make mention of it to me or to anyone that I know of. Perhaps he came at last to the knowledge that my prognostication was coming true and that, if he complained, I would only remind him of it. This is mere supposition of course, but I often wondered if I would be forced out, asked to resign, so had determined I would rather take Bernard Shaw's advice and get kicked out. This situation lasted for fifteen years, with the result that my former happy association with Milner was soured for the last few years of his life, and it was left to Alan Richardson, the next dean, to settle the uncomfortable situation and to appoint as Master of the Song School a sympathetic spirit to be of help to the music rather than a hindrance.

Earlier in my time there, Milner had made attempts at chanting the services that were not too successful. I had the impression that he somewhat fancied himself in the role of precentor, but he soon gave it up and did not try again. On one occasion the choir was put off by his starting the creed (at matins) with the first two words only when they were used to *I believe in God.* How they managed to start I do not remember.

Milner died in 1963. He was kind enough to leave me fifty pounds in his will. In addition I was given some small items from his pottery collection as well as a coloured eighteenth century print of the Minster towers taken from Saint Leonard's Place, and several of Walter de la Mare's books which one day I hope to read.

ITINERANT ORGANIST

One of the by-products of the office of Master of the Music at the Cathedral and Metropolitical Church of Saint Peter of York was invitations to play organ recitals, some of them of a prestigious kind such as the opening of a new organ or a rebuilt or restored one. Soon after the war's end, before the resumption of normal cultural activity with the rise of mechanical reproduction and the Third Programme of the BBC, music was not too plentiful. Hence what was a makeshift substitute was often relied on to fill the gap. It was a continuation of the pre-war state of affairs such as Melville Cook used to arrange in Leeds Parish Church where once he, on the piano, played César Franck's *Symphonic Variations* to my organ accompaniment. The orchestration lent itself readily to this treatment and worked well. The combining of the contrasting tone qualities of the two instruments left me with a fondness which appeared now and again over the following years, eventually bringing about my seventy-first opus, of which more later.

In November 1947 I played a recital in London for the Organ Music Society, a prestigious body founded and run by Archibald Farmer and Felix Aprahamian. This took place at Westminster Chapel in Buckingham Gate on the impressive Father Willis/Rushworth organ of four manuals. The programme included the Bairstow *Sonata* and my *Impromptu*, the Bach D major, the second concerto by Matthew Camidge, two Guilmant pieces, Stanford's *Fantasia and Toccata* and, to finish, Franck's *Final* in B flat.

Melville Cook, who had been organist at Leeds Parish Church since 1937, founded a chamber choir called the Leeds Guild of Singers, and I took part in a good many of their concerts. Based at the Parish Church, they moved around locally and also to other locations such as Beverley Minster, Selby Abbey and churches at Ilkley and Headingley (St. Chad). The programmes were always interesting and varied. A particular favourite was the *Missa Brevis* of Kodaly which, as a result of making its acquaintance here, eventually found its way into the Minster choir's repertoire and was used regularly. In the Brahms *Liebeslieder Waltzes* Melville forsook his baton for the treble end of the piano and allotted the bass to me. Several recitals with Douglas Hall provided the pleasure of accompanying his violin in sonatas by Ravel, Poulenc, Walton and Turina, in and around Leeds and Bradford.

∥O∥

The Minster's full and correct designation 'The Cathedral and Metropolitical Church of Saint Peter of York' and that of the Archbishop 'Primate of England and Metropolitan' both speak of matters of importance. Thus for special events to do with the Northern Province, the Minster has become the natural and obvious choice. One of these, early in my days as organist, was a service of thanksgiving for the Prayer Book of 1549 in its four hundredth year, and attended by Doctor Cyril Garbett, the Archbishop at the time. It was broadcast on the BBC Third Programme at 6.00pm on Wednesday 18 May, giving it country-wide coverage. It also enabled Gerald Knight, director of the Royal School of Church Music, the opportunity to send me his gratuitous assessment of the choir's performance.

There was a problem, however, in that I had, by some mischance or carelessness, undertaken to play a recital at Leeds Parish Church that same evening; the kind of nightmare scenario that seems inevitable however careful one can be. 'Organist to make taxi dash between recitals' was the Yorkshire Post's way of broaching the subject, and went on to explain that I would be there at the service until I had finished conducting the anthem when Allan Wicks, the Assistant Organist, would take over. All worked out apparently, according to plan, and Leeds was able to have its share of the Healey Willan *Passacaglia* among other pieces. It is not related how I reached home afterwards after a fairly active day.

Incidentally, a Yorkshire Evening Post headline of the same date intimated 'York Minster sets BBC a puzzle', referring to the problem of how to cope with the choir in motion as it sang the Litany in procession. The report says that it is 'a problem involving the strategic installation of microphones among the spaces of the Minster', a situation which has become easier with the passage of time and microphones of greater sensitivity.

◖O◗

One of the events we always enjoyed was the annual combining with the cathedral choirs of Durham and Ripon in the three venues in their turn. This had taken place early in the twentieth century and had, I believe, lapsed at some time. It was a going concern again during Bairstow's tenure, and, on one occasion (and perhaps others) included additional choirs. There is a photograph in the Yorkshire Post of 2 July 1936 which, while featuring the regulars – Bairstow, Moody (Ripon) and John Dykes Bower (Durham) – also included HK Andrews (then at Beverley Minster, later at New College Oxford) and William Ellis of Newcastle whose choir made a fourth that year. Also in the photograph is Sir Walter Alcock, up from Salisbury, who had written his evening canticles in A for the occasion, which he conducted. Bairstow conducted his anthem *Blessed City, heavenly Salem*. Directing such a body of highly trained, dedicated, intelligent and sensitive singers, with their potential for expression, variety of tone colour, to say nothing of full-blooded, inspiring volume of power, is a major pleasure indeed, especially when increased threefold beyond one's normal assignment.

The June 1949 meeting at York took in the choirs of Newcastle Cathedral, with their organist Kenneth Malcolmson, and Carlisle with Doctor FW Wadely, active there since 1910, who I used to meet now and then in the following years, notably as one of my doctoral examiners at Durham; he with his Cambridge doctorate, a rare thing at that time (including of course Vaughan Williams and Walford Davies) but even rarer in later years. This time we had Bairstow in D, Greene's *O clap your hands together* for introit, unaccompanied, Wood's *Glory and honour and laud* and Samuel Wesley's *Exultate Deo*, all of which made a magnificent sound, hardly possible to forget. The only mishap, due to my carelessness, was that I had inadvertently told Carlisle in my hand written instructions that the other Wesley anthem was *In Exitu Israel* instead of *Exultate Deo*. So the poor unfortunate choristers had to remain silent for that item. Doctor Wadely was extremely kind and understanding. That was in the days when there was no secretarial help, nor any of these ubiquitous computers to spew out masses of duplicated commands.

It may have been at this meeting that I aroused Doctor Moody's displeasure by placing the Ripon choir in what he thought (no doubt quite correctly) was a junior position in the procession. It had not occurred to me that it mattered who went first or who followed. It had become my care to arrange all the movement and the extra seating in the nave, and I had worked out a viable system. It was therefore not much of a help, in the midst of trying to marshal some ninety-odd bodies, to be taken to task in that manner. He did quieten down, though, when I assumed a probably over-apologetic stance, and I think my plan was adhered to. Looking back, that was probably the best way to deal with this somewhat testy gentleman, rather than a head-on collision, especially as I was forty-three years his junior. On another occasion he ventured to tell me that when wearing one's full-dress doctor's academic dress in full technicolour (which Professor Hutchings referred to as the Party Frock), it was wrong to put on the hood over the gown. That of course is the case with Oxford, and no doubt with the Oxford gown he wore for his Lambeth degree. But no strict rules about the Durham use ever came to my notice, and I was happy to acquaint the learned doctor of the fact.

Another time, when we were to sing Psalm 150 to our usual single chant, composed by the Reverend George Surtees Talbot (a one-time minor canon at York and thus of some significance to us), it happened that the four treble notes of the first half of the chant were identical with a chant of Moody's which, incidentally, was in the York chant book and had been in regular use there for many years. True to form, he did not scruple to make his feelings known, though to what purpose is hard to fathom, and done without regard for its effect on the other person, who was busily engrossed in rehearsing it.

As I have gone about making use of past pocket diaries for ideas as to what I should bother to write about, it has been borne in on me increasingly how full and interesting a life I have led. Very few days in sixty-six years of diary days are void, and many are filled with several entries. It is patently clear that a great deal has had to be left out of this account. Quite rightly, because so much is repetition; the Minster activities went on each day the same, but with notable happenings from time to time which are probably of some interest in a tale of this sort. To the player, recitals are always fascinating due in so many ways to the endless variety of organs. To the reader, with nothing to hear and only a list of pieces to look at, the attraction can soon wear thin, but there remains here some record of what was deemed an acceptable offering in the programmes at the time. My hope, then, is to sum up a total of sixty-six years of non-stop playing, a total which is not wildly inaccurate.

Inexorably as time went on I became immersed in many other activities that filled each day with a variety of matters needing attention – the inevitable state of affairs in a cathedral organist's life. One's chief care of course was the choir, which occupied one's thoughts most of the time. As well as the extra-mural ploys, correspondence took up a good deal of time and effort and it was not until I was married that I was blessed with the luxury of a secretary, and that very domestically. The planning of recital programmes is a time-consuming operation; there was practising to be done and new repertoire to be learned after what might be called the chores had been dealt with.

Requests for organ recitals started modestly with six in 1947 which included Durham and Wakefield cathedrals; the eight of 1948 taking in Blackburn and Carlisle cathedrals; and the thirteen of 1949 among which were Beverley Minster, Salisbury cathedral, Birmingham Town Hall, King's College in Cambridge, and the opening of the Harrison organ in the Barony Church in Glasgow. Also among these recitals was one of the dreaded (by the recitalist that is) half-hour events on diploma day: a rather terrifying affair at the Royal College of Organists in its old location in the Kensington Gore premises by the Albert Hall where no help was forthcoming from the dead acoustic. One was conscious, inevitably, of the hall full of expert, knowledgeable folk who nevertheless were listening sympathetically and, one hoped, not too critically. But all was well. Afterwards I received a letter which gave very great pleasure and which I quote in full for no other reason than to show the affectionate and kindly attitude of the King's organist Stanley Roper who it was always a joy to meet, which was seldom – alas:

Chapel Royal, St James's Palace, S.W.1

24 July '49

You won't mind a little letter of congratulation and gratitude from me, will you! For you played splendidly, in fact I think the charm of the Bach Trio has rarely been equalled, and I know how grateful all were for this experience. I kept you in mind during your long journey last night, hoping your mind was dwelling all the time on the pleasure and example you have given us. For I suppose you had to face that rather tedious return to York and perhaps in a crowded train. It was good to have the little chats together this week and a delight to catch your eye now and again yesterday [at the council meeting]. Bravo – and very many happy years in the grand old place.

Yours, S. No reply of course.

A more encouraging letter than this can hardly be imagined. The trio was the third movement of the fifth Bach Sonata; the fugue was BWV 537. John Dykes Bower observed with a twinkle that I actually *phrased* the pedal part in the trio. This was an indication of his experiences as an examiner for the RCO diplomas where he had found that, even if the phrasing of both manual parts had received due attention, little or no regard had been paid to the shaping of the bass line, such as a good cellist or bassoon player would apply to it. The rest of the programme (all chosen from the set pieces for the Fellowship and Associateship examinations) was the Mozart *Fantasia* in F minor and major, K 594 (not an easy piece, in fact according to Sir William McKie the most difficult he knew), Whitlock's *Pastorale* and the first movement of Mendelssohn's fourth sonata.

Three days later I gave a recital at the Minster, and then set off on a tandem tour of the West Country, starting at Salisbury where I joined

David Swale who was teaching in the choir school there and singing in the cathedral choir. (At this time Derek Sutton was there too, also teaching and singing, strengthening the York link that was begun by Cyril and Mimi Jackson. Cyril was canon precentor at Salisbury, having been minor canon at the Minster during my choristership.) For almost three weeks David and I pedalled our way along roads not yet overcrowded with traffic, enjoying the scenery and visiting countless places, picturesque and interesting: Exeter, Truro, Looe, Newquay (which offered us the best sea-bathing we had ever experienced in this country); Boscastle, Bude, Tintagel, Glastonbury (where in the church the cleric clearly did not believe me when I told him where I was organist – we wanted to try the organ but I cannot remember if we did); Minehead, Porlock, Wells, Bath, Tewkesbury, Worcester, Stratford, Pershore, Evesham, Broadway, Warwick which still had its Hope-Jones organ; Market Harborough and thence to Peterborough for the train home. The tandem served us well, providing healthy activity and only proving tiresome when on more than one occasion the chain broke, needing an expert to join it up again.

The Worcester visit was memorable: we called on the cathedral organist, Sir Ivor Atkins, then nearly eighty years old with fifty-two years in the post. He took us on what seems now like a whirlwind tour of the cathedral, the library and the organ, with a marvellously youthful enthusiasm. He even took us to the very spot in the north nave aisle where, during a rehearsal, Elgar had called his attention to the place where Handel had put the second violins above the firsts. This had obviously impressed him.

◖●◗

Back to work once more in York – and round the country. Soon I was playing the organ with whose sound I had become familiar through the weekly Wednesday broadcast recitals by GD Cunningham. I listened to them over a long period and became familiar with a good deal of the repertoire. He always included a transcription: one I remember was the finale of Beethoven's fifth symphony. This was, of course, Birmingham Town Hall. At the time of my recital there, George Thalben-Ball was city organist. My main work was Healey Willan's *Introduction, Passacaglia and Fugue*, which I had recently learned from the original

Schirmer edition of 1919, that Sir Edward had passed on to me one day with the injunction 'You'd better learn this'. It provided the mainstay of many a programme for some years. The press critic, however, failed to mention it in the Birmingham Post next day (6 October) but commented generously on my pedal technique and what he called the agreeably fresh ideas of my own; and ended his piece, 'This was one of the most pleasing performances heard at any guest recital since the series began': this despite what he referred to as the one or two 'unfortunately salient visitors' accidents' – I had not yet come across Cunningham's sagacious advice: 'Never leave a tuba lying about'. The Bach D major *Prelude and Fugue* at the end became, he said, a crazy steeplechase, which I am sure it was. The four Schumann sketches with their 'constant triple measure and other similarities do not make a really satisfying suite' but my 'extremely well-chosen colouring did much to define their separate characters, and (my) firm but lilting rhythmic impulse was wholly delightful'. The writer's initials were JFW and he earned my gratitude. 1949 came to an end with the usual Christmas doings and my third and last *Messiah* in Leeds Town Hall with the Philharmonic Society and Olive Groves, soprano, among the soloists.

It was not long before I came on to the council of the Royal College of Organists, my first appearance there causing me some trepidation – among such giants as Sir Stanley Marchant (late of Saint Paul's Cathedral and then Principal of The Royal Academy of Music) but knowing several already, chiefly John Dykes Bower.

◖●◗

For most of the time I was at the Minster I was kept rather busy with visits to places near and far, and was quite often away, which meant leaving the assistant in charge. I took it that all was well during my absences: no adverse comments from the Dean or others came to my notice. But it seemed that opinions from further afield began to appear which were unfavourable, and whisperings were to be heard relating to the Minster choir and its performance, allegedly because of my absences for organ recitals. The choir achieved somewhat of a bad name; there may have been some justification, for no choir can be on top form all the time. This troubled me of course.

Looking back, the post-war period saw a tremendous advance in the standard of cathedral music. Recordings of some top choirs were beginning to be produced, choirs in universities, whose duties were less onerous than the daily slog (sometimes twice daily) required in cathedrals. This allowed them time for rehearsal resulting in a high degree of perfection. When committed to disc and tape this soon became the norm, and anything not measuring up to that level was apt to receive criticism. With a full programme of music to produce on minimum rehearsal it was inevitable that some services went better than others, and even included a disaster of some proportion once in a very long while (which could also happen in the 'higher' echelons, let it be said). One does not disregard the positive advantage of a tight schedule of singing together, bringing in a close mutual understanding between the performers. It was a thoroughly enjoyable and fulfilling occupation, engendering a great deal of enthusiasm and dedication.

One wondered whether those who wished to be critical concluded that it was the obvious result of the choirmaster's absence that the choir's standards should fall. Any choir has its ups and downs but gradually at the Minster we reached a state of stability for many years with a succession of splendid head choristers and a dedicated body of songmen. Not that it was always easy to recruit the lower voices: at one period we were down to a single bass which, at a certain matins, necessitated my singing a lead from the console, yards away, up aloft, to the hilarity of all, as the off-stage voice did its best to head off an awkward situation. This was in the days when the full choir was still present for morning weekday services: the congregation probably numbered no more than four or five on those occasions. Leaving the assistant in charge was perfectly legitimate and the choir's training and their constant singing together enabled them to carry through on their own any situation they were faced with, regardless of who happened to be at the organ. And there were always assistants of the highest quality, Allan Wicks being the first I had.

CONDUCTING AND DIRECTING

Usually there was conducting to be done at the Minster services, of an intimate kind, unlike the orchestra and the Musical Society where broader gestures were needed. It was necessary to scale down one's physical activity so as not to constitute a distraction to the worshipper, and it was surprising how effective minimum movement could be. A cathedral choir is an intelligent body and can respond to the slightest directive or facial expression. What is done in rehearsal can, and should, have a strong influence on the performance. As mentioned above Dean Milner-White had a firm dislike of that word, maintaining that the choir's mission was for God's glory and not for their own puffing up. Moreover, when properly briefed they were capable of singing something perfectly on their own with all the necessary understanding. The conductor, when present, was perhaps only necessary to set them all off at the same time and to negotiate them through a tricky patch. After all, anything that was accompanied on the organ had to be managed without a conductor. The choir was used to this having, without being aware, formulated the way of doing it with complete success time after time. In my early years at the Minster it was customary for only one organist to be present at a service, either the Organist or the Assistant as the complete complement, and it worked very well. Only once did I forget to book Allan Wicks for evensong while I gallivanted off to Leeds for a reception to honour Vaughan Williams, but the choir carried on, on its own, saving my bacon.

A feature which today may seem remarkable – in the days when there is a marked tendency to have everything conducted, even to the smallest amen – is that only unaccompanied pieces were conducted. Those with organ were left to the choir on their own, unconducted, to look across to the singers on the opposite side and to use their own individual intelligence and expertise. The unanimity, and the spirit and know-how, are noteworthy as shown by the archive of tapes recorded over many years by John Rothera.

I do not dispute the fact that conditions may have altered quite radically in the intervening period, necessitating conducting most of the time, what with girls' choirs, fewer services, longer holidays and the constant search for complete accuracy. Our care and our great love was to deliver the music – the intangible – in the best way possible to meet the needs of the members of the congregation. Appropriate music had been chosen in advance. It was then up to us to put it across to them as eloquently as we could. This meant that we all had to understand what we were singing, and that very much included the conductor whose responsibility was to explain what was necessary and to make sure that his message had reached his singers. That is the first prerequisite. But certainly, listening to one's best efforts of so long ago, it is possible to take with a pinch of salt most of the criticisms that were aimed at our product, in the knowledge that we never did anything less than our best, and whatever was short of perfection was, after all, only human and was the lot of every choir under the sun. I hope that almost thirty-seven years of doing this has reached its target wherever and whoever it might be. Music that is unleashed with mere notes and ignorance of its full significance is better remaining silent – or in the wings.

Musical activity away from the Minster included the directing of the York Symphony Orchestra as well as the Leeds Philharmonic Society of which I became chorus master. All these were to be fitted in, each with its weekly rehearsal, to say nothing of meetings of various kinds, some of them municipal, which were not always to one's taste and were sometimes grudgingly attended. My connexion with the Leeds chorus brought the great opportunity of conducting *Messiah* in that imposing building of Leeds Town Hall. The orchestra in 1947 was the Northern Philharmonic and Allan Wicks was the society's chorus pianist.

I enjoyed this great treat three years running, having for soloists the first time Kathleen Ferrier and Peter Pears as well as Ada Alsop and Trevor Anthony. At the performance of 1948, joined by the Hallé orchestra, the *Yorkshire Post* critic Ernest Bradbury found that several instances recalled Sir Edward Bairstow's 'splendid interpretation'. The same critic commented that '... Mr Jackson knows how to get the best from his singers: and I think he must have succeeded last night beyond the expectation of anyone. The "Phil" have not sung like this for more than ten years ...' When Sir Malcolm Sargent was engaged as conductor I was informed that he wished to do *Messiah* as well: this was the cue for me to withdraw from the scene altogether.

||O||

In York since the year of the birth of Mozart there has existed a music club that had as one of its founders John Camidge (1735-1803), organist of the Minster from 1756 to 1799. It became known as York Musical Society and was always under the direction of the Minster organist as a matter of course. Under TT Noble it flourished producing the great choral works, numbering around two hundred singing members. Still in a healthy state under Bairstow its numbers decreased somewhat. After a rather lean period due to the Second World War and to a difference of opinion with Sir Edward, the conductor who had resigned, the position came to me for the next thirty-three years. The chorus of the Musical Society had constantly to be reminded to keep looking at the conductor and to enunciate the words clearly. At times it was very hard work, but this usually paid off in performances. Our greatest achievement I think, apart from the yearly Bach *Passions* and the Beethoven *Missa Solemnis* was the B minor *Mass*.

Sir Georg Solti so rightly said that a conductor should be the servant of the composer. Of course this applies anywhere in the field of interpretation, in which the interpreter must try to know and feel what the composer experienced at the moment of composition, and not be anxious to display his own ideas to the detriment of the music's life or the composer's instructions.

I had never had any instruction in conducting, so, in at the deep end once more, a way had to be found to do it when I also took up the direction of the York Symphony Orchestra (YSO) in 1947. This is exactly what happened at the start of Mr Noble's connexion with the YSO. Shortly before leaving to take up his post at Saint Thomas' Church, New York in 1913 he told the orchestra 'When I came to York I had scarcely had a stick in my hand, and you have taught me all I know about conducting ...' Here was I in the same position and wondering how to cope, but what experience I had had with small combinations and the dance band in the army were a start.

Orchestral and choral performance was very different from the music in Minster worship. A baton was used and I had to pick up what I could in the way of tips, one of which was to regard the baton as an extension of the hand, not a load for it to carry. Iris Lemare, an experienced conductor, was then living near York, putting on the occasional concert with her Lemare Orchestra. I was very grateful for the one piece of advice she gave me when asked; this was, simply, to give a good down beat. Which may seem too simple and not very helpful but was an excellent basis from which to start, the rest following in due course. Another hint on conducting was from Basil Cameron who, as president of the YSO, came up from London for a celebratory concert in 1967. He evidently saw that my beat lacked something (not surprisingly) and told me to use the same motion as when hammering a nail into a wall. That too was very welcome advice, and I dare say that there were many other points in addition that needed correcting.

It was of course possible to pick up tips by watching conductors such as Sir Adrian Boult with his economy or Sir John Barbirolli who, for several years, came with the Hallé giving concerts on three successive evenings in the spring of the year. I was allowed in for the rehearsals, which were of the greatest profit. He too was economical: at one of the concerts he appeared to be doing nothing at all in the pizzicato movement of Tchaikovsky's fourth symphony, standing stock-still as seen from the audience. Those concerts, such a welcome addition to the York music scene, were given in the Rialto cinema owned by Mr Jack Prendergast whose son (my pupil for a while) became well known as John Barry, writer of a great many film scores.

The YSO was a body whose palmy days were with Tertius Noble who had founded it on coming to York from Ely Cathedral in 1898. His popularity drew together the best local players into what was spoken of (by Samuel Coleridge-Taylor) as the best amateur orchestra in the country when he conducted it (as did Elgar, Edward German and others). Noble was greatly aided in the running and leading of the orchestra by Editha Knocker, who also taught some of the string players, being an authority on violin playing and author of books on the subject which she had studied as a pupil of Joachim. Basil Cameron learned from her and played in the orchestra under his surname Hindenburg, which he dropped when hostilities began in 1914, adopting his second Christian name for surname.

When Doctor Bairstow arrived at the Minster he was expected to follow on where Mr Noble had been active; but it seemed that his interests lay in the choral rather than the orchestral scene. Not that he was lacking in sympathy with or knowledge of the symphonic repertoire. The reason was most likely that, being an amateur body, however well-regarded, its standards could not be high enough for him. He chose to share the conducting with Miss Knocker.

For many years – nearly three decades – it kept going, though lacking somewhat its former distinction, until the war came and the orchestra ceased its operations. Then at the end of the 1939-45 war determined efforts were made to revive its fortunes. In 1947 I took over the baton despite my inexperience and, with the faithful few weekly attenders, struggled to produce some worthy results. It was not easy – the lack of a full complement of instruments at rehearsals was a continual frustration, such as when, without cellos or basses, I was reduced to playing their part on the piano with my right hand and conducting with the other, as was my habit, being a left-hander. It was a relief not to have to bother with diction: there were other problems. Those Monday evenings were inclined to be a drag, but we kept going.

Concerts had not been undertaken for many a year and whether to launch out in that direction was much debated and eventually approved, though in a modest way for a start. The hall of the Mount School was an early venue with Herbert Howells' *Puck's Minuet* among the items. At the Folk Hall in New Earswick (the model village built by Joseph Rowntree) a mile or so north of York, Schumann's piano concerto was performed with an incompetent pianist who had received some exaggerated encomiums from an unreliable source. In the same hall, and probably at the same concert, Beethoven's fourth symphony was lacking a second horn for some reason, perhaps because the inexperienced secretary had failed to book a comer-in. There is no doubt that the ultimate responsibility rested with the conductor who stepped into the breach at the last moment, unrehearsed, and *sang* the important two notes at the end of the *scherzo* in his best second horn tone quality.

Gradually things improved and it was thought that the orchestra should have a president. Sir Benjamin Dawson, who with his pianist wife was a pillar of York's music, agreed to fulfil the role and was a most faithful supporter. He attended all concerts, always expressed most encouraging comments, and presented percussion instruments that were helpfully selected by James Blades, the well-known percussionist. In 1966 Sir Benjamin was succeeded as president by the prestigious conductor Basil Cameron who retained happy memories of his violin-playing days under Tertius Noble's conductorship. We were greatly encouraged by his visit to the concert in 1967.

Amateurs that we were, we could eventually attempt pieces like the Sibelius Violin Concerto. With some ten rehearsals (not all fully attended) the players would begin to take in what the music was wanting to communicate. We all tried to service the music as well as we could.

Different halls were used. The Tempest Anderson Hall in the Yorkshire Museum saw several visits, one of which had not only Tchaikovsky's fourth symphony in its second half but, to follow, Walton's *Music for Children*, which, as it turned out, was superfluous. The Minster had Schubert's *Unfinished* which was more difficult than I had anticipated, partly perhaps because of its sharp key. Saint-Saëns' Third appeared with Frederic Waine (the orchestra's assistant conductor) playing the organ part. But perhaps the greatest triumph was the B flat piano concerto of Brahms for which the fee for the soloist Denis Matthews was paid by one of the viola players, Beatrice London. To aim so high had, up to then, been unthinkable and quite beyond the society's means. Miss London's welcome gesture proved a turning point in the orchestra's fortunes and its policies. Colin Horsley came to a Minster concert in March 1967 to play the fourth Beethoven piano concerto. *Harold in Italy* figured (in the hall of Saint Peter's School) with Cecil Aronowitz playing the solo viola part, and in the same place Jack Brymer joined us for Mozart's clarinet concerto. Another pleasant memory is of the Brahms double concerto with the Tunnel brothers, John and Charles. In the Minster we also did the Hindemith organ concerto with Martin Neary as soloist, which was creditably and stoically played by the orchestra as well as by Martin but not received with a great deal of appreciation.

Denis Matthews' visit was a great day in the life of the orchestra, an inspiration to the body of amateurs who accompanied him, giving him their finest playing, as Keith Pemberton said in his 1968 press report. Denis Matthews had been slightly exercised about the cello solo in the slow movement of the second Brahms piano concerto but as the principal cellist was Moray Welsh there was no need to fear; 'serene beauty' was the quality that came forth, in Keith Pemberton's press report.

Occasionally during my tenure as conductor of the YSO I had played the solo part in a piano concerto, such as Saint-Saëns' second, Franck's *Symphonic Variations*, Mozart's C minor, Beethoven's third (as arranged by Liszt, of which I had inherited a copy from my boyhood teacher Arthur Ayres at Malton, along with the rest of his music) and Ravel's *Concerto for the Left Hand*: the last two of these in a concert conducted by David Blake. I also had much fun with *Rhapsody in Blue* in the somewhat inappropriate setting of York's ancient Guildhall.

An event of considerable importance to me happened in 1979, when the orchestra very generously undertook to play the symphony I had submitted in 1957 for the Durham doctorate, causing the Yorkshire Post critic to question why it had taken me twenty-two years to put on a performance. Perhaps he did not realize that it is not all that easy to secure performances of one's products. The orchestra then was only just ready to tackle it and the players did a creditable job for which I am very much indebted to them: they worked hard, and the audience appeared to appreciate the result, in the Sir Jack Lyons concert hall of the university.

My spell as conductor of the YSO came to an end in 1980 when at last, being tired of perhaps ten or a dozen weekly rehearsals prior to a concert, with variously incomplete combinations of instruments aforementioned, I suggested that fewer rehearsals would be more enjoyable, yielding better results. Understandably such a scheme did not appeal to the players who welcomed the regular discipline so it was agreed that another conductor should be sought, ending my thirty-year stint. In taking this stance I had been influenced by the recently formed Guildhall Orchestra joined by the city's professional players who could manage with less rehearsal time. But there was room for both and the symphony orchestra continued as before, reaching commendable standards as time went on and probably comparing favourably with the Noble era.

MARRIAGE AND MONTFORT L'AMAURY

The year 1950 dawned, which turned out a significant one for me, and not only for the commemoration of Bach's death. Priscilla and I had first met in amateur theatricals at Malton in the mid-1930s, but it seemed that, if at that time we did have any feelings for each other, we were content to wait until the war was out of the way before proceeding with any commitment.

Priscilla's family had been Quakers from George Fox's time, and I had been vaguely interested in the movement having come to know her two aunts who lived in their family home at Huttons Ambo two miles from Malton, one of whom, Kathleen, a violinist, was devoted to chamber music. She had sought me out to join a trio in which the Vicar of Malton's daughter Helen Cardale played the cello. Kathleen's sister Janet was a fine artist, as were several members of her family including her father John William Procter, Priscilla's grandfather, who illustrated most beautifully with many delightful and sometimes amusing coloured drawings a journal written by his wife Elizabeth (née Dymond) recording their three-week 400-mile journey on holiday with pony and trap in 1878. Dod Procter RA was well known; Ernest Procter, her husband, was first cousin to Priscilla's father. They joined the Newlyn artist fraternity in the 1920s along with Laura Knight, Alfred Munnings and others. Ernest's portrait of Delius is in the National Portrait Gallery and Dod's famous *Morning* of 1926 has its place in the Tate. Priscilla's sister Elizabeth (Betty) took after her aunt and produced much work of a very high quality of technique and inspiration. Priscilla herself is talented in the same field but was unable to make use of it – or her musical abilities on the piano, to my regret – since the rearing of our family inevitably took precedence.

And on her mother's side the artistic talent was also to be found in her mother and other members of the Adams family, including her grandfather Samuel Henry Adams (1856-1951) who founded the York firm Adams Hydraulics. He was a civil engineer and in 1930 published an exhaustive treatise with the title *Modern Sewage Disposal and Hygienics*, an impressive work more than 450 pages long, lavishly illustrated and packed with diagrams and information of all kinds. It became a standard work on the subject. Unusually for a work of this kind it ranges widely among countless byways of history, art, architecture, fashion, taken from a myriad sources and providing compelling reading – aspects not expected in a book so named are met and dealt with. The author declares that 'Although essentially for men, it is for women too'.

I am not sure that Dean Milner-White would not have preferred me to remain single, but he accepted the situation readily and was ever kind and encouraging to us both, remarkably so since Priscilla's Quaker faith may not have been all that his high Anglican persuasions could permit. His letter from Kirkwall, Orkney, where he was on holiday or retreat when our engagement was announced, begins:

My dear Francis

Blow on blow!!! Nothing but percussion instruments boom in my ears! Even in this lonely solitude sound the drums of fate! Of happy fate, I hope. And nothing in your letter gives me greater pleasure than to hear you have known each other sixteen years.

It concludes, in retrospect quite prophetically:

God bless you both, and may He write a divine symphony out of your life together, one lasting many years and growing always lovelier in His work and His love.

Bach's anniversary was important to us organists, so Allan Wicks, Frederic Waine (director of music at Saint Peter's School) and I gave six recitals of his works during the summer, each containing one of the sonatas and also one item by another composer. It was the home team's affair and an expression of our devotion and gratitude to the incomparable master.

Allan played the *Scherzo* by Duruflé, the *Litanies* of Alain and Liszt's *BACH*. Freddie's choice was Jongen's *Menuet-Scherzo*, the Franck *Pastorale* and Stanford's *Prelude in the form of a Chaconne.* My contribution was the *Suite Modale* of Flor Peeters and the two Dupré *Sketches* which had so galvanised me when I heard them, up there with the composer at the Minster console, for his recital a month earlier. France's most famous organist Dupré was often in this country – and many others. His recital at Leeds Parish Church the previous November followed a fortnight after mine there, as announced by a poster containing our two names in large scarlet letters – at that stage something I never expected to see: just as some years later at San Francisco Cathedral I shared a poster with Duke Ellington.

One day at evensong not long after Christmas we sang *A Spotless Rose* by Howells. Unusually, at the end the Dean's Verger told me how moved he was by it, particularly the portrayal of 'on a cold, cold winter's night'. I wrote to Howells telling him of this, thanking him for his composition and receiving this characteristic reply:

3, Beverley Close, Barnes, SW 13. Prospect 5119

28 January 1950

My Dear Francis,

If a man loves a building as I do York Minster it's a comforting and encouraging thought that one's music has been heard from time to time within its walls.

If a fellow who has written a tune knows it has been sung and played and loved by friends of his in such a place he feels enormously encouraged: and is enormously grateful.

If the singers in the choir find his music acceptable (and even 'singable') then again he's more than glad of it.

If the Dean is so kind as to write to him, and the friendly verger is made to shiver at a cadence not to be found in a Harmony Primer or bought at Woolworth's, then his reward is complete.

So you see, my dear Francis, my pleasure in your letter is fourfold: and (most sincerely and seriously) I am most grateful to you and all concerned in the performances.

Yours ever, Herbert Howells:

PS I am marking the proofs of 'Te Deum' and 'Jubilate' of 'Collegium Regale', done for King's College, C[*ambridge*]. H[*erbert*].

Which puts me in mind of the choir practice when copies of the Howells' Gloucester evening service were being put out for the first time. We already had the evening *Collegium Regale* in our repertoire, and the copies of the new service looked exactly like it. This prompted one of the choristers to announce 'Oh, it's another Collium Rayjeel'.

The first day of February 1950 saw (and heard) the second (and last) performance of a piece called *Invocation* which I had written the previous year for the Peterborough Arts Festival at the behest of Douglas Hopkins the cathedral organist, and which Maurice Miles, conductor of the Yorkshire Symphony Orchestra, generously allowed into his programme in the Rialto Cinema in York. At this late stage I can recall little of the performance of the music, but the Yorkshire Post critic Ernest Bradbury was tolerant, claiming that 'the music follows a logical course. The short themes are well-knit, and a mild bitonality affords a certain freshness of harmony that stimulates the ear agreeably and makes for pleasant listening'. He also made the point that 'One suspected that the performance was by no means as good as it might have been' but as I say I cannot remember... What I do recall is, at a prior rehearsal somewhere in Leeds there was difficulty with a clarinet phrase which after a couple of further tries to sort it out (and wasting valuable rehearsal time) turned out to have been written a semitone higher or lower than it should have been. That was my doing, and not much of a boost to one's confidence. The thought of it, half a century and more later still causes minor twinges of embarrassment.

As to the Bach commemoration, the ultimate work to choose to do him honour must surely be the B minor *Mass* – referred to constantly by my faithful housekeeper Mabel Taylor as 'The Minor Mass'. (Perhaps that second letter of the alphabet held other connotations for her, though she was a calm and self-controlled lady.) The Leeds Philharmonic Society came to the Minster on 20 April to join the York Musical Society and the Northern Philharmonic Orchestra led by Douglas Hall. The soloists were Elsie Suddaby, Muriel Brunskill, Alfred Hepworth (in the Minster choir as a chorister, then a songman) and Henry Cummings (bass). The following day I was to be in London so we all travelled there together and enjoyed the journey in a somewhat lively mood.

Between April and November there were nineteen recitals, including that on the eve of my wedding, two in London – Saint Margaret the Queen, Streatham Hill and Saint Gabriel's, Cricklewood, where Lionel Dakers was organist. It was very interesting, also, to play at Saint Bees on the famous Willis lovingly watched over by Colonel George Dixon with William Coulthard as the organist of the church. At Lytham there was the dedication of the organ, and a meal in the vicarage that was partaken in the room where a genuine Van Dyck portrait hung along with others of similar value.

I gave a piano recital at Selby at the invitation of David Gedge during his time as organist of the abbey, including Chopin's third *Ballade* in the programme: also another for the Thirsk music club containing Bach's first *Partita*, Beethoven's opus 90 sonata, the Brahms *Variations on a theme of Handel* and Ravel *Valses Nobles et Sentimentales*. But it became clear that it was not the piano but the organ that people preferred to hear me playing.

On 9 August, upwards of seventy choristers arrived from the four corners of England to fill in during the Minster choir's holiday. It was a course organised by the Royal School of Church Music, lasted a fortnight, and was under the expert tuition of Edred Wright, assisted by Doctor EP Brice and Frederic Waine. The press account notes that, though they had never met before, there was a service to be sung the day after their arrival. It was an intensive but enjoyable and instructive exercise which culminated in a broadcast of evensong on 22 August (at 3pm in the Home Service) at which the *Magnificat* and *Nunc Dimittis* were Walmisley's in D minor. Great play was made of the possession by the Minster of the composer's manuscript and that it was to be used for the organ accompaniment for this occasion. Notice had been given in the Evening Press, our York newspaper, of the intention to use the manuscript; in fact Dean Milner-White joined in a photograph of the instructors 'examining' it. I was fully determined this should happen; indeed I think it was my idea in the first place, but when the time came I quite forgot and had to make do with the boring day-to-day organ copy as the realisation came when the service had begun and was well under way. However, the truth was never revealed. There was a singular lack of interest, and no comment whatever.

The very next day at evensong the Minster choirboys were singing *Let the bright seraphim* for the delegates assembled at Leeds for the congress of the Incorporated Association of Organists who had travelled over to York for the afternoon. It was a 'Boys Only' service and was followed by a short recital in which I included the Dupré *Sketches* yet again. Such gatherings require a certain stoicism in view of the welter and close proximity of organ recitals. The fraternity, eager however for the next onslaught, moved smartly on to Selby Abbey for an early evening recital by John Dykes Bower (as yet unknighted), of which part was broadcast and attended by the Princess Royal, Princess Mary. The programme included Stanford's *Sonata Britannica*, beginning with the Bach B minor (a work he played constantly in his recitals) and ending with Alcock's *Introduction and Passacaglia*. There was more on the following evening, at Leeds Parish Church, in which Melville Cook played Jongen's *Sonata Eroica*, a favourite work of his.

September saw my third participation in the annual series of monthly Saturday concerts in Huddersfield town hall that continued regularly for many years. These featured, in addition to an organist, a solo singer and a choir, one of the many that flourished in that very musical locality. At that time admission to the gallery could be had for one penny – an old one at that. They were given their share of the Willan *Passacaglia*.

Late in October there was a 'JS Bach Bi-Centenary Festival' in Leicester Cathedral in which I gave a recital of his works. One critic commented that 'the programme was particularly well balanced', beginning modestly with the *Prelude and Fugue* in A major and ending with the 'massive' *Toccata* in F that 'eclipsed all else in sound and size'. Included along the way were the third *Sonata (Trio)*, the *Saint Anne*, three chorale preludes and the *Fugue Alla Gigue*. The cathedral organist since 1930 was George Gray, who after the 1914–18 war had been a pupil of Bairstow at York. He contributed a similar programme in the Bach series, along with those of Doctor Willis Grant of Birmingham Cathedral and Harold Dexter who later became organist of Southwark Cathedral. Kind comments on my efforts about brilliance, clarity, spaciousness and brilliant registration were duly noted, gratefully, if somewhat surprisingly in those early prentice days.

A day or two before our wedding, a welcome letter came from Doctor Noble, then aged eighty-three, who had kept in touch with Mr Scaife for nearly forty years after he left York. His sight had become worse but he had bravely done the writing with his own hand, producing an uncertain result that was only just readable. It is another letter I am proud to possess:

Oct 26. Rockport Mass USA

My dear Jackson

We are delighted to hear of your engagement, and of your wedding day next Wednesday. We send you our heartiest good wishes for a long life of great happiness. We will think of you next Wed-day. Do you know that newspapers take seven weeks to get to my front door?! Letters come as usual most regularly, and air mail is very fast, often only two days.

You are certainly going to have a glorious time in old York next June.* Are you doing Gerontius. You will enjoy the Barbirollis, they are lovely people and John is a wonderful conductor.

I hear from Scaife pretty regularly, so get news of the Minster and the work of the choir, how I would love to hear some of your services.

I trust you can read this.

Our best to you ever sincerely

T Tertius Noble

*The first of the triennial York Festivals.

The most notable recital was on the last day of October, the day before I was to be married. It had been fixed first, was unchangeable, and I could not be released from the contract. (I had taken the opportunity to include a Guilmant wedding march in the programme as a sop and a nod in the direction of my imminent change of status.) Thus there was no stag night but, to ease my load in view of the next day's doings, so that I should be in good form to stand its rigours, a car with driver was hired for the forty-mile drive to Denby Dale which was splendid – until during the recital there came down one of those thick freezing fogs we used regularly to have. We could have managed very well without it, and the only course was for me in the passenger's seat with the window open to keep the driver informed how near he was to the verge: white lines were not so plentiful then. Progress was lamentably slow – and extremely cold – but home was achieved without incident.

Not surprisingly I awoke next morning with a really bad headache – which again I could have managed without; not a good beginning to the happiest day of one's life... Steps were taken to alleviate my condition and all was well by two o'clock on the feast of All Saints, largely due to the ministrations of the best man, David Swale. The full choir was in excellent form: they sang *Audi Filia* for the first time in its four-part version and Melville Cook played us out with the *Toccata* in F (by Bach – not Widor). Dean Milner-White tied the knot and the Canon Chancellor, known to us all as Freddie Harrison, gave the address. He and the bride were well acquainted, she having acted as his secretary for a time.

Our honeymoon began at Lastingham, but after three days a move had to be made for the next recital. This was at Sunderland, in Saint Gabriel's church. Fireworks were let off that Saturday night, a day early because November fifth was a Sunday. We thought it was quite a nice celebratory occurrence. We then moved on to the Lake District where the honeymoon began in earnest, in a lovely house at the southern end of Crummock Water where we thoroughly enjoyed the peace, the autumn colouring, and the chance to recover from the welter of preparation which is the unavoidable result of these activities.

We came back to York and settled in to the splendid Minster Court house that would now be run properly for thirty-two years. It must have been a daunting situation that faced Priscilla in the wonderful, handsome organist's house, with the minimum of help: no cook, no housemaids as in previous regimes, and hospitality needing to be administered frequently and often unexpectedly. She also took on the organising of the Minster flowers, deploying another of her decided gifts of flower arranging, on a tight budget for almost a third of a century. My own great good fortune was to have a most competent secretary, experienced formerly in the service of Canon Harrison and Lord Halifax, and always available! Even after the family – Alice, William and Edward – arrived in the 1950s this secretarial help continued, hugely reducing my office work and earning my continual gratitude.

Recitals at Leeds and Huddersfield soon followed, and on 9 December the re-dedication of the famous Five Sisters window took place. The glass had been removed for safety during the war and was now back in place. The Dean imaginatively had seen that the feminine nature of the project should be carried through and arranged for the singing to be done by members of Women's Institutes from all over Yorkshire. This entailed holding rehearsals in outlying places as well as making a female voice version of *Audi Filia*, transposing it down a semitone to C major. It seemed to work well.

It is, or should be, a cathedral organist's job to produce compositions that are needed for special occasions. Dean Milner-White had introduced the nine-fold kyrie at the Eucharist and it was apparently a scarce choral commodity. Bairstow obliged with two that were never published. It then occurred to us that adaptations could be made using music from other movements or unused scraps that sometimes are present. It was decided to approach Henry Ley to do this and he quickly produced several *Kyries* that served us well for a time and were published by Novello.

As this kind of situation was apt to occur now and again, the fact that one might be able to meet it oneself began to dawn and, with the Dean's encouragement as related elsewhere, home products began to appear. Two early attempts, *How bright these glorious spirits shine* and *Ave Maria, blessed maid*, were accepted by Year Book Press (later Banks) and Faith Press respectively, the latter being an anthemized version of the hymn in the *English Hymnal.* The former was kindly put on at Salisbury Cathedral soon after its publication during one of several visits when I stayed with David and Rachel Willcocks.

My attempt at a kyrie led on to a setting of a complete communion service that was taken on by Oxford University Press to my great delight. At least, it was at first; then second thoughts came along with the disappointing news that the creed would have to be omitted. The Dean, however, graciously undertook to subvent its publication, separately, to my grateful relief. This was the first sign of the trend which eventually brought about the demise of the composed setting of the creed, resulting in the loss of one of the significant features of the service, and causing recourse either to an uninspiring muttering or something sung in unison that hardly lifts the spirit as a good choral setting would. It is hard to see the logic of this since there seems very little difference between the creed and the other choral portions in terms of their expressing the sentiments of the silent worshipper.

Next came a *Benedicite* (in March 1950); an evening service, followed a few years later by a *Te Deum and Jubilate*, all published by Oxford University Press, all in the same key and known domestically as 'Me in G'. This is a key to which I have often been drawn when starting a piece, causing me to find another one; for example *Division on Nun danket* for organ (Novello) started life in G and then rose to A, no doubt to its advantage. Looking back to the time when working on the evening service, I am fairly certain that, at the back of my mind, I was presumptuous enough to imagine that it could be another 'Coll. Reg.' in the Wood-Howells line. I don't think I got as far as proposing its dedication to King's, but I did play it to Boris Ord on one of his York visits and well remember his noticeable wince at the final cadence of the *Gloria* with its jazz-influenced chromatics, and his stern injunction that there should be no such thing. He was of course perfectly right, and it is fortunate he caused me to have second thoughts because it was lifted straight out of the Dance Band store of ending clichés. I was grateful for this advice for I wonder if that would have caused it to be turned down by publishers. Perhaps my trying it on was an earnest of things to come, when so-called jazz invaded the sacred precincts. Way on into the next century, or even earlier, it would have been distasteful to behold the *avant-garde* of yesteryear appearing as outworn and only fit for discarding. Jazzy music belongs to the music hall, and there is plenty of life left in the traditional, true style of church music.

However, some fourteen years later Boris' successor, David Willcocks, dropped me a line with the happy information that 'Francis Jackson in G' was the setting of the canticles to be sung in the broadcast of evensong from King's College, Cambridge, on 20 February 1963, which was probably the first of its several appearances on that programme. Even in the final throes of preparing this memoir a broadcast of 'Me in G' was chosen for the Wednesday broadcast of choral evensong from Winchester College under Malcolm Archer's direction on the day after my ninety-fifth birthday. Other pieces appeared over the years, a list of which is at the end of this book for your delectation.

Recitals for 1951 numbered twenty-six, one per fortnight on average, which left my assistant Allan Wicks plenty to do to keep the flag flying successfully, and causing no complaints. Looking back, it is surprising that the Dean was tolerant of my absences. Only once was I taken to task, and that was for being away on a Sunday in Manchester recording Liszt with Gordon Thorne in the town hall, for which, if I remember correctly, I received no recompense. But as a general rule it must have been accepted that it was necessary for outside activities to be undertaken, both for refreshment and for the missionary element. (The cathedral's organist inevitably had some value as a travelling salesman.) But there was also the pressing need to augment the salary paid by the Minster, which at that time could hardly be described as princely.

There were two or three broadcasts and recordings from the Minster including a ten-minute spot at 9.20am on each of the May Sundays, all recorded in one session, with short pieces by Bach, Vierne, Whitlock, Bossi, Boyce and Schumann. The broadcast of choral evensong for the eve of Saint James had Elvey in A for the canticles and Ouseley's anthem *I saw the souls of them that were beheaded.* Among the recital venues were King's College, Cambridge, and Peterborough Cathedral with the co-operation of Bram Gay who I accompanied in the Purcell *Trumpet Sonata* – discovered a few years earlier in the Minster library at York – and the Haydn concerto. The cathedral choristers sang *Let the bright seraphim* and I, as often about that period, let off the Healey Willan *Passacaglia.* This took place in an Arts Week supported by the Arts Council of Great Britain. The Willan came up again in May at one

of the six recitals in Saint Paul's during the Festival of Britain. I chose
also the first chorale of César Franck as being the kind of music suitable
to that acoustic. Douglas Hopkins had once told me that his experience
there as assistant organist had taught him that slow music was the
most effective with so much resonance to contend with. Nevertheless I
also played the Bossi *Scherzo* and had no adverse comments.

I cannot forbear to quote from a letter sent me by Cecil Clutton,
if only to show how enthusiastic he could be. Sam, as he was known
universally, became a firm friend in the ensuing years. He was a
tremendous power in the organ world, a prolific writer and adviser,
possessing a profound knowledge of the whole field. He was also an
authority on clocks and their history, as well as being a racing motorist.
His appreciation of the many things in which he was interested used
very often to cause him to declare, as here below, that they were the
best he had ever come across:

> I feel I must just write and thank you for your recital at Saint
> Paul's. I thought it one of the most supreme performances on
> any organ I ever heard. It was certainly the only recital at Saint
> Paul's I ever enjoyed, and even found intelligible. Your taming
> of the acoustics was completely masterly. In fact the whole thing
> left me quite lost in admiration.

Experience of the Minster's acoustics had evidently come in useful.
The Willan appeared again, as the final item; and two more of the
six recitals (half of them) each ended with another *Introduction and
Passacaglia*, those by Alcock and Reger.

There is a point probably worth making: it seems that the frequent
mention of Healey Willan could indicate a closer association than in
fact existed. Certainly from 1952 I was in touch with him from time
to time by letter; meeting him on recital tours that usually took me
to Toronto, and my admiration of his *Passacaglia* was a factor in our
friendship, which I valued highly. That splendid work proved a valuable
recital piece, which I often used and was immensely privileged to play
in his presence more than once (eliciting no grievances – even though
I am not certain that my tempi were always what was indicated in the
copy). So far as any of my compositions are concerned I cannot claim
any of his influence, as has been suggested. What is likely is that he and

I each took our influences, such as they are, from some common source, though I suspect that mine came from France to perhaps a greater extent. But I am not sure that a composer can judge correctly on his own products; I find it difficult.

The two-week-long York Festival began with a recital in which I did not include the Willan. Two days later the choir of Leeds Parish Church joined with the Minster choir in a concert of English church music with Max Rostal playing Bach's unaccompanied *Partita* in D minor at the half-way point. For the York Musical Society's concert Maurice Miles brought the Yorkshire Symphony Orchestra to play the *Fourth Symphony* of Edmund Rubbra and to accompany the Fauré *Requiem* with Elsie Suddaby and William Parsons as soloists. This latter work was in the early stages of becoming known and popular, and was not difficult to put on. It all went smoothly at the previous night's rehearsal; so much so that I brought it to an end quite a while before the scheduled time for finishing, to the immense pleasure of the players. I then was informed that such a thing was not done – the union hours must be adhered to, but I had not seen the necessity of doing again what had been perfectly well performed, and did not want to tire and bore everyone when all was satisfactory. No doubt I could have made out that one passage or another could be improved and had it played over again, but sometimes it is wiser to under-do the rehearsing. And the performance was all it needed to be: Ernest Bradbury in the Yorkshire Post noted that 'the singers and players responded with that necessary degree of warmth – intense yet detached – that lends such an aura of holiness to the *Sanctus*, such an ethereal quality to the last movement *In Paradisum*'.

For these concerts – and others – Dean Milner-White had conceived the idea of substituting at the start a spoken prayer with a sung one. On this occasion the Minster Choir sang William Byrd's *Christe qui lux es et dies*. Mr Bradbury's reaction was that 'It is not possible to imagine a more beautiful beginning to an evening of music-making'.

The music for the Minster services during that fortnight was the best of our repertoire, chosen with great care and printed in a special pamphlet. There was no plain day; evensong was sung every day in addition to the Sunday Matins and Eucharist. Thereafter followed the summer series of recitals in the Minster, given by Kurt Wolfgang Senn of Berne, Harold Darke, Melville Cook, Allan Wicks, Harry Gabb and me.

▐O▌

Then in less than a week Priscilla and I were off on our summer holiday – four whole weeks of it, which was what the Bairstows had usually taken, regardless of the fact that the choir had only the inside of three weeks, from Monday until Saturday, including their two free Sundays of the year. Thus our first summer holiday together was planned as an adventurous and eventful one, naturally more so than those usually taken within this island at the time and reflecting the post-war freedom to travel. Previous extended holidays had included the round of cathedrals undertaken in 1933 with Dennis Laughton (comfortably in his car) where I was graciously allowed to 'try' the organs; and the post-war tandem tour of 1949.

This year, 1951, in Priscilla's mother's Morris Minor we set off at 3.15pm (later known as 15.15) reaching Huntingdon for the night, thence next day to Canterbury and Dover, crossing to Boulogne on the *SS Dinard* ferry. The next night we spent in Poix at the Hotel Cardinal, reaching Paris by way of Beauvais with the cathedral's astronomical clock and immensely high vaulting, at 155 feet said to be the highest in gothic architecture. It was in the early stages of driving on the unaccustomed side of the road, and taking the greatest care to keep doing that, fixing one's attention firmly on it, that, approaching a roundabout I kept resolutely to the right while turning left and going round clockwise. This resulted in a near head-on collision with a very surprised driver coming from the opposite direction who confronted us with an inexhaustible supply of 'Alors!' as he emerged from a very narrow concealed entry between blocks of houses close to each side of the road.

We did a good deal of walking about Paris, the city being new to me. Priscilla had been there in her teens and remembered the Galéries Lafayette, which we visited, and were duly amazed.

To the Louvre and to a flat not far from the Arc de Triomphe in order to return the cuff-links (rather valuable) left behind in York by Pierre Fournier, the famous cellist, during the York Festival. There was no-one in his flat, and an American-sounding gent in an upper or lower one who was unaware of his fame, and appeared not to be acquainted with him either, agreed to pass the links on to him. Having heard no more afterwards we had to assume that he was as good as his word. To Montmartre next to see the splendid view of Paris from the Sacré Coeur.

While in Paris we managed to hear two organs, perhaps the best known: Saint Sulpice and Notre Dame. This was on our first Sunday in France, 19 August, when after an early start we found our way to the former by 10am, via the Métro. There was to be a service at 10.15am, but no indication as to whether or not the organ would sound. We sat at the back and tried to follow the service that was said by two priests: one celebrating and another on the Gospel side with a microphone. Not being conversant enough with the French tongue, and certainly not up in the Roman Catholic service, we had almost given it up till the time came for administering the communion, when the organ started up with an offertoire. At any rate we had heard the organ. But the priest had hardly finished the service when the organ began again in the flashy French style so I made my way up the side aisle to hear it better from a distance, but it came to an end too soon. So we looked about the church and found a remarkable reredos at the east end, consisting of a window as the frame, and behind it pictured rocks and clouds with the Blessed Virgin Mary all lit from a skylight at the top. Then the organ began again, I suppose to start the 11.15am mass; Bach in G minor, not the big one.

Then to Notre Dame. Inside it is not very impressive, at any rate at first rather dark. The *Grand Orgue* is high up in the west gallery but it had done its bit for that morning, so we went off to have lunch hoping to hear it later, at 2.30pm

Returning to Notre Dame we found their *Vêpres, Nones* and others, about five services altogether, had begun. Plainsong was being growled at an inordinate speed to the accompaniment of the chancel organ by a few priests in vestments and a (probable) choir in mufti. There were various obvious differences of opinion amongst the singers as to how the words fitted the chant, and then there was a hiatus. Everything came to a standstill, a priest came in late, everyone stood up, and what looked like the choir-master went to a telephone (we heard the bell ring) and had a protracted conversation leaning over a desk. At first I thought

My mother Eveline May née Suddaby (1889-1974) with her spectacular head of hair, described as being the colour of a field of ripe corn.

My father William Altham Jackson (1888-1944) in his twenties.

My brother Paul stands by me, early in 1918, while the Great War plies its relentless way and our father is out there doing his share.

Jacksons all: Aunt Sybil holds the horseshoe for good luck at her Ayton cottage with her brother's family and its latest and last occupant Angela Bliss. On the left, elder brother (William) Paul.

*The recent York chorister,
Eton-suited, 1929.*

*The same, cassocked
and surpliced, in August
of the same year*

Edward Cuthbert Bairstow, my example and inspiration.

Again the family, at East Mount, Malton, some dozen years after the Ayton group.

The May 1936 production of Tilly of Bloomsbury at Malton with (extreme left) Priscilla; next but one back row Helen Cardale; me (centre) as the Reverend Adrian Rylands; last but one, Priscilla's brother John Procter who later married Helen. I then became his brother-in-law some 14½ years after.

Mus.Bac. 1937 Durham, photographed by the Precentor, the Reverend HY Ganderton, who was also Head Master of the Chorister School.

A slightly unfocussed picture by Mrs Macdonald of the EMG gramophone with its 'Oversize Horn' and its clockwork wind-up motor, where the pre-war record sessions took place at Coll Earn. (Page 42)

The first organ opening, at Crossford, Lanarkshire (June 1938), at which the donor Sir John Colville (Secretary of State for Scotland, later Lord Clydesmuir) took off his shoes to accompany one of the hymns.

The winner of 'The Stick' at Tidworth Pennings Camp 1941, excused guard duties for being allegedly the best turned out.

Somewhere in the western desert, North Africa, September 1942 (Page 73)

Italy, December 1944

Day Two of my 37-year (less a week) sojourn as Master of the Music, 'hereinafter called the organist', of the cathedral and metropolitical church of Saint Peter of York, 9 October 1946.

158

With the Minster choristers, on becoming their guide and mentor in October 1946.

In the Practice Room when it was in the Choir School.

The dean who appointed me, Eric Milner-White.

Fernando Germani who came to play a recital in 1947.
Photograph © The Northern Echo

*All Saints' Day 1950 at Priscilla's mother's house, Clifton, York: best man
David Swale (behind Julia Wilkinson), and matron of honour Betty, Priscilla's
sister. Our nieces Bridget Procter, Mary Griffiths and
Judith Procter complete the group. Aunt Sybil had made a quick exit from the
quire to the south quire aisle in order to be the first to congratulate me on my
improved status.*

*On our first summer holiday together
in 1951: Priscilla and Madame
Reveleau, his housekeeper, in Ravel's
garden at Montfort L'Amaury.
(Pages 168-9)*

With Healey Willan at Trinity College School, Port Hope, Ontario, during the 1954 summer choir school.

The kind of thing up to which we got in our early Acklam days, photographed by Enid Dunkerley.

The three children wearing the hats I brought them from my 1961 American tour.

Two sketches I made in France on our way to Switzerland in 1951: Saulçet near S. Pourçin, and our camp near La Roche, August 23-27.

*A Canadian photograph dated 18 May 1961 showing (second from left) Leo
Sowerby, next George Maybee and his mother,
David and Rachel Willcocks, FJ, Peter Partridge.*

*Sam Clutton took this with my
camera: Marcel Dupré on his organ
bench at Meudon on the evening of
Whit Monday,
19 April 1971.*

Fred Pratt Green, author of the harvest hymn 'For the fruits of his creation'
which became widely used at that season.

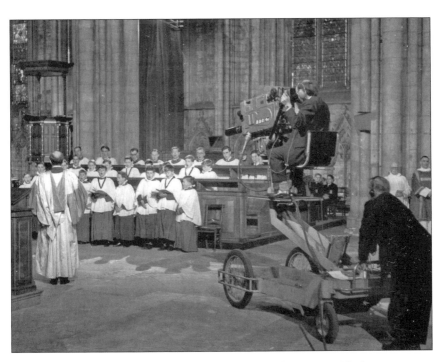

Camera and action: the BBC televises the Minster Choir.

Writing our Bach tributes outside the Tomaskirche in Leipzig, 20 July 1985:
Philip Sawyer, Iain Galbraith, John Kitchen, FJ.
Photograph taken by Winnie Hamilton

F · A · J
2 · X · 97

Fanfares enough   will sound – forgive this duf**F**
Laudation where   true poets might despai**R**
Of words to be fit instruments.   Our ple **A**:
Return again, glad day!   More years attai**N** –
Eighty for Jack son   is   no cul - de - sa**C**.
Advance! we cry...   A century! say **I**,
Tuning weak strings to wish you all good thing**S**.

M · H ·

The 80ᵗʰ birthday acrostic, illustrating Mary Holtby's amazing facility with
words.

it was the tardy priest who was responsible but I think that that was probably the end of one of the services and the Grand Orgue should have come in with an extemporisation to tide them over to the next one. Anyway it didn't, so they gathered themselves together and began afresh on the growling. After a while the chancel organist pressed the bell and in came the *Grand Orgue* for the first time with fine crashing noises in the modern style. The organist's other interludes were of contrasting natures, one of which used a remarkably fine clarinet or cremona of enormous power that filled the building. This process took us till after 4pm, and after we had seen them all leave their places and come and pay homage to a statue of the Virgin, incense and all, we had a short play-out and that was that. I must not forget the amateurish performance of Arcadelt's tune and another by a few selected voices (male, be it said) during the collection. It was like a village concert both to hear and to see. The whole behaviour of the choir was like a rehearsal, or like a studio performance at a broadcast. I suppose vestments are reserved for the priests: at any rate we had witnessed a similar practice at Saint Sulpice, this time a server at mass in sports shirt and – shorts. Which brings to mind the notice on the door of Chartres Cathedral reminding us that it was God's house, a cathedral and not a museum, and that *shorts*, amongst other things I have forgotten, were '*un incorrection grave*'. There and at other cathedrals we were prayed not to 'circulate' during the offices. (Another notice in Paris begged us not to lean – *appuyer* – our bicycles *and* cars against the building – an office of some sort.)

We left Paris next morning bound for Versailles, but met with a diversion of the most unexpected kind, and memorable indeed. Driving along we suddenly saw a sign to Montfort l'Amaury, a name of immense significance, the place where Ravel lived. Here was a chance we could not possibly miss to see what there was to see. According to the guidebook it was a pretty place, with a view and woods (the forest of Yveline it turned out to be), but the rather flat and uninteresting road did not promise well. It was really quite a thrill to turn into the road leading to Ravel's own village.

So we arrived. It seemed an old town, with narrow streets and hardly room to move. An enquiry immediately gave us the location of the sacred spot (and a guide pamphlet too, stating that said house was *'prochainement musée'*) up to the *Place de l'Eglise*, to the left and the first house after the hospital. And, there it was; no mistaking it; with a plaque saying Maurice Ravel had lived there from 1921 to 1937. But it was all shuttered – we didn't know then, after a mere five days in France and half a day in the country, that that is the habit – it looked as if it might be a museum already. So we spied through the wrought-iron gateway into the garden and saw geraniums in pots. We rang the bell, watched by an old *dame* from a safe distance. This produced nothing so I ran after the old *dame* and asked her. 'Oh, it is inhabited by a very old woman, over eighty, and is to be a museum when she dies.' 'But cannot one enter now?' said I. 'She is too old, one must not disturb her.' Further probing of a younger *dame* brought no more encouragement, so we would walk down the narrow lane to see if we could see the garden-front of the house. But there was little chance of seeing anything. The lane dropped steeply from the road, with a high stone wall on either side and a hedge on top of the garden wall. It then returned, steeply, up to the road, arriving at the other end of the house and leaving the garden in the shape of a triangle. However, one had seen perhaps a square two yards of the front of Ravel's house above the hedge, so one was lucky with that. We would take a photograph, then, of the house from the road, and go and find an hotel.

But as we climbed the lane, what should we notice but that one of the windows was now open. At least our eighty-three-year-old was active enough to open a window. Hope began to spring again; and there, as we gained the road, was a sweet grey-haired old lady with a shawl over her head, leaning out of the window talking to someone on the road, and talking in firm quick tones too. Without further ado I approached her and asked if one could see the house. The reply I cannot remember accurately, but did not sound encouraging. She then peppered her friend, now retreating down the road, with one or two remarks, maybe about us, I don't know. We then began our conversation anew. *'Vous avez un appareil photographique, n'est-ce pas? Attendez.'* She would open the gate and allow us to take a photograph of the front of the house, which she did, and did not take long about it. She was remarkably active for eighty-three and seemed to miss nothing. It was about 6pm by this time and the sun was behind the house, so whatever photographs one tried would have to be manually timed exposures. Priscilla took the old lady on to the terrace whilst I photographed them both from the ground level below with the house in the background.

She must have liked our faces, or was perhaps impressed by our interest, because she said she would just be able to show us his bedroom, which opened on to the garden. So in we went. 'Sa chambre', said she after rapidly throwing the shutters open – 'just as he left it'. The bed lay alongside the inner wall and had a gold-coloured counterpane and a canopy over it with silky balls along the edge. His bathroom adjoined, also overlooking the garden, with a geyser to the bath and such as his nail scissors all neatly arranged on the dressing table, and his brush and comb on another near the window. This was almost too good to be true. But more was to follow. We were directed to see the kitchen that was up a narrow, winding deal staircase up to street level, or a little above perhaps. This was the window we had seen open, and it gave a magnificent view of the church. A photograph was duly taken 'from Ravel's kitchen', and I hoped it was not on the same exposure as the previous photograph (camera film had to be wound manually then).

I had asked, out in the garden, if he used to work on the little balcony. 'Non', was the reply, 'dans son bureau avec son piano'. 'Oh yes,' I observed, 'he used to work at the piano, of course.' And it now seemed we were to be shown his bureau, eventually. I very much wanted to see it and his piano. The next one to be unshuttered for us was a tiny room containing the balcony (which as I remember was covered in wisteria). It was only big enough for two, tête-à-tête-wise, and had a miniature sofa upholstered in a similar gold plush, with a well-worn spot for sitting. I sat in it.

Next were two sitting rooms and the dining-room – all strung out in a line with windows to the garden and a passage at the back on the road side of the house which went on going up and down in short staircases, and turning tiny corners though continuing in the same general direction. One sitting room had a low table set out with coffee cups and there was a black and white carpet in squares set diagonally. The decorations were dark as a rule – one had not much time to take them all in – and the rooms had an oriental touch about them, mainly because of the darkness, and also due to the antique furniture and ornaments. One of these rooms had a cupboard let into the wall, with glass doors and china and metal, maybe pewter, teapots and the like, all lit up by strip-lights. The dining room was bigger than most of the other rooms – about the same size as the two sitting-rooms perhaps – and had a small, low, round table in the centre and a semi-circular one, more one's idea of a dining-table when opened out, against a wall.

Next was a little book room about six by nine feet mainly lit, I think, by electric light. Shelves were from head-height upwards, the books covered in old leather binding. The only author's name I remember or even saw was Voltaire. At the far end in the middle was Ravel's gramophone, a cabinet standing on the floor, the front of which I opened and longed to look in the top and to find his records, if any. On top of the gramophone was a yellow vase containing Trembling Jockeys long since turned brown and which, if one could have understood Madame's explanation, had something of a history. The word *Angleterre* entered into it and one wonders if someone had brought them to him from England.

But next came the great thing. The corridor dropped two or three steps and we came into a small room with black wallpaper, a grand piano with an oil-lamp on the player's right hand side, oil portraits, and a little mahogany set of shelves fixed to the wall on which were set out some tiny china ornaments and other *bibelots* for which one knew of his fondness – one was a white and gold upright piano. This was it. '*Son bureau*'. His office? Study? Music-room? Anyway, since he did not work on the balcony, this must be the room where *L'Enfant et les Sortilèges*, the *Violin Sonata*, the two concertos, *Boléro* and the *Duo* were written – the last first, unless he had finished it before going to Montfort. I found out later that *Boléro* began life in Saint Jean de Luz.

The piano and the lamp were the ones in the photographs we have seen of him. I sat on the stool he sat on, and played a morsel of the *Minuet* from *Le Tombeau de Couperin* which was there on the desk. The piano was out of tune and sticking badly, so was somewhat hampering. On my left was a rack containing a little music – some Mendelssohn, Liszt's *Transcendental Studies*, some orchestra scoring paper, and his piano works from *Menuet Antique* to *Valses Nobles* bound up with a hand-made paper covering. *Le Tombeau*, the only subsequent piano work was loose on the music desk. Also, of his music, was the complete ballet *Ma Mère L'Oye* done out for piano (by him?) and bound in the same paper. I had no idea this was published.

It was while I was rummaging amongst the music that Madame Reveleau (for that was her name) seized hold of Priscilla's hand, covering her with confusion, and remarking most definitely and loudly that it was *'une belle main'* and would brook no denial. (Priscilla says all that performance was so she could have a good look at her ring.) And this was the lady who had kept house for Ravel and attended to his daily wants while he was writing his music there. It was a remarkable thing to meet her, who had been in such close touch with him – as remarkable as seeing the things he had had around him, exactly as he had left them. Sentimental? Well perhaps. Or just French maybe. But anyway it was of absorbing interest to us both, and a more intimate connexion than any museum could be, even places like Elgar's birthplace, full of his Order of Merit, paper-cuttings and such, all set out under glass cases. And here there was no speck of dust anywhere.

The next thing to do after bidding Madame Reveleau *'au revoir'* and promising to send her something from England, was to find a bed. We tried the Duchesse Anne, not mentioned in Michelin, and were unimpressed, so drove on a little further towards the station, coming upon the Hôtel de l'Arrivé that seemed to be on both sides of the road at a fork. This, though plain, seemed attractive and at any rate French, with its plane trees and chestnuts, cut back, in the yard, and French people sitting under them chattering. A staircase opening directly off the yard brought us to a corridor and our bedroom at the end of it. It was being modernised, though the sanitary fittings would have caused Adamsez, the firm founded by Priscilla's grandfather Samuel Henry Adams, no little amusement. The window opened wide, as they all do, leaving a square hole with no casing, and had a bar across to lean on when opening or closing the shutters, or merely for gossiping purposes, with some nice wrought iron work underneath it. By this time we were jolly hungry, having missed a proper lunch or even a picnic at Versailles, and having been diverted from tea by Ravel and Madame Reveleau. So, having seen a notice advertising the evening *repas* as being at 7pm, down we went at 7pm to the spacious if rather bare *salle à manger*. After some time rolls were brought and we hoped for more. But no, being French they would take their time over the sacred business of eating, and when, my headache having reached its zenith, the soup arrived in its tureen and was deposited on our table (after everyone else had been served) we fell to with more than French gusto.

After a comfortable night, disturbed a little by hooting motorists and a cock crowing just outside, we dealt with our *petit déjeuner*, packed (as we thought) all our belongings and departed to see the church and to take one further photograph of the Ravel *maison* in case it had been too dark the night before. Madame Reveleau saw us from the kitchen and, I thought, dodged smartly out of the way in case the *Anglais* were going to be further nuisance. The church we found very pleasing. It was the usual French shape, classical, apsidal, and with a wonderfully light feeling (the sun was bright and coming in through the old windows) and seemed to have a feeling of height – that the whole church was high up – which may merely have been because it *is* high up. The twenty-seven or so sixteenth century windows we inspected in some detail and found them colourful and in good order, and a dear little modern-looking organ at the back asking to be played.

So we bade leave of Montfort l'Amaury, passing THE house on the way, and driving through the wonderful woods, miles long, to a village called Saint Léger, perhaps 10 kilometres away. Turning the corner we were astonished to be hailed by a Frenchman, and could not but pull up. He asked us if we were from Montfort l'Amaury and the Hôtel de l'Arrivé. 'Yes' said we, very puzzled. 'You have left a *valise* there. They have telephoned to ask us to stop some Anglais in a red car and tell them.' At first we could not believe it, but it was obviously us. So with a warm handshake (*'toujours à votre service, Monsieur'*), we turned round and back we went, through the lovely woods and – yes, past THE house, with sniggers from us both (the gate was open now) to the Hôtel de l'Arrivé. It was our big suitcase that I had left almost in the middle of the road. It was very clever (*habile...*) of them to have caught us up as we might have been at Chartres before discovering it. So, more handshakes, forty-odd francs for the telephone, past Ravel's house yet again and on to within two and a half miles of Chartres, the approach to which city from the Versailles direction is striking.

From ten miles distance we had seen the cathedral with its two spires, and watched it grow as we came nearer, and change from a grey silhouette to something three-dimensional. We were looking for a place for our picnic lunch, having decided it was best to eat regularly after suffering acute pangs the previous day, headaches and such-like. The sun was bright, the clouds high and white and quite a breeze blowing. So we turned off the road into a cornfield in stook with the intention of regarding the cathedral in peace whilst eating. The picnic kettle was put on, and I thought it would be nice to have a photograph of the scene, which necessitated the camera of course. But where was the camera? Clearly, after searching the car high and low, we decided it was not there. It must then be at Montfort l'Amaury in the shop where we bought postcards and children's books. These latter must have fascinated us so much that we did not notice the absence of camera. This, at least, is what we hoped. All the other gloomy possibilities presented themselves to our minds in quick confusion, and in the end there was nothing for it but to go back to Montfort l'Amaury to see if the camera was there.

The prospect of having to go back yet again was not so funny, this time perhaps thirty kilometres, even though it did mean seeing our friend's house once more. But as we ate our sardines in the cornfield, with the magnificent prospect of Chartres cathedral in the distance, we realized we had partly to retrace our steps to get to our next objective, Fontainebleau, at any rate as far as Rambouillet. We thought we had better 'do' Chartres cathedral as we were so near, and try to enjoy it even though we did not know whether the camera was in the post-card shop or what had happened to it. There the cathedral stood, boldly and alone, and it was not until we were almost upon it that any town was visible. Inside a sombreness is given to the building by its glass, such as no photograph can give the likeness of. The rose-windows were, according to my diary entry, like big snowflakes. Its height is one of its features (like Beauvais which we had found so enormous on seeing a French cathedral for the first time on our second day in France), and the wonderful carvings round the outer part of the screen in the choir and apse, and the *grand orgue*, stuck like a huge limpet, high up on the south wall of the nave, almost touching the roof. Talking of organs, one expects this one to be played from up there (a nerve-wracking business to be sure) and another smaller one in the choir to be used for accompaniment. Here in Chartres one found a console in the choir but no organ, which led one to suspect electronicism. I would have loved to play lots of the organs we saw, but it takes time and is always a little embarrassing, especially when a foreign language is involved. It was great fun bringing into play one's schoolboy French, which at times was effective and improved the more it was deployed.

This visit done, by about 4.30pm we drove back again and retrieved the camera, given up rather grudgingly by Madame in black, large and slow, who first asked *'Comment est il, cet appareil photographique?'*, apparently unmoved. This I could not at first understand but, on being further asked how big it was, I outlined the shape of it and was given it back.

En route for Fontainebleau we made for Rambouillet again, for the fifth time past IT and along the road to Saint Léger, the best kind of road one could have chosen for repetition. It had been 'one of those days', but we had seen Chartres and the view of it from our luncheon cornfield, which will not be forgotten for a long time.

On leaving Chartres and Versaîlles, as well as visiting Fontainebleau, our route lay through Montages, La Châpelle d'Angillou and Chêne Vert to Bourges with a cathedral of scarcely imaginable immensity and fabulous gardens on its south side. Next through Moulins, and, turning off the road to Vichy we found a camping place near La Roche in a grass field where we spent two nights and a day recovering from our exertions and enjoying the hot sun, grasshoppers, dragon flies, clouds and blue sky.

Then on we went to Geneva and Lausanne, and to Berne where we stayed for three nights. Our continental holiday contained one professional engagement – a recital at the Berner Münster, whose organist Herr Senn had played at York earlier that summer. This was my first recital on the continent, the seventh in the series of Abendmusik in Berne. It was a programme entirely of English music, by Stanford, both Wesleys, Purcell, Blow, Walond, Me (with my *Impromptu*) and Parry. Looking back more than half a century I was somewhat sceptical about the wisdom of it and, having no memory whatever of the occasion, my attempt to decipher one of the press cuttings was reassuring. With the help of Langenscheidts German dictionary I learned that 'to hear English music covering 300 years is a rare (*seltenes*), instructive (*lehrreiches*) and attractive (*reizvolles*) event (*ereignis*)'. This is as far as I felt the need to go with the laborious process of translation; one day I may find a German friend or scholar to reveal the whole truth.

And now the homeward trek. From Berne by way of Neuchatel, Orbe and Vallorbe we found a hotel on a hill above Lac des Joux, a fairly big one in which we seemed to be the only guests. The views were wonderful and the cowbells pleasant and peaceful. Crossing the frontier at Vallorbe, through Pontarlier, with a long run down the Jura mountains to Besançon, Gray and Langres, we stayed the night at Chaumont and the next night at Rheims, having passed Saint Dizier, Chalons-sur-Marne and Vitry whose badly damaged church was being repaired.

||O||

Three days later we left Boulogne for home and straight back into the daily round: Musical Society (*Carmen* and *Orpheus* Act 2, Gluck), Orchestra (Haydn *Oxford* Symphony, Schumann Piano Concerto), the Old Chorister's Reunion, recitals in Rotherham, Leeds Parish Church (including Rheînberger's Eighth Sonata) said to be 'organ music without tears and ... keenly enjoyed' (Yorkshire Evening Post, 4.10.51). This was brought about by a statement of Melville Cook's to the effect that 'The organ is not a popular instrument in the way that the piano is popular, and recitals have to draw their support from the more limited circle of music lovers'. This may still be the case half a century later, but there came a time, as I believe, when recordings of organ music surpassed in number those of the piano. Then there was a concert at Richmond with a string orchestra conducted by Iris Lemare when we played Bach's *Clavier Concerto* in A and the *Concertino for Harpsicord and Strings* by Walter Leigh, but using a piano. The last item was the *Serenad* by Dag Wiren, always enjoyable. There were five more Sunday morning ten-minute broadcasts in December, containing *Sleepers Wake*, *In dulci jubilo*, *The Holy Boy* and others. And of course there was *Messiah* with the YMS, and the Nine Lessons and Carols on Christmas Eve – the climax to the year's round of daily services with the Minster Choir.

Immense care was taken over the annual carol service, described by Dean Milner-White as the Minster's Christmas present to the city of York. And indeed the citizens showed their appreciation by flocking to fill pretty well every seat in the building, incidentally damping down the resonance considerably. The Dean had plenty of experience of the service. It was in fact he, as is well known, who introduced it on becoming Dean of King's College, Cambridge, at the end of the first world war, basing it on Bishop Benson's invention at Truro in the 1870s.

Milner had a genius for innovation (for other things too, glass, enriching the furnishings, things artistic) such as improving liturgies; and here he scored a big success with the carol service on Christmas Eve at King's. There was a dissenter, however, a don who was devotedly attached to his Christmas Eve evensong. As I heard Milner relate, a compromise was reached by including the *Magnificat* amongst the carols. This, however, did not work. He was always meticulous at York now, to choose pieces he regarded as true carols, and was reluctant to allow, for instance, Kenneth Leighton's *Lully lullay* and *Three Kings from Persian Lands afar*, a candidate for the Epiphany procession which never made it … David Swale's *This endris night* accompanied by both organ and piano was a favourite, as was Walford Davies *O little town of Bethlehem* to set the scene at the beginning of the service.

It seemed that the period between Christmas and Easter was usually fairly quiet. The next year began thus, though at home we were in a state of anticipation so that, before any extra-mural affair could come about, one early morning Alice came into the world, at home in Minster Court, leaving Priscilla and me newly parentised and overwhelmed with happiness at our unwonted status. We had wondered when she would choose to arrive, and if it might be on the Feast of the Purification. On that morning we were consecrating a bishop for the Manchester diocese for which ceremony the nave was full, as usual on such occasions; those present included Norman Cocker of *Tuba Tune* fame, organist of Manchester Cathedral who had an interest in the new bishop. But Alice had other ideas – two days later was soon enough.

I had been to Lincoln perhaps twice to seek help with preparation for the DMus examination from Doctor Gordon Slater the cathedral organist, but finding the travel rather demanding I took the advice of Doctor AJ Bull of Richmond, a friend from my Catterick army days, who strongly recommended Doctor Benjamin Burrows as having much success with correspondence. I found his tuition excellent for his concise comment and also, probably, because his handwriting was almost illegible, needing a good deal of poring over which concentrated the mind wonderfully. It was not easy finding time for study, and the history was rather a toil that I did not enjoy particularly. This was before the time when recordings of ancient music were readily available to those not in a university or music history institution. I was not pleased with my efforts and inevitably failed to satisfy the examiners, though in what specifics one was not informed.

And then the extra-mural musical merry-go-round got into gear once more, with the *Hallelujah Concerto* in Hull City Hall, with my once more joining the Yorkshire Symphony Orchestra under Maurice Miles, though that particular work was probably a slightly inappropriate choice for a Lenten concert, sandwiched between Debussy's *La Mer* and the Dvorak D minor symphony. But nobody minded. Later that month the Musical Society did Vaughan Williams' *Sea Symphony*; and soon after that the YSO had Raymond Cohen for a Mozart violin concerto and *The Lark Ascending*.

Becoming more and more involved in lots of activities, by 1952 the thought of trying again for the degree of DMus had gone rather to the back of my mind until, a month before the examination, I suppose noticing that I had not sent in my entry, Professor Hutchings telephoned wanting to know why. Having worked less intensively since the first attempt, I was at first doubtful. However, as I looked more closely into the situation it seemed that another shot could be a possibility: I was still able to write eight-part counterpoint with reasonable ease, and was fairly confident of the rest except, of course, for the history. So an intensive month's revision began, as well as an earnest onslaught on that rather tiresome subject in that conveniently slack period, ending with the desired result.

I had taken myself to Durham for three days 'submitting myself' (as the instructions direct) for the degree of DMus. Canon Pattinson was a great help and comfort during my stay with him and his wife in the lovely precinct by the cathedral known as The College (which by that time I knew well, due to all those previous examinations) understanding, as he did, the amount of stress one is under. He had been friendly from my early days at York and was keenly interested in music and organs.

The next stage in my quest was to produce the Exercise – a substantial composition to illustrate the candidate's prowess, musicianship and knowledge of the ins and outs and intricacies of the craft. In army days, with the chance to read poetry, I had kept in mind the need for a libretto for a possible choral work with orchestra, and the favourite that emerged was Spencer's *Epithalamium*. There came, however, no musical ideas or inspirations, and in any case the poem would be too long, so nothing was done until the first examination had been surmounted. The ultimate decision turned out to be for a symphony, a form known only too well from the numerous and infinitely various examples one had listened to, played piano-duet versions of, and knew by heart in many cases. It is not a task to be undertaken lightly or wantonly for the first time. But that is what happened and what in the end it turned out to be, five years later.

Occasionally I came across Herbert Howells who attended RCO meetings. I was having lunch near the RCO where I was examining when he spotted me and told me that he was working on a piece that he had been stuck with for some years. It was now coming easily and rapidly. This was *Hymnus Paradisi*, in memory of his son Michael. Shortly after my appointment to York I had shown him a *Magnificat* and *Nunc Dimittis* I was rather pleased with. His comment was that there were too many seventh chords: I was still under the influence of Ravel's quartet, which is full of them; it had grabbed me almost to the point of obsession, and that was to blame. It was kind of him to take the trouble, to make a diagnosis so rapidly, and I was grateful.

One of the more notable happenings later in the year was the Three Choirs Festival at Hereford where I was responsible for the voluntaries after the four evensongs. This involved taking a week off, that is six days between the first two September Sundays, allowing for a day of driving at either end. This festival was the first of the two during Meredith Davies' stay as organist of the cathedral and conductor of the festival. It was pleasant to renew acquaintance with the Hereford scene after nineteen years, with the welcome entry to the other events, not only musical ones but lunch with the mayor, the bishop, and tea with the dean, as well as generous hospitality with one's allotted host and hostess. The only disappointment was the weather. Whereas lovely warm golden days had been the norm up until then – as I informed Priscilla whose first experience of a Three Choirs Festival this was to be – we were hard put to it to keep ourselves warm. Was this perhaps an early indication of the global warming phenomenon that was to come and exercise a later generation? My four voluntaries went ahead as arranged, the last one being, perhaps inevitably, the Willan; preceded by the Bach *Toccata* in F, Stanford's *Fantasia and Toccata*, and, first of all, the big G minor Bach BWV 542. Among the works performed were *Cantiones Sacrae* by John Gardner in its first performance and, conducted by their composers, *Hymnus Paradisi* (Howells) and Dyson's setting of Acts, Chapter 27 (*St Paul's Voyage to Melita*), a splendid work scarcely ever performed. I happened to bump into Howells under the staging at the west end of the nave where he had been rehearsing. He greeted me with 'Hello Francis; are you coming to hear my tune tonight?' My reply was certainly affirmative, and enjoyed and admired the 'tune' was.

Also at the Hereford festival, in the street outside the Green Dragon, he confessed to me that he had written an evening service for York, by the same token as he had provided several cathedrals each with a setting which was to express its own ethos. This was good news, and I waited and waited for it to appear, but with no result. Many years later at one of the York festivals it arrived, at the behest of the organisers, but it did not occur to me till many more years had passed that he had expected the Dean and Chapter to commission the work. I ought to have realised. However, it came, was copied, and received its first performance. Novello later published it, though it did not seem to be the kind of work that would sell many copies. We found it heavy going and, sad to say, had to abandon it. I hope and expect that Herbert received his commissioning fee.

The same thing, unfortunately, happened with Benjamin Britten when he came to a York Festival in 1954. He said he would love to compose a magnificat and nunc dimittis, having evidently enjoyed the choir's singing. Again nothing happened, for which I was to blame for not realising that he would need to be commissioned. What kind of a loss this was is interesting to speculate. Commissioning can be an uncertain business and I have not always been wildly enthusiastic about Britten's church music. I was then still pretty innocent about the more commercial side of music. He and Peter Pears joined a lunch party at Minster Court, when Ben took a great fancy to Priscilla's mother, as he confessed to me, on account of her happy demeanour. I was interested in Britten's view of *Gerontius*. At that time both of us professed to dislike it – he quite vehemently – but some time later he was conducting a performance of it. For myself, during my teens I remember Bairstow doing it in the Exhibition Building (in the York city art gallery) and I attended the rehearsals, so it came to me quite early. I had a much more positive opinion of it on becoming reaquainted some decades later.

||O||

Recitals came, were dispatched and dealt with. It was fascinating to meet an instrument you had no knowledge of except, no doubt, from a list of the stops sent to you beforehand, sometimes with the builder's name, sometimes without. It is crucial to know who the maker is, as with works of art and musical compositions. One certain fact is that whichever organ you are concerned with, it is unlike any other for several reasons – its position, free-standing or in a 'lethal' chamber [Cecil Clutton]; the acoustic, resonant or dry; the voicing; size (anything from six stops to sixty or six hundred). No wonder that it can be so easy to become hooked on organs and immersed in 'organ crawls', an attitude with the attendant danger of focusing on the mechanics (wind pressures, action) rather than on the music they are there to serve.

It was always gratifying in future years to make a return visit such as to the Victoria Hall, Hanley, where in 1960 I played the inaugural recital of the North Staffordshire Organists Society and then those celebrating its twenty-fifth, fortieth and fiftieth anniversaries. It was always pleasant to tread familiar ground, but the greater percentage of recitals were in new venues and they could be just as agreeable, unknown territory though they were. Hospitality was generously provided and was always different. Unusual things could happen, such as the fee that was a bag of coins – the takings. This was agreed to beforehand, and the cashing-up on reaching home was interesting (but no buttons).

Somewhere, I do not recall where, my kind host and hostess were clearly unaware that extramural activities such as recitals were usually part of an organist's bread and butter rather than a benevolent act. A fee had never been thought of. But when somehow the matter was raised it was embarrassing, especially at meal times, when in an uncanny way any subject brought into the conversation seemed to relate to the uncomfortable situation, and there seemed to be no way to deal with it: one just wished for the visit to terminate. How it ended I do not know, but the wisdom of settling such matters at the beginning was strongly brought home to me. There were, however, very occasionally times when it was a pleasure to donate one's services towards a worthy cause such as money for a new organ.

By no means are all churches wealthy, nor are they practiced in mounting concerts and availing themselves of financial aids that can be available to ease the fundraising efforts. Also sometimes it appeared that the value of, indeed the necessity for, effective advertising had not been realised. Organ recitals are a minority interest – the polar opposite of a cup final or even of a run-of-the-mill football match – which can profit greatly from the services of the local newspaper and radio station, let alone an eye-catching poster displayed at the actual venue, and other more subtle artifices employed by those who have the skill and the inclination to use them. An enthusiastic remark by a first-time experiencer of a recital of mine, to the effect that 'This is the way forward!', was a veritable shot in the arm, the like of which can be a rare event in one's progress.

Certain recitals stand out for some reason, such as Norwich Cathedral or Saint Peter's Eton Square, London, for the Organ Music Society when I stayed with CS Lang and Garth Benson in their ménage at Artillery Mansions. There were twelve recitals that year (1952) and various broadcasts from the Minster, one of them to Norway, as well as two choir programmes and two evensongs. A particularly significant broadcast was when Alec Redshaw brought his singers from Grimsby to do a late evening programme of the works of Healey Willan in which I played the *Passacaglia*. It was very special because the composer himself, over from Canada, was there in the north transept under the Five Sisters window, on the recommendation (at second hand) of Bairstow who regarded that as the best place to hear the organ. This was my first meeting with him, and he graciously signed my (Schirmer) copy declaring that we were 'pals'. We came to know each other quite well and corresponded fairly often. The recital had begun at ten in the evening and was at that juncture live, perforce, recording not yet having become the norm. Afterwards the choir's arrival back in Grimsby, plus Doctor Willan, must have been well into the following day.

Two days later, Advent Sunday saw *Sleepers Wake* as the anthem at evensong, with a small orchestra tucked in between the choir stalls. This now happened annually, solos being done by the boys and men of the Minster choir. Dean Milner-White was not totally in favour of having this rather lengthy Germanic piece for the anthem in an Anglican setting, but allowed it to happen, only once persuading me to do *Jesu, Priceless Treasure* instead. It was very fortunate that the orchestra could be formed from local musicians who were generous enough to give their services. It would have been impossible for me to ask for the means to pay them, in view of the Dean's feelings. That would very probably have put an end to it.

After a few years it occurred to me that the players would welcome joining in other parts of the service; not the psalms of course but the hymn, always *Lo he comes with clouds descending* to its 'Helmsley' tune. And then, why not the Magnificat and Nunc Dimittis? So the beautiful *Short Service* of Edmund Hooper (1553-1621) was suitable for the strings, but not for the oboes. It worked well, however. Other possibilities came to mind, resulting in my scoring Bairstow's 1940 service in G, of a suitable character for Advent, and I was surprised how well Bach's choice of two oboes, cor anglais and strings (leaving out the trumpet, for which the organ substituted in our cantata set-up) suited Sir Edward's music. For some reason I believe the arrangement was only used once. Of the 1952 performance the Yorkshire Post critic Ernest Bradbury thought that it 'must have come very near to the style of performance that Bach himself directed'. He continues, 'the effect of this timeless music, as evening darkness enclosed the high vaults of York's beautiful Minster may be imagined … and it is a matter for gratitude, if not pride, that the highest standards continue to be upheld at York'.

Sleepers Wake was always greatly enjoyed by the performers, a miniature version of the great Palm Sunday event, the *Passion according to Saint Matthew*, which had been going since Doctor Bairstow started it in York in 1913 on his arrival from Leeds. Its truncated version starting at 3pm lasted a little over two hours. For the full performance a larger number of players was needed, and the setting-up took up a good deal of time and effort. Here again it was most generously supported by willing musicians, some of whom came some distance to take part.

The nave was full, and a frequent attender was the Princess Royal, over from Harewood House, some twenty miles away. The soloists came up from London and elsewhere and then, with but an hour and a half's rehearsal with the orchestra, all was set in place. The lovely soprano Honor Sheppard came from Manchester, as did Sylvia Spencer bringing her oboe, and her husband with his flute. More than once Gordon Clinton came to do an inimitable Christus. Once we had the magisterial Astra Desmond; there were some memorable evangelists, Eric Greene, Gordon Pullin and (perhaps our favourite) Wilfred Brown whose shortened life was an immense sorrow to us all.

At this period, in Minster Court we had as our next-door neighbour the retired bishop of Hull, Bishop Hubbard who took the place of a canon and was much liked by everyone. Shortly before Christmas that year he took me as his guest along with Allan Wicks to the dinner of the Oxford Society. This, as I recall it, was a prestigious affair in the Station Hotel in York, and I remember that one of the first guests we saw on arrival was a formidable-looking lady we did not know. Wondering about her identity it occurred to us that possibly she was none other than Lady Margaret Hall in person. But we never found out. (All the world knows that Lady Margaret Hall is an Oxford college.)

Two entertaining guests joined us at home during the year – Hilary Chadwyck-Healy in the summer and in December Henry Ley with the fund of reminiscences which he enjoyed as much as we did, hearing as well as seeing his amusing heavings and the scratching motions of his fingers as he laughed with huge delight.

Another visitor we remember with pleasure about the same time was Sir George Dyson who spent an evening with us. He was attending an antiquarians' conference, and cut one of the sessions at Castle Howard in order to attend evensong when by sheer coincidence we happened to be singing his evening canticles in D. He was in the organ loft listening in the tribune above the archway in the choir screen (where the console now is) and after the *Magnificat* came excitedly to where I was in the console's old position, evidently very pleased and saying 'It's quite symphonic, isn't it?' Over our evening coffee, among other subjects I particularly remember his regretting having lost the opportunity of finding out (at second-hand) from someone he had met who had experience of the Handel commemorations in Westminster Abbey in the 1780s, someone who would have known exactly how singing was done at that period, so soon after Handel's death. Arguments about authentic performance were raging for a time after the war, and Sir George wished he could have put in his oar to help quell the controversies. But then, in his early years (he was born in 1883) no-one was concerned with matters of such unimportance as they were considered to be at that time.

||O||

Having begun to hone my speech-making skills on organists' associations from time to time, Newcastle Cathedral choristers were my speech 'victims' for their prize-giving early in 1953, and I dare say that my recital (with the Willan) on the previous evening was the more successful of the two events. This was during Kenneth Malcolmson's time as organist. More Willan was dispensed at Keble (Oxford), Chester and Bristol, the last on the splendid Walker cathedral organ built soon after Tertius Noble's York rebuild of 1903 by the same firm, to which it bore quite some resemblance.

In the early summer my adjudication skills, however negligible, were put to the test for the benefit of the Essex Musical Association at Chelmsford. Here again one's inexperience assured that a more fortunate matter was a concert in which I conducted the *Serenad* of Dag Wiren and Kodaly's *Matra Pictures*, both delightfully entertaining works. Doctor Cecil Armstrong Gibbs was a power in this Association. He and Bairstow were friends and I had enjoyed some of his songs, among them *The Bells, In the Highlands* and *Five Eyes*. He had been much moved (he told me) on coming into the Minster some years before during evensong one winter's afternoon as darkness was falling, to hear the psalms in progress in the distant quire. He described its effect and I set to, trying to identify the particular chant that had so impressed him. After some long cogitations and suggestions all was revealed. It was just a simple single chant, by WR Bexfield (1824–53), consisting of a mere ten chords, all of them triads, nine of them in root position, and Doctor Gibbs had remembered the exact key – 'f minorish' as he said, although it begins in C minor but ends in the dominant of F.

PSALM CXXXVII.

213

W. R. Bexfield.

The fact that such slender resources could produce so profound an impact was in accord with a favourite ploy of Sir Edward's – the juxtaposition of triads – which he used quite often in his compositions, for example at the end of the *Benedictus* of his Communion Service in D, and which Stanford's *The Fairy Lough* may have suggested to him. The single chant of Christopher Gibbons produced a similar effect, appropriately for the words 'I will wash my hands in innocency, O Lord …'.

It was at this time that we learned of the death of Doctor Noble on 4 May 1953, the day before his eighty-sixth birthday, a sad day for Britain as well as America with the departure of a well-loved man whose stock was of the highest and who had reached the status of a legend in his lifetime. I was so fortunate to have had the privilege of meeting him. His only descendant, Philip (1903–1979) who would have been a mere nine years of age when leaving York for New York (on his father's becoming organist of Saint Thomas), paid more than one return visit and presented a handsome clock in memory of his father at the centenary of his birth in 1967. It graces the Camera Cantorum, the choir room off the south transept, along with his portrait, a fine photograph no doubt taken at the end of his stay in York as he left for the New World.

Mitchell Hall in Marichal College, part of Aberdeen University, had its organ rebuilt in 1953 and I played a recital on the fine instrument. My reason for mentioning it here is the headline to the critique next day that stated 'An organ recital to enjoy, not endure'. This was pleasing to me, naturally, but probably spoke of some experience which had put off the writer and inclined to turn him – and others, no doubt – from attending organ recitals. Certainly in this kind of performance the range and diversity are perhaps as wide as in any other, if not wider and for more than one reason: the style of the player, the type of organ, the acoustic, let alone the choice of pieces, and to say nothing of the likely ecclesiastical temperature in winter especially, or the hardness of the pew seating; but all such factors contributing to the fascination which can possess the devotee of this kind of concert-going. The approved composers in this particular programme included Boyce, Bach (BWV 564), Mozart (K 594), Peeters (*Modal Suite*), Stanford, Duruflé (*Scherzo*), and Dupré (in B).

This was the year of the Queen's coronation, and back at home in York due recognition was paid to it. This was mainly in a performance of *Merrie England*, that very popular composition of Sir Edward German. This was to take place in the Museum Gardens, and that is how it began. We had not gone very far however before raining started, causing York Musical Society, Lemare Orchestra, soloists, and some, most, or probably all of the audience to beat a hasty retreat into the Tempest Anderson Hall close by, there to continue the operation. This was June.

Next month was held the first royal garden party after the coronation, only to be beset by the same problem. 'Umbrella Day' proclaimed the Daily Telegraph, 'queues in rain', though Priscilla and I were not unduly incommoded. But we were delighted to count among our fellow guests Sherpa Tensing with his wife, and Sir Edmund Hillary, safely down from the summit of Mount Everest. For this privileged event we had to leave our holiday farm in Northumberland (appropriately named 'Minsteracres') with Alice, seventeen months old, in the care of Priscilla's sister Betty. On our return it was interesting to observe Alice's momentary bewilderment on seeing her mother again having become used to her aunt's somewhat similar looks.

At the end of March 1954 the Musical Society put on Dyson's *Canterbury Pilgrims* in the York Art Gallery, and shortly afterwards at the symphony orchestra's concert I played the second Saint-Saëns piano concerto, which Frederic Waine conducted. Mendelssohn's *Italian* Symphony was played before the interval.

The second of the York Triennial Festivals came along in June, lasting for three weeks, and including a variety of events. Of these the one that attracted most interest was the Monteverdi *Vespers*, a work that had scarcely ever if at all been heard in this country. Walter Goehr conducted the Sheffield Philharmonic Choir, York Minster Choir and the BBC Northern Orchestra. Among the half-dozen soloists were Alfred Deller, and Wilfred Brown our much loved tenor who provided distant falsetto echoes from the north transept, while Allan Wicks and I had an organ apiece to play. The novelty of the unfamiliar work caught the imagination of the public who flocked to the Minster for it. It was broadcast and was followed by many performances across the country and again at subsequent York festivals.

The Minster Choir, unused to appearing at anything but services, acquitted themselves of 'A Procession of Church Music over Five Centuries' (the title bearing the imprint of Dean Milner-White). This comprised seventeen choral items ranging from the York Masses (circa 1500) to Vaughan Williams and Howells, taking in Minster organists Nares and Bairstow, with representative works by Tallis, Byrd, Gibbons and their successors. Interspersed, and played by Allan Wicks, were examples of that 'peculiarly English musical form the voluntary' according to the critic Ernest Bradbury, who wrote generously of the concept and of the choir's presentation. There were operas by the English Opera Group: Britten came for his *Rape of Lucretia* and there was *Love in a Village* and Lennox Berkeley's *A dinner engagement.* Fernando Germani, from Rome, and I gave organ recitals.

There was a performance of Walton's *Façade* in the Theatre Royal in which Edith Sitwell herself and Peter Pears declaimed the poems, observed from the wings by Britten (holding a glass of whisky) and myself sharing a score. The final concert of the festival was Britten's *Saint Nicholas* for which he was unable to stay. We did, however, have a distinguished cast, among them George Malcolm, piano, Alexander Young, tenor, the English Opera Group String Orchestra, with Allan Wicks and Frederic Waine at the two organs. For the young Nicholas we had the services of a Minster chorister Terence Precious who managed his repetitive role 'God be glorified' splendidly, despite the awkward note he is given – the E – which is the very one where normally the voice changes from chest to head – even a semitone up or down would be easier. But the composer's problem is understood; and some choristers will find no difficulty in tackling it. No doubt the break is apt to vary slightly in individual boys.

||O||

A direct result of the visit of Healey Willan to York (towards the end of 1952) was an invitation to take part in a fortnight's summer school for choirboys, a venture of the diocese of Toronto. In 1954 it was a thrill to be in Canada for the first time. I crossed the Atlantic in the *Empress of France*, taking five days to do so, a more leisurely way than became one's lot in the years that followed. For company I had Alec Redshaw whose choir had come to York for the broadcast of Healey Willan's works two years before. Alec had several adjudications to do around and about in Canada. As we sailed up the Saint Lawrence River, schoolboy memories of the Plains of Abraham and General Wolfe (baptized at York in Saint Cuthbert's church, half a dozen stone-throws from the Minster) inevitably came to mind. There was mounting excitement as we approached Quebec: one lady hoped desperately that we should see 'the shadow' and kept up her aspiration in clarion tones. To me it was puzzling, since daylight was fading and I wondered how a shadow could be produced. At length Quebec was reached and her ambition was achieved: there, in all its glorious illumination was the famous and imposing C.P.R. hotel, the *Chateau* Frontenac. (I had just finished reading *The Frontenac Mystery*.) I was not yet used to transatlantic pronunciations; even some years later, and further south over the border, I heard a minister of religion asking someone about 'painings'. The mystery was solved when I realized that his church was mounting an art exhibition.

The first few days in Canada were spent at or near Bracebridge, some hundred miles north of Toronto, in a wooden holiday home by Lake Muskoka. Here I was briefed about things to come by John Bradley who, with his mother, was taking a break from the heat of Toronto. A row-boat was available and was a relaxing pleasure. John was organist at Rosedale church in Toronto and taught at Saint Andrew's College, Aurora. In later years, each time I was in North America we would meet, and he became a great and much valued friend of the family for more than half a century. Soon after that first meeting I had a *Fanfare* published by Oxford University Press, which I dedicated to him. Another piece composed at that time, *Scherzetto Pastorale*, was, like the *Fanfare*, included in one of the Oxford organ albums; this I inscribed to Brian Snell, one of the choristers at Port Hope. Our friendship has lasted, likewise, another fifty years plus. After Port Hope it was cemented very firmly by my being their family's guest in Glenrose Avenue for most of my lengthy stay in Toronto. Brian's parents Muriel and Grant Snell were my kind and willing hosts and, oddly enough, living but three minutes or so from Doctor Willan's house in Inglewood Drive, just across Mount Pleasant which they had not realized until then. It was exhilarating to spend time with Canadians *en masse* as well as a few from the United Kingdom who had gone there years ago, some like Healey, retaining their native accent and taking in the more relaxed, carefree manner of the Canadian.

Doctor Willan was the Director of the summer school for choirboys, with John Bradley as organiser. I was chosen as a representative of the 'Old Country', which they wished to include among the staff. This was to take place at Trinity College, Port Hope, east of Toronto on Lake Ontario. There were some fifty boys and half a dozen staff. In addition there was another similar event at Camp Hyanto, at Lyndhurst along the lake to the east with another similar group.

The two-week stay at Trinity College, Port Hope, was happy and full of enjoyment and achievement. The main difficulty we were faced with was the poor state of the boys' voices. Too much raucous shouting during games had spoilt many of them, and the head-voice was rarely to be found among the entire number. Services were sung on most days and at the afternoon evensong on one of the Sundays the Governor General Vincent Massey attended.

There were, of course, rehearsals, talks (Doctor Willan on plainsong), ad hoc concerts, outings, parties and fun generally. At one of the impromptu concerts, having sat observing one of the turns, I was descended on by the participants and dragged up front, somewhat to my bewilderment, to have a ceremony of a sort performed. I was installed as 'Big Chief Double Diapason', complete with appropriate head-dress which had large feathers attached upon a school cap. Worse was to follow when Healey, pretending to be a choirboy, had to have his voice tested by me. Clad in blue shorts (with his underpants dangling below), sock-suspenders showing, a white T-shirt with the badge of the course stamped all over it, and a school cap. For his audition he sang *A Perfect Day* (a favourite of my Suddaby grandmother) about three octaves too low, having first made gruesome attempts to show me his singing voice. Then, needing another song, I asked him if he knew *Who is Sylvia?* to which he replied 'No Sir, I've never met her' Neither did he know the name of the composer. When I told him it was Schubert, he said 'Do you mean Schubert The Moose, Sir?' This went down well with the boys who had so christened the antelope's head in the dining room when adopting it as their mascot.

Healey was universally popular; chats with him, hearing his views on any subject, his ideas and philosophies as well as his reminiscences, stories and jokes (usually inclined towards the *risqué* were always stimulating and edifying. I recorded in a letter one of his pronouncements: 'There are very few things in this life you need take seriously; very few people, and least of all, yourself'. One day the subject of the American composer, Dudley Buck (1839-1909) came up for discussion. At this time, some forty-five years after his death his work was suffering summary dismissal along with others of his generation; since then reassessment has treated him more kindly. But on this occasion Healey's opinion on a certain composition of Buck's was asked. His immediate explosive comment left us in no doubt: 'Oh that's Buck at his Dudleyest'.

As well as being university organist, Healey was also vice-principal of the Toronto conservatory of music: the principal was Sir Ernest Macmillan, the very successful conductor of the Toronto Symphony Orchestra. While in Toronto preparing for my recital to the Canadian College of Organists, I went with Healey one evening to a meal with him and Lady MacMillan in their enchanting roof garden with tall trees for shade (though the sun was near to setting) and occasional coloured lights. My letter to Priscilla of 23 August contains this description:

'Sir Ernest was rather frightening at first – a heavy face, grey spiky hair, and a posing, important Beechamesque manner. But one could very soon get underneath it and he was gracious, kind and thoughtful. Healey said later that he is a precocious child who will show off before an audience, but on his own is nice. His figure is like Edward Lear's drawings and he seems to trot about, or bob like a robin .... Gorgeous cold ham and salad, cantaloupe melon and ice cream, coffee, all in the open air. Eventually we went downstairs ... and had records until 1.30am.'

The original suggestion for the venue of my recital during the three-day CCO congress was Yorkminster Baptist Church, but Doctor

Willan considered this *infra dig* for an Anglican cathedral organist from England, despite the appropriate name and the splendid organ. He therefore directed that the university's Convocation Hall should be the chosen place, with its four-manual Casavant, an excellent instrument with but one hazard. The Solo Organ stops-knobs were divided, half on each side, facilitating who knows not what crises, with the need to look to right and left to see which stops were in or out. Healey's practical solution was to use one of the three pistons of each division as a 'Cancel', leaving two only for the stops but necessitating two movements instead of a single one. The programme contained the Dupré *Noel Variations*, and I kept Bach till the end: the *Toccata* in F that I played at a moderate pace. This pleased Doctor Willan who said it was good to hear a 'man's Toccata': and since then I have often wondered what epithet he would apply to some of the more *scherzando* accounts one is liable to encounter at times.

An important and unexpected result of the Ontario Diocese Summer School at Port Hope (though it might have been always in the mind of John Bradley as the moving spirit and organiser) was the emergence of the Saint George's Choir School in Toronto which started a valuable tradition by supplying Saint James' Cathedral with its chorister boys, and has done so ever since to the great benefit of all concerned.

The cathedral in Kingston, at the eastern end of Lake Ontario (the opposite end to Toronto) is classical, reminiscent of Saint Paul's. At this time and for some years its large choir, of sixty-three boys and forty-eight men, was under the inspired direction of George Maybee and one of a very few such formations in North America. When I played there he was in London with the best section of the choir singing services at Westminster Abbey, leaving behind sufficient forces to keep things going at home. His choral results were remarkable and justly famous. At Christmas time there was usually hilarity when the carol *Past three o'clock* came round. The words 'Born is a baby, Gentle as maybe' were, as he himself admitted, far from being an accurate assessment of a somewhat powerful and strict disciplinarian.

Some years later another visit was made to this country by the choir, this time including York. This was rather forced upon us by those organizing the trip, and occasioned a huge amount of activity which, over and above our normally full schedule of day-to-day duties, was rather more than we could comfortably manage. To borrow beds for the thirty boys, to find a room suitable to make a dormitory to put them in, as well as finding hospitality for the twenty men of the choir was a formidable undertaking, largely tackled by the Minster's Chapter Clerk, Brigadier Haddon. His army connexions were invaluable in the borrowing of beds, and a dormitory was provided by the local training college nearby, over the city walls. Then how to feed the boys (Priscilla's domain) and where? Our large kitchen was just big enough but trestle tables were needed. The boiled eggs – two and a half dozen – were greeted with puzzlement; evidently an unknown commodity at home. Most of them ended in the bin. Sausages fared better. It was a rewarding time, and greatly enjoyed and appreciated all round.

Before leaving George Maybee it is probably worth mentioning his gleeful account of his claim to have brought about the marriage of Sir William McKie (considered to be a confirmed bachelor) by introducing him to his future Canadian wife Phyllis Birks, forming a union that proved a complete success. Sir William's biographer, Howard Hollis, however, states that they met in the Bahamas in 1945. Was this at the hands of George or was he using an excess of imagination? George, himself unmarried, did not reach a great age, and Sir William, born in Melbourne, spent his final years in Ottawa after a full and active life in England, latterly as organist of Westminster Abbey.

A HOME AND A HYMN TUNE

Having become settled into an ordered routine – a fairly tightly packed one – and the family increasing (William arrived in February 1954, two years and two weeks after Alice) Priscilla and I felt it prudent to look ahead and plan for whatever should befall us later on. We had the superb dwelling – the organist's residence ever since Noble's arrival in 1898 – a tied house that we would be required to vacate at the end of my tenure of the post. We would then have to find somewhere to live, and probably even earlier should anything go wrong: there were already signs that there could be problems with the Headmaster.

We therefore began to look around, keeping our eyes open for possibilities. These took the form of a countryside situation, an old property, within easy reach of York, and not costing a great deal, to fit in with slender resources and my not over-generous salary. (This, on my appointment was £400 per annum. Noble's I believe began at £200 in 1898, and Bairstow's was £400.) Our favoured area was somewhere between our native heaths, York and Malton, eastwardly – the Yorkshire Wolds in fact – and bordered by the A64 and the A166.

After some cruising around and making a few abortive moves our efforts became focussed on a property in Acklam, a small village seven miles south of Malton and thirty minutes' drive from York. Acklam is on a slope halfway up the wold, facing York and its Plain, the top of the cottage garden being 420 feet above sea level. Ivy House was solid and cosy-looking, of stone, modestly proportioned, and the last house at the southern end of the village. We were very much taken with the appearance of the cottage, but had no idea whether it was available. Certainly it was inhabited, though it appeared to be in need of quite some attention. Our enquiry at the neighbouring inn was helpfully met by Mr Howard the owner, who undertook to find out if there was a chance of its being for sale, and we awaited information from him, though not necessarily with a great deal of hope.

The 1955 summer holiday was drawing near, and the inevitable preparations, packing and the kind of turmoil that attends these activities was going ahead. These eventually came to an end; the car was loaded, Priscilla and the children were all aboard, I was about to close the front door and lock it, when the telephone rang. Oh dear – did it need to, just at this moment? Another minute and we would have gone, safely out of range of the tiresome instrument. Shall I shut the door and pretend I hadn't heard it? What might be the annoying consequences of answering when we could have been free of all that kind of thing, to which our day-to-day lives were perpetually subject? Heart in mouth I lifted the receiver. Mr Howard, good as his word, had asked Mr Harrison, and he was willing to sell. What a start to our holiday. Shut the door. Firmly. Goodbye to Minster Court for a month, and drive off in a state of high glee.

At that time there was much thought about re-housing and doing away with what were considered out-worn, sub-standard cottages, lacking damp courses and possessing a ceiling height of less than seven feet six inches. Conservation was not yet a going concern. The inhabitants of Ivy House were, I think, worried that it would be condemned, and were relieved to be able to leave its fate in the hands of others. And for a while after we had taken possession its fate was still none too certain. It appears that we saved it by moving in promptly, thus preventing the authorities from finding it empty which, we understood, would have enabled them to have it demolished. So the holiday was enlivened by continuous plans and discussions. How wonderful it was going to be to have a place of our own, to do with it whatever we wished, with a whole quarter acre of garden and sixteen damson trees, some within sight of their pensionable age; somewhere for the children to cavort and to learn about country life. It has the most lovely views across a small valley over rolling fields towards a distant aspect of the Plain. Seeing it from the high point down the village street constantly puts me in mind of my first, boyhood impression, formed when on cycling trips exploring the neighbourhood with a friend. The effect is that the road appears to come to an end at our cottage. Closer inspection, however, reveals a ninety degree turn to the right; not the most convenient manoeuvre for traffic, farm vehicles, and least of all for the lengthy fiftyish-seater school bus that twice a day has to gingerly creep its way round with only inches to spare between us and the Half Moon Inn opposite.

But we still had to do the purchasing, so had to temper our enthusiasm for the time being. How much would it cost: was it in fact capable of restoration: could we afford to do all that was necessary? Meeting the owner to discuss terms was a somewhat daunting procedure: a formidable character, native to the district, with accent and tone-of-voice to match. On asking what sort of figure he required, I received the firm, forthright reply, complete with the straightest, sternest look, denoting there was to be no denial: 'A hoondred an' fott-ty pound'. At which my heart missed a beat. I cannot now recollect the amount we had in mind to afford; but what seems over half a century and more later to be a trifling sum was to me at that moment rather a shock. Where was that amount of money to be found? Could we really go through with the project? It would be a risk, but one we surely ought to take. So the deal was struck and ways and means seriously considered.

Sometime during my later teens I had been urged by my father to take out an insurance policy. Not realizing fully the advantage this would be, I was inclined to resent the paying of the yearly premium of a pound or two. Then came the time, at long last, when I was to reap the benefit I had never really comprehended: the policy matured and I received a cheque for ...almost *a hundred and forty pounds*. This was within something like three or four weeks of the purchase of the cottage, so we could not be blamed for divining some kind of providence at work. We were now the proud owners, assured of our own roof to cover us, come what might. It was our very own property: the conveyancing was done on 23 February 1956.

Much work was needed and was possible through being spread across many years as money became available. By the time of my retirement the cottage, re-named Nether Garth, was as we wanted it, serving our modest needs and affording us untold pleasure, satisfaction and security. For those first years it was ideal for brief visits with the children on Wednesday half-days and for holidays until the latter became more adventurous. A real cottage existence it was, with its paraffin lamps and cooker, bathing in front of the kitchen fire in water brought by bucket from the pump outside, and candles to light us to bed. Electricity was still several years in the future, but the characteristic odour of that ancient mode of lighting so evocative of country cottage living (learnt in one's extreme youth in Auntie Sybil's cottage) was still with us for some time to come, with its accompanying daily maintenance – trimming, filling, cleaning of lamp chimneys, not to mention the locating and purchasing of the necessary fuel.

Not only did we change the name of the cottage – something I am inclined, on occasion, to regret – but some years later, I was outside the cottage when a huge, shiny motorbike pulled up. Its driver asked the way to some street, the like of which is not found in Acklam. Acklam possesses two roads; one appears to be referred to sometimes as Main Street; the other is anonymous. So I at once realized that he was in the wrong Acklam, and he quite cheerfully set off to the Middlesbrough suburb, some forty miles, which is technically West Acklam. This led to confirming for myself that ours is East Acklam; the rest of the story belongs to a hymn tune.

||○||

Earlier that year – Easter morning in fact – breakfast time was enlivened countrywide by the Minster organ's account of the Widor *Toccata* (and one or two other pieces). What more suitable piece of music for that joyous day, despite the brickbats hurled at it by so many, among them our revered Vaughan Williams who wished he could invent an organ on which it could not be played (I have encountered several). This piece was Sir Edward's regular post-Easter Day evensong voluntary, eagerly awaited and greatly appreciated. And on the previous Sunday, the yearly Saint Matthew Passion was made memorable by the singing of two of the soprano arias by a Minster chorister, Beverley Jones, who, as well as possessing a voice of a rare quality, was a first rate musician with a natural understanding of the music's expressive potential. The only rehearsal he had was a quick run-through with piano and, on the day, a few bars with the orchestra. For the next two years he had no rehearsal at all. In later performances his baritone contributions were of immense value. During his choristership the Queen's coronation took place, and he was one of the two York representatives invited to join the composite choir, the other being Tony Hopper. Beverley had a notable success in the Musical Society's performance of the Brahms *Requiem* in November when he tackled the soprano solo and its long taxing phrases with complete confidence 'capturing the sensitivity and mystery of the music and somehow piercing to the heart of this great musical document' as reported in the Yorkshire Evening Press by Percy Lovell, director of music at Bootham School.

The other work at this concert held a special interest. This was the first performance of the posthumous *Five Poems of the Spirit* by Sir Edward Bairstow, the composition of which had been encouraged by Dean Milner-White who chose the words, and described the event in his characteristic manner as 'an occasion unrepeatable ever'. Mr Lovell thought that 'the settings are of considerable distinction, peeping occasionally beyond the bounds of the late-Romantic choral idiom with moments of great beauty...' containing, as they do, the distillation of the composer's individual style. The performance was attended by Sir Ernest Bullock who had completed some of the orchestrations left unfinished at Bairstow's death. The work has not been performed as much as it deserves, but the year 2009 saw a very beautiful recording of it by the choir of Saint John's College Cambridge conducted by David Hill, along with other works by Bairstow on the same compact disc.

This question of neglect is apt to give rise to a thought that from time to time can claim one's attention. There are works by composers who are little known which can reach as high a level of inspiration as those by established composers; and they will receive due recognition in certain quarters but not the unquestioned and universal attention accorded to the well-known figure who can be trusted to provide a work which will be acceptable. With Bairstow in mind I can take as an example his *Six Variations on an Original Theme* for violin and piano, which is a work of great merit both technically and musically, but is never, to my knowledge, ever played except again through the good offices of the CD in a recording by Fenella Humphreys and Malcolm

Tyler. Violinists in general who naturally know all about Paganini, Ysaye, Kreisler, Mozart, Beethoven *et al* can be forgiven for being ignorant of what goes on in other fields of music, and never to have come across the name of an organist such as Edward Bairstow. But in the case of this piece of his, full of beauty, variety and invention, and being expertly laid out for both instruments, it can only be regretted that it is not being made available, for the pleasure it can provide for the musical public. It is tempting to speculate how different could have been its fate had it borne the name of, say, Elgar or Holst. No wonder Kreisler pretended to be Pugnani – and others. Published by Oxford University Press in 1932 it has been out of print for many years.

A significant turning-point came about later that year. In Denmark, a tour was arranged for me by Kjeld Tofte-Hansen whose acquaintance I made when he visited York. There were six recitals during the seventeen days Priscilla and I enjoyed in that delightful country. We found an affinity with its people and were much impressed by its orderliness and quiet confidence. Before setting off, however, I had the pleasure of playing a Sunday evening recital in the Three Choirs Festival at Hereford on the splendid Willis cathedral organ.

My Denmark programmes were largely of English music that I hoped might be of interest, though Bach and others were not excluded. It was, however, more than a little surprising to meet the kind of organ that was to be my lot for the engagements that had been so kindly and meticulously (not to say entirely *gratis* too) organised for me. Of the sophisticated modern aids to stop-pulling and pushing that we in England were now beginning to regard as necessities – our right, in fact – there were none. Tracker action, straight stop-jambs, stops with lengthy shanks that would need an assistant to manipulate, and a pedal-board of unaccustomed dimension, all had to be wrestled with, almost literally. The show had to go on; and go on it did, as gradually the logic became clear. There was no need for our constant changes of stops; there were other means of attaining the desired quality of tone, so appealing was the voicing of all the stops and with such responsiveness, like a harpsichord, brilliant, full of vitality, and hugely stimulating. This was a new experience, entirely unexpected. I recalled, with some gratitude, my association with the mid-Victorian tracker organ in Malton church, with features not dissimilar to the Danish ones. So, the baptism years stood me in very good stead on many occasions. Here it was a rapid turn-around – an emergency almost – a baptism by fire for which I have given great thanks ever since I underwent that experience. I learned what an organ really was meant to be, and was glad to find, as time went on, that such a feeling was infecting the organ scene at home as well as in other countries. Most of the organs I played, if not all, were Marcussens, at Odense (Thomas Kingo Church), Aabenraa, Haderslev cathedral, Randers, Herning and Viborg.

There was a recording in the concert hall of Radio House which was broadcast, and a visit of special note to the Marcussen organ works at Aabenraa, shown round by the director himself, Mr Zachariassen, who was most welcoming. The whole exercise was very memorable, full of interest and very great pleasure. Another tour there, equally happy, came about some years later.

Back in England the recital schedule contained two in Edinburgh's MacEwan Hall (April and November), two in Chelmsford Cathedral (May and October), dedications or re-openings at Kendal (Zion Congregational Chapel) and Middlesbrough Town Hall (on the day the sputnik made its remarkable entry on the scene) plus Saint Mary Redcliffe (Bristol). The recital in London's Temple Church was in the presence of Henry Willis III and his guest and fellow organ builder G Donald Harrison from across the Atlantic.

A different kind of dedication was held at York when the Air Force memorial, the astronomical clock in the north transept of the Minster, was unveiled by the Duke of Edinburgh. For this service the Dean wished me to write an anthem for which he provided the words – 'arranged them' as he put it – a blend of his own and texts from the bible. Beginning 'Remember for good, O Father, those whose names we commemorate before thee', they continue with his poetical thought – 'They went through the air and space without fear; and the shining stars marked their shining deeds'. It was published by Novellos and appeared as a supplement in the August *Musical Times*. This drew from Gerald Knight, Director of the Royal School of Church Music, an appreciative and encouraging letter:

My dear Francis, I just wanted to send you a wee note to thank you for producing that lovely music in the Musical Times. It's rarely that my interest is kindled by the anthems etc. there, but this time it very definitely is. I hope you'll go on composing... Every good wish and congratulations

Ever yours

Gerald 2.viii.56

The anthem was used at evensong for several years afterwards on Battle of Britain Sunday in early September.

Archbishop Garbett, who should have taken a leading part in the service, was prevented through illness. He died nearly two months later at the end of the old year. Thus his magisterial presence and powerful pulpit pronouncements became memories for us. Not long after my appointment as organist ten years earlier I had received a directive from him via his chaplain and the Minster succentor Hugh Frazer that he required the note G for anything he was to sing – he was unable to manage anything like the intonations introducing the creed or *Gloria in excelsis.* I duly produced the note, and his admirable attempt very nearly made it, perhaps three-eights of a semitone below, but in a wonderfully resonant tone quality which brooked no denial, perfectly and distinctly audible to all and with no electronic aids whatever. The Princess Royal came to his funeral.

His successor Michael Ramsey came from Durham and was enthroned in late April. He stayed with us for five years as Primate of England and Metropolitan until he became Primate of all England ... at Canterbury. These services, of which I saw many, were always impressive and well attended. Varying as they did according to their purpose – bishops' consecrations having the most predictable pattern – they all required careful preparation, briefing, and a cool head.

In 1956, the tenth year of my Minster appointment, extra-mural recitals were beginning to reach a peak – thirty kept me busy, and Ronald Perrin keeping things going during my absences. Among them were two broadcasts of the Poulenc concerto, one for the overseas service and the other actually in the Light Programme. This was before this delightful work gained its tremendous popularity.

But the recital that attracted the most attention – on 10 March – was the re-opening of the famous Schulze organ at Armley, in Saint

Bartholomew's Church. First, I feel I should express the thoughts I ought to have felt at the time concerning my engagement for this event. It did not occur to me then that the obvious person to do the recital was Melville Cook, the chief Leeds organist, on whose territory I was encroaching. Whether he had any view of the kind I have never learned. But in any case it would have been difficult if not impossible for me to ask the BBC to transfer the invitation to him, so I proceeded with it to the extent of choosing the Bach D major *Prelude and Fugue* for a start – a brave (or foolhardy) decision, with its dicey solo pedal scale at the beginning. I played it quite frequently at that period, usually with success. However – and it was a broadcast of considerable interest to the organ fraternity – it was not to be my prerogative to provide a hiccup which would enliven organistic conversations for some time; not the organist, but the poor unfortunate organ. For in the course of finding somewhere to place a microphone inside the organ, one of the engineers had dislodged some woodwork which fell on to the pipes. The disastrous result did not reveal itself despite checks. It was not until after the announcer's descriptive prologue, when I began to play, that the full extent of the mishap was to be heard, such drastic mistuning as is never to be found even in an organ neglected for long enough. To say that the effect was dramatic and electric was an understatement: for me it was shattering, and it was all I could do to keep going in the hope that things would improve. That is all I can remember. How the rest of the programme fared is not even a ghost of a memory, and no recording exists of which I am aware. But certainly it provided a topic for quite a while. It could even have raised the suspicion that it was a judgement on me for trespassing on another's patch. As to the cause of the *débâcle*, the idea has been expressed that a sudden rise in temperature could have played its part to some extent. We must be content to leave the mystery unsolved and take pleasure in the unique instrument restored to robust health by Harrison and Harrison some years later.

An equally doubtful choice of the Bach D major was made for one of the Royal Festival Hall recitals (at 5.55pm) when it was the first item. I do not recall anything untoward however, and continued with Hindemith's second sonata and Vierne's first symphony more or less satisfactorily, I hope.

A rather special recital in the popular Saturday concerts at Huddersfield Town Hall took place in October of that year (1956) after the organ had been restored by the Willis firm. Henry Willis (the third) was present with his wife, and both sat in the hall throughout my rehearsing. He told me that he loved hearing his organ 'being turned inside out' and I imagine that he bore me no ill will for having insisted on there being no rocking tablets for the couplers below the console's music desk, which was his custom learnt from across the Atlantic. I had been taken on as adviser, and all was successful enough, the only idiosyncrasy being the Krummhorn which for some odd reason I specified as sixteen feet instead of eight. But at no point do I remember its being held in question by anyone. Its beautiful pipes had been shown me one day by Mr Willis in the factory, they having been recently completed.

At York in the Minster, the annual *Messiah* by York Musical Society proved satisfactory, as Percy Lovell's generous critique indicated, 'such an alive and vivid version of a great work, which is sometimes made a museum piece by an over-solemn approach'. The Lemare orchestra again came along to play splendidly for us, and the superb soloists were Heather Harper, Helen Watts, Cyril Hornby and Gordon Clinton. It was rewarding to have musicians of high calibre for our concerts. A notable one was Joseph Cooper who came the following year to join the YSO in Rachmaninoff's second piano concerto. His relaxed manner, playing entirely from memory, was notable and I was interested too, to find the orchestra that is required more modest than I had imagined; more Mozartian perhaps. But the spring concert that year had only local talent for the solo part of the Schumann concerto when I passed the baton to Freddie Waine and did what I could on the piano.

Healey Willan was a prolific composer, and at one time had completed twelve short masses for his church choir. He was apprehensive about writing the thirteenth because of the bad luck that might ensue, but on a subsequent visit I learned that all was well and that two more had been accomplished without any ill effect. He was also, quite naturally, hopeful that these works might be taken up in other countries, England particularly, not perhaps being aware of the subtle difference in style prevalent here. It might be the truth that our preference was for a more advanced style of composition, for better or worse... He had already written an evening set of canticles for the Durham–Ripon–York annual get-together. This was at Lionel Dakers' suggestion – to be something like Stanford in A – and it duly appeared and was in regular use at York afterwards. Also frequently sung was the motet *Gloria Deo per immensa saecula* for five voices, a fine work in contrapuntal style, a method he used less frequently but in this case with conspicuous success, affording enjoyment to the (unaccompanied) singers.

The connexion with Healey Willan continued happily, and I kept in mind the wish I heard him give voice to during my Canada visit of 1954, which was that he would value greatly a Lambeth degree. Certainly his work for the church, including membership of the synod, was deserving of the honour. It was casually expressed, *en passant*, but I remembered, and wondered what would happen if I tried to do something about it myself, soliciting the support of others including Vaughan Williams. It did not seem out of place that I should do so. Sir William Mackie, sympathetic with transatlantic matters, complimented me on what he called my initiative, and Vaughan Williams' pretty legible holograph letter was distinctly positive. He had written from 10 Hanover Terrace, Regent's Park on 5 October 1955.

> Dear Dr Jackson,
>
> It will give me great pleasure to back your application for a Lambeth degree for Dr Healey Willan – he is a fine composer and organist – and we, in this country certainly ought to make some public recognition of his work.
>
> Yours *[indistinct]*
>
> R. Vaughan Williams

Both composers shared the same birthday, 12 October.

However, after making my approach, a rather flustered Dean burst into the house one morning, as was his wont (there was no need in those days to keep the front door on the latch) waving a letter from Geoffrey Fisher, the Archbishop, taking up the subject and giving me to understand that I had strayed beyond the bounds of my station – a mere organist: a layman – having the audacity to write a letter to the head of the Anglican church! Later, the Archbishop's secretary divulged that Vaughan Williams had hoped to be present at the ceremony but was prevented at the last minute. Nevertheless, all proceeded as hoped for; and we saw the degree conferred and had a cup of tea as well.

||O||

The following year, 1957, was as action-packed as we had come to expect, and with one or two unusual items to stimulate interest (if that was really needed). The birth of a second son, a festival and a visit by the Queen, sixteen recitals, two radio recordings and the unusual pleasure of accompanying Gioconda da Vito on the day I received the doctorate.

The work on my doctoral Exercise, the symphony, had proceeded over the years, slowly at first but gaining in pace as it progressed, until the fourth and final movement was sketched out in thirteen days. Then began the intricate process of orchestration followed by a fair copy, to be bound in a certain way with the title 'up the back, not across'. To produce the full score, all neat and accurate, was a job requiring patience, endurance, a peaceful situation with no interruption and of course unlimited time. Happily we had recently bought the cottage fifteen miles away on the Yorkshire Wolds, and this was the ideal place to go to ground for a few days to give my whole attention to the matter.

So I forsook York, Priscilla and the two children, handing over all Minster duties to Eric Parsons, my excellent assistant. With ink, pen, ruler, paper, food and, I hoped, all other necessities, I set to work without a single distraction, no telephone, no callers, with only one end in view. There was even less of a need to bother with feeding as time went on, in my almost totally static condition. Nor was there a keyboard for checking anything doubtful. How long it all took I do not know but finished it was, to my great relief – though of course with the nagging thought that once more the examiners might not be pleased.

To the bookbinders it duly went in time for the deadline for its presentation. I considered the means of getting the rather bulky article to Durham, the packing, postage and all that it entails. I then had the brilliant idea that I could be my own courier, persuading myself that I was perhaps due for a bit of a jaunt after all the lengthy concentration.

Durham is so lovely around the Cathedral, and perhaps the crocuses would be out again in the College as they obligingly always were, providing their silent consolation on so many other exam excursions. So up the Bailey, I dumped my precious load unceremoniously, like a baker delivering his bread, the milkman his milk, or the postman out of whose job I had done him.

So far, so good; but what next? To wait and hope, or to forget all about it, having no idea how long it would be before any decision reached me? Back then to the daily round, to the choristers next morning and the many other things to take one's attention: matins with the boys, evensong full choir, the Musical Society's evening rehearsal, then a good night's sleep and plain day to follow.

Half way through the morning the tiresome telephone chose to ring. I picked up the receiver to hear a sonorous voice say 'Is that Doctor Jackson?' 'No' I replied, 'Mr Jackson'. 'Oh no, it's Doctor Jackson', countered Professor Hutchings. He must have seized upon my product at once and spent most of his time examining it. To judge by his rapid decision he appears to have had few doubts, and I could only be very touched by his thoughtfulness in relieving me of the anxiety of waiting, and letting me know in what was a very characteristic way of his.

Great rejoicings of course in the front hall of 1 Minster Court where the telephone was, and an explanation needed for the children. This was readily furnished by Priscilla, to the effect that because of some cogent reason they would not understand, Daddy was going to be called Doctor Jackson. At which, contrary to all expectation, William's face fell: 'I want to call Doctor Jackson daddy'.

I was told I could use the new form of address forthwith, and what is more, I could sport the beautiful cream damask and palatinate purple hood as soon as Messrs Gray would supply one. 'Make very broad your phylacteries', advised the good professor, referring to Matthew 23, verse 5. For the conferment I hired a set of full dress robes; afterwards, through the kindness of CS (Robin) Lang I was able to borrow the robes he no longer used in his retirement from Christ's Hospital. After a while he suggested I might like to buy them, which is what the Dean and Chapter did for me for £30, a gift I value greatly.

Our second son, Edward, made his first appearance just three weeks after I had been declared a doctor – sharing his birthday with the Dean and Shakespeare. A friend was impressed that these two 'achievements' (his term) should have come about so closely together. (Nowadays the congratulation would probably give rise to the omnipresent rejoinder 'no problem' which can certainly be the case when everything is safely done and finished.)

There was also another York Festival, the third, lasting for three weeks and mounting nightly performances of the mediaeval mystery plays in the ruins of Saint Mary's Abbey. As previously there was a very full supporting programme of music culminating in the Monteverdi *Vespers* conducted by Walter Goehr.

There were organ recitals by Eric Parsons, my splendid Assistant Organist, soon to leave York for Saint Mary's Cathedral, Edinburgh; by André Fleury of Dijon, and myself. I also broadcast the Bach *Passacaglia* and my *Toccata, Chorale and Fugue*, recently completed and dedicated to Healey Willan on his seventy-fifth birthday. An especially enjoyable evening was afforded by Bach's music in which the Musical Society's performance of *Magnificat* and wedding cantata (BWV 120a) were praised next morning in the Yorkshire Post by Mr Bradbury. Likewise commended was the Boyd Neel orchestra for its accompanying, its fifth *Brandenburg Concerto* and the harpsichord concerto played by Thurston Dart. A concert of contrasts involved the Minster Choir with Byrd's *Great Service* and Mozart's music for organ played by Derrick Cantrell, then in office at Manchester Cathedral.

I joined Gioconda da Vito in a Bach recital when she played two of his works for solo violin, before and between which his organ music provided contrast. The final item, which so impressed Ernest Bradbury, was the Vitali *Chaconne*. In his Yorkshire Post critique he writes that she moved from her position in the Nave to a platform on the organ screen 'where we saw her black-robed figure looking most diminutive beside the high organ pipes, and yet the tone of her instrument carried perfectly to the west end of the building. She had preferred to play without the lights, and for the second half of the recital only the fine perpendicular organ screen was illuminated, and yet the encircling gloom could not diminish the radiance of all this music, or its performance'.

A happening which no doubt helped further to fix the memory of this recital occurred halfway through the *Chaconne*. The E string collapsed and she finished the performance without it, and with no hint of any crisis; such was her professionalism.

The visit of the Queen, which was to include the York Cycle of Mystery Plays performed open-air in the ruins of Saint Mary's Abbey, was eagerly anticipated. A certain doubt hung around the probability, since the weather – at midsummer – was problematical. Jim Bridge, the groundsman tending the Dean's Park that morning, pointed out to us that the daisies were closed. He was right, the rain came down determinedly, so plan B was put into operation: an organ recital in the Minster. The programmes had been elegantly printed, just in case, and were pressed into service. The pieces were chosen for their attractiveness – voluntaries by Boyce and Samuel Wesley, a Bach *Liebster Jesu*, the Vierne *Berceuse* and *Variations on a Noel* by Dupré. Seats were taken and I began. Soon Her Majesty stood up and began a tour of the Minster conducted by the Dean. Thus the music turned out to be suitable, soft enough not to intrude on the spoken word, except for the riotous finish on full organ. It was a happy event; I was presented to Her Majesty. Alas for the Mystery Players, their disappointment was a sad thing for them.

The festival over, there was no lack of interesting things to take part in. The Musical Society produced Sir Arthur Bliss's *Pastorale*; the Rossini *Petite Messe Solennel* on Saint Cecilia's Day in the orchestral version with the YSO, and the Brahms *Alto Rhapsody* with Shirley Minty; these in addition to the usual Saint Matthew Passion and *Messiah*. The YSO did Beethoven's fifth symphony, as well as Rachmaninoff's second concerto with Joseph Cooper as already mentioned.

Organs to play were at Gloucester and Hereford Cathedrals (on successive evenings), Saint George's Hall, Liverpool (with Willan and Dupré), in Edinburgh at Saint Cuthbert's and the McEwan Hall. For the Organ Music Society, at the West London Synagogue, the programme included Leo Sowerby's *Chorale Prelude* on the Vaughan Williams tune to 'For all the Saints'. This was requested by Mr Archibald Farmer (joint founder of the society with Felix Aprahamian) who provided a programme note enthusiastically commending the piece with its ten variations and its insistent crotchet rhythm.

The Royal Festival Hall audience heard Buxtehude, Bach in C 564, and the Franck *Final* on 4 December. I think it was this concert that my cousin Elsie Suddaby came to. In the same venue two months earlier I was delighted and privileged to hear my *Benedicite* sung by the choir of Saint Paul's under Doctor John Dykes Bower in a concert of English church music. For this I added strings to the organ accompaniment, played by the Kalmar Chamber Orchestra, with Harry Gabb at the organ.

Sir William McKie, organist at Westminster Abbey had brought about a congress of organists that year – the first one of an international nature – attracting candidates from all over the world, with a fair sprinkling from America. Among the latter were David McK. Williams, Searle Wright, Gordon Jeffery, David Craighead, Lewis Elmer, Marilyn Mason and Leo Sowerby, the last being well-known as a composer. My afternoon recital preceding evensong was the first event in the congress, and I had chosen and learned specially Sowerby's *Toccata* which began the programme and was thus the first piece of music to be heard in the Congress. It was a huge thrill to meet him afterwards and to have him write a complimentary inscription in my copy – not, unfortunately, including my name. I came to know him quite well when I played, first in Chicago and, on a subsequent tour, in Washington Cathedral when he was director of the College of Church Musicians. He was pleased that I grasped what he intended for the last four bars of the *Toccata* where the continuous semiquaver movement ceases and big crotchet chords finish the piece: I kept them in the same tempo whereas, he said, usually a sudden slowing of the tempo was done.

Leo had studied with Respighi who, he said, 'gave himself airs'. A few years after this, on one of my American tours, in his bachelor apartment he cooked us a steak each before my Washington Cathedral recital, which is a nice thing to remember; just as it is to recall having an egg fried for me by Sir Jack Westrup, Heather Professor of Music in the University of Oxford, before catching my morning train to Southampton after playing at Balliol the previous evening (18 November 1956). This occasion is etched on my memory, since I had arrived without a copy of Vierne's *First Symphony*. The situation was saved by Philip Taylor, organist of Magdalen, who possessed a copy and kindly lent it at the eleventh hour.

For the inauguration of the Edinburgh Festival in August I had been asked by Herrick Bunney for two fanfares 'played by military brass and drums' as the music critic of the Times wrote, which 'were the composition of *Frederick* Jackson, of York, who, perhaps taking the hint from Walton's Coronation *Te Deum*, made splendid use of the antiphony of trumpeters and organ in opposite transepts of the cathedral' (Saint Giles) – unconsciously though. One of the fanfares fared well in a solo organ version that was published and twice recorded. At that stage it was of interest to find out anything there was to know about the effect of one's composing efforts.

Another fanfare I had composed was published in an Oxford album of six pieces, by Armstrong Gibbs, Douglas Guest, Geoffrey Bush, Sidney Campbell and Henry Coleman. The first three fared tolerably well in an *Organists' Quarterly Record* review, though Doctor Campbell's 'excruciating cadence' spoils the album. 'Why' asks the assessor, 'why must composers try to be "original" in just this way?' Henry Coleman is lacking originality, though sounding pleasant, 'which we cannot say of an appalling *Fanfare* by Francis Jackson. This merely sounds like an outburst of bad temper'. I was thrilled to see this honest opinion for the first time decades later on 8 March 2010. To have so distinguished myself without really trying and, though I might possibly have taken it to heart at the time, no harm was done to the progress of the piece: indeed, did not Doctor Campbell himself broadcast it from Windsor one Sunday morning? In the same review he again is not spared the rod, where his *Exultate* seems to be wishing 'to work off some pent-up fury', jumping from key to key with a complete disregard of harmonic logic and ending with a 'modern-conventional "wrong-chord" cadential passage'. Alas, it is not possible to please everybody.

On that front my communion service, eight years old, seemed to be making some headway. I heard from Douglas Coates that he had used it at the London church of Saint Cuthbert's, Philbeach Gardens in May, and on the second Sunday in Lent it had been sung at the Cathedral Church of Saint John the Divine, New York – no less – under Alec Wyton. I expect and hope that the creed was included, as it was in the days before it was thought best to be handed to the congregation to mutter, rather than to have their spirits lifted by some helpful singing.

In early September I played the Poulenc organ concerto at an Albert Hall Promenade Concert, conducted by Basil Cameron. Afterwards I was able to board an 11.45pm train, back to York at 4.43am in time to take the milk train to Whitby, arriving there at something like five or six in the morning. It was a lovely day, Priscilla and the children were staying at Sandsend and the tide was out, so I walked the three miles north on the sands to join them in time for breakfast.

‖O‖

About this time something quite unexpected attended my feelings towards a certain hymn tune, from which I learned the impossibility of being able to predict the reaction of the listener to a piece of music – or work of art, or anything else. It all began when I took a dislike to playing *All through the night* when the choir and congregation were singing 'God that madest earth and heaven'; a good tune, perfect for its original purpose, and a secular one (not that there is any harm in using some secular tunes in church: this has been done from time immemorial). Another factor is that many Welsh tunes are repetitive, with the same phrase appearing three times (*Llanfair* and Saint *Denio* are other examples). This, however, has not prejudiced their popularity or durability. Where secular tunes are concerned, everything depends of course on their quality, and this is not necessarily very high, in the case of some that have been produced in recent years, and in a plethora.

So, in an effort to find something else I sketched three or four tunes of which I retained one; in E flat, *in five-four time*, which was sung for the first time at the 1957 Old Choristers' Reunion at the Minster. By then it had become clear that two beats on 'God' and two on 'earth' were unnecessary (bar 3 was always in common time). And then, of course, it needed a name. I considered Purey-Cust, the Dean of York who founded the Old Choristers' Association in 1907, but eventually decided that a place name could be more appropriate than a personal one. We had recently bought our Acklam cottage, but this presented a slight problem since another place of the same name exists as part of Middlesbrough. On a map printed around 1900 that is called West Acklam. Ours according to the war memorial in the church is called East Acklam, though not so on any map I know of. But this solved the problem and abolished any ambiguity.

A year or two later it so happened that I was at a gathering of musical Methodists at Hoddesdon and had taken a tape with me with illustrations for my talk. When we came to the end of one of these the next example followed immediately, so I let it play on – it was all accidental, I swear – and I was startled to observe the Reverend Doctor Francis Westbrook, the chief Methodist musician, becoming excited. Afterwards he declared that this was just what he wanted for a hymn he was including in the supplement to the Methodist Hymn Book which he was in the process of preparing, entitled *Hymns and Songs*. Duly it appeared there with the words 'Through the love of God our Saviour' and was spotted by John Wilson and Cyril Taylor whose wish for the tune to have different words caused them to approach Fred Pratt Green. He produced a three-stanza harvest hymn beginning 'For the fruits of his creation, Thanks be to God'. This quickly gained wide acceptance joined with *East Acklam* and soon appeared in some thirty hymnals as well as in several collections made by churches and schools, the sum total reaching sixty-seven in just over half a century. I counted it ironic, too, that one book should reverse the order, awarding first place to *Ar hyd y nos* and summarily demoting my effort.

Needless to say, the words sometimes had to be changed to suit the odd (in more than one sense) whim so that, for instance, the first line would become 'For the fruits of ALL creation'. 'Silent growth while men are sleeping' found no favour with a certain sector of the gentle sex; but even some of those who did not wish to grind that particular axe, male or female, could interpret that line as denoting wide-awake women while the chaps slept. It was inevitable, I suppose, that someone would like the words so much that they wished to produce their own tune for them. This happened. In America. In the same country an amateur organist domiciled in Old Hickory chose the tune on which to compose a voluntary for a competition; but it failed to bring him any reward. But before all this I received two other hymns from authors who had liked the tune, neither of which has, as far as I know, been published. And the tune has appeared set to another hymn 'Gift of Christ from God our Father', and yet another 'Into darkness light has broken. Christ has been born' and another 'For the wonder of creation, God's name be praised'; and all this came about because of a whim of mine and my efforts to displace *Ar hyd y nos*, plus the tape recorder that didn't stop where it was supposed to.

Again it was rather ironic, surely, that when the new Methodist Hymn Book appeared in 1983 I found my *East Acklam* with its Pratt Green words provided with a second tune – none other than *Ar hyd y nos*. More ironically still, Fred's words have appeared in the new Australian Hymn Book recently with – guess which tune – *Ar hyd y nos*: as far as I know not as an alternative, but the *only* tune.

Then a Canadian organist arranged the hymn as an anthem, with brass and organ, but quite differently from my own effort which was published by the RSCM in 1989. This latter was among a collection of six anthems for harvest entitled *Crown of the Year* among whose composers were numbered Richard Shephard and Prince Albert. I also provided a rather lush harmonization for the last verse for the 1993 Three Choirs' Festival at Worcester when the singing of the hymn was led by the choir of All Saints, Worcester, Massachusetts. This version then appeared in *New English Praise* (Canterbury Press 2006); it ends with six notes of descant of which four are the tune an octave higher. More than once I have been approached to provide a descant to fit in with the overdone practice that seems to be the fashion nowadays. My attitude is that a descant is unnecessary. This feeling was reinforced when one of the school hymn books contained, without any reference to me, a most unsuitable one which had practically no relation to the tune and caused me to make a protest that received neither acknowledgement nor reply.

The Reverend Doctor Fred Pratt Green, poet and greatly respected figure in the Methodist church, worked in York at one time and lived in Muncaster, a suburb of York. I regret I was quite unaware of this until May 1993 when, happening to be in Norwich where he was then living, it was my great pleasure to make his acquaintance through the good offices of Ronald Watson. Four months later he celebrated his ninetieth birthday. He wrote more than three hundred hymns (nowhere near the seven or eight thousand of Charles Wesley, as he admitted, but a healthy total nevertheless) and I am greatly privileged to be counted among the elect who are associated with his work. Requests to use our joint hymn, to print it or to include it in a hymn book, have come from many different places and still do so. One was from the Presbyterian Church of Ireland. It appears in both the American and Canadian hymnals as well as in the one used by the Sisters of Saint Paul de Chartres in the Philippines. Locations as far apart as Chicago and North Berwick, Norwich and Calgary, Ballybrack, New Brunswick, Dringhouses (York), Nebraska, Australia and Pickering (North Yorkshire) have asked for it. Hymn conferences have included it, and the dioceses of Bradford, Bristol, Canterbury, Leicester, Llandaff, Salisbury and York have used it for their diocesan choirs' festivals; Dulwich, Harrow, Boston (Massachusetts), Gloucester and Monmouth have printed and made use of it. Little did I contemplate such a state of affairs when I scribbled those sixteen bars. Broadcasts of it have been heard on Sunday Half Hour, Songs of Praise and the Daily Service where, unfortunately, I have more than twice undergone hearing *Ar hyd y nos* instead. Walking in the Lake District in 2009 and entering a remote church I found the hymn in *Ancient and Modern Revised*, words and tune, as was my usual ploy, and sometimes I signed it. This time – it was the organist's copy – a clear instruction read 'Not this' and gave the number of *East Acklam*'s substitute, the predictable one. I signed my tune, but not before putting an unequivocal 'NO' to the unwelcome directive. Such was my work of supererogation: I don't think it is entirely blameworthy, though disappointing and none of my business what tunes are used in other churches.

Most composers would, I suppose, like to think that their works might be durable enough to go into the general repertoire, like the Beethoven and Mozart symphonies, and be played and heard for ever. They should remember, however, that with each new composition the corpus of music has become that much larger, and anything added to it has to be increasingly excellent to find a place among it. Fashions change too and what, for instance, were once usually referred to as 'those dreadful Victorian tunes' have undergone a striking resurgence which should be salutary to any creative person no matter how popular he may be during his lifetime. If he by any chance proves not to be a Bach, a Chopin or a Gershwin, perhaps he might be well content to look down from heaven – fairly continuously – and hear the one tune he left on earth raising the roof of mission church or cathedral anywhere at all on its surface, to the joy and satisfaction of all those who participate in recreating his musical microcosm, sounding as fresh and spontaneous as on the day it was written.

As I say, fashions change, so I do not expect those sixteen bars to gain, much less retain, immortality. If by chance they did, well and good, but there is always a possibility that someone may dislike playing them as much as I disliked playing *All through the night*, and feel that Fred's words are worthy of something better.

||O||

The following year (1958) was not quite so full, but was busy enough with fifteen recitals, two broadcasts, three rather interesting concerts, two with the YSO including the fourth *Brandenburg Concerto*, Beethoven's first piano concerto with Keith Swallow as soloist, Walton's *Music for Children* and Tchaikovsky's Fourth symphony, which was quite a big assignment for the amateur York Symphony Orchestra as mentioned previously. The YSO joined in with the Musical Society in a concert in the Minster to celebrate the diamond jubilee of the English Folk Dance and Song Society. Keith Swallow was again involved, in a piano concerto by Arnold Foster founded on country dance tunes; also in Vaughan Williams' *Fantasia on the Old 104th Psalm Tune* for chorus, orchestra and organ, first heard at the Gloucester Three Choirs Festival in 1950 – a rousing final item. Other composers represented were Peter Crossley-Holland, Holst, Parry and Ethel Smyth in the centenary year of her birth. The soprano soloist was Stella Kemp-Welch, whose husband Noel had come to York from Saint Michael's College, Tenbury, as chaplain to Saint Peter's School. He later joined the Minster choir in the bass line.

Another unusual event, in the Art Gallery, was the AGM of the YSO that was followed by a rehearsal of Elgar's *Cello Concerto*, taken by Bernard Shore, the solo part played by orchestral member Kathleen Anderson. Then after an interval there was a performance in which Bernard Shore played the solo part on his viola in Elgar's arrangement. A special pleasure in the Minster was accompanying Bernard Shore once more, in Holst's *Lyric Suite*, with organ, then on the piano a beautiful work, *Romance* from a suite by Benjamin Dale that is never heard.

Saint Mary Redcliffe was a delight as usual, reckoned as Arthur Harrison's finest organ; this was during Garth Benson's tenure as organist, a fine player and good company, whom I had first met in his time as organ scholar of King's College, Cambridge.

Our Ash Wednesday broadcast of evensong had for its anthem that very beautiful piece *I have lifted up mine eyes to the mountains* by Richard H Walthew, a piece which should be far better known and which is published by Stainer and Bell. This was in advance of the regular yearly BBC inclusion, by Saint John's Cambridge, of the Allegrí *Miserere*. The *Magnificat* and *Nunc Dimittis* in E major were by John Clarke-Whitfeld (1770-1836) of Hereford Cathedral and Cambridge; a delightful piece of no great consequence which we used to enjoy. After one performance some years later, I had an abrupt message from Dean Jasper (1975-84) delivered by the Precentor, forbidding its use on any future occasion with no reason vouchsafed. This was one of two similar and unique happenings in my 37-year spell, both from the same person. The other time it was a creed I had written – in E flat I think – which was vetoed, and I have no idea why. I should have gone and asked, but the thought did not occur to me. Dean Milner-White would have come to me himself sympathetically, with a properly thought-out case, and submitted to counter-suggestion without any uneasiness or fear of being stood up to. I saw nothing wrong with the piece and hope I may unearth it one day from the welter of accumulated matter if only to try to find a reason for its banning. If it is any good it would also be ready for use against the day when the creed is reinstated as a valid and regular choral item in the Eucharist.

In July the Royal School of Church Music held a Festival Service in the Albert Hall under the direction of Gerald Knight. The singers were drawn from choirs affiliated to the RSCM in all parts of the United Kingdom. Four organists took part, Doctor John Dykes Bower of Saint Paul's to play for the service; Sir William McKie to provide a Middle Voluntary; I to play before the service and Doctor Sidney Campbell of Canterbury Cathedral the music afterwards. One hundred and fifty bishops were present who were attending the Lambeth Conference.

Of course the Minster work carried on as always, fulfilling, not without anxieties, and the greatest privilege. The choir had by now reached a state of stability that lasted for many years.

The sad news of the death of Doctor Vaughan Williams came on the BBC news on 26 August and there was a commemoration in Westminster Abbey on 19 September before a full congregation. Many were the tributes paid him.

A rather special recital, on my forty-first birthday, happened in the chapel of Saint Michael's College, Tenbury, which was a commemoration of its founding by the Reverend Sir Frederick Arthur Gore Ouseley in 1856. We used to sing some of Ouseley's music in the Minster services. In my recital programme Dr Heathcote Statham, who had been organist there in his younger days, was commemorated with his wonderful *Rhapsody on a Ground*; other pieces were my own *Toccata, Chorale and Fugue*, then a year old, and *Voluntary XXVII for Double Organ* which paid tribute to the composer John Blow on the 250th anniversary, the previous day, of his death on the first day of October 1708.

Later in October, Leeds held its week-long Centenary Musical Festival with artists such as Otto Klemperer, Menuhin, Britten and Pears. In my Parish Church recital I played the Frank Martin *Passacaille*, as well as the *Choral* by Peter Racine Fricker who was in the church to hear it. Of the former work Ernest Bradbury noted that 'in a heavily discordant yet ruthlessly logical *Passacaglia*' there was built up 'wave after wave of effective sound all brilliantly focussed on what Doctor Vaughan Williams once called the European wrong-note system', all this under the headline 'A recital where time was forgotten'.

Recitals numbered twenty-seven in 1959, taking in Gloucester Cathedral, the Temple Church, Newcastle City Hall twice and the City Temple. Two of special interest were the Italian Church in London, the first recital on a beautiful organ built by JW Walker and, by the same builder, the organ in Saint Helen's at York which I helped to design and which turned out to be somewhat of interest with its tracker action. This system – traditional and proved over centuries – came to occupy me to a large extent and was very much the right true system to be employed, as I saw it. I advocated it as much as possible but realized that larger organs found the modern electrics quite satisfactory. Nevertheless tracker action gathered momentum and has been very much reinstated after its sojourn in the doldrums for many years.

As well as two evensong broadcasts, there was *Israel in Egypt* by the Musical Society, and the YSO, with Raymond Cohen in the Beethoven violin concerto. There was also a commercial recording of two Liszt works, *Missa Choralis* and *Via Crucis*, with the BBC Singers under Gordon Thorne. This took place in Manchester Town Hall, causing trouble with Dean Milner-White as already related. Gordon's premature death not long afterwards was a great sadness.

Incidentally, my involvement with music other than for church or organ would have gained Bairstow's approval. One of his constant adjurations was to take an interest in as wide a spectrum as possible, broadening our outlook. This was taken as a command, to be faithfully carried out.

One day at evensong the Minster organ went disastrously wrong: the pistons and composition pedals decided to dish up all manner of crazy combinations which I believe was due to the perishing of the insulation on the wires of the electric action, and to dampness. This was very similar to the 1929 situation when the organ reacted to the effects of the lovely new heating plant that had been so welcomed. The woodwork cracked and things were so serious that the cost of repair amounted to the huge sum of £4,000. Harrison & Harrison did the work then. Now, forty years on, the cost was very much higher. This time the work was done by Messrs JW Walker and included making some amendments to the tonal scheme, bringing in more colour and less force of volume. Opportunity was taken to raise the pitch by part of a semitone to do away with the distress caused to orchestral instruments, oboes especially, which found it irksome and difficult to tune to the same pitch as the organ.

The recital I gave at Saint Mary's Church, Swansea on 20 October came to an end in what at that time was an unusual and surprising way. The Dupré *Noel* variations, having reached their uproarious finish, our Latin-tempered Welsh brothers and sisters burst into immediate and lavish applause. Nothing remarkable in the twenty-first century, but unheard of fifty years before, catching me very much on the hop and not quite sure of what to do. (At York, Dean Milner-White had made it very plain that – as his firm instruction bade the enthusiastic festival concertgoer – 'The audience will understand that in a cathedral church there can be NO APPLAUSE'.) I managed to gather myself together and bowed as best I could from up in the rather cramped organ loft. However, nobody appeared to be any the worse for clapping their hands together in the house of the Lord; nor, as was eventually to become the norm everywhere, for drinking coffee or holding prestigious dinners in cathedral naves, something quite unheard of not all that long ago.

OVER THE POND

The following year was true to form, with thirty-five recitals and the usual two Wednesday evensongs on Radio 3. An unusual concert at Barnsley, Pitt Street Methodist Church, had for its first half an organ recital of some forty-five minutes ending with the third Franck *Choral*. This was followed by Mendelssohn's *Lobgesang* performed by the Barnsley Music Society's chorus and soloists, for which I supplied the accompaniment.

A Festival Hall recital in March ended with the *Passacaille* by Frank Martin – a tough nut that I took to America a year hence thinking it would be appreciated there. It was less well advised for playing at Middlesbrough Town Hall on 11 November but probably safer at the Royal Festival Hall, though I did not receive any opinion. I played it in several recitals (among them Saint Luke's, Chelsea, in November) until it appeared to be lacking in the kind of appeal that was needed. It was the final item in a half-hour broadcast from the Minster in November, a programme which included the first broadcast of a *Prelude for a Solemn Occasion*, a piece I had written for a projected collection springing from the International Congress of Organists the previous year (1957), but which came to nothing, so far as I am aware. It was published by Banks on its own.

My old schoolmaster during my choristership, George Arthur Scaife, died on 22 May at the age of 85. He had been Master of the Song School for 48 years and had given succeeding generations of choristers a thorough grounding in the basic subjects under a strict discipline, for which a great deal of gratitude was felt and acknowledged.

The previous day had been one to rejoice in, when the Minster organ was newly refurbished and at evensong was celebrated. 'The organ shall not sound until after the Dedication. The Choir enter in silence. The Dean and Canons go to stand between the Organ and the Choir.' The organ was 'dedicated anew … Then shall the Organ sound and the people sing *Let all the world in every corner sing* ….' And there in the nave the seal was set as 'after it, while the congregation *sit*, will be played: *Fugue* in E flat … Bach'. This essential piece had left an undimmed impression on my 1930 choirboy memory as played by the then organist, Doctor Bairstow. But in those hardier (and perhaps more respectful) days we all, choir and congregation, *stood* there in the Quire to those immortal strains. The earlier restoration had lasted a whole year (1929-30), and all we had for that length of time was the black Schiedmayer grand piano. (The Hammond organ was just beginning to make itself felt.) Now, thirty years on, Sir Edward was remembered in his D major canticles, and the anthem (composed by erstwhile cantabrigian colleague of the Dean's, Patrick Hadley) *My beloved spake*, was Dean Milner-White's inspired choice for the occasion.

During the recital which came later, the Great G minor fugue called forth special comment from Ernest Bradbury in the Yorkshire Post '… in such performances … we can … appreciate that Bach's fugues are to music what the Minster itself is to architecture – a masterly construction of lines, curves and shapes as graceful in structure as they are strong in tension'. Other items, as well as the Bach *Fantasia* to precede the fugue, were Mozart K608 (the *Fantasia* played by Sir Walter Parratt at the opening of the organ in 1903), the Statham *Rhapsody on a Ground*, Gordon Phillips' *Toccata*, the Dupré *Noel Variations*, and (further tribute to my predecessor) Bairstow's *Toccata-Prelude on Pange Lingua*.

Haydn's *Creation* given in the spring in the Minster by the York Musical Society elicited kindly comment from Percy Lovell who thought that Haydn 'would have been pleased with the clear and firm singing' of the chorus in the midst of their arduous preparation for the Bach *Mass* in B minor for the next York Festival. He was not so complimentary, quite rightly, about the amateur orchestra's contribution that had passages some members found too taxing. I had hoped to provide encouragement by enlisting their participation, though I had been warned against it. I had also in mind the saving of expense, but the experiment was not repeated, except in *Messiah*, which they found easier.

The fourth triennial York Festival of 1960 followed the trend of its predecessors culminating once more in the Monteverdi *Vespers* under Walter Goehr, who also conducted the Bach *Mass* with the combined choirs of the Ambrosian Singers and the York Musical Society. My recital contained Bairstow's *Sonata*, Flor Peeters' *Variations* (opus 58), and Leo Sowerby's fine *Toccata*.

As 1961 began, Sir William Harris, organist of Saint George's Chapel at Windsor, announced his retirement and on 23 January the Dean had written asking if I would like to be put on the short list of applicants. I thought it would be good to have a look and was interviewed in the pleasant setting of the deanery. I also called upon Sir William who failed to see any reason that I should leave York – not that he was wishing me any misfortune or unhappiness: it was the scale and magnificence of the York building he was concerned with, as compared with the royal chapel. It was a most interesting visit. I had a good look round, the while thinking how the three children, aged 9, 7 and 4 years would fare – let alone Priscilla. And I thought of Windsor's geographical position, different in some ways from our northerly location – the north was where we were created and where we belonged, and really the niggles and annoyances at the Minster which came along in the ordinary course of events seemed of so little account two hundred miles to the south, as a kind of homesickness came across me. Of course I could not leave York, so I wrote asking to withdraw, receiving a reply from the Dean in the same kindly, sympathetic terms as the first letter. It said:

> Dear Dr Jackson, I wish it might have been otherwise, but I cannot quarrel with your decision. We all much enjoyed your visit.
>
> Yours very sincerely – Eric Hamilton (Bishop)

Despite the ongoing Minster duties and recitals, variety was never lacking, and the days were filled to capacity. Pupils there were, committees to do with the various societies, with the Corporation's Entertainments – a sub-committee, planning of the Minster service music, organ pieces to be learned. On top of everything else, Iris Lemare suggested I might write something for her January orchestral concert. She was always wanting to help young musicians and I believe performed works by Benjamin Britten in his younger days. Having been fascinated by the hymn tune *Mantegna* by Vaughan Williams, I agreed with Iris that variations upon it would bear the title *Homage to Vaughan Williams* and this is what I worked at and then conducted in the Rialto Concert Hall at York (to kindly newspaper comment from Percy Lovell). Vaughan Williams had died three years before. Later, at the request of Doctor Herbert Sumsion I conducted it at the Gloucester Three Choirs Festival, this time to not-so-favourable criticism by my fellow Yorkshireman Ernest Bradbury. But one day soon afterwards Ursula, Vaughan William's widow, came to lunch and heard a tape of one of the performances about which she said nice things.

The year proved to be of more than usual interest. Previously we had had more than one royal visit, but here was another, a special one: a wedding. There had been other royal weddings before, two in the thirteenth century and most famously that of Edward III with Philippa of Hainault in 1328 when both were around the age of sixteen. After the long gap of more than six centuries this one was sure to raise more than considerable interest. The Queen's cousin Prince Edward, Duke of Kent, was to marry Miss Katharine Worsley of Hovingham, a name familiar to us at Malton eight miles away, particularly regarding local cricketing considerations.

To discuss the music the Dean and I met the bride- and groom-to-be at Hovingham, and I sang as best I could at the piano Bairstow's introit *I sat down under his shadow*, a choice morsel which was immediately decided upon. The Dean was keen to have *Audi Filia*, the words from Psalm 45 about a marriage, which I had set for the reinstatement of the Five Sisters window, and was sung at our wedding. This too was chosen. As to the organ music and what is referred to as 'The Wedding March', I later sent a tape with four likely pieces, avoiding the Mendelssohn (and Wagner) from which to choose – two by Bach: *Toccata* in F and the *Saint Anne Prelude*; *Grand Choeur Dialogué* by Gigout and another *Toccata* in F. This was of course the Widor which at the time I thought was a highly original and very excellent idea. So the planning was completed. A good deal of water had to flow under the bridge before it became reality.

There were twenty-one recitals in this country, two of them at King's College, Cambridge, with Frank Martin again and Vierne's Third Symphony: two January evensong broadcasts, the first for the Conversion of Saint Paul with his well-known words from Corinthians 'Though I speak with the tongues of men and of angels' as the anthem in Bairstow's setting, and Nares in F for canticles.

Herbert Howells and I were one day in the King's College organ loft at the same time, when he dropped a remark about some aspect of academic dress. Very soon afterwards it was announced that he was to receive a doctorate of music from Cambridge, *honoris causa*. I think it was on this occasion that I told him of my admiration of the Collegium Regale *Magnificat* and *Nunc Dimittis*. He replied, 'Well Francis, if I heard that music without knowing who composed it I would be wild about it', or words to that effect. At a cathedral organists' conference in Saint Paul's he thanked me for lunch on the previous day. At once I grasped that he was taking me for David Willcocks, on checking with whom I proved my supposition to be correct, and passed on his thanks.

||O||

The Westminster Abbey recital for the First International Congress of Organists in 1957 – half an hour long – had far-reaching consequences, for among the American contingent was Robert Baker whom I had not met previously. He was organist of the Fifth Avenue Presbyterian church, New York, and was to have his organ rebuilt or replaced. He wanted me to play the opening recital and would arrange for his friend, the agent Lilian Murtagh, to fix other recitals to make the visit worthwhile, which duly took place in 1961. The only fly in the ointment was that the organ, the cause of the whole operation in the first place, failed to be ready in time. However, although other tours came about at three-yearly intervals, none of them took place in Fifth Avenue Presbyterian Church.

I had to clear my absence from the Minster with the Dean. The tour was planned to last for eight weeks (3 April-26 May). Negotiations with the excellent Lilian Murtagh were well advanced when I broached the subject, and there was an awkward moment when he appeared to be going to raise an objection: 'But you will be in the hands of Agents'. Well yes, but how else can it be done? However, the moment passed and permission was granted. He may have not greatly liked my forsaking the Minster for so long – though the show would go on unhindered in the capable hands of Ronald Perrin – and he must have realized that my visits to all those foreign parts were in a way a kind of missionary expedition. Not that the Minster was always correctly designated – Yorkminster Cathedral was a not infrequent appellation; and there was confusion, too, with Westminster Abbey. Once I was blatantly designated Sir Francis Jackson, *aetat* a mere 44, at Methuen (whose second syllable has the accent).

So came about my first North American recital tour, taking off on Easter Monday for Toronto, landing at *Malton* airport, a sop for any homesickness I might have been feeling, bearing in mind the town of my birth that shared the name. After an active term culminating in a Saint Matthew Passion, Holy Week and Easter, a little cessation would have been welcome but instead it was a matter of being plunged into an entirely different life, one I had not experienced and could only imagine. Not that it was going to be anything but enjoyable and rewarding; merely unknown and unexpected, and the excitement of it all would provide the necessary stimulus.

There were to be sixteen recitals, and I took five different programmes: with more experience I would have submitted no more than two. The most popular one, with Willan and Dupré, was taken up seven times; two others three times each, the one with Vierne III and Hindemith III twice, and the Martin, Parry, Hindemith and Peeters once only. There was perhaps some advantage in having a variety, for playing the same pieces too often was likely to interfere with spontaneity. For their part the organs possessed certain basic similarities that tended to ease the planning of registrations at each fresh venue. One feature (on which we in England had come to depend) most, if not all of them, lacked was the Great and Pedal Combination Coupler. This was at first disconcerting but was eventually made up for by the plentiful supply of General Pistons, which had not yet become part of our standard equipment at home.

It was not only the organs: temperature caused an unusual situation in my first recital south of the forty-ninth parallel – at Evanston – where somewhat extreme wintry conditions were in operation, snow and frost, but inside a temperature of 78 Fahrenheit. This was quite unheard of in any English place of worship – in my experience, at any rate – and constituted a hazard in that the pages of my scores, on becoming deprived of their accustomed moisture content, curled up to an alarming extent, taking quite a while to straighten out and become usable.

A certain amount of crossing of the border separating Canada from the United States was necessary, but not as laborious an undertaking as between countries east of the Atlantic. I began at Montreal, and at Ottawa was given hospitality by Gerald Wheeler, organist of the cathedral and Jennifer his wife. Gerald had worked at Saint Paul's Cathedral with John Dykes Bower and had not long been in Canada. The Norman and Beard organ was a great pleasure with some beautiful flutes, a 'superb trumpet that sticks out horizontally at the congregation' and some 'gorgeous classical noises' as I informed Priscilla on 5 April. After the recital I was told of the tremendous effect that Hindemith's third sonata had had upon a young teenage boy in the audience. He was very much impressed with the beauty of it, and this was somewhat of a surprise to me, having not yet myself reached that exalted state of appreciation of this music. I had not taken it into my repertoire too willingly, and this was the only occasion, out of the many performances I gave, that any remark, favourable or otherwise, had reached my ears, and I was sorry not to meet the boy. There was one comment, however, which was rather interesting but which did not relate to the music. It concerned a misprint in the title of the third movement, which is based on an old German tune, *I bid her then*, when the 'i' became 'e'.

Grace Church, Toronto was the next port of call, where Derek Holman ran the music. Then across the border to Evanston and an Austin organ with a rather confusing system for adjusting the pistons. You pressed and held the piston, the while changing the stops. This led more than once to accidental changes that were rather inconvenient.

Having met Alick Maclean in Scarborough in the early 1930s, it was of the greatest interest to meet his son Quentin. This was at Grace Church on the Hill, Toronto, when he was in the audience (and so was Healey Willan who, on account of a choir practice, arrived too late to hear his *Passacaglia*). Quentin Maclean and Healey Willan were great friends. Maclean was extremely well known in England as a cinema organist in the 1930s but he was also a fine player of Bach with a splendid technique. He cut a similar figure to that which I remember of his father and was indeed an impressive and somewhat awesome, large-built person. At my Toronto recital in 1961 I remember feeling a little dwarfed in the presence of two such eminent musicians, even though Healey was the easier and less formidable of the two. Quite soon afterwards Quentin Maclean died of cancer, to Healey's great grief.

This leads me to the somewhat macabre statement that, several times during my life, meeting eminent people in like manner has been followed not long afterwards by their death. I am aware that it is sheer coincidence and worthy of no more than passing mention; but such things do intrigue me. Apart from Quentin Maclean perhaps the most notable is Marcel Dupré; the account of my meeting with whom is written elsewhere. This was just six weeks before his death. Another was G Donald Harrison, the eminent organ builder who attended my recital at the Temple Church on 16 June 1955 with Henry Willis III who afterwards introduced me to him. He died a year and two days later. I was also just in time to see Ruth Draper several times on what I believe was her last London appearance, on the evenings of RCO examination days when I was at a loose end. Finally, when I went to Lyons in 1983 at the behest of Patrice Caire to help in the judging of the Improvisation Contest, the panel was in the extremely capable hands of Pierre Cochereau. He was vital and energetic, full of fun and – younger than I – good for many years to come. It was therefore a shock when he died suddenly shortly afterwards.

At Chicago airport I was met by Jack Goode and his wife and was staggered by the enormous scale of the skyscrapers along the Lake Shore Drive, and driving under the post office that had allowed the road to be put through it (or the post office to be built across it). Mr Boe, organist of Saint Luke's, arranged an evening meal at his house at which a fellow guest was Leo Sowerby, at that time organist of Saint James' Episcopal Church in Chicago. He was rated the chief composer of church and organ music in the United States. I had already met him at the 1957 International Congress at Westminster Abbey and was to do so again at Washington Cathedral a few years later. He was friendly and unassuming.

Next to Portland, Oregon, after which, on making my way to the next recital in Christ Church Cathedral, Victoria, British Columbia I changed planes at Seattle where a rather extraordinary happening occurred. Along with the other passengers waiting for the connecting plane I strolled about to fill in the time and keep the circulation going, taking little notice of anybody else, when suddenly a middle-aged lady asked me 'Are you Francis Jackson?' Thousands of miles from home and surely far enough away from any place where I could be recognised, a slight feeling of irritation was the first reaction – can I not be left alone even on the furthest distance America can offer from York, England? But only momentary; she was delightful and quickly quelled my puzzlement. She gave me her name – it rang a faint bell – and explained that she had been a great friend of my grandfather's family (he died in 1904), knew them all well in the vicarage at Ebberston near Scarborough, my father the youngest of them being then in his early teens. She had caught the facial resemblance. This was not perhaps quite so remarkable since she was aware that I was to visit those parts, though still some distance away. She was still in touch with my Aunt Sybil, my father's eldest sister, after some years' residence in Victoria and we had plenty to talk about on the flight there. Her name, Jessie Walker, was vaguely familiar from its mentions when my aunt was visiting us at home, but had been of little interest to me at that young age, with next to no prospect of my ever meeting her. I never came to know anything of her family history or her activities, and at that time she must have been aged around eighty. I heard from her again at York, just before setting off on another tour of the States in April 1967; she hoped to be in the gallery for my recital – alas I have no record or remembrance of whether she made it. The audience at my 1961 recital was said to number one thousand.

I was staying at Sidney, British Columbia, close to Victoria with the family of Gray Campbell, publisher of books, whose wife Eleanor was a great friend of Priscilla's before she left England with her Canadian husband. This was a God-given respite, of three or four days when my need for rest and quiet was rigorously respected. I was also shown some of the beauties of that delectable part of the world (of which a local newspaper quoted my expressed opinion that it was like the south of England), including ascending the staircase to the console of the carillon for a demonstration by Mr Berginck, a somewhat hair-raising procedure, with minimal protection (as it seemed) between all the girders, struts and supports of the skeleton bell tower.

This happy and welcome interlude had to come to an end, and I was duly taken to Sidney airport for the plane to Edmonton, but not before I had crossed the Strait of Georgia to play in Saint Andrew's Wesley United Church in Vancouver. And this was a notable occurrence – or its aftermath was. My host bought two newspapers for me to read on the plane about my efforts of the previous evening. We did not expect, on opening the *Vancouver Sun*, to see a headline claiming 'Musical Message lost by Organist'. Our dance was turned into mourning, though not for long. The writer – a young singer apparently – who admitted that he knew nothing about organ playing, found my playing 'most unsatisfactory'. There was too much middle and bass tone, and 'absence of normal musical values, phrasing, cadence, dynamic change, rubato, accent, rhythmic tension, etc.'. I was observed 'at work at the console, such a busy man! Poking and pushing and pulling things, one eye on the music, one on the instrumental adjustments, hands and feet flying'. On further scrutiny, the initial shock was somewhat allayed as we realized that a 'loose terminology, a completely erroneous conception of organ performances, and a veritable braggadocio of unauthenticated musical terms' (as appeared later in a letter from an anonymous correspondent) left the reader 'with little accurate information about the concert'. So, with some apprehension the other paper, the *British Columbian*, was consulted. Suffice it to quote the headline 'Organ recital delights large church audience'. I was able to board the plane more or less content. I think this can be rated as one of the two most derogatory pieces of press coverage ever directed at me. There were others, of course, varying in the extent of their criticism, some more deserved than others. After all, considering the wide variety of opinions held by critics, whose experience of performance may at times be outside their range of experience and preference (let alone the bewildering types of venue, acoustic, standard, and the training they had undergone) there is bound to be uncertainty in what is reported, and one learns to take whatever comes.

Several years – decades in fact – later, I was conducting *Messiah* in the Minster with the York Musical Society and securing what was generally considered to be a very satisfactory performance. The following day I bought an evening local newspaper and eagerly prepared to read its opinion, for which purpose I sought a well-lit shop window, to be taken aback to find something similar to Vancouver, causing me to wonder if the writer had been at some other concert altogether. I later learned that he was a student, with the initials JC (but with no religious connotation, as suggested to me by a canon of the church). He, too, duly received his just deserts by the same medium in the course of the next few days.

In Vancouver I was delighted to meet again Hugh MacLean, erstwhile organ scholar at King's College, Cambridge who had given the first broadcast of a piece of mine called *Toccata, Chorale and Fugue* and had used the *Toccata* as the final voluntary of a rather famous long-playing disc of evensong in the college chapel, in which the Stanford canticles in G were a notable item. He possessed two pianos on which we amused and rather complimented ourselves with an *ad hoc* sight-read account of Vaughan Williams' *Introduction and Fugue,* a fine piece written in 1946 for Cyril Smith and Phyllis Sellick that is seldom to be heard.

Edmonton's unfinished cathedral, lofty and slightly resonant, contained a very pleasing organ, and my stay with Hugh Bancroft and Eldred his wife was very enjoyable. Southward next and into the United States once more, to Sioux Falls in South Dakota state; then to Akron, Ohio, some 40 miles south of Lake Erie. Next, to Canada once more, renewing acquaintance with Kingston and George Maybee. At Saint John New Brunswick, a letter I wrote to Priscilla reported that the recital here 'was a great success' and that 'There had not been a big do since 1934 so it was really quite a bold venture' for those who promoted it.

On to Saint Martin in the Fields, Philadelphia, where I was wonderfully entertained by Quaker friends of Priscilla's, Tessa (née

Rowntree, of York) and Jack Cadbury. Next to Saint George in Stuyvesant Square, New York, where Charles Henderson was the organist; then Pittsburgh where I spent some time with an old York chorister Percy Procter and his wife. He seemed to be relishing still his mischievous behaviour as in the days when Tertius Noble was at the Minster. Many years afterwards, both having moved to the States, they met, Percy reintroducing himself to Noble and withholding his name, describing himself as the worst behaved boy he ever had. 'Is it Procter?' immediately volunteered Noble, who evidently had cause to remember him all that long afterwards.

While in New York I stayed at Union Theological Seminary with Robert and Mary Baker. It was he who caused this tour to happen; he became a wonderful friend. I did a master class there and also spoke at the dinner of the American Guild of Organists, which was designated a Banquet. I was taken to the Cathedral of Saint John the Divine – said to be an eighth of a mile long – where Alec Wyton's choir sang 'Me in G'. My letter at the time says that the Cathedral was not so impressively large: 'the Minster is bigger…' Saint Thomas's church on Fifth Avenue was also on the schedule, with all its TT Noble connexions, and a meeting with the then organist William Self, who I was to meet again some years later in Worcester, Massachusetts, at his church of All Saints.

On my way to Washington I stayed at Baltimore in order to meet Arthur Howes, leading light in the Organ Institute, with whom at that time I had a common interest in the Organ Reform movement. The organ in the National Cathedral at Washington had what must have been the unique feature of an adjustable pedal-board. This could be raised or lowered by the pressing of an appropriate button, and was there to accommodate the widely differing physique of the two organists. Paul Callaway was, I think, somewhat below average height, while his assistant Doctor Richard Dirksen was very much above it. The height of the seat was also variable, which meant quite a deal of care to attain the right adjustment of everything, but could assure a completely comfortable situation for organists of whatever shape or dimension. It was here that Jack Cadbury was sent into raptures at the start of a piece of mine called *Diversion for Mixtures*, a kind of toccata *perpetuum mobile*. And in the south transept I witnessed the unveiling of a musicians' window which prominently displayed the name of Vaughan Williams – a compliment to English music.

My Washington host and hostess, Bill and Nancy Tufts, welcomed me to their spacious house in the countryside not far outside the city. Nancy, an authority on handbell ringing, had published books on the subject. The house stood within sight of the Potomac River, and had, to my great delight, wisterias growing in profusion among the lush grass, to the extent that their plentiful seedlings were considered a 'nuisance' – something I could never have labelled one of my favourite plants. It was no trouble at all to have one of those seedlings dug up for me to bring home to Minster Court, where it flourished, having spent four days at the bottom of my suitcase as I discharged the last of my commissions in Bermuda.

Here I had come from Washington, leaving at 18.15, changing planes at New York's Idlewild airport and thence, in a Viscount, landing in Bermuda five minutes before midnight where I was met by Sir Hereward Watlington who, with others, came right up to the plane to meet their guests, such were the easy conditions and lack of restriction. It was a surprise, on stepping out of the plane, to be greeted by the unexpectedly warm air, and the narrowness of the roads, like English country lanes. The organ for my recital in Devonshire church was a Willis, of the familiar pattern so often met with back in England.

The tour of the USA ended in time for me to get back to England early in June. There was no direct flight, which meant a return to New York for arrival in old York in time for a rehearsal of the wedding of the Duke of Kent to Miss Katharine Worsley the following day. Priscilla met me at Heathrow with a hiccup to report. The anthem *Audi Filia* that had been proposed and approved, was found on closer scrutiny to contain some words that were considered unsuitable. Which words they were I never found out, but it is Priscilla's firm conviction that it was the phrase 'forget also thine own people and thy father's house' that went against the grain. My own supposition that the mention of the Queen 'in a vesture of gold wrought about with diverse colours' might have been a stumbling block too, though less likely. The Dean's choice of an alternative for the royal wedding was the second of Holst's *Two*

Psalms, 'Lord, who hast made us for thine own' which served excellently well.

It can be imagined what a heyday this created for the press at the time. I was alerted by Priscilla (in almost her first words to me on arrival at Heathrow) that on no account were we to say anything about it to any reporter; such was the strict injunction from on high. What it was thought I would say I cannot imagine, for I was completely ignorant of the situation. We managed to achieve King's Cross without incident and had taken our seats in the York train when, sure enough, a reporter found us, though how he did it I have no idea. I cannot remember how I dealt with him, but he had to accept that it was impossible for me to make any comment as I knew nothing whatever about the matter. The previous evening, Priscilla had been tracked down at her uncle's London residence and, in reply to her assurance that she knew nothing about it, she was informed 'Well you must know something; you're his wife, aren't you?'

The anthem *Audi Filia* was now published by Oxford University Press on the understanding that it was to be used for the royal wedding: it was therefore embarrassing to have to go back on that assurance, although I had no part in dealing with the situation, being in America. I hope the publishers were not too upset. Occasionally since then appreciative comments about *Audi Filia* have reached me which I have found somewhat surprising but of course encouraging.

Incidentally, it is never remotely possible to foretell what kind of a reception one's works will have. Benjamin Britten appeared to regret the success of his *Te Deum* in C, which he regarded as sub-standard: 'I wrote it at school', he said disparagingly in my hearing.

Back at home, all was well – the choir was in good shape. A recital at Norwich Cathedral followed; more rehearsing, and then the wedding itself just under a fortnight after leaving Bermuda. The Widor *Toccata*, which was the 'Wedding March' as the couple left the ceremony, seemed to have been a very popular item. For several months afterwards and even longer, I had requests by post for 'the music at the wedding', to such an extent that I typed out (with carbon copies) a stock of lists of the entire programme of music used during the service. Would that photocopying had been possible then. After a long time it dawned on me that it was simply the Widor that was their interest. It took quite a while to come to an end. After the wedding service, we drove the sixteen or so miles to Hovingham for the reception in the grounds of the Hall, which was certainly something to remember on that sunny summer day.

‖O‖

There were other musical matters to be occupied with as the year unfolded. The annual congress of the Incorporated Association of Organists took place in York during August. As President, I was required to give an address at the meeting in the Guildhall, so something to talk about was to be thought up – more broadcasts of organ recitals? Organs in Spain would be good for us to hear… And then – oh yes, the Widor's supplanting of the Mendelssohn for the wedding march would fill quite a useful space: why have a march anyway; why use a makeshift version for the organ when there was ample material available among the considerable repertoire of genuine organ music; and why (here was a thought that would never enter our heads here in the next century) use music in church which was written for a secular purpose and which, moreover, had come to be so misused in the music hall whenever there was any suggestion or mention of marriage? The subject proved a more fertile one than I had anticipated. A lively series of press opinion and letters ensued, continuing for quite a while.

In the course of the animatedly interested comment from many quarters that ensued for some time, I gathered the *Toccata* was used at Widor's church, S. Sulpice, for royal affairs and for weddings and suchlike to do solely with the composer's family, and that a strict embargo was imposed on its use for any other purpose. I heard it hinted more than once that I had set some organists a problem; those who were probably not in the virtuoso class or had an inadequate instrument, which would have rejoiced the heart of Doctor Ralph Vaughan Williams as mentioned earlier. Subsequently, there was a certain amount of discussion in the musical press as to the speed at which it should be played, for Widor changed his mind more than once, as the various editions show. As is well known, his own recording of it must be by far the slowest performance ever, one certainly not taken as a yardstick by some enthusiastic players one has heard who (probably) manage to negotiate the rapidly repeated chords with great *élan* at a furious pace.

Forceful opinions on both sides, letters to the Yorkshire Post and the Times; a Daily Record feature with the headline *Wedding 'Battle'* and picturing eight young people, some anticipating marriage, all in favour of keeping the usual choice: 'A wedding wouldn't be the same without *Here comes the bride*', said one. Herbert Woodhouse in 'The Star, Johannesburg' quoted and seemed tacitly to concur with my somewhat dubious statement that to take the Mendelssohn from the stage and present a travesty of it at a church wedding was 'almost sinful'. Also on my side was Doctor Erik Routley, well-known as writer on church and music matters. His long article in the British Weekly in late October delved deeply into all angles and suggested several optional pieces for the exit of the happy couple such as the Bach *Fantasia* in G, *In dir ist Freude*, Karg-Elert's *Nun Danket*, or 'almost any Bach', as well as several hymns to avoid: 'OPL' (O perfect love) and Crimond; most weddings being 'strictly idolatrous, sentimental and religiously depressing occasions' – an utterance which, in its turn was duly dealt with as could be expected.

There was another controversy for the organists' congress, concerning the concert at Castle Howard. It was my idea to have the music of a single composer – who but my so greatly admired Maurice Ravel – the idea being to introduce this very special music to some who were not aware of it and who, I felt sure, could not but be overtaken by its attractiveness. However, such turned out not to be the case. '200 Organists didn't revel in Ravel' according to our local newspaper. Some preferred to remain outside 'to enjoy the evening air and so missed the very well written *Trio* ...'. True, the Violin Sonata and the work for violin and cello are not easy to appreciate at a first hearing, but the *Valses Nobles et Sentimentales* are not problematic. The *Trio* likewise was 'nearer to our experience and left us thinking that perhaps Ravel was not so bad after all'.

Another matter to enliven the scene arose as a result of the organ recital given by Ronald Perrin in which, the headline stated, 'Minster organ disappoints by over-restraint' and 'They've taken the guts out of the Minster organ', referring to its restoration a year earlier. At the time there had been similar criticism of the changes that were made, which appeared to be opinions held by adherents of the pre-baroque revival, whose worst fears were perhaps being realised. The recitalist, however, was not to be blamed: 'It was well planned; and it was well played'. In the end all was well. Saturday's Press reported that 'If Monday's Minster organ "had its guts taken out" they were all back again last night'. The listeners, who had for the earlier event been seated in the nave some distance from the organ (and with the enormous space of the transepts and the central tower between them and the sound source to traverse) were now much nearer to it, feeling decidedly happier; the concluding item (Dupré in B) 'left us all wanting to cheer'.

Midway through the following month, catching us all refreshed after our summer break, the enthronement of another archbishop was held. Doctor Donald Coggan began his thirteen-year spell before himself departing for Canterbury as had his predecessor at York, Michael Ramsey, whom we had welcomed to the high office just over five years earlier. I had written a fanfare (in G) for the enthronement service, an item which on previous such occasions had been supplied by brass players. The service brought forth another letter that gave much pleasure, from Bishopthorpe, dated 14 September 1961.

My dear Dr Jackson

I want you to know how deeply grateful I am to you for all that you did to make yesterday's great service so beautiful and so great an offering of praise to God. I cannot tell you what the music on such an occasion means to me.

I realise that a great deal of work has been entailed for you and for the men and boys of the choir. I should be grateful if you would convey to them an expression of my very sincere thanks. I so much look forward to meeting you, in the organ loft or elsewhere!

Yours very sincerely, Donald Ebor

In fact, the new Archbishop made an early opportunity of a meeting, calling at Minster Court soon after his enthronement and we became acquainted. Edward, aged four, had been told and had some idea of what to expect. He formed the notion that a throne would be needed, so he used all available cushions to construct one. Unfortunately, order had to be restored among the soft furnishings so the Archbishop had to manage without a throne on that occasion. However, as he and I came down the stairs from the drawing-room, Edward was standing below in the hall transfixed. I thought I detected some puzzlement, as if he could not understand why the Archbishop was not arrayed in all his fine robes – cope, mitre, staff and all.

It was always a pleasure to see Doctor Coggan on his visits to the Minster; he was always interested in the music. One Saturday, he came up to the organ loft for evensong, and I allotted him the job of giving the note for the unaccompanied anthem which I was to conduct, for which purpose I pulled out the appropriate stop and placed a sixpenny piece on the key to be pressed. This was to be his fee for his service, but he left it behind. The canticles were the controversial set written for Saint John's College, Cambridge, by Michael Tippett – the second of the two performances we ever attempted. His tactful comment was that it was 'a breakthrough...'

Once, he and Mrs Coggan came to an evening party that we held in aid of the Royal College of Organists, and in our turn we went to Bishopthorpe for a musical evening in which I took part in the C minor piano quartet of Fauré. He turned the pages for me and was clearly bowled over by the passionate music.

When in the mid-1970s I embarked on the biography of Sir Edward Bairstow and told Doctor Coggan, he jumped in quickly and eagerly, asking to be allowed to read the proofs. He admitted to possessing the necessary skills for this purpose, and I was naturally surprised that someone in his position would wish to bother with such a task and apparently to take pleasure in doing it. However, it was twenty years or so before any proofs were ready, by which time Lord Coggan was retired from his office of head of the Church of England and was living in Winchester. But he kept his word, returning the corrected material in a very short time, with only very few errors overlooked.

||O||

Back to 1961: I revelled in playing the organ of Saint George's Hall Liverpool on 18 September, with its huge variety of tone and enormous power. The Liverpool Daily Post decided that I had attacked the Mozart *Fantasia* K 608 almost in a temper, which pleased me, having never regarded it in that sort of light. But that is certainly a valid concept. The writer (of initials NB) was convinced that Mozart, 'a non-organ composer, had some of the greatest ideas of all' and that Mendelssohn's Fifth Sonata 'sounded tame and trite in comparison', and I wondered how much of that was my doing. He was, however, kind enough to say that he hoped I would go back there again soon.

At one of the evensongs of the Three Choirs Festival at Hereford, the *Magnificat* and *Nunc Dimittis* I had composed at the behest of Melville Cook was introduced for the first time. It became known as the Hereford Service and was experimental in being in two voice parts instead of the usual four, so that any combination of soprano, alto, tenor, or bass (even, improbably, alto and tenor only) might work. I think it had a modicum of success for Novellos reprinted it, though as ill luck would have it, at the very moment I sent them an SATB version hoping for its conversion to respectability. But I took comfort in the knowledge that its unusual format (with trebles and tenors on the upper line, in octaves, and altos and basses likewise on the lower) had escaped the notice of John Dykes Bower who heard it at Hereford, imagining it to be the usual layout for four voices.

Over the years I was to meet Boris Ord occasionally, at the Cathedral Organists' Conference, or when I played at King's. He was always good company, interesting and amusing. Priscilla thought that playing the organ in a rather crouching position wearing his black gown he resembled a large black beetle. Once, when he came for one of Dean Milner-White's newly introduced Epiphany processions, he took me to task (in no measured terms) for taking the carol 'O'er the hill and o'er the vale' too slowly.

During his last illness David Willcocks took me to see him. He was in bed, reading, and said practically nothing. A sad visit. This was after evensong in the chapel when David had let me play the final voluntary. I chose the first movement of Guilmant's first sonata, and David related to Boris how I was thrown into confusion, while playing it, by an edition which was different from the one I possessed and had failed to check beforehand. On 30 December Boris died aged 64, his *Times* obituary appearing on the first day of 1962.

The first recital of the New Year was delayed for a week and a day when I was struck down by an attack of influenza. The venue was Godalming, with its newly rebuilt organ in the parish church. The Surrey Advertiser and County Times reported that 'one lover of organ music … travelled by motor-cycle from Rochester, only to be disappointed'. However, he made the trip again, a distance of sixty or seventy miles in January conditions. Most of the recital was broadcast later on the BBC Third Programme.

That same month, two distinguished guests graced the annual dinner of the York and District Organists' Association. Marilyn Mason, from the University of Ann Arbor, Michigan, well-known recitalist who was playing a concert in the Minster, made a speech describing the organ as one of the best she had ever played (which is a widely held view, and is my own opinion, to be sure). The other speaker was Sir Thomas Armstrong, Principal of the Royal Academy of Music and for a spell of two years President of the Incorporated Association of Organists, in which office I had succeeded him. He commented on the difficulty of recruiting boys into church choirs and regretted the passing of boys' voices from the London scene and that it would be increasingly difficult to get men for the choirs later. This was an early recognition of the problem that would have to be faced sooner or later.

The York Symphony Orchestra's spring concert contained the Beethoven *Eroica* Symphony in the first half. After the interval Frederic Waine took over the baton for the *Hebrides* overture and the César Franck *Variations Symphonique* for me to play the piano part.

It is perhaps worth mentioning a headline in the Daily Mail of 16 June: 'Cathedral recital is a sell-out' which charted a fairly unusual situation, organs being not the most popular of concert instruments. This was Coventry where there were estimated to be 1500 in the audience – a rare occurrence for an organ recital. There was much interest at that time in the new cathedral built beside its bombed predecessor, and the organ, only recently placed there, was likewise a special attraction. One of the items I included was the recently published work of Brian Brockless, *Prelude, Toccata and Chaconne*, which the composer kindly came to hear. The cathedral had been consecrated only three weeks before this, and among the events included in the celebrations was a work I wrote for speaker and organ founded on the biblical Daniel stories. Entitled *Daniel in Babylon*, it was written and performed by John Stuart Anderson for the first time on 10 June 1962, and it contained poems he composed especially to go between the scenes. Later I set the poems to music for unaccompanied choir and in this form the work received a good many performances. It was followed by a similar piece, dealing with the life of William Tyndale the translator of the bible. We called it *A Time of Fire* on account of the burning of books and, eventually, of Tyndale himself. Both works were later recorded on the Amphion label in Leeds Parish Church, with the inspired co-operation of the Saint Peter's Singers conducted by Simon Lindley.

Of the thirty recitals of 1962, four were inaugurations: Carlisle Cathedral; Whitworth Hall (University of Manchester); Bute Hall (University of Glasgow) and Bradford Cathedral. A press cutting from the same year headed 'Latest Wills' and dated 20 September 1962 contained the information that my good childhood friend Cecil Hylton Wybergh, of Exmouth, Devon, and previously of Escrick Park near York where I came to know him, had left the sum of £85,401. Coincidentally among the other twelve names appeared another linked with my choristership, that of John Ireland, of Washington, Sussex – designated 'musical composer, famously writer of symphonic music of a high quality', the song *Sea Fever* (Masefield's poem) widely sung, and his morning and evening canticles in F which were regularly used at the Minster and popular with the choir, as was his anthem *Greater love*, which begins with the words 'Many waters cannot quench love'. He had lived in a converted windmill.

A variety of happenings proved 1963 to be an eventful year. Perhaps the chief of these was the ending of Eric Milner-White's notable tenure of the deanery, held for twenty-two years from 1941. He died on 11 June aged 79. His work on the stained glass proved of great benefit, at the time when a good deal of it was to be replaced after its exile for safety during the war. He was an acknowledged expert when Dean of King's College, Cambridge, and this is said to have been a prime factor in his being appointed to come to the Minster's aid at a critical juncture: not that all his procedures have since received universal approval – which, of course, is likely to happen in any walk of life. There can be no doubting the Minster's good fortune in having had the benefit of his devoted care of all the Minster's facets; chief among these was the music. For his own exequies the service and the music were the same as he had prepared for Lord Halifax. Rather than the Order for Burial, it followed 'the more ancient and solemn Form of Requiem habitually rendered in this Cathedral on All Souls Day'.

Requiem aeternam by Walford Davies began the service and Charles Wood's Phrygian setting provided the ninefold *Kyrie* and the rest of the sung liturgy. The hymns were 'Let saints on earth', 'Rock of Ages' and 'The King of Love' to the tune Saint Columba.

Earlier in the year – on the Sunday before Easter, its accustomed day – the Saint Matthew Passion attained its fiftieth yearly performance, of which Doctor Bairstow had conducted thirty-two. Despite its being a truncated version when first put on at York in 1914 by Bairstow (lasting two hours and a quarter instead of three hours and three-quarters) it had attracted an audience to fill the Minster's nave. Some had made lengthy journeys to attend. Opportunities to hear the work at that time were rare before the coming of broadcasting and recording – or the motorway. The Golden Jubilee presentation offered a welcome chance to mark the occasion, and it was not difficult to decide what form this should take: naturally, to do the whole work without any omissions. This received enthusiastic approval, not least from Ernest Bradbury whose long article in the Yorkshire Post in advance of the performance remarked upon the fact that the earnest searching for authenticity in performance, an activity which at that time was engaging the minds and energies of performers far and wide, had done nothing, or very little, to cause the heart to leap up. He praised Bairstow's approach, despite its unaccompanied chorales and piano continuo which were frowned upon by the pundits, but which 'lit up the mind and the imagination, and brought Bach's message home as today's performances seldom do' (that is, those of the 1960s). His critique of our performance, bearing the headline 'Uncut Version of Saint Matthew Passion' was most generous, proposing that 'In a sense, the work that Doctor Bairstow started in 1914 has at last borne fruit', and observing that at York 'everybody who has heard past performances has been aware that they have been taking part in an experience that leaves them profoundly moved. Palm Sunday 1963 has made history in York Minster': a performance without cuts and 'of the highest calibre'. The Princess Royal came from Harewood for the performance, as she had often done in previous years.

After this major change in the half-century progress of the great work in York, other changes came about. For the following year it seemed that something rather less Herculean should be attempted (though not a return to the incomplete Saint Matthew), Bach's *Passion according to Saint John* therefore was the obvious and perfect choice. This provided us with a challenge and a chance to savour more of the majesty of his supreme creations. And so continued the yearly alternation of these two works until my departure from the scene in 1982 when the reins were taken over by Philip Moore.

Towards the end of April the Leith Hill Festival was held. Founded by Vaughan Williams and held each year with his close involvement, its aim was to encourage singing in towns and villages by public competition and one or more concerts by the combined competing choirs. It was after Vaughan Williams had died that I once took a hand in the adjudication process. The conducting then was in the hands of Doctor William Cole, who directed a concert version of *Hugh the Drover*, VW's opera of 1914. There was always a preliminary ritual singing by the combined choirs, of a part song expressly written by Vaughan Williams to his wife Ursula's words: 'What is the meaning of spring this fine spring morning' is how I remember the start of it. It is not possible to come by a copy of 'Song for a Spring Festival' since it is (or was then) closely guarded for the sole use of the Leith Hill festival choirs.

The month of May had three pleasurable happenings. William was admitted chorister of Saint George's Chapel, Windsor, where he came under the benign influence of the organist Sidney Campbell and began the daily singing of the offices within inches of the tomb of poor Anne Boleyn and in the midst of so much history. In due course his young brother Edward joined him.

Priscilla and I paid visits to Adlington Hall and Addington Palace within nine days of each other, respectively on the eleventh (in Cheshire) and twentieth (at Croydon, Surrey). The former visit was for a recital on the famous and unique organ of circa 1670 which had not long before been restored to playing condition by Noel Mander, after lying in a ruinous state and seemingly beyond any hope of repair for close on 150 years. This was an engrossing enterprise, and in complete contrast to the kind of organ one was used to, with its mere thirteen stops and no pedals. Required also was a completely different choice of pieces: the usual great Bach works were impossible.

An item which I included at a later visit (on 4 July 1980) was chosen as being appropriate for American Independence Day and as a gesture towards American relatives of the Legh family (owners of the Hall) who were present. This was *Moon River*, that evocative waltz tune by Henry Mancini. It turned out after all, however, to be less feasible as an organ solo than I had anticipated (and was totally anachronistic in any case) but the situation was saved by the sporting collaboration of Joan Rodgers who sang it (with complete and entrancing effect) along with other unusual bedfellows, Handel, Haydn, Dvorak. Neither was Gershwin overlooked: his *Summertime* was the penultimate piece in the programme. The final item was one of Scott Joplin's Rags – *Fig Leaf* – demonstrating the fact that advantage was being taken of the opportunity to include pieces that were forbidden in sacred buildings, as was the practice at that time.

The Addington event was a very special one. Once used by the Archbishops of Canterbury, the palace now housed the Royal School of Church Music, and was being graced by the Queen who stayed for three hours, had lunch, and heard – and enjoyed – some of the students' efforts. I was to be honoured with a Fellowship, along with Doctor Leo Sowerby, the American composer, George Maybee of Kingston Cathedral, Ontario, and Mervyn Byers, organist of Saint Andrew's Cathedral, Sydney, who had formerly been organist of Selby Abbey and Bridlington Priory. Accommodation being limited in the palace, lunch for an overflow (of which Priscilla and I formed a part) was kindly provided by Sir William and Lady McKie down the road at a Croydon hotel (Sir William was still organist of Westminster Abbey). Arthur Hutchings, still professor of music at Durham, was one of the new Fellows. I have a recollection of his informing Her Majesty that on a visit she had once made to the university, the students, in their anxiety to appear all clean and presentable, used up every drop of hot water in the system. This was very typical of Professor Hutchings who had a plentiful store of amusing tales that he relished to relate.

For three weeks in June and July came the fifth of the York Triennial Festivals which had proved so successful since their beginnings in 1951. There was the customary variety of events, recitals, concerts, of which Rossini's *Petite Messe Solenelle* was of particular interest. In its original form with harmonium and piano for accompaniment, and with four excellent soloists, it was the home team's (York Musical Society) contribution to the choral concerts. The Britten *War Requiem*, under Meredith Davies' direction was broadcast, with the Huddersfield Choral Society, the BBC Symphony Orchestra and the Minster choristers, perched up on the pulpitum. Monteverdi's *Vespers*, which in previous festivals had proved a novel and striking work for the final concert, was displaced by Michael Tippett's *Child of our Time* under the baton of Norman del Mar with the London Symphony Orchestra and the Sheffield Choral Society. Allan Wicks returned to the Minster from Canterbury to present a daring organ programme entirely of the music of Messiaen, *Les Corps Glorieux* and *Messe de la Pentecôte*, which at that time was a revelation to frequenters of organ recitals.

A second appearance of mine in Saint George's Hall, Liverpool, included the Bairstow *Sonata* and Hindemith's Third, but the press write-up favoured Frank Martin's *Passacaille*, although by far the most praise was reserved for the final item, the *Toccata and Fugue* in F of Bach.

In October I took part in a concert of unusual interest in the Duke's Hall of the Royal Academy of Music in London where Eric Greene conducted a choir of blind singers in *Zadok the Priest* and Rossini's *Stabat Mater*. Called 'Pro Canto Singers' the choir was Eric Greene's idea and, with much patient preparation, a remarkable success. Vaughan Williams' *Serenade to Music* was also performed by sixteen soloists, as at its first performance in 1938: on this occasion six of the original number were there to join in. At the end of the month it was my privilege to play the Father Smith organ at the west end of Cambridge's University Church which had been recently restored by the firm of Hill, Norman and Beard. David Willcocks turned the pages.

Then back in York once more was the symphony orchestra's second concert of 1963. This began with the *Jupiter Symphony* followed by a delightful *Villanelle* by Stephen Dodgson. After the interval came the Fauré Suite *Pélleas et Mélisande* and, to finish, the Bach *Concerto* in C for two harpsichords which, said the critique next day, called out 'a torrent of applause from the large audience'. For this performance, and through the generosity of the Castle Museum authorities we were privileged to borrow the two-hundred-year-old harpsichord made in York by Thomas Haxby, still in excellent working order, which it was my own good fortune to be playing. Percy Lovell, then director of music at Bootham School, had taken the trouble to bring and to play his own, modern instrument. Considering what hazards can present themselves on occasions such as this, when different instruments are involved with, for instance, possible divergences of pitch, this exercise was remarkably free of troubles. There was 'a serene and sustained gaiety' causing the writer of the press review, CH Schofield, to express the encouraging idea that help of a financial nature was deserved by the orchestra 'who, in the Bach and Fauré made rings round many a more highly-publicised body of players'.

The orchestra's next concert the following March was also of a special nature, as far as its mostly amateur members were concerned. It took place in the Minster (there being at that time no concert hall of a suitable size in the city), a building whose acoustics could be either an enhancement or a hazard. Not only was Beethoven's *Coriolan* Overture there at the beginning, a prelude to Mozart's fortieth symphony, with Handel's sixteenth and longest organ concerto (in F) up to the interval. Frederic Waine who played it was also there at the organ for the final work, the third *Symphony* of Saint-Saëns, and Mrs Whitworth had for her partner in the piano duet the Reverend Noel Kemp-Welch, then chaplain at Saint Peter's School and previously Warden of Saint Michael's College, Tenbury. It was certainly a memorable event; the generous press review ended by pronouncing it 'an evening of distinct and decisive characterisation to reward a larger-than-usual audience'.

||O||

At the Minster, Dean Milner-White's successor was appointed. Being naturally curious as to who would be our next dean we had been looking out for any indications that might tell us something. One day, sure enough, a car was espied outside the Deanery, plainly visible from our house. Recourse to our AA Handbook revealed that it bore a Nottingham number-plate. John Dykes Bower, when I next saw him, immediately suggested a cleric he knew of, vicar of one of the churches there. That proved wide of the mark but we were in the right locality. Our neighbour Canon Reginald Cant wrote to me on 2 November with advance news that the next dean was to be Alan Richardson, professor of theology at Nottingham University and previously canon of Durham.

In the meantime, in February 1964 a Yorkshire Post headline said 'Frugal dean left £93,377' and gave details of Dean Milner-White's many legacies – fifty pounds each to five of the junior Minster clergy and myself 'in gratitude for their splendid services to York Minster and its Dean'. His secretary, Margery Green, observed that he spent freely on cultural interests and on schools, allowing money inherited from his father to accumulate interest over the years.

Alan Richardson became his successor with all due rites and ceremonies at 3.00pm on Friday 29 May. Thus began a different kind of regime so far as the relationship of dean and choir music was concerned. There was a new feeling since I was free to put on what I liked without reference to a dean or anyone. Not that any tremendous change was perceptible; and all proceeded happily as before, to the evident satisfaction of all. One exception happened, however, when a canon thought we were doing too many anthems in Latin. This was easily dealt with, and one is inclined to wonder how Dean Milner-White would have reacted half a century later, when even the canticles are in Latin; this he would simply not have tolerated or even bothered to consider.

Just a fortnight before the Dean's installation I returned from a North American tour with twenty recitals under my belt including Washington Cathedral and former haunts at Toronto and Kingston. The first, at Bethlehem, Pennsylvania, provided me with somewhat of a lesson on the subject of jet-lag. Still being on English time and feeling in need of rest, I fell into a deep slumber only to wake up by a miracle a mere half hour before the scheduled starting time. This, as far as I was concerned, was one o'clock in the morning – not the hour of the day to feel at one's best. However, I managed to struggle through and had no complaints, but was in some doubt myself, hoping the audience's assessment was not as negative as mine. The last recital, at New London, Connecticut, was distinctly happier (as were the rest) and enabled me to be on the homeward trek, via New London, New York, London and York – in that order in the space of twenty-four hours. Having given nine recitals before going to America and another twenty-four afterwards, a fairly healthy total of fifty-three resulted for that year.

Next door to the RCO, in the Albert Hall, the fourth Handel organ concerto took me to a Prom to play. Later I visited the Mariner's Church at Dun Laoghaire near Dublin, and Canterbury Cathedral, then at Selby High School played a piano recital organised by David Gedge, organist of the Abbey and not yet translated to Brecon Cathedral. I attempted Couperin's *Dix-huitième Ordre*, Chopin's *Third Ballade*, *Movements Perpetuels* by Poulenc, and Ravel's *Le Tombeau de Couperin*, all six movements. The reviewer of the Irish recital, though grateful to me for going such a distance, thought little of the music, Bach excepted – Stanford, Fricker, Peeters, Dupré ('of an uninspiring mediocrity') – and myself, whose *Toccata, Chorale and Fugue* 'seemed to have been written to justify the composer's professional status rather than from any creative musical conviction'. Perhaps I should have sent an apology.

The His Master's Voice 'Great Cathedral Organs' series (reissued on fourteen CDs in 2011) was at its beginnings, and I was included in it. The producer was Brian Culverhouse. Two notable works were Norman Cocker's *Tuba Tune* and the Healey Willan *Introduction, Passacaglia and Fugue* which elicited no other opinion than 'There's an awful lot of echo in York Minster': this from the composer himself – no less. The recording had taken place in early March, a month before the start of the American tour. It turned out just possible to send a (proof) copy of the disc to Doctor Willan in advance of my meeting up with him in Toronto. After some days with him, without comment and my departure being imminent I ventured to ask if he had received the disc, to receive the reply already quoted. And nothing else. But I did, twice, play it in his presence and he did not appear displeased.

In November the Musical Society gave the first UK performance of *Urbs Beata* by John Joubert, which he conducted in the Minster on the twenty-first. It had already had its first performance in Saint George's Cathedral, Capetown, just a year earlier. Taking part in the York performance were the Leeds 'Young Phil', Gerald English, John Cameron and the Manchester Mozart Orchestra, playing to a packed audience who responded warmly and appreciatively. For the first half of the programme I had the great pleasure of conducting César Franck's *Symphony*, a work I knew well and enjoyed: it was chosen because the orchestration was pretty well identical with the Joubert. *Zadok the Priest* was also present.

||O||

Sam Clutton and I were quite often in touch, and when he had an organ built for him by Noel Mander for his London home, Peter Hurford and I made a recording on it. We did one side each of a long-playing record under the 'Abbey' label, Peter seeing to Dandrieu, Couperin and three of the Bach *Allein Gott* chorale preludes, while Mendelssohn, Brahms and Hindemith (*Sonata* II) fell to my lot, plus the Bach *Ach bleib bei uns* and the Dorian Toccata – for its antiphony. The record with the title 'An organ for an organ scholar' was issued in 1966, soon after the organ was installed.

The house organ, which had only ten stops, had been very craftily designed to fit into a room with a ceiling but 7 feet 9 inches high. With its two manuals and tracker action it was intended for earlier music, which Sam liked to play. I gave a public recital on the organ when it was in Saint Peter's, Bethnal Green (it had been erected here before being delivered to its Blackheath destination), having in its programme Mendelssohn, Vierne and, as in the recording to come, Hindemith, 'thereby demonstrating that an organ designed primarily for the earlier German and French repertoire can be effectively pressed into the service of some modern and romantic music if used with sufficient judgement and skill', as Austin Niland wrote in an article following the event.

The organ is now in the music faculty of the University of Cambridge where no doubt its individual character, formed with so much care and devotion, is of value for students in the study of music of earlier periods. Sam's life came to an end unexpectedly in Saint Martin in the Fields while listening to the new organ placed there, and in Saint Paul's Cathedral there was a memorial service and commemoration for him on 16 April 1991.

There was an unusual concert in July at Sledmere House near York, in aid of the Imperial Cancer Research Fund. This was supported by many of the nobility, and the chief guest was Princess Marina. The house possesses an impressive three-manual organ, a special interest of Sir Richard Sykes whose family have lived there for many generations. This organ replaced an electronic (Hammond) instrument that I knew in my Malton days, when I gave piano lessons to the young Polly Elwes, of television fame later, and her brother and sister. Their grandfather was the celebrated tenor Gervase Elwes.

Taking part in the entertainment were the actress Margaret Rutherford, lutenist Robert Spencer and John Stuart Anderson, clad in his impressive 'Daniel' raiment. He and I presented part of the monodrama *Daniel in Babylon*. Naturally the Widor *Toccata* was required and brought the proceedings to a satisfactory conclusion. A rather special memory is of the final curtain call when it was my pleasure to appear with Margaret Rutherford on my arm. She had performed extracts from *The Rivals* and *The Importance of being Ernest*.

Early in 1968 Gordon Pullin and I gave a concert in the excellent hall of Bootham School where he taught classics (combining it with the role of tenor songman in the Minster choir). The songs were by Bairstow and Ravel with a few of mine from my time in the army. The Ravel *'Histoires Naturelles'* were a challenge and wonderfully enjoyable.

A second monodrama *A Time of Fire*, which concerns the life of William Tyndale as mentioned before, was given performances in Norwich cathedral, Cromer parish church, Bristol and Wymondham Abbey. At this last I shared a copy with Doctor Statham. John Stuart Anderson, who commissioned the music from me and who provided the libretto, played Tyndale as usual and Brian Runnett the organ. There were two favourable accounts, one of the Norwich performance in the Eastern Daily Press 'the writer's initials GWG' calling it a 'Spiritual Experience'. The eminent critic Basil Maine said that the 'congregation at Cromer parish church ... heard *Tyndale* in the Broadland Singers' highly-valued performance. After a lifetime of listening to music, one does not easily judge any performance to be memorable; but this Passion Sunday experience I can only describe as such'. Much later in 2004 a performance took place in Ely cathedral, with Richard Rastall (a professor of Leeds University) as Tyndale, the chorus and vocal soloists of Saint Peter's Singers of Leeds under Simon Lindley, and Jonathan Lilley playing the organ.

Brian Runnett succeeded Doctor Statham at Norwich Cathedral, but tragically lost his life in a motoring accident in August 1970 at the age of 37 after a mere three years in the post. During this short spell he had made a notable contribution to the life of the cathedral and was greatly missed. About this time I was asked to write a *Festival Toccata* (and evening responses) for the West Riding cathedrals' yearly gathering to take place at Bradford. I dedicated it to Brian's memory and it was published some thirty years later incorporating revisions which dispelled some vague doubts I had felt at the beginning. After the long silence following its initial appearance I brought it out in its revised form at York in August 2011. However, in the meantime, a memorial recital for Brian took place in Norwich Cathedral on 13 July 2005, when it was played by Graham Barber who had served as organ scholar to Brian for the three years of his tenure as organist. Also in the programme were the *Prelude and Fugue* in E by Krebs (of which Brian had made a notable recording), three of the *Christmas Meditations* dedicated to Brian by Arthur Wills, one of the *Trois Danses* of Jehan Alain and the *Variations and Fugue on an original theme* by Max Reger, opus 73.

I was asked to help with the restoration of the unique historic (1609) organ in Hatfield House. This was to be restored by Noel Mander and I was charged with the business of arranging details. To this end, Edward and I called there on his way back to Windsor for the Christmas services. We had lunch with Lord and Lady Salisbury and were shown some of the house. Later, the restoration having been carried out, a celebration took place in the London organ works of Mander, attended by members of the Salisbury family. Pieces not requiring pedals such as I had needed for the practically contemporary Adlington Hall organ came in useful with, of course, the essential addition of the *Earl of Salisbury's Pavane* by William Byrd.

||O||

More and more the thought is borne in upon me as to what a deep divide there is between the two kinds of music, the 'pop' kind which is so much the concern of 'the music business', and the other that in my army days was referred to as 'long-haired music' (before the fashion for long hair among the male population, it was the preserve of the 'Arty'). Nowadays, apart from the Promenade concerts, Classic FM and perhaps a few other crusading spirits, it is plain that a great deal more public support goes to popular music. There are possibly two main reasons for this: little or no chance of experiencing it in the home or place of education; and, perhaps as a direct result, a kind of fear that 'classical' music is too 'upmarket' or 'posh', only to be understood or appreciated by intellectuals. What is wrong with the right kind of 'posh'? Is it not possible that a few minutes could be devoted daily as a normal activity to musical appreciation in the school curriculum? To someone fortunate to be attuned to the wonders of music, what gives rise to such aspirations is the wish that its delights and benefits could be shared by all. After all, somewhere among the almost infinite variety of music that is to be had – orchestral, choral, chamber – in its wide-ranging combinations (solo instruments, organ even) there is something to suit all tastes; not forgetting opera, which has risen dramatically in popularity in recent years. And there is always the chance to sing together. The vital thing is that children and their families should be introduced to music in a purposeful and encouraging way. Contact with music would surely have some effect, as demonstrated in the life of a chorister.

It has sometimes been thought that a chorister's education has suffered on account of the long periods spent in musical activity and services, but many would defend such a form of stimulating education. Naturally it is suitable for the more musical child – and not every one of them is necessarily keen on that type of music, or sold on religion. Nevertheless, most of those who are put to it find they enjoy it, are able to develop any latent musicianship they may have, and find a firm basis for whatever branch of music they eventually follow. It has been an immense joy and satisfaction that so many choristers of mine have made their way into the musical profession, and in a variety of ways. Who would have thought that one of them (Jeremy J Beadle) should have become a regular broadcaster on opera, the second Viennese school and all that is avant garde and up-to-date: or that another who became a lecturer at Manchester University (Robin Walker) should have become, as well as a first class pianist, a composer of the most modern works, some for brass band, a forty-part motet in 2002 and a second one shortly afterwards. Another (Anthony Smith) became a singer and yet another an assistant cathedral organist (Peter Backhouse at Saint Mary's, and then at Saint Giles, Edinburgh). And there is Richard Egarr making a great success as harpsichordist in Holland as well as director of the Academy of Ancient Music in succession to Christopher Hogwood. Not only has he made many notable recordings including the Handel organ concertos, but he conducted the band playing on a barge during the Thames river pageant, part of the Queen's Diamond Jubilee celebration in 2012 (Priscilla and I were able to attend his wedding in Amsterdam, on our way to our 1981 summer holiday on Lake Maggiore).

Even those who took up non-music professions have usually made a success of the way of their choice, gaining scholarships, choral scholarships and prestigious posts. The musical bug nevertheless had infected and caused them to enter into whatever facet was of interest and enjoyment. Whether or not it is the affection for music that was at the foundation of their devotion to it in later life, it is good to know that they have found a purpose and, I am sure, enjoyment in pursuing it. I include among these the one who for a time held a semi-musical job as helper to a musician, the most celebrated English composer of his day, Michael Tippett. This is Christopher Senior, whose father was a vicar choral at the Minster and later Vicar of Helmsley. There are others, and the percentage is higher since the second war.

John Sutton's enthusiasm was organ playing and, though his daily bread came as a result of business, he kept up his technique to the extent of making a long-playing disc, and that in the Guards' Chapel. Then some time later he was kind enough to include Priscilla and me in a visit to Venice sponsored by his firm, which was a memorable and enjoyable time seeing the sights and a performance of *La Gioconda* at the Verona Opera Festival in the amphitheatre there. I was not able to leave Venice without being able to say we had been in Saint Mark's, moreover that I had actually played the organ through John's diplomacy and with the most pleasant welcome of a priest. All I did was extemporise. On many a Sunday morning John had stood with his fellows in the choir stalls waiting to process out singing Psalm 150, while I 'covered' the washing of the eucharistic vessels using the York chant by George Surtees Talbot as my theme (which never failed me for nearly thirty-seven years). That is what I did in Venice, being the first idea that occurred to me.

In view of a chronicle of choristers such as this, it would appear that there is no disadvantage in a child's devoting more time to music than usual. It is difficult to decide whether their brightness is attributable to their chorister training or to their innate intelligence. Admittedly they are chosen for their potentialities, and these are inevitably developed, so it is probably a combination of both. But certainly the background of daily singing, learning and performing at a high level of excellence in the matchless beauty of our cathedrals cannot but bring out qualities which could otherwise lie dormant. I have heard it said that the optimum period of concentration by a young person is an hour and a half at a stretch per day – at least application of the most useful kind – so after that what could be better than to deploy one's talents in a completely contrasting way, contributing another facet to the character. There is, I am quite sure, nothing to be said against a chorister's training from the education point of view: I cannot help regarding it, in fact, as nothing but an advantage. I have never failed to be grateful that it came my way. I would have been most unlikely to become organist of York Minster had I taken any other course. A succession of excellent head choristers made a notable contribution to the choir's success. One thinks of Colin Hardy, John Sutton, Ian Morton, Roy Bean, John (York) Skinner, Christopher Senior, Beverley Jones and many more, who knew their job, inspiring confidence throughout the choir and providing an example for their successors to follow.

||O||

In the mid-1960s cathedral choirs and some university college choirs began travelling – an expensive business requiring a good deal of organisation – to places like Europe, America, Russia, Scandinavia, and even Australia. For our part at the Minster, our almost daily duties kept us occupied and seemed to us the thing we were put there to do. But we allowed ourselves the occasional short trip. There was the annual foregathering with our near neighbour choirs of Ripon and Durham, in rotation. This amounted to evensong preceded by rehearsal – and perhaps a row on the river at Durham. Thus York was deprived merely of one service; and this was in the days before visiting choirs were available to plug any gap in the run of daily sung services.

There was a visit we paid to Halifax Parish Church during Dean Richardson's time for a special celebration. The boys distinguished themselves with 'Let the bright Seraphim'. They and I paid a similar visit to Aysgarth School on the afternoon of their free day, a May Wednesday in 1969. The choice of pieces could not avoid including both the Stanford *Bible Songs* to which we were so very attached. A recital at Ampleforth by the Minster choristers included Stanford's

Song of Wisdom – an equal favourite with the *Song of Peace*, which ended the programme – and *Mein glaübiges Herze* from Bach's cantata 68 with *obbligato* instruments and harpsichord.

But the most significant excursion at the time was to Malines, with which York had a connexion dating back to the time of the Conversations in which Viscount Halifax was a moving spirit. Cardinal Suenens was in office. He had come to York some time before, preaching on a Sunday morning to our amazement in perfectly clear English and without a note to help. During our stay in Malines he invited some of us to dinner and was a charming host. He was also present at the recital the choir gave in the cathedral. At the same event we were also greatly honoured by the presence of Flor Peeters, who had been organist there since 1925. I had met him occasionally and briefly, once when he was playing at Ampleforth and was brought to see the Minster. It was then that he signed his name for me, writing it from right to left. He also autographed his *Concert Piece* with the kindly message 'To my estimated colleague Francis Jackson'. He was most appreciative of the choir's performance in his cathedral and rewarded me with a warm hug.

Nearer home, a concert in Blackburn Cathedral during John Bertalot's tenure included Charles Wood's six-voice service in E for the songmen to sing and the *Song of Peace* of Stanford for the boys. This was a piece I had taken to in a big way during my chorister days when Elsie Suddaby revealed it to us at one of Sir Edward's musical Sunday afternoons in the Minster, and which has retained its attraction in full measure ever since. Therefore, when Philip Lowe in 2009 asked me to make an SATB version for a choir festival at Rochdale (which I had already done for the *Song of Wisdom* and the *Song of Battle*) I enjoyed doing it, hoping the while that I would do nothing to impair its inherent beauty. Reports afterwards seemed to indicate that it had served its purpose on that occasion under the direction of Andrew Carter. The Blackburn concert concluded with the *Mass in G minor* by Vaughan Williams, sung of course without accompaniment. Organ was provided in the first half by John Marsh who was studying at York University, and as organ scholar at the Minster was my valued assistant. I was sorry to have to miss meeting Mr Heath when he was visiting York while Prime Minister. I had gone to Carlisle to do a television programme with Andrew Seivewright, so left it in the hands of John to show him the organ. Beforehand I wrote to explain my absence and sent my most recent published long-playing record, receiving a kindly letter in return. However, he declined the invitation to play the Minster organ.

A recital I remember with particular pleasure was in the church at Tittleshall where, as well as the excellent two-manual Binns organ (for Mendelssohn 4 and Hindemith 3), I had the unalloyed happiness of a two-manual Goble harpsichord belonging to my old friend Doctor David Baldwin, on which the Couperin *Dix-huitième Ordre* and Bach's *Italian Concerto* sounded as colourful and vibrant as I had ever known them, due I'm sure more to the wonderful instrument than to my playing.

Other events around December 1968 included a piano recital for the Thirsk Music Club. This included *Le Tombeau de Couperin* again (as at Selby) with Couperin's own *Dix-huitième Ordre*: and at the York Art Centre (housed in Saint John's Church, Micklegate) Ravel appeared again with his *Valses Nobles et Sentimentales* and his two pastiches '*A la manière de ... Borodin/Chabrier*'.

‖O‖

Eric Milner-White, who had come from Cambridge as dean in 1941 was keen to have a university on his doorstep at York and worked hard along with others, to bring one. This came about eventually in 1963 complete with Music Department run by Wilfrid Mellers, David Blake and Peter Aston. It soon carved a solid niche for itself in Academia, and when the Sir Jack Lyons concert hall was built and an organ was to be included, my advice about it was sought. Who should build it was of course a crucial matter. The firm JW Walker was doing splendid work as always, and I would have chosen them. But much in the forefront then was Maurice Forsyth Grant, popular with the avant-garde, and it was his firm (along with Messrs Degens and Rippin) who erected the three-manual totally unenclosed instrument, claiming a firm place in the organ-building realm.

Its inauguration took place on Thursday 27 November 1969, and it was my privilege to play that evening. Not only one privilege but another as well, in the shape of a brand new work written especially for the occasion. For this world premier I was given thirty days in which to prepare all thirty pages, in a not-too-readable manuscript, the final of its nine movements being a toccata with many notes I found so hard to read that I had to request a clearer copy. This duly arrived – the work of a student I think, beautifully written, making it possible to learn and perform. To turn the pages and to manipulate stops I had the luxury of a Minster Organ Scholar on either side of me (John Marsh and Andrew Wilson-Dickson), all three of us arrayed in our dinner jackets as was the custom then. It was quite a struggle, but was rewarded by Wilfrid's standing and enthusiastically applauding when it was all safely delivered – he who had composed it, the university's head of music, Professor Mellers. The title is *Opus Alchymicum*; an interesting work. I believe that originally the dedication was to me, so when, much later, a recording was made by Kevin Bowyer and the dedication was assigned to him, that was a pleasure to note in view of the great amount of trouble, not to say accuracy, that this process demands. It was the second item in the opening recital, following a voluntary by James Nares (Minster organist aged 19 in 1734 until 1756). Next came Bach's monumental *Passacaglia* and (to keep up to date) two Messiaen pieces, *Joie et clarté des Corps Glorieux* and *Dieu parmi nous*. Afterwards a very enjoyable dinner was undertaken at which (Priscilla says) I pulled Wilfrid's leg about his music calligraphy, suggesting that his next organ composition should be more readable.

This was not the only event welcoming the organ. On the next day at lunchtime Frederick Rimmer brought entirely contemporary works from Glasgow – Hindemith, Persichetti, Nielsen and himself. (I had first met him in the mid-1930s when we were returning from Durham after taking a Mus. Bac. Examination, he then being organist at Saint Paul's, Princes Park, Liverpool.) For this recital, all seats were 2/6d (half-a-crown or 12.5p). From Saint Albans on the following day came Peter Hurford to play 'Music of the French Baroque and JS Bach' for six shillings a seat, he and I more expensive than Fred with his long and taxing Nielsen piece *Commotio* (if that is what it was).

It was good having an organ in the city (or just outside) of the most modern way of thinking, its new voice clearly to be heard on a recording some years later when it answered well for my concerto (of 1985) in the crisp acoustic of the Lyons hall, providing a striking contrast to its companion piece, Percy Whitlock's *Organ Symphony*

(1938) in the Minster's rich milieu. Both were first recordings and were brilliantly served by the university students' orchestra directed with wonderful enjoyment for us all by Doctor Jonathan Wainright. He had come to the Minster to run the new girls' treble (or soprano) line of the choir, soon moving to the university and afterwards becoming head of the music faculty, succeeding Professor Nicola Lefanu who had taken over from Professor Mellers.

Still in 1969, the Minster was in the midst of its trauma of restoration, the tremendous operation to save it from falling down. Its life was drastically disrupted for five years during which, though matins was abandoned on weekdays, evensong carried on with the organ enclosed in what was said to be the largest polythene bag in England – probably the world. My reference to the state of things in the annual report of the Friends of the Minster notes that 'The two Wednesday Evensongs broadcast on 8 and 15 May took place in spite of problems caused by the restoration. The balance test, always an exacting job, was not made easier by loud hammering. By contrast, the utter peace during the actual broadcast was blissful. Neither the polythene bag nor the depletion of the Pedal and Solo Organs has hindered organ recitals, broadcast or otherwise'. However, the number of attenders fell dramatically in the summer series – understandably.

There was another new-style organ to be launched, at the King's School, Worcester, in College Hall, close by the cathedral. The organ was built by the Malvern-based firm of Nicholson who used pipework and casework from a dismantled London organ to create an essentially new instrument, a sprightly two-manual of seventeen stops that was just the one for Hindemith (Sonata 1), Sweelink, Stanley, Bach, Couperin and the Dupré B major *Prelude and Fugue*. The director of music then was Harry Bramma who provided generous hospitality for Priscilla and me. He moved to Southwark seven years later to take charge of music in the cathedral, and then to be Director of the Royal School of Church Music.

That year was a full and varied one with a total of forty recitals between Bath, Bristol, Dundee, Edinburgh, Carlisle, Bangor, Durham, Newcastle, Jersey, Exeter, Oxford, the Whitworth Hall of Manchester University – and plenty more, plus non-organ pursuits such as the YSO concert with the Strauss *Oboe Concerto* and some of Walton's *Façade*; a trip to Ireland with Barry Rose to make a recording on a rather special organ in Down cathedral. This was originally built by Samuel Green (1740-96) and its character had been carefully preserved when the time came for it to be restored by Harrisons in 1914. Among the pieces, some of Stanford's were almost a *sine qua non*; a slightly cynical commentator hinting that I *would* do that wouldn't I because Stanford was born in Dublin, a distance of seventy miles away by crow.

An organ which had a special significance was that in the church on the Thames at Cookham, the one that Stanley Spencer used to love to listen to, sitting as close as he could to enjoy the articulation of the pipes, a feature that was lost at a rebuild and which he very much regretted. It was a thrill to see his pictures, painted all around where I was playing.

Perhaps what provided most pleasure and satisfaction with the York Symphony Orchestra that autumn was when I handed the baton over to David Blake and took to the piano stool for Beethoven's third piano concerto and the one written for the left hand by Ravel in 1930. This had long been a favourite of mine from its early days, released from its commissioner Paul Wittgenstein's six-year exclusive rights of performance, and of whose existence I became aware only on reading the composer's obituary in the newspapers at the very end of 1937. There seemed to be some interest, to judge by the full audience, whether in Beethoven, Delius (*Walk to the Paradise Garden*), Rossini's *Italian in Algiers* Overture, or the novelty of half a pianist doing what he could within quite severe limitations. The right hand being unemployed provided me with the opportunity to dispense with a turner of pages – if one was needed (which it was for safety in my case, though I knew it well by heart) – but it did not apply to the unfortunate Wittgenstein who had no right arm, having lost it in the 1914-18 war.

BBC EVENSONG AND PARIS

Another organ was soon to appear at Blackburn Cathedral, of which I had a hand in the designing. Messrs JW Walker provided the splendid instrument of three manuals, a feature of which was the thirty-two foot reed. This received the appellation 'Serpent' for which I initially got the blame (or credit) though it was John Bertalot's idea. A miniature portrait of the serpent appeared on the knob. I think John wished to have as picturesque and unusual a name for his Thirty-two Foot as ours at York; this had the name of 'Sackbut' as long ago as the 1820s, which had been restored in 1960 after losing it for a space.

When time came for the launching of the new organ, I was invited to play the opening recital. This programme, to include the Bach *Passacaglia* and *Dieu parmi nous* of Messiaen, was to be recorded for broadcast and I was commissioned to write a piece. I decided to try for a sonata (in G minor). A few days before the event a headline in our excellent evening newspaper informed the world that 'Minster organist has to learn his own composition'. I had stated that, though I had written the music and put it on paper (over a period of a month), I still had to learn to play it and that it was none too easy; moreover it still needed to be finished – which mercifully it duly was. A headline of 2 January notified anyone who might be interested 'Organist's Sonata almost ready' for playing on the tenth of the month; a near squeak with no more than a week to go, but not an uncommon situation. At the recital all went well, except for a cipher caused by a small wood chip which found its way down between two of the manual keys – the kind of occurrence that is likely to happen where a new instrument of a complicated nature is concerned. In the final movement opportunity was afforded the Imperial Trumpet to reveal its commanding presence by means of a showy fanfare such as Spanish organs are wont to revel in with their *chamade* horizontal reeds.

Oxford University Press published the sonata soon afterwards. It was the first of six sonatas I produced for similar situations, the second being at York for the completion of the Minster's restoration in 1972; then at Armley and Doncaster for two famous Schulze organs; and the fifth for Percy Whitlock's centenary at his Bournemouth church of Saint Stephen. The sixth came into being for the recital celebrating the 2004 restoration of the Armley Schulze, thus it was my second effort for that important organ.

In constructing recital programmes it goes without saying that acceptable music is the top priority. This can be difficult when so many differing and unknown tastes have to be catered for, so it is inevitable that a wrong guess can at some time be made, as perhaps at Geneva in March 1970 in the English church of The Holy Trinity. The critic first of all noted that my *métier acompli* stood me in good stead, as well as the 'atmospheric and elegant registration' that was in evidence. He regretted, however, that the choice of compositions was not up to the standard of the interpreter – no *inspiration veritable* nor well-known composers from *Grand Bretagne* represented. Stanford, then, did not qualify with his *Fantasia and Toccata* (his 1894 piece), nor Wesley *père* or *fils*, William Mathias whose excellent *Variations on a Hymn Tune* figured; nor my own tripartite toccata piece. He could have had a point, of course, there being no Bach – not that he could be counted a Great Briton – but it was unfortunate that, at that period, I occasionally left him out, a course which I came to deprecate and to discontinue. Apart from going through that stage I have always included his wondrous creations, which never fail after countless hearings. However, the writer was gracious enough to pronounce the recital a success from the performance angle and expressed 'indebtedness' for my efforts. And his views were certainly worth taking seriously even if he were a lone voice.

One day early in 1970, out of a clear blue sky came a bombshell, unexpected and disturbing. The BBC was going to do away with the weekly Wednesday Choral Evensong, cutting down the number of broadcasts to one a month and promising programmes of cathedral music in indeterminate quantity. Naturally this caused great alarm not only among the choirs and organists who were concerned with the production of these services, but, as was soon revealed, with a huge body of devoted listeners and worshippers over the length and breadth of the country and beyond. The reason proposed was a reorganisation of broadcasting procedures, a matter which was also the concern of other departments of the BBC. It could appear that religion was thought to be on the wane and was the care of only a small minority. How wide of the mark this proved to be was soon shown over the next month or so by a vigorous press coverage in which the Yorkshire Post played a resounding role. Its music critic Ernest Bradbury produced a long and powerful article and there were many letters, all – except one – deploring the proposition. The maverick admitted to a lack of fondness for the spread of the 'goat-bleat' to the treble section of Anglican choirs. Another complaint was the craze for high notes, but their exploitation under the pretext of 'reconstruction by the Master of the Choristers' – a point of view not easy to follow. He confessed also to finding the counter-attraction on Radio 2 too much for him.

The Yorkshire Post of 16 February reported an early reaction to the situation:

'The Master of the Music at York Minster … plans to present a petition to the BBC protesting against a proposal to cut Radio Four's weekly Choral Evensong to once a month. With the Dean's approval, Dr Jackson has placed two notices in Minster porches urging people to support his call that the BBC should continue with existing arrangements for broadcasting Choral Evensong. He decided to get up a petition when letters supporting his views followed publicity in the Yorkshire Post last Friday. On Saturday he said, "I knew there was a firm body of support for the retention of weekly Choral Evensong broadcasts. I shall leave the petition notices on view for another fortnight. The letters I have received to date are very encouraging". The Wednesday afternoon broadcasts had been running continuously for 44 years. "I want the programme retained because it shows Church music of the past 500 years – which is unique in the English speaking world – in its proper setting, ie Divine Service." '

A few days later the response was encouraging:

'Petitions campaigning against the BBC's decision to stop the Radio Four Choral Evensong programmes on Wednesday nights are being sent all over the country by York Minster's organist. This is an extension of his campaign two weeks ago, when he put petitions up in the Minster entrances. Since then, he has received about 500 signatures. As a result of the publicity, people from as far south as Exeter have written to him pledging their support. He said he had replied to them all, sending well over 50 copies of the petition in an effort to gain more support. He also wants all the other church and cathedral organists to join him, and distribute petitions in their own areas.'

For six weeks the situation remained in this state of uncertainty and anxiety, when suddenly the wireless gave the encouraging news that evensong was to continue, to the huge relief of a great many people. On 28 March I sent a letter to the Editor of the Yorkshire Post to express my gratitude for such wide support, part of which I quote:

'The campaign came into being during a telephone conversation I had with one of your reporters and the encouraging total of more than 20,170 has been contributed by devotees of the broadcast living as far apart as Saint David's, Colchester, Glasgow, and Belfast, as well as from all parts of Yorkshire. Your own part which was acknowledged in Thursday's issue of the Yorkshire Post, cannot be over-estimated. It will be noted that the decision has been taken before I have had a chance to send the signatures to the BBC. They had been arriving every day and the total has been rising steadily. I shall, however, send to Lord Hill a summary of the number of signatures and their origin, with the aim of reinforcing the BBC's decision to reinstate the programme.'

Having been a participant first as a chorister in 1929 when York Minster used to broadcast 4pm evensong weekly on Tuesday (with

Westminster Abbey on Thursday) and having been left to play a broadcast (without any rehearsal, probably 5 September 1939) when Sir Edward and his assistant Owen Le P Franklin were absent, there is a certain attachment one cannot avoid feeling towards this rather special event. And I was not alone.

The weekly broadcast had continued, untroubled, for a further forty or so years, for a short period adding even another evensong, on Fridays. It then entered the mind of the Corporation that Wednesday was not the day to be broadcasting a full-blown cathedral evensong every week. No, Sunday was the day for spiritual activity. Once a month was to be enough, with programmes of church music from time to time. Here again was cause for despondency; and what could be done? It was going to be very inconvenient for a choir to do its normal morning Lord's Day duties, to be able to manage a full run-through rehearsal of evensong and then to be on top form for the transmission. However, it continued thus for a while until Wednesday was reinstated. Then, most unexpectedly, the service remained and continues on Sunday in addition by means of a recorded repeat – a surprising outcome very much welcomed.

||O||

A tour across the Atlantic followed in April and May, starting with a few days acclimatising with the family of Priscilla's niece Judith near Washington, before moving on to play fifteen recitals. That year's itinerary took me to the four points of the American compass, including Elon College (Greensboro), Newark, Princeton (where I was the guest of Lee Bristol), New York, South Bend, Dallas, Houston, Grace Cathedral in San Francisco (where my name appeared on the same bill posting as Duke Ellington – just the two of us) and San Diego, before going north to Vancouver, Kingston and Halifax (Nova Scotia). Then back home for twenty-four more recitals, among them Westminster Central Hall, Hurstpierpoint, Dublin (Saint Peter), King's College (Cambridge), and another piano recital at the Margaret McMillan College at Bradford. Two other events I remember with pleasure were with the York Musical Society: Kodaly's entertaining *Matra Pictures* and two Stanford works, *Songs of the Fleet*, ever popular, and *Phaudrig Crohoore* which we enjoyed. It deserves to be better known. There were forty-six recitals all told this year, east and west of the Atlantic.

In the summer a contingent from the Birmingham School of Music (headed by Gordon Clinton, a favourite and frequent Christus in our Bach Passions and at other times) joined us in the *Dream of Gerontius*. This turned out to be one of those occasions when everything conspired to generate a compelling atmosphere, which lives on and is fondly remembered. A second collaboration in the same work took place at Scarborough with the Choral Society, which created a like impression.

I flew back to the United States in August, this time to New Jersey to take part in an Anglo-American boy choir training course at Westminster Choir College. In Princeton University chapel I conducted a choir, two hundred and twenty-five strong, of men and boys. This was organised under the sponsorship of the Royal School of Church Music of England and the Music Commission of the Diocese of New Jersey and was at the conclusion of the course. The choir was composed of singers from many parts of North America including distant Florida and the Canadian border. Present were many of America's leading figures in ecclesiastical music, among them Gerre Hancock, organist of Saint Thomas Church, New York (a successor to T Tertius Noble) and Doctor Ronald Arnatt.

During the ceremony I received the honorary Fellowship of Westminster Choir College. This was presented to me by Doctor Lee Hastings Bristol, a significant figure in the college and in music generally around the country. I was Doctor and Mrs Bristol's house-guest in their beautiful home, in the grounds of which he had built a music room to contain a two-manual tracker organ in the baroque style fashionable at the time. He nicknamed the music room 'The Supplement', he having been much occupied with production of an additional book to the American Hymnal known by that name. One of his projects was to publish a collection of organ pieces, based on tunes contained in the book which bore his name, as the *Bristol Collection*. The tune I chose to use was an old American folk tune to the words beginning 'Jesus walked this lonesome valley', the tune having the final two words for its title.

Then followed our Lakeland summer holiday; a popular location with the family where Crummock Water was excellent for swimming and for sailing in the Mirror dinghy, named *Dipper* by William. This was an exercise at which Alice, William and Edward became adept following the line which was a continual attraction to Priscilla's family. Her father had spent many years in his hobby of building sailing boats named *Owl One* and *Owl Two*, as well as the dinghy *Owlet*: these had provided their trips and holidays on the Ouse, Derwent, Humber and Trent rivers and imbued them all – and the next generation – with a partiality for this pursuit.

||O||

The next year contained five inaugurations including Southwell Minster, Pershore Abbey and Saint Matthew, Northampton, among the total of thirty-two recitals, one in Notre Dame, Paris (with Wesley's *Andante en Sol* and *Sarabande pour le matin de Paques*, which of course is by Howells). There were more – at the Festival Hall, Keele University, New College (Oxford) with its brand new Grant Degens and Rippin organ (the notion of David Lumsden). This last coped well with my first sonata, which I played also at Bury Saint Edmunds and was broadcast. There were two accounts by the YSO of my *Brigantia Overture*, an evensong broadcast from King's of my G major canticles under David Willcocks and, at York, the Minster Choristers' Speech Day with John Dykes Bower presenting the prizes. Sylvia Rosenberg came for the Symphony Orchestra's autumn concert to play the Brahms violin concerto; and composer Gordon Jacob came with his wife and two small children to stay with us for a night or two on an examination stint.

On Sunday 18 April 1971 I was to play in Notre Dame for three-quarters of an hour before the 6.30pm service. On the morning of that day, by arrangement Robert Neuville took Sam Clutton, my son William and me to S. Sulpice where we witnessed the extraordinary (to us) performance that has been going on week after week on Sunday morning, and probably has done from time immemorial. We were there in good time and climbed the spiral staircase leading to the rear gallery. It was rather like Saint Paul's; in fact so is the whole building, in style if not in plan. Some imposing plaques let into the wall informed us, as we drew nearer, of the name of the builder of the organ and of its date (1862). Indeed we weren't allowed not to notice all this, since it appeared again on four wooden panels above the choir organ so that the organist could see it as he sat there to play.

Already people were there, and an air of expectancy. There was a tape recorder at the ready, with earphones, in the gallery at the south side of the organ. A woman in her late forties seemed *au fait* with it all, and it was she who, in due course, turned switches to bring on the wind, shortly after which the Master himself arrived, accompanied by his devoted wife. As we prepared to meet the great man, his wife was in command of the proceedings and informed him, close to his ear in loud tones '*nous avons l'organiste d'York*' – twice. Dupré nodded in agreement, smiled, shook my hand, and greeted the next comer. Then we all went into the console apartment and were disposed in our various positions. I was told by Madame Dupré to sit on the bench – a capacious affair allowing ample room without incommoding the player – at the treble, or south, side of the console, while William and Robert stood on the red-carpeted, curved stairs leading up to it. Same on the left, a young organist from Switzerland and his companions on the stairs. At intervals one of the doors on either side opened admitting another onlooker, the ladies, as I observed, eliciting the coveted, ready smile from *le maître*. But never a word from his lips, even during the pauses, which were considerable. Talking, however, was not eschewed by Madame Dupré and the regulars.

By this time a few more people had come and we were all welcomed, though Monsieur Dupré himself bestowed nothing more than his winning smile. He was not really interested in us, though we were welcome to be there if we wished – and after all, this was the form, the ceremonial. We worshippers had come to sit at the feet of the great man, and we were going to witness the act in all its primeval splendour, whether we were from England, America, Switzerland (which some of us were) or even if we were JS Bach himself. The show would go on as always, and the onlookers – a different lot each Sunday plus some regulars – were an essential part of it. One wondered how much difference it would have made if one day none were present. But that would not happen – could not happen – to so great and well-loved a man, especially as far as the gentle sex was concerned. There would always be enough feminine admirers to bring him delight and to cast his smile upon, as well as Fulbright scholars in search of the truth, and revering interpreters of his music from England and anywhere else.

As he took his seat at the console, clad in his coat and beret (by permission of the church, he once told me, if not of the Pope himself) it was difficult to believe that this was the man who had thought up the all-but-impossible intricacies of the G minor prelude and fugue, the brilliance and cross-rhythms of the B major, the dancing character of the *Noel Variations*. And when he began to play, this impression grew even stronger. Gone was any flash of youthful vigour and imagination. What came out of the organ was the kind of improvisation one might have heard in a minor English cathedral in 1920. Not even a chromatic seventh chord to colour the even tenor of the lengthy improvisation nor yet a change of colour from the eight-foot *'fonds de tous claviers'* played from the lowest of the five manuals.

Nevertheless it was Marcel Dupré who was playing, and the music was in every way appropriate to the service. This was exactly what Widor would have been doing from the time of his non-appointment in 1862 until his retirement seventy-two years later, and Léfébure-Wely before him, and so on. Here was a living tradition which would one day be given new life at the hands of a younger man, a tradition going on till doomsday and which would lose its appeal immediately the famous Master relinquished the reins, until his successor should build up his own particular band of devoted followers and the mystique that surrounds the world-famous virtuoso. One wondered inevitably who could possibly succeed him. Certainly no assistant was in evidence, such as Dupré himself had been in the days of Widor. Maybe the next organist will be taken on as casually as was Widor in 1862. Introduced to the *curé* by Cavaillé-Coll who had just finished building the organ; asked to play for a service, then afterwards confronting the *curé* to know whether he had been appointed, and being told 'come next Sunday', and so on each Sunday. Not a secure beginning for a tenure stretching to eight decades.

An assistant stop-manipulator efficiently and somewhat fussily pushed and pulled at one side and then hurtled round the front of the console to do the same at the other, scattering all in his path and nearly squashing me against the back panels. During one of his improvisations – perhaps the communion – this man said to him *'j'ai l'impression qu'il attend'*, meaning the officiant. Dupré did not comprehend, so it was said again and he drew to a close. Dupré's command of the registration was noticeable. Even if he appeared to be not quite with us some of the time when away from the console, he was well able to control the centenarian monster with its curved stop terraces and its multifarious ventil pedals, couplers, *tirasses* and all. The reeds seemed to be out all the time (as indeed the ear had no difficulty in discerning) and were brought into use by five or six pedals along the centre in front of the pedal board. It was interesting to see Dupré run his foot along them in a glissando from left to right releasing them all, causing somewhat of a clatter. He knew, naturally, exactly where everything was, and what to do with it and when. It was quite a distance for him to reach to the upper stops, and he was obliged to support his leaning body on the terrace below the stops with the hand that manipulated them. I saw his foot on the swell pedal once only – at the beginning – as he pushed it down and hooked it there.

But though he had control of the organ, the same could not be said of the music. Suddenly, during the half-hour interlude between services, the D major fugue began, and I was at once galvanized by a panic. Of all the pieces for him at his time of life to attempt, this was the least advisable. And my worst fears were realized, for after half a minute or so he had left the track and was improvising in the style so that only those with a thorough knowledge of the piece would have been aware of his straying, until he picked it up again. But not for long. This seemed to happen two or three times until the last couple of pages went off comparatively hitchless. Unfortunately hitches there were throughout the performance, due in some measure to his deafness, and there were notes that hung on after their time, due partly to his misshapen fingers which caused notes to sound adjacent to the ones he meant to play, and partly to the malfunctioning of the coupling mechanism. In fact at times so many notes were missing that Bach was all but unrecognisable: the even-numbered notes in the subject when played once in the pedals, solo, were absent, presenting us with only the tonic and mediant, in quavers. Nevertheless it was an astonishing achievement, thoroughly professional (which goes without saying) and an object-lesson in how to cope when the unexpected happens. We had taken part in a unique and unforgettable experience, one which in a short while would come to an end.

No doubt some little attention to the action was needed after sixty-six years. But what a miracle. An organ of one hundred and nine years of age, practically untouched, still doing its work perfectly adequately, at the hands of an organist within a fortnight of his eighty-fifth birthday; an organist who at the age of eight was taken by the builder of this organ for a walk by the Seine to fill in time before giving his first recital, discussing together the unusual compass of the manuals and pedals at S. Sulpice.

Then came a loud, interminable improvisation, at I don't know what part of the service, in which the organ sounded like a monster harmonium. I don't know whether he used the mixtures – the layout of the console was so bewildering, one could hardly make out what was in use and attend to the music at the same time – but there was little, if any, evidence of them. The reedy noise went on and on and became in the end so boring that it caused me to propose leaving. There was still another mass to be gone through and the company seemed all set to sit it out. They seemed in fact perfectly happy and to be enjoying themselves, Guilmant's grand-daughter among them, now in her late middle age.

So eventually we withdrew, but it was not yet all over. The Master came out and disappeared into his tiny corridor-like room and out the other end, while Madame showed us the priceless keepsakes hanging on the walls – a picture of Cavaillé-Coll *lui-même* signed and inscribed to Widor, a picture of old S. Sulpice, one of Louis Nicolas Clérambault (1676-1749) who was organist there – and a bust of Widor on a marble shelf in front of the mirror which occupies the near end wall of the small room. I had the temerity to ask Madame Dupré if we could see them and their organ at Meudon, and she, with characteristic French courtesy, readily agreed. I could not tell her exactly what time, so left it to Robert to telephone her. Being at Poitiers during the day we could not be in Paris before 6.40pm, so we arranged that 7pm should be the time of arrival. We went to Poitiers to see the remarkable Cliquot organ in the cathedral built in the 1780s and still working faultlessly. Unluckily on our return there was a formidable queue for taxis, so we spent three-quarters of an hour waiting for one. The distance was greater than we had anticipated, added to which the taxi got thoroughly lost causing us to arrive half an hour later than we had arranged, despite the train's arrival half an hour ahead of schedule.

Having arrived at the front gate (which was quite impregnable, boarded up and possessing no handle) we pressed the bell and better pressed it, but to no avail. The house was some distance away, up the path, but no-one obeyed our summons. Wondering whether we had travelled in vain, our next move was to ask the neighbour (at 42 Bde. Anatole France) to be told that we were to try at 38 where his children lived. So we rang the bell on the gate and a young man, announcing himself as the grandson of M. Dupré let us in, in company with a large and bouncy Alsatian who, he said, was 'not naughty' but quite safe. This was the grandson of whom Dupré had told me once in York: two *petites filles* and – wait for it –'Meester Dominic'. And here he was, letting us in, most politely. The new house, built in the garden of the old, was inhabited by the three grandchildren. Orphans they were, said Madame Dupré, their mother having died, and their father killed in a motor accident. They ran the house still and were students. Marcel and Madame had their meals with them, in fact dinner was being finished as we arrived and we felt slightly awkward at our very late appearance.

However, Dominic took us up to the old house and put us in the salon, which was just as one would expect it to be – a place of a former era, a home of sixty years ago, comfortable, warm, faded perhaps, but with elegant settee and chairs in Louis XIV style. A handsome glass-fronted bookcase with curved legs contained tidily bound books of what looked like organ music and, as he told us later, the books which Guilmant compiled with the themes he had set his class for improvisation. Another batch contained the same thing as done by Dupré. Each series took up something like eighteen inches or two feet of shelving, and that of Guilmant was written in beautiful 'how do you say?'. 'Gravure' I volunteered; but he didn't hear it. I asked Madame if he had kept the themes given him to improvise on, but she said not all. She talked as if she knew a lot about organs, so took a good deal of the brunt of visitors' curiosity. Her whole life seemed to be given over to keeping her husband going, and she certainly did a wonderful job. They were obviously very devoted and very touching to see together.

Off the salon, which is not large, opened a fair-sized hall which could seat two hundred with ease. This was built by them especially for the organ. Set out in the front half were some one hundred chairs – and more in the gallery up a spiral, organ-loftish staircase. And at the end was the organ which had come from Guilmant's house just up the road. Its tin pipes were gleaming: they had been cleaned not long ago. The organ was raised up two or three steps, and on the right was a piano with an ornamental cloth over it – the instrument on which I suppose his pianist daughter played the work he wrote for her and himself. On the piano was a large reading lamp with a huge parchment shade on which was written some music in black and red. I think it was from a work of his, perhaps a fugue in D minor. Madame Dupré sat on the right between organ and piano, Sam on the piano chair turned round, I on a large tapestry one pulled out from the left against the organ and *le maître* on the bench, with his back to the organ. In English he began to talk about his beginnings as an organist – Rouen, his father, Guilmant – and twice (to his wife's mounting anxiety) we heard about his eight-year-old walk 'on the border of the Seine' with Cavaillé-Coll. She said he had told us that '*deja*', which he probably didn't hear. Madame told him three times to '*montre l'orgue*' and he eventually began to move in that direction, but had to be reminded about '*le vent*' which proved a little difficult to convey to him. However, he opened a door on the left of the organ case and, slowly operating one of those old-fashioned progressive switches, produced the desired result and came and sat the other way round on the bench.

'I am going to make you a little improvisation to show you the stops of the organ.' And a very similar process as the previous day in S. Sulpice was begun – slow, 8-foot common chords with random adding of stops, all played from the bottom of the four keyboards until the swell oboe and trumpet (and *fonds* of course) were shown not only in their solo capacity as in the *Choral* in A minor but in canon with the swell to pedal. Most of it worked. One was aware again how his reflexes carried him through, in the act of doing the thing he had enjoyed devoting his life to and which had long ago become second nature. Abruptly he left his chordal playing and began a fugue on quite a simple subject, and I wondered how often he had used it before. It was fairly correct if not very inspired, and in an easy, andante tempo. I think the registration was added to and once more the harmonium effect was created. I wondered what the cromorne sounded like, and the mutations, and the flutes alone, and it was not until I was out of the room getting my camera that I heard the cromorne being tried. I asked Madame's permission to take a photo (for which I had carefully prepared the camera before arrival) and though I had intended the picture to include all four of us, using the automatic shutter, Sam insisted on taking it because it would, he said, have been impertinent to impose himself on the group. I had to give in to avoid both keeping everyone waiting and finding a stand for the camera. Then I wondered whether I had set the camera right and if there would be a photograph. I need not have worried; the result was excellent.

Sam thought that Dupré thought Sam was me, and spoke mostly to him. There was certainly no talk of York, or, in fact, any thing other than Dupré and those bearing on that subject. So I doubt even if he was aware that either one of us had come from York (or London) even when I mentioned that he, when in York, had played a two-piano duet with me at Minster Court and listened to some of the *Planets* ('Holst' said Madame immediately) on the gramophone. Dupré flashed an instant gesture of recognition, but said nothing.

He told us that he never knew nervousness until he came to play in front of Guilmant whose pupil he wished to become. He has an obvious reverence and love for his old master, whose house was within a few yards of his own at Meudon 'close to the station' as he said several times. He pointed out to us the place where Guilmant's garden began and where the house stood before it was demolished to make room for apartment blocks.

Perhaps the most interesting point about his training was what he told us about his lineage as a player of Bach. He had played the D minor *Toccata and Fugue* the previous morning at S. Sulpice from his edition, naturally, the book being brought in by his helper whose suggestion it was. This was the only time his hands left the bottom manual – to do the echoes on the *Récit* manual. He did not wish to boast, but he had learned from Guilmant to play Bach, and Guilmant had learned to play Bach from Lemmens who had learnt from J.S. Bach's youngest son. He wasn't boasting, but there the fact was and he couldn't escape it: he was in the direct line of succession. And I wonder how much of value the busy weekly tape recorder will capture of the 'art spontané, mais fugitif … les modéles d'improvisation proposés par le plus prestigieux chef d'école de la musique d'orgue contemporaine', which is the aim of the 'Association des Amis de l'Art de Marcel Dupré'.

We then began to take our leave. Dupré said he would 'put us to the sta*tion*' (giving stress to the second syllable) so we left the house by a back door, from another entrance hall off the salon, wandered up a narrow lane and across the road to the station. Here was the most famous of living organists, in a navy coat and rather shabby hat, looking like any other elderly man, seeing off his guests, probably an unwilling host: we shall never know, because there was never a flicker from either him or his wife to suggest we were thought a bore and a nuisance. But it was a wonderful visit, one that remains vivid in the memory.

||O||

The next month brought a most welcome and touching letter from Canon Reginald Cant, our opposite neighbour, a saintly person, universally loved and respected. That it was five months early for its purpose only added to its acceptability, its lonesomeness giving space to savour the affection it conveyed, and forming an earnest of what was to come later in fuller measure.

3, Minster Court

13 May 1971

Dear Francis

I think that this month you celebrate the 25th anniversary of your appointment as Master of the Music. As I am departing for the continent today and don't return till the end of the month, I may miss a celebration of the event.

I don't intend, therefore, to leave without sending a word of thanks for your presence here, for all the beauty you have given us and for all the fame you have brought us.

All congratulations for the past, and all good wishes for the future.

Yours sincerely, Reginald Cant

||O||

The start of my two-year spell as President of the Royal College of Organists was in 1972, following William Cole, Ivor Keys, Sir David Willcocks and Sir Jack Westrup (in reverse order) and many lustrous names before theirs, one being of special significance to me who had held the distinction forty-four years before – Sir Edward Bairstow. It was in the remarkable building in Kensington Gore that my connexion with the College began (aged eighteen), and my council membership, first noted in the 1953/54 Calendar. [Then for a spell the RCO lodged in Saint Andrew's Church, Holborn and afterwards in Southwark Cathedral where it has happily carried on under the benign influence of Peter Wright the Cathedral's organist and his presidential successor, James O'Donnell, organist of Westminster Abbey.] I had been a member of the RCO council for a good many years, taking a keen interest in its affairs: now a closer involvement was possible. The day-to-day running of the college, though, was in the very capable hands of the Clerk, Barry Lyndon, and the Secretary, Sir John Dykes Bower, who as the retired organist of Saint Paul's Cathedral in his turn had succeeded the former organist of Westminster Abbey, Sir William McKie. Apart from the chairing of meetings, perhaps the most onerous presidential duty, and the most exposed, was the twice-yearly presentation of diplomas and the presidential address that presented itself as a major undertaking.

I had read Sir Edward's addresses in back numbers of the *Musical Times* – lengthy and of serious import, as he pursued his lifetime's missionary endeavours towards improving the cause of music that was so dear to his heart. This was an example that should be followed, one felt, and was nothing if not daunting. But I received some reassurance from Barry Lyndon: all that the audience wanted was 'to hear the President talking'. I managed to fulfil that commitment, somehow, and was suitably rewarded by the decision of the *Musical Times* to refrain from publishing any reference to my painstaking efforts. This was probably a disappointment to me at the time, and somewhat mystifying. There were, no doubt, many valid reasons which will never be revealed. However, on looking at those four talks after having forgotten them completely for almost forty years, it has been reassuring because I managed the original task without grumbles, and (if I might venture) I enjoyed coming into contact once more with the topics I had dealt with.

The first address was perhaps not so difficult, because it was the occasion of the presentation of Armorial Bearings to the college, the gift of an anonymous donor. Music therefore did not take as prime a place as it might have done and gave me the chance to expatiate on heraldry about which I knew nothing despite my sighting of all those dozens of shields every time I sang a service in York Minster in my younger days. My interest in the subject was awakened, incidentally causing me for a while to bring heraldry to the attention of my York choirboys. The RCO occasion, on 27 January 1973, began with a brief piece I had written for it. The title could only be *Heraldic Flourish*, and it had the immense distinction of being played by the most famous organist of the day, Doctor (later Sir) George Thalben-Ball who very recently had received the honorary Doctorate of Music from Birmingham University, in the robes of which he appeared for, I believe, the first time.

Six months later I was dealing with the organ, its history, design and development, with the purpose of highlighting the work of three men who had contributed greatly, by their writings and with their profound and wide knowledge, to the many aspects of the instrument and were to be made Honorary Members of the College. First, in alphabetical order, Felix Aprahamian 'an acknowledged authority not only on his special subject of French organ music but also on the entire organ music repertoire' in the words of Sir John Dykes Bower, presenting him. An entrancing writer and critic on any aspect of music, his literary style was always a joy to read. Then Cecil Clutton, who was from an early age a regular contributor of articles to *The Organ* quarterly, all packed with sound knowledge and unbounded enthusiasm. *The British Organ* of which he was co-author with Austin Niland 'is a standard work on the subject. As secretary of the Organs Advisory Committee of the Council for Places of Worship, his efforts to secure the proper treatment of the organ as a musical instrument have been untiring'.

The third recipient was, through illness, prevented from receiving his certificate of Honorary Membership in person: Doctor WL Sumner was also 'a noted scholar who generously shares his knowledge in assisting the schemes for organs up and down the country'. He made 'major contributions to Grove's *Dictionary of Music and Musicians*, and his book *The Organs of St Paul's Cathedral, London* is a work of immense learning and interest'. It was a rare privilege for me to be the one to make the presentation of the College's Honorary Membership to three so distinguished persons.

My third attempt, of the following January 1974, dealt more with music but began with some remarks about 'the unique nature of the building' in which we found ourselves. The façade of the building, a fine frontage in Kensington Gore facing the Albert Hall, had been re-decorated during my term as President, bringing to life the frieze of classical figures in relief. I was quoting a phrase that had produced a slight snigger on a previous occasion, at a time when anything Victorian was 'dreadful' and before Sir John Betjeman urged us to revise our opinion of the architecture of that period. Similarly with music: though there was much of value there were also disappointments such as with the third symphony of Louis Spohr of which I presumed to remark that 'we all found a lack of invention and overmuch reliance on too meagre thematic material', which is very much the same assessment as that found in Grove's *Dictionary*. (Later, I am wondering which came first.)

It was the fourth and final of these Presidential outpourings that was the easiest – a gift, one might say – coming as it did within something like a month of the centenary of the birth of Edward Bairstow, who I came to know so well and to value so highly as man and musician. His tutelage, which I enjoyed for ten years, and his friendship were beyond price, and an immense gift vouchsafed to so many people, for which I give continual thanks.

|O|

Earlier, shortly before Easter in March 1972, another notable event was acted out when the Queen came to distribute the Royal Maundy. This takes place every alternate year in various places, but in celebration of the Minster's semi-millennium it came a year earlier, interrupting the cycle. There was a good deal of planning for the service. I went with the Precentor, Canon Paul Burbridge, to Buckingham Palace to discuss and work out procedures. This was all very informal and friendly, involving traversing passages below ground level where central heating pipes and such necessities are to be found in some profusion. All the arrangements were in the hands of the official staff, but our suggestions for what was to be sung were accepted. We had recently taken up *O Sacrum Convivium* by Messiaen, which was very suitable for Maundy Thursday, but we learned that for this particular service it was not necessary to stick to seasonal works, and that, in fact, anything could be used. So this piece was approved, along with five other anthems, two that were Lenten and penitential – Wesley's *Cast me not away* and *Hide not thou thy face* by Farrant. The more dramatic Battishill *O Lord look down from heaven* and Bairstow's gentler *I sat down under his shadow* completed the quota of music covering the two distributions of the Maundy money, along with *Zadok the Priest* – an unmistakably festive piece, written for a coronation (by Handel of course). This is the only one that appears regularly at every Maundy service. Apparently, so familiar is Her Majesty with its topography that she knows where she should be at any point of the music, and can estimate whether they will finish before it stops: it is the last piece in this part of the service. The Chapel Royal choir had journeyed north to join with us for the occasion; they were under the direction of Harry Gabb, an old friend from army days at Catterick: good company always and a fine musician. The service was broadcast and an LP recording was made by Harry Mudd and issued under the Abbey Records label.

A special treat for us was to join in having lunch with Her Majesty with the chance to meet her and talk as with any ordinary person in a relaxed and normal manner. And the menu was all in French, tempting us with *JAMBON DE YORK GARNI, SAUCE CUMBERLAND* and *BISCUITS CUILLIERES* giving the date as *Jeudi le 30 Mars 1972*; but it seemed that the printer was unable to manage *MAISON DU TRÉSORIER* for the Treasurer's House venue where these delights were partaken – (which could be because he realised it was not edible).

Easter came – and went – and somehow another visit to Paris happened, so soon after last year's. The journey from York, including a choppy crossing of the Channel took ten hours, landing me at Gare du Nord at half past ten. My dearest wish was for sleep; but such was the hospitality of my host and hostess, Monsieur and Madame Neuville, that the elaborate and memorable meal (with shrimps and avocado pear and much more) delayed it until two in the morning. So I felt thoroughly initiated in the French manner of keeping body and soul together. But next morning, having woken at 5.45am, a large (English?) breakfast of bacon and two eggs was had at about ten o'clock. Then a walk to the Trocadero and to Notre Dame to rehearse for Sunday's recital. Here I was very much looked after by François Carbou, one of the organist staff. The original console had been replaced by one of English or American style, which was somewhat of a relief to one not conversant with the French way with ventil pedals and other conveniences. After the recital it was fascinating to visit the cathedral museum (after hours) to see the Cavaillé-Coll console of 1868 that Vierne had used during his thirty-seven years there. And his spectacles, and death mask.

This visit had been arranged by Robert Neuville, a young friend of Cecil Clutton's who, though not an organist himself, was able easily to effect an assignation at any organ, such as S. Séverin, Trinité, S. Sulpice, Notre Dame, which from our perspective in this country were pretty well unattainable. But the organists were usually ordinary, approachable people. This was certainly the case with Jean Langlais in César Franck's church, Ste. Clothilde. He let me play between services as well as asking me for a theme for improvising which I found great difficulty in singing to him but which caused him no problem. It had only seven notes, but they were quite sufficient for his purpose, in the characteristic French style: would that I could have had a mobile phone with me of the kind that records and performs lots of other marvels.

The French language, which I would have liked to know more fluently, was always of interest, especially when concerning two of my organ pieces as they appeared on the Notre Dame programme: *Prelude for a Solemn Occasion* and *Diversion for Mixtures* took on an exotic flavour (I thought) as *Prélude pour une fête solennelle* and *Divertissement pour les mixtures*. Away from music it was rather entertaining to see what we call a fridge described as an *Installation Frigorifique*, though how generally this is used I do not know, my dictionary giving *glacière* and other names as well. Similarly at Montfort l'Amaury, for the first time we heard Madame Reveleau call a camera *un appareille photographique* which the dictionary does give – these terms more leisurely than ours but taking a little longer to say.

Another visit to Ravel's house at Montfort had to be undertaken, this time in wind and pouring rain to find *Le Belvédère* shuttered and workmen pulling it about, Madame Reveleau no longer there. She would have been aged around one hundred and three. It seemed that the information we had gathered on a previous visit (*prochainement musée*) was being put into effect. There was no hope of going into the house, but I pulled up two seedlings from the cherry tree in the garden that were growing in profusion in the lane outside. One of them has flourished mightily in our garden at East Acklam during the succeeding forty years, producing several second and third generation descendants of Ravel's *cerisier*. Its girth has become considerable and, if I am correctly informed, it has exceeded the normal lifespan of its genus by a good ten years.

At home there was no shortage of events to keep us busy and interested. The Minster choir gave a recital at Bradford Cathedral as April was ending, with Geoffrey Coffin (my Assistant) to accompany and to play Alain and Howells. Among the choir offerings were Messiaen, Rachmaninoff, Haydn, and anthems, including Bairstow's *Of the Father's love begotten* with its hugely enjoyable and climactic final chorus.

The first of the three June Saturdays to which the Dean, Alan Richardson refers in a kindly, welcome letter (quoted below) was when the Durham, Ripon and Lincoln choirs joined in the first performance since 1868 of Samuel Wesley's cantata *Confitemini* with the Northern Sinfonia Orchestra and four soloists, Honor Sheppard, Barbara Robotham, Philip Langridge and John Noble. John Marsh, our organ scholar, had searched it out and prepared an edition towards his degree at the university. With its fifteen movements, some strong choruses and solo and duet numbers of variable quality it was interesting and enjoyable, increasing our knowledge of and regard for this interesting man.

A week later the Fauré *Requiem*, preceded by anthems (one of them Holst's *Psalm 86*) brought us to Lincoln for a joint concert with the cathedral choir with whose director, Doctor Philip Marshall, I shared the conducting. The *Requiem* (which was anathema to Francis Poulenc) was fully appreciated by all, listeners and performers, and drew a grateful response from Mr J Watson who I did not know and who had come from Goole: his letter the following day said 'Nothing can surpass the lovely English cathedral tone of the boys' voices singing as with one voice. They were superb. One forgot the dampness outside and the chill of the Minster while basking in the warmth of such grand music. I shall never forget those boys' music'. Such comments were liable to come from time to time and are an encouragement which is necessary in the course of a life of continuous performance. A cathedral choir's daily purpose is to convey a cogent message to whoever is present, and they cannot know what effect they are having (apart from a mutually unexpressed feeling that may come at times) making helpful sentiments like Mr Watson's very much valued, so much the more because of their rarity.

The third date the Dean refers to is the annual evensong of the three northern choirs, this year at Ripon, always a jaunt to anticipate and enjoy.

The Dean wrote:

> The Deanery, York, YO1 2JD
> 18 May, 1972
>
> My dear Francis,
>
> Thank you for sending me a copy of your arrangements for June 10, 17 and 24 – your excellent programme for York, Lincoln and Ripon. I am very glad that all this is happening. Here at York 1972 is the most important anniversary since 1927 and will (so far as I can see) be the most important one until 2027! I am glad that you and the choir and the other musical people are combining so splendidly to make the year a success, and it is high time I sent you a word of appreciation. In particular I wish to record my appreciation (and that of many other people) for your *Sonata giocosa per la Renascita di una Cattedrale*, which contributed a note (or rather many notes!) of distinction to the very happy Festival on April 28.
>
> No reply to this inadequate Thank You is called for.
>
> Yours ever, Alan

||O||

York Minster, incidentally, is a cathedral and used to be known as such. The 'Minster' word, when following 'York's' last letter, avoided the juxtaposition of two identical hard-sounding consonants, eventually becoming universally used. Derived, I am told, from *monasterium*, it was brought into use for a big church. There is, however, one notable exception I know of: at Kirkdale near Helmsley where the tiny Saint Gregory church, romantically set in a valley of trees, assumed the title.

Nineteen seventy-two was a significant year for the Minster. The brand new York Cathedral completed in 1472 was consecrated on 3 July that year. It was fortuitous, then, that the building's five-year rescue programme was finished in time for services of thanksgiving on dates within four and two days respectively of the original exactly five hundred years later – one on the patronal festival of Saint Peter, with the Archbishop's sermon, and another a day or two afterwards for the Friends of the Minster with the Archbishop of Canterbury to preach.

The architect who devised the restoration programme, Bernard Fielden, asked me to write a commemorative and celebratory piece to be played before the Friends' service. What resulted was another sonata which I called *Sonata Giocosa* (which more appropriately should have been *Goiosa*) *per la renascita di una cattedrale*. (I have no idea why I used Italian.) The hymn tune called *York* composed by John Milton's father came in extremely useful in all three movements; its melody is an interesting shape and bears repetition. Also the words which are usually put to it (Pray that Jerusalem may have peace and felicity) seemed to be appropriate for the situation after so much turmoil and anxiety. This all happened at the height of summertime.

In early June the choral societies of Ripon and Scarborough joined with York in the Minster for the B minor *Mass*, Bach's great choral work, perhaps the greatest of all, again with the Northern Sinfonia Orchestra and with Barbara Robotham, Elizabeth Simon, Kenneth Bowen and John Carol Case for the solos.

Two productions of *A Time of Fire* (John Stuart Anderson's monodrama with my music) were among the festival events. This came in for criticism by a music critic who as a general rule appeared to regard his role as literally critical – disapproving – no doubt with the laudable object of trying to be helpful. 'A vital spark', however, was found to be missing from the production. It would be instructive to know how general was this assessment.

Later in the year it was stated from the same source that the choir had the wrong kind of accompaniment for the Kodaly *Missa Brevis* and for Vaughan Williams' *Vision of Aeroplanes*, which the composer had read to me the day we met some thirty years before. This work is not easy, and its unusual subject intrigued and fascinated us. However we were evidently unfortunate as the Lyons Hall organ seemed to overlay the sound of the choir 'like a widespread headache'. This work and the other motet by Vaughan Williams, *The Voice out of the whirlwind*, were both 'rather dull' and Bach's *Jesu, Priceless Treasure* 'is not one of Bach's masterpieces anyway...' Also 'The choir needs to find its own identity' was the headline on 13 November. Plenty for us all to think about, to be sure; and we have to accept that when we put ourselves in a vulnerable position we have to be prepared for whatever judgement comes our way.

There were opinions from happier writers concerning a recital on the rebuilt Leeds Town Hall organ, which was broadcast. Ernest Bradbury's headline in the Yorkshire Post of 14 July said 'Sonata highlight of recital'. This was my second one and (if I may) he ended with 'It is a magnificent piece, and was commissioned for the Builders' Festival at the Minster last April'. As if that were not enough, three days later the Yorkshire Post passed on William Coulthard's idea of the same affair: he was lucky, he said, to have been present. He had attended recitals by eminent organists from all over the world, but could not recollect one that thrilled him more than this one; another instance of producing an effect you are unaware of, and wondering why it should come about. That I should quote laudatory words such as this is done not without certain misgiving, certainly in no spirit of showing off and puffing up – simply as George Mallory said about climbing Everest: 'because it's there' – my aim and hope is to provide a true and valid account of what has come as a result of things I have been concerned with.

||O||

When Ramsay Silver left Oxford University Press to take over Banks' Music Publications in York, he signed me up as editor of his new Eboracum Choral Series, asking for a carol to start it off. Having put aside for possible use words I had received on a Christmas card, whose provenance I know nothing of, 'Can I not sing but hoy' were what I chose to set. It was soon completed, and published, though it turned out to be more of a part song than the simple carol that Ramsay probably had in mind. On a trip to Cambridge I ventured showing it to David Willcocks who very kindly put it into the next Nine Lessons and Carols service at King's College. It has not found universal favour, probably because at first sight it appears not to be concerned enough with religion – the usual kind of shepherds, snow, angels and the traditional scenario. It begins:

Can I not sing but hoy,
Whan the Jolly Shepherd made so mych joy?
The shepherd upon a hill he satt;
He had on him his tabard and his hat
Hys tar-box, his pipe, and his flagat;
Hys name was called Jolly, Jolly Wat,
For he was a gud herdés boy
With hoy! With hoy!
For in his pype he made so mich joy.

© Banks Music Publications 1972. Reproduced by permission.

He did, however, see a star 'as rede as blode' and, having 'gon faster than a pace; He found Jhesu in a sympyll place'. So all turned out well in the end, and the printed copy was Number One of the Eboracum Choral Series. In the space of forty years the series has climbed to more than five and a half hundred items, not all of which have I had a hand in editing, by any means.

Of that year's thirty-nine recitals, four were on new or rededicated organs, and one of them was only part of a concert consisting of organ solos to allow the boys from Vienna to rest their voices during their famous choir's Minster appearance. The parish church organ at Saint Neots was one of the restored organs, and a piece was commissioned for the opening recital. In considering what to write, it occurred to me that it was time to try a straightforward prelude and fugue. Some forty years later I might have thought otherwise, having heard a rumour that fugues were no longer in vogue – a surprising idea. Is not a fugue one of the enduring musical forms, unquestioned and unchallenged? However, no such doubts bothered me then, and I set to work, proceeding with not quite the fluency to produce in time something that would do.

Even as I walked through the churchyard to the recital I was trying to solve some problem or other. But all was well for the moment, the piece was accepted; only one dissatisfied listener I heard of thought it was 'the same old stuff' – probably an adherent of what Vaughan Williams called the European Wrong Note System (or similar words). This discouraged me a little and I put it away and forgot it. But reading an article by Simon Nieminski some years later, giving my piece a more honourable character, I put it through a careful revision that now went easily and satisfied me sufficiently to submit it for publication. An excellent recording of it was made on the Doncaster Schulze organ by Joseph Sentance during his time at what is now called Doncaster Minster. As the prelude began with a rippling motif I thought it would do no harm to give the piece a name. Why not *The Brook*? After all, that is how Bach's name sounds in English. And then it was rather nice to discover that the church at Saint Neots, with the river running by, stands in Brook Street: all a happy coincidence occurring of its own volition.

||◯||

Coming now to the age of fifty-five, had I given any thought to the matter I would have realised that I had ten years more at the Minster if all continued happily. By and large it did. My appointment was done on a fairly casual basis, somewhat similar to that of Widor's. No mention of any contract had ever been made; my eventual Minster total of thirty-seven years was worked out on something like a gentleman's agreement and I was fortunate indeed that so far nothing untoward had come along to make insuperable difficulties. Sadly, this was to change in years to come. In the meantime my recitals carried on, alongside the Musical Society chorus and the Symphony Orchestra, packing the days with activity which never ceased, plus plenty of other things as well.

Since the re-founding of the Song School in 1903 the choir practice room had been in an upstairs room of the school building in Minster Yard. In the mid-1960s the Camera Cantorum was opened in memory of Dean Milner-White, a commodious high-ceilinged room off the South Transept and adjacent to the choir vestries. This effectively brought all the choir's activity within the Minster's walls. The wall-space begged to be filled. Gradually this was achieved through the gathering of portraits of the organists and choir over the years. These go back as far as James Nares, appointed in 1734 at the age of nineteen. His three successors (and an unsuccessful fourth) and a large photographic portrait of Doctor EG Monk (organist 1859-84) taken in Dublin also contribute to the interest, along with other photographs of former Minster choirs (and Healey Willan) and an oil painting of John Naylor. The latter was given soon after the choir moved from their quarters across the road in the Song School. Those members of the Camidge dynasty (as one might call it) following Nares, and whose three generations ran the music for one hundred and three years from 1756, are represented by pastel portraits which came to us by one of those fortunate coincidences one dreams of, which happens of its own accord and is far better than one could hope for.

It happened that there was a series on the BBC entitled 'Organ Gallery', in which interviews with various organists were conducted by John Lade. When my turn came in September 1972, for one of the items I was to play and talk about I chose the second of the *Six Concertos for the Organ or Grand Piano Forte* by Matthew Camidge who had been organist of the Minster from 1803 to 1842. Soon after the broadcast I received a letter from Rachel Teasdale, resident in York, with the news that portraits of the Camidges were in existence and in the possession of her sister-in-law Mrs Margaret Teasdale, a descendant of the Camidges. I had known about the portraits, having seen an illustrated article on the Camidges in an issue of the *Musical Times* dating back to the early 1900s, stating that they were in the possession of the organist of Beverley Minster, John Camidge (1853-1939) of the fifth generation of the York line. I had sometimes wondered what had become of them in the years following his death.

In case it is puzzling to those reading this to find there are four portraits and only three Minster organists, the simple reason is that the fourth generation, Thomas Simpson Camidge (1828-1912), was not appointed to succeed his father John (in office 1842-58) as he must have confidently expected considering such ample precedent, and especially since he had shouldered the full responsibility of the job for some ten years after his father suffered a stroke. Being obliged, then, to remove himself from York – and his feelings at being discarded can well be imagined – he secured the appointment of organist at what he called

Hexham Abbey *Cathedral.* Subsequently he moved to spend the rest of his life in The Mumbles, a few miles south of Swansea. His son John, then at Beverley Minster, remained unmarried and was custodian of his ancestors' portraits.

So, furnished with instructions as to where in Retford to find Mrs Teasdale – and conveniently on my way home from somewhere I cannot now recall – I was thrilled to see and to recognize those four faces, now in their true size and colour, and moreover in perfect condition. It was a great moment. Soon it began to appear that Mrs Teasdale, in her charming but limited accommodation, was having some difficulty in being able to house them, and frankly confessing her inability to find a solution to the problem. This, of course, was my cue to come to her aid and to pluck up courage to make the obvious suggestion, having in mind the spectacular effect they would have in our elegant new rehearsal room, being of the right, generous scale for the purpose, and providing the welcome colour element as well as filling the 103-year gap in the two-and-a-half century-long depiction of Minster organists. My suggestion was welcomed, a great deal of gratitude expressed, the canvasses stacked into the boot of the car, and homeward with the precious cargo. They were then re-framed having lost their originals, and each with its metal label duly hung in the Camera Cantorum. Here they provide continuing pleasure in what surely is their right home.

A CENTENARY AND DOWN UNDER

Immediately before I started the North American visit in 1973, Edinburgh had heard my *Brigantia* overture conducted by Gerald Gentry and played by the members of the Youth Orchestra. I heard their excellent playing on a recording. I had been to North America three-yearly since 1961, and this was the fifth tour, fitting in some interesting places. Beginning with Dundas (Ontario), Rutgers University (New Brunswick) came two days after, with Miami (Trinity Episcopal) similarly. In planning my itinerary Lilian Murtagh, my splendid agent, usually managed that length of interval between recitals, though it varied, sometimes allowing me a little longer breathing space. Once, in 1967, there were four on successive evenings on the way west to British Columbia – Saskatoon, Calgary, Edmonton and Victoria – all cathedrals except the Knox United Episcopal church at Saskatoon.

While in Miami I had the thrill of meeting Reginal Foort who was living there, the organist who was a hero of my boyhood with his frequent cinema organ broadcasts. I had a very enjoyable dinner with him in the company of David Thurman, the organist of the church where I played. He was then aged eighty and had been in Miami since 1951 playing at a synagogue and a crematorium. My letter home says that he was looking no more than sixty-five, and that he had been taught by Sir Walter Parratt at the Royal College at the same time as Thalben Ball. David also took me to see whales and dolphins doing a miraculous performance in the seaquarium.

Another unexpected visitor was Mrs Teasdale who had given the Camidge portraits to the Minster choir practice room. She was with her son William (thus a Camidge descendant) visiting from her Retford home in England. I sent news home of the audience, that 'they liked my sonata and the Dupré B major, so I played the two sketches (Dupré) as at Rutgers with great effect. They stood up again to applaud'.

Then to Saint Thomas, New York, once occupied by Tertius Noble and now by Gerre Hancock. Imagine my amazement to find in the audience none other than George Thalben-Ball, over from London, with Carlo Curly (not yet famous) who was chaperoning him around New York. After a master class in Kingston Ontario, onwards to the west coast, Los Angeles, where there were three organs in the church coupled together – in the east and west ends and one between them, of classical design. The wise Lilian Murtagh obtained three days' rehearsal for me to learn how it all functioned, which was not a moment too long. I was glad that every manoeuvre turned out successfully. This concert was unique in another way: I was left to my own devices (which is a great relief from interruption) and do not remember meeting anyone, though I must have been led to the organ and had it turned on for me. But I left the church speaking to no-one and returned to the hotel on my own. It was strange, then, to hear sometime afterwards the opinion that this was the best recital of the series ... one person's verdict.

Boystown was next, appropriately named, with its big school for boys; then Georgetown where I played at Christ Church, whose organist was Ronald Stalford. He became a close friend and came later to York for a term to act as Assistant. Having been a student at Washington Cathedral at the School of Church Music run by Leo Sowerby, he became eventually his executor and responsible for his publications. Lastly to Princeton, where the company of David Drinkwater and George Huddlestone was a pleasure. It was of interest to receive a letter from David after the recital saying he had had so many calls thanking him for having me play.

||O||

Of that year's forty-three recitals in the old country, twelve included my *Sonata Giocosa*, among them Buckfast Abbey, Saint James (Piccadilly), the town halls of Birmingham and Manchester, Ellesmere College,

Bath Abbey, King William's College in Castletown on the Isle of Man, and York during another festival, to which the Duchess of Kent came. That piece was still more or less current news since it was but a year since the completion of the Minster's restoration for which it was composed. For another reason, that recital was a kind of landmark. I was attracted for the first time to a Reger organ piece having come across a performance of the Opus 135B. (I had previously decided that his orchestral works were better.) Having never been motivated to learn any of Reger's works I resolved to mend my ways, choosing to include Opus 135B in this festival programme. As I worked on it, it was increasingly hard to learn, so much so that it was not going to be fit to play in public. I thought I had left ample time but I was wrong. Geoffrey Coffin's ready help with the odd few bars of one hand got me out of the problem in a rather shame-faced state. I did manage a performance on my own in a Newcastle church – successfully I hope – but have given up thoughts of playing any more Reger, which I count as a defeat and a disrespect to this worthy composer.

Two days before, I had been in the church of Saint Wulfram in Grantham in a most enjoyable collaboration with Sir Charles Groves and the Royal Liverpool Philharmonic Orchestra in the first Guilmant symphony with organ. It was a great pleasure to work with Sir Charles who was always sympathetic and unperturbed. I had first met him twenty-four years earlier on a similar occasion in Manchester Town Hall for a broadcast of the second of Rheinberger's concertos on the very day (if my archive is truthful) of the birth of his daughter Sally. I was rather tickled, as well, to be complimented by Maurice Johnson, head of Northern Regional BBC music, for actually Watching The Beat…

I composed an *Evening Hymn* to the words of Sir Thomas Browne for the Exultate singers directed by Garrett O'Brien, who sang it for the first time in Saint John's, Smith Square, on 20 July 1973. And just before this a letter, written in the Royal College of Music, came from Herbert Howells who had recently written his York *Magnificat* and *Nunc Dimittis* and had been in touch with Priscilla, delivering it piecemeal while I was (as he had once said) 'enchanting the Americans'. I had hoped he might come for its launch. His characteristic letter ran:

Saturday 9 June '73

My dear Francis:

Many thanks for a very kind friend–just–back–from–the–Watergate Paradise (and freshly in contact with the horrors of HH canticles) and ready to let us hear that he's none the worse for his USA look-around. It was good to know you are back, and well.

And now that there's so much to face up to in York we hope all of it will not be too much of a burden for you both, and for the choir and Geoffrey [Coffin, Assistant Organist].

I wish I could be there for the Minster's start for it all. But I'll be with you, in my 4pm thoughts on Friday, and keeping fingers crossed for everything you'd wish for: and not only on Friday – but even until Rachmaninov's very last Bell has sounded on the evening of 1st July!

It was so kind of you to say you'd like me to come on Friday. I wish I could!

Love to you – and (please) my greetings to all the members of your choir. Herbert

||O||

October 1973 saw the annual dinner of the Royal College of Organists, most conveniently for the President and his Wife, in York, and in surroundings that could not have been finer – the Georgian Assembly Rooms a short distance from the Minster. The Duchess of Kent, herself an organist, who had spent her young life only a few miles away at Hovingham and had been married in the Minster twelve years before, was to be our most distinguished guest of honour along with the Dean of York, Doctor Alan Richardson. Great was our sorrow when illness prevented Her Royal Highness from being with us: nevertheless the event turned out extremely happily.

After the dinner, formalities and speeches, a short walk brought us to a recently restored and beautified Minster where, seated in the nave, we saw the vaulting, stonework and pillars in their pristine brightness as Bach's great *Fantasia* in G greeted us at the hands of Geoffrey

Coffin. We then heard two pieces of magical quality which fitted the mood of the moment to perfection, Bairstow's *Nocturne*, rarely heard, with its long, leisurely winding melodies in the opulent key of D flat. This was even upstaged by Karg-Elert's *Fuge, Kanzone und Epilog* in which the organ was joined by the ladies of the Chapter House Choir conducted by Andrew Carter, and the violin of Jonathan Trout. This equally rare work, based on the intonation to the creed is, like the Bairstow, in a luxurious key (F sharp) and bears out unmistakably the composer's feelings: 'I love this piece tenderly', writes Karg-Elert, 'it was written, frankly, in a vein of exaltation, and savours of holy water and consecrated candles … That is the Catholic side of me…' The majestic fugue with its commanding short introduction is followed by the ethereal *Kanzone*, which eventually increases in power and ends on a chord of the dominant against which for the first time the violin is heard. Its first note, only a semitone above its lowest, is a stroke of genius and quite unexpected. Here on this evening, in a miraculous way it seemed to fill completely the entire space of the transepts and the tower as it wound its way upwards to hover over the angelic voices making their debut with 'Credo in unum Deum'. Having reached several leger lines and quoted from a previous similar work *Jesu deine tiefen Wunden*, the violin gained the topmost tonic note and stayed there like a star till near the end when, returning to its lowest string, it climbed once more and took its place high over the prolonged oscillating 'Amens' to reach the ultimate perfect fifth over the organ's final added sixth. The only regret was that it had to come to an end. No wonder Stanley Webb's critique (in the RCO Year Book 1974-75) reported that so ended 'a memorable occasion in a mood of exultation'. We felt that the Duchess would have taken pleasure in it, and were sorry she had to miss it.

‖●‖

Naturally, as well as the joyful, interesting things that came our way were the more sombre ones. At the start of 1974 Priscilla and I were in Edinburgh where I was to play in the McEwan Hall on 18 January. We were staying for a couple of nights with the organist of Saint Giles' Cathedral, Herrick Bunney and Mary his wife. We had left their telephone number with my brother knowing that my mother was not well, so it was not too much of a surprise early that morning to be

290

called from the bathroom to the telephone to hear from my sister-in-law that she had died. She was some months short of her eighty-fifth birthday and had been failing for some time, living for a while with Paul my elder brother and Joyce his wife in Malton, having been on her own since my father's death aged fifty-six in 1944. The recital went ahead as planned and we returned home to York the following day.

Three further melancholy events took place in June. On the first of the month was a memorial service for Frederic Waine in the Chapel of Saint Peter's School where he had been in charge of the music before becoming Warden of the Royal School of Church Music in Addington Palace. He and I were associated in more than one York musical institution and were often in touch about some matter or performance concerning the Symphony Orchestra, the Musical Society or something else.

Sidney Campell's death on 4 June was very sad for us, especially for William and Edward who as choristers at Windsor had enjoyed their time with him to the full. I first came to know him way back in his Ely days and counted him a good, reliable friend and support.

Another friend of long standing, Walter Emery, died on 24 June. We first met over organ pieces I wrote which were being published by Novello of which he had the oversight. He was always generous with advice and helped me considerably with the registration of Bach.

As noted above and alluded to in my RCO presidential address, 1974 saw the centenary of Sir Edward's birth. An early hint of what in the way of celebration was to follow appeared in May, which was a concert in the Minster by the York Symphony Orchestra, the programme containing the *Coronation March*, which he had entered for a competition in 1902. There had been one hundred and ninety entries and 'top brass' adjudication, three 'Sirs': Frederick (Westminster) Bridge, Charles Hubert Hastings Parry, and Walter Parratt, but neither Bairstow's nor the winner's efforts have been handed down to later generations and we do not know whether this 1974 performance was a world première. My beginnings of an organ transcription await consummation...

Slightly earlier than the RCO Diploma presentation in Kensington Gore, and in anticipation of the anniversary, in York we had celebrated Sir Edward's centenary with five events. June held three concerts in close succession. Happily, it was York's turn to host the annual combination of York, Ripon and Durham Cathedral choirs which fell on his birthday, 22 August. At evensong there was Bairstow in D – just the thing for a joyful gathering of some eighty or ninety highly trained singers in the resonant spaces of the Minster – and for the anthem, that special piece *If the Lord had not helped me.* That was at four o'clock and, with ninety minutes interval for sustenance, the forces were re-assembled for an early evening concert of church and organ music which included his Choral Ballad *The Prodigal Son,* a late work (1939) of which he was particularly fond but which has not, unfortunately, caught on.

The following Friday there was a concert of his secular works in Saint William's College, that splendid ancient timbered building at the Minster's east end, a venue which was certainly very familiar to Sir Edward through his countless attendances at functions there, among them the annual Choir School speech day at which he usually took the opportunity to say something controversial that was eagerly taken up by the local *Yorkshire Evening Press.* It was also here that a concert of his works had taken place to celebrate his seventieth birthday, in the darkest days of the war, August 1944. Now, thirty years on was a unique opportunity to hear again some of his music that was not so well known as that he wrote for church use, but still containing the same high level of inspiration and faultless craftsmanship. These qualities are especially evident in the *Six Variations on an Original Theme* for violin and piano, dedicated to Sybil Eaton in 1916, a friend of long standing.

She regularly took part for very many years in the Saint Matthew Passion in the Minster each Palm Sunday. Her main role was the obbligato of the aria *Erbarm dich,* which was always sure of its most expressive interpretation at her hands and under the inspired direction of Sir Edward. The violin *Variations,* being the high spot of the programme, were placed as the last item, providing an ethereal ending to the event. The two-piano *Variations* had come earlier, midway between vocal items and part songs. Both works are finely fashioned and worthy of being better known.

The next day was the Minster's patronal festival of Saint Peter and also the annual Festival of the Friends of York Minster. It was my privilege to give a memorial address in the august presence of a goodly number of its members and several Bairstow relatives, chiefly Sir Edward's daughter Nancy (Mrs George Brown) and his most famous pupil who became organist of Westminster Abbey and then Principal of the Royal Scottish Academy of Music and Drama in Glasgow, Sir Ernest Bullock. In the north quire aisle of the Minster the Friends of the Minster erected a stone tablet containing the names of the organists up to that point – twenty-seven of them since 1474, a span of precisely five hundred years. It commemorates the centenary of one of its noblest occupants, whose daughter was present to unveil it.

At evensong the Canticles were sung to his unison service in E flat of 1923, and the anthem, *Blessed City*, one of the greatest pieces at the disposal of church and cathedral choirs, which made its appearance annually, at this service. The E flat *Magnificat* and *Nunc Dimittis* are a finer conception than might be expected: though he was writing for an incomplete choir he gave nothing less than his best. In the evening there was a memorial concert in Huntington church where Sir Edward and Lady Bairstow are buried. Information about the event unfortunately is in short supply. One of the evenings saw a dinner party in our big Minster Court dining room for the Bairstows who had come for the commemoration. This was organised and carried out by Priscilla with her unfailing unflappability.

The second of our broadcast evensongs on 17 July (two at a time, a week apart, was the pattern at that time) had Bairstow in G (of 1940) for canticles and *Lord, thou hast been our refuge* for the anthem. We also recorded this on a long-playing Centenary Disc of his music along with the double-choir version of the *Te Deum* and *Benedictus*, the three introits of OUP, *Lord I call upon thee*, and the organ sonata.

It was my resolve to include a piece of his in every one of my recitals through the entire year. This did not prove completely possible, but I managed it in twenty-eight of the forty-three I gave; and in exactly half of *them* the *Sonata* figured, the rest having several *Nocturne* appearances, the *Prelude* in C, and *Evening Song* in various measures. There had also been an earlier concert in March, an earnest of things to come, given in the Minster by the Royal Artillery band, into which I contributed the *Nocturne* and the *Prelude* in C.

The summer series of organ recitalists made our contribution as each programme contained one of his compositions: Melville Cook was over here from Toronto; Dudley Holroyd of Bath Abbey; Gwyn Hodgson, erstwhile Minster chorister who had a post in Denmark; Rodney Baldwyn of Pershore Abbey; Geoffrey Coffin, Assistant at York; and myself.

Durham also remembered its Professor of Music in a recital in which the cathedral choir, conducted by Richard Lloyd, sang six pieces of his church music in two groups of three to begin and end the concert; *Blessed City* forming a rousing start and *If the Lord had not helped me* (one of Bairstow's most deeply felt works) a peaceful ending. Both sets of variations were there, the *Sonata*, and songs, notably four of the *Songs of the Spirit* (his swan song) sung by Gordon Pullin. As at York, Nigel Harrison was violinist, Charles Macdonald partnering me on the other piano, and Alan Thurlow, then the cathedral's Assistant, not yet moved to Chichester, for accompanying the choir.

Especially memorable was the event in Wigan parish church on 12 June, recalling Bairstow's seven-year spell there as organist. David Cutter, then holding that office, conducted the choir. As well as *Save us, O Lord* and *Jesu the very thought of thee*, they included the delightful arrangement of the lovely Angers Melody *The day draws on with golden light* and, remembering his close association with Ernest Bullock, native of Wigan, his *Give us the wings of faith*. The *Prelude* in C, the *Scherzo* in A flat, the *Toccata-Prelude on Pange Lingua* and the *Sonata* all found their way on to that programme. This all made a deep impression, as shown in David's lovely letter to me the following day:

> 'I cannot let this day close without writing to you. Judging by the comments that have reached me during the day, our efforts last night have made an enormous impact on those who were present... "Experience" and "dignified" are the two words most frequently being used... One of the choirmen said ... that they had felt inspired by the accompaniment, and as the evening went on, they began to realise that it was no ordinary occasion.'

The busy, eventful year was not yet at an end: more activity would certainly be in store, so something of a relaxing nature was undertaken in the shape of a short visit to Paris. Edward, then aged 17, and I took off on 15 August and found that capital in a relaxed mood enjoying plentiful summer warmth causing a thirst which required frequent slaking, somewhat to the disadvantage of our budgeting, but we enjoyed to the full places of interest such as the Père Lachaise cemetery where lie so many familiar personalities, among them Rossini, Oscar Wilde, Voltaire and Chopin. For the latter some admirer had placed a candle that was burning peacefully in the calm air. We did a good deal of walking and of course a visit to the Musée Maurice Ravel at Montfort L'Amaury was obligatory – my third – where I took Edward's photograph in the same place and position as Ravel was once pictured on his balcony.

||O||

No such musical experience as the concert which followed the 1973 RCO dinner in York happened a year later. At last in October 1974 we were able to welcome Her Royal Highness to an event at London's Savoy Hotel which proved no less enjoyable than that at York. The Bishop of London (Doctor Gerald Ellison, a Vice-Patron of the RCO) proposed the toast of the College, producing in the course of his speech a pencil once belonging to Sir Walter Parratt, organist at Saint George's Chapel when the bishop was a chorister there. And it turned out that his two sons and both ours had also been Windsor choristers in their time.

The RCO Year Book report was written by that genius-with-words Gordon Reynolds, a contemporary of mine I had known since teenage years. We had first met in the organ loft of Beverley Minster at the hands of Doctor HK Andrews the organist, not yet moved on to New College, Oxford. 'The President's speech', he wrote, 'like a good musical composition, reached a climax – and that climax achieved an element of surprise'.

Speaking to Her Royal Highness, I as President said:

'Looking forward to tonight, several members of the College Council have been putting their heads together and have written organ pieces which we have collected and had bound into a small volume. You are an organist yourself, but we are not going to ask you to play them at sight here and now. We are not even able, alas, to ask the composers to play them one after another, all eleven of us, so that there would be a kind of musical General Election to find the best one. You come from a beautiful part of a very special county, so we have taken the title from your home village and called the collection *Hovingham Sketches*. We hope you will accept it as a token of our warm appreciation of your presence here tonight, and we hope that the pieces themselves will give some pleasure – and that you will enjoy playing them.'

Gordon ended his account of the proceedings: 'with this delightful, indeed historic, presentation the formalities of the evening were concluded. Members and their guests were free to extemporise verbally at their own tempo upon the themes suggested – or upon any other'. He then enlisted the titles of the eleven compositions, each with its composer.

That being accomplished so pleasurably, I gave no further thought to the matter: I had never considered publication for what was after all a private gift to a royal personage, so when, quite some time later, three of the composers – Peter Hurford, Richard Popplewell, and Arthur Wills – enquired about the possibility of publication of their pieces, they went ahead with their individual publishers. The remaining eight – those by Arthur J Pritchard, William Lloyd Webber, Bernard Rose, Eric H Thiman, Harold Darke, George Thalben-Ball, Herbert Howells, and myself – were undertaken by Banks, then under the direction of Ramsay Silver, some nine years after their launching, in an attractive pale blue cover with a print picturing Hovingham Hall, the Duchess's first home. This brought from her a signed copy and a grateful letter in her own hand.

As a kind of postscript, a wonderful letter came from Gordon Reynolds, setting the seal on the memorable happening and the considerable effort made by many towards its success. The letter ran:

Chapel Royal, Hampton Court Palace, East Molesey, Surrey

15.10.74

Dear Francis

Last Wednesday was quite splendid. I do congratulate you on presiding over the finest end-of-term-of-office proceedings I have ever been to. HRH so obviously enjoyed being there and everyone was so friendly (I could hardly believe they were organists). It occurred to me, having relieved you of your poem, that you might not know why! Barry Lyndon asked me to write an account for the Year Book. I was so delighted to hear it in your delightful speech and felt I must quote a bit. I shall write to Paul Jennings and ask his permission... Many thanks for the loan.

'Lo, God is here' [an anthem I had written which they had been singing at the Chapel Royal where Gordon Reynolds was organist. I had set the trebles a slight problem without being aware.] went down like a bomb (no, that doesn't sound right – anyway it went well and we all liked it very much). What I call 'the hard entry' is the boys' one in bar 34. They were a bit dim in rehearsal.

Again, our most grateful thanks to you and your wife for a lovely evening.

Yours ever,

Gordon

The poem he alludes to has given me so much pleasure by its subtlety and brilliance I venture to hope that it may similarly enchant readers of this tale. My copy, cut from the *Observer*, bears the author's signature obtained from him at no less a place than East Bergholt where he was an observer at a master class I was giving.

Seated One Day

'THE SYRINX of olden times, which was to become the FRESTEL of the minstrels, is still used in the Balkans and by the goatherds of the Pyrenees, who burble limpid tunes by blowing into their PIHARETS or PIHURLECS . . . the organ also includes reed-stops; their ancestors may be found in the Greek AULOS . . . as also in the Chinese CHENG or mouth-organ . . . the Romans used them, as is evident from the TIBIA UTRICULARIS. From this instrument originated the Breton CORNEMUSE, or BINIOU, the CABRETTE of Auvergne, the Italian ZAMPOGNA, the Spanish and Portuguese GAITA, the Scottish BAGPIPES, etc.' – *Organ Music. Leduc.*

Up in his loft the shy FRCO
Pours splendour on the shufflers-out below
Whose thoughts now run more on the Sunday joint
Than mounting majesties of counterpoint
And only six or seven, whose souls are finer,
Stay for the climax of the great G Minor
Or for the player's public-private dream
(Since Improvising On A Given Theme
Was one of many subjects passed in, all
In that odd building near the Albert Hall).
O, what musician stands comparison
With maestros of the Willis or the Harrison
And Harrison? O artists in the round
Rearing colossal palaces of sound
Or, if a dreamy air be thought the best
Drawing sweet sadness from the Voix Celeste!
Here in my verse your ancestry I blazon,
Ye ancient heroes of the diapason.

Long before Europe knows of loud-voic'd choirs
The goat-foot God with *syrinx*-note inspires
And Balkan shepherds burble limpid tunes
First played by Fauns on far-off Afternoons;
Bach wrote some down – not all; the rest'll
Only be heard on *piharet* or *frestel;*
Only where Bretons guard their lambs and ewes
Is heard the full magic of the *cornemuse*
See how the organ owes an ancient debt
To the wild *bagpipes* and the loud *cabrette,*
See, where the southern light grows ever brighter
The Portuguese wakes echoes with his *gaita*
Which, like the *cheng* amid the paddy crops,
Sounds even reedier than French organ stops.
For *cheng* and *aulos, biniou* and *flute*
All issue forth from music's ancient root;
Now your great engine keeps them all in station;
Here, at the fount of music's console-ation

By art the wild notes now are organised,
By art the song of Pan is Christianised: -
Hail to you, organists, who, behind a screen
Each day reveal the God in the Machine.'

Paul Jennings
Observer 11.1.59

‖O‖

Another visit to the metropolis in October, shortly after the RCO dinner, brought yet one more performance of Bairstow's *Sonata*. This was in the Royal Festival Hall, with Stanford's *Fantasia and Toccata*, the *Passacaglia* of Alan Ridout and two Bach Preludes and Fugues – the *Wedge* and the G major respectively – for start and finish: except that, as one critic said 'As an encore, Dr Jackson played with great élan and verve his *Diversion for Mixtures* – a splendid end to a most enjoyable and interesting recital'. 'ANA' was the writer, who spotted that I obviously had great affection for the Sonata and commended the performance. Felix Aprahamian in his immaculate programme note was sympathetic, afterwards in the Sunday Times on 20 October, a little less so: 'of Sir Edward Bairstow's *Sonata* only the central *Scherzo* (recently republished to mark the centenary of his birth) redeemed conventional respectability with a touch of rhythmic verve'. Of the two other critiques one said the *Sonata* was 'a fine example of the between–the-wars cathedral style, ... projected with authority in the grandly ruminative outer movements and virtuosity in the central Scherzo'.

And thirdly, Nicholas Webber thought it 'provided an object lesson in craftsmanship. It was certainly fitting that the composer's successor at York should be giving it at a Festival Hall premier, particularly since he has made the first recording (Canon Records CNN 4977). ... the unusual layout of the three movements ... make it a neglected work of exceptional interest ... Jackson played with splendid verve and assurance, going on to one of his own pieces as an encore'. Alan Ridout was present to hear his *Passacaglia*; he 'and the recitalist both received a well deserved ovation'. (ANA)

In view of the fact that Bairstow was a native of Huddersfield, his *magnum opus* for the organ was an essential item on the newly constituted parish church organ there. In the Examiner newspaper Malcolm Cruise wrote that 'The Great Sonata written in 1937 when Sir Edward was on holiday in the Isle of Arran is a work of great beauty. Its melodies, its harmonic progressions, and its devilishly difficult but exciting *Scherzo* [in planning the work Bairstow wanted the central movement to be 'a real devil'] all combine to make this a piece which sticks in the mind. And Dr Jackson made a superb job of it, finding his way about the new console almost as if he had designed it himself'.

There remained twelve recitals of the year's total of forty-three, of which half a dozen included the *Sonata* – Marlow (Buckinghamshire), Mirfield, Glasgow (the RCO recital at Renfield Parish Church), Manchester Town Hall, Huddersfield (the inaugural recital on the newly rebuilt organ in Holy Trinity Parish Church), and the Durham commemoration already mentioned. Heworth (part of York) had *Evening Song*, which was also heard at Roundhay (part of Leeds) alongside the *Prelude* in C and the *Scherzo* in A flat. I like to imagine that we celebrated the great man with something approaching adequacy: certainly it was a labour of love, most interesting, hugely enjoyable, and an expression of much gratitude.

Before the end of this centenary year there was just time for one more event which, while not intended as one and happening quite inadvertently, was a new edition of the York Minster Chant Book, used by the choir daily and containing the music for the psalms. The first edition had emerged in 1916, the work of Doctor Bairstow helped by GA Scaife, his colleague in the Song School. There was a second edition in December 1929. And for the third it seemed that 'Christmas 1974' which, the preface states, was an appropriate time for its launching. There were, however, fifty-three chants printed a second time at the end of the book, the purpose being to take care of the great festivals: Ash Wednesday, Good Friday, Ascension Day, Christmas Day and the Sovereign's Accession when special psalms were used. A fine collection, it was firmly based among the classical chants but included more recent ones, notably seventeen of Bairstow's own, and five remarkable ones by one of the Minor Canons of whom he thought very highly, the Reverend George Surtees Talbot (1875-1918). These all remain in my edition, along with additions by PC Buck, Andrew Carter, Edgar Day, Philip Marshall, Stanley Vann, and William Wolstenholme, in addition to two by LL Dix which replaced two others of his introduced in 1929.

As well as ten of mine, one does not forget Mr Scaife's contribution; he basked in the reflected glory of his dual-purpose E minor-major chant every First Evening of the month with Psalm 6; that and a Benedicite (which sadly has not survived) being his contribution to the repertoire.

TT Noble, on departing from the Minster in 1913 for Saint Thomas (New York), was allowed to leave five of his chants, and only one other composition, the Morning and Evening service in B minor, which apparently passed Bairstow's exacting standards – or just escaped his likely unfavourable and prejudiced judgement. He had a low opinion of Victorian church music and might have been inclined to place Noble's works among it. Bairstow's immediate and laconic reaction to my telling him I had seen Noble conducting the Magnificat and Nunc Dimittis at the 1934 Gloucester Three Choirs Festival, for which he had used an accompaniment for full orchestra, was 'It's not worth it'. One suspects that it avoided the chop at York purely on sufferance. Now, more than half a century on, it has achieved a certain period charm and maintains a secure place in the majority of cathedral repertoires.

‖❍‖

One had to be ready for anything and there was always something new happening. Over the years commissions have come by various different routes: telephone calls, letters and personal requests. Once when giving a recital overseas it was suggested that I might be commissioned to write an anthem for a commemoration of the church's foundation. I was asked to name a fee – on the spot – but wriggled out of that since it needs careful handling. The commission came later, along with a libretto and a *photograph* of a cheque. The amount however was rather less than I had anticipated and a letter was sent conveying that message, which brought forth the reply that it would be increased by fifty per cent. But I never had any news as to the reception of the piece and hope that it proved suitable for its purpose.

In February 1975 in the Roman Catholic church of Saint Teresa, Clarendon Street, Dublin, my rehearsing up in the west end gallery was objected to vociferously in loud tones by an elderly gentleman who would not be reasoned with. My noises were authorised and, as always, the recitalist is granted opportunity to become used to an unfamiliar instrument. There were several other folk present which made me unwilling to engage in an unseemly verbal contest, but what I tried to convey to him in as polite a manner as possible had no effect. His proper course was to speak to a member of the staff. I do not remember how the matter was resolved; I am sure I continued playing, and the recital was accomplished as planned.

Back to my hotel, and to bed with the wireless informing us all of the day's happenings. The unwelcome news came through that Doctor Alan Richardson, Dean of York and our next-door neighbour, had suddenly died. This was unexpected, of course, although he was known not to be in the best of health. His verger said that 'After the Dean had given the blessing and received the alms he told me he didn't feel well. I helped him into the vestry where he collapsed'. He was sixty-nine and had been at York for eleven years, running Minster affairs in a quietly efficient manner, but shouldering for its full five years the trauma of the restoration, leaving him but three years to enjoy its successful completion.

But now, in two days' time, there was to be the important service of enthronement of Archbishop Coggan's successor, Stuart Blanch, in which the Dean's part was an important one. The service went ahead, and then there were the funeral arrangements to make at once. The Archbishop of Canterbury came to preach and the hymns were: 'Christ is made the sure foundation', 'The King of love my shepherd is' to the Dykes tune and 'O thou who camest from above' (Hereford) with Gibbons-Bairstow 'Jesu grant me this, I pray' sung by the choir, and Psalm 121.

We then waited to learn who we were to have as the next dean – always an uncertain time. We did not have to wait long to learn it was to be Ronald Jasper, the mainspring of the new liturgies. Up to this point we had been able to cling gratefully to the ones we were brought up with and were perfectly contented to carry on using. But now the prospect looked somewhat different. What happened next was all rather sad. Everything had been going along perfectly satisfactorily and we could see no necessity for altering it. The dictum of Lucius Carey, Lord Falkland, told me by our good minor canon John McMullen, came to mind: 'If it is not necessary to change, it is necessary not to change'. But others were insisting that it *was* necessary. The regret at this point was the changing of the liturgies, but later my relationship with the new Dean lacked the personal contact I had been used to from previous years: letters would be pushed through the door, the sight of which was never welcome; or I would receive a verbal message through some other person. I had been used to having a dean bursting through the front door (we never locked it in those days) discussing whatever matter was needed in a reasonable manner. However, it was possible to continue, but without the unalloyed pleasure that once had been the norm and fortunately without any noticeable fall in the standard of the choir's performance that I was aware of. Extramural activity carried on as before in its interesting and varied manner, which was a kind of lifeline. There had been an idea put forward, though not too officially, that I should cease taking outside jobs, spending the whole time looking after the sung services. But it must have been realized that this would be unpractical; and what was an Assistant there for? Any cathedral organist was expected to show his face in the outside world for one purpose or another.

It was some time before I had the chance to play in the Netherlands: this came, first, in April 1975 when I went with the Chapter House Choir and Andrew Carter, its conductor, for a short tour involving appearances in Dordrecht, Leiden and the Catholic Cathedral of Saint Bavo in Haarlem. This afforded the valuable opportunity to see for myself the nature of the famous organs of which that country possesses so many and was a very enjoyable episode as well as being informative.

In celebration of his centenary year, Ravel's *Toccata* and *Jeux d'Eau* as well as his *Trio* formed part of a concert entirely of his music in the Tempest Anderson Hall. Unfortunately it was not well attended, which was probably an indication that this composer's music had not begun to be appreciated by the city's music lovers; or alternatively, that the artists at this recital though well-known in Manchester were strangers to York's concert-goers. The programme also had Ravel songs sung by Gordon Pullin, among them the *Histoire Naturelles*.

On 19 December there was a concert of carols by candlelight by the Chapter House Choir. There were also hand bells, a speciality of members of the choir. Geoffrey Coffin had put up a chamber organ, and for this occasion I wrote a partita, using a Somerset Carol for variations. With one manual and a small number of stops not a great amount of variety was possible but there was a single pedal stop – a sixteen-foot reed which lent a distinct character to the tutti as well as possibilities for a certain type of solo work. One variation was for pedals alone (with manuals coupled) and had references to the big G minor Bach fugue. Ever since, sporadic working at it, titivating and adding now and again a new movement, has brought it no nearer completion (with the best will in the world). The tune in question (number 32 in the *Oxford Book of Carols*) has a certain similarity to 'God rest you merry gentlemen'. There is the odd reference to the Messiah overture, and a none-too-discreet likeness to the *Variations on a Noel* of Dupré, as well as a nod in the direction of Rachmaninoff. It will not be a bad thing to have it in a final, finished state.

One morning in 1976 Priscilla answered a telephone call from a Peter Ashmore asking to speak to me. 'The Queen has asked me to find out if you are free to come to lunch on Tuesday 26 October. am Master of the Household...' at which my first reaction was that someone was pulling my leg – only for a moment though. The diary was at hand and, *mirabile dictu*, nothing there. Then followed the Master of the Household's voice – 'Good, I will send you a card and perhaps you will be good enough to acknowledge it'. It arrived next morning. How in the world was I chosen for one of the lunch parties?

A fortnight later my fellow guests and I were met at the imposing Palace entrance by members of the household. They were welcoming and friendly and, soon after introductions were made over aperitifs in a small drawing room, the Queen and the Duke plus two corgis joined their guests. We were all introduced and they mingled until there was a general stir and our host and hostess led us into the nearby dining room. Here the oval table was laid for twelve, the Queen and the Duke sitting opposite one another in the middle of each side. We had previously been shown a table plan at the same point as the guest list. On the Queen's left was Hugh Scanlon (of the TUC) with Doctor Moulton on her right. I sat on the left of Lady Elizabeth Bassett, Extra Lady in Waiting to the Queen Mother, who was very sweet and kindly with on my left Doctor Moulton who makes bicycles with small wheels and, formerly, cycles which folded but were not popular. We were soon able to touch on the subject of organs. He felt a certain responsibility for the one in his Wiltshire church which one of his forbears had given the time for whose restoration could not, he was fairly certain, be far off. He could not remember who the builder was and asked for suggestions. My first and only one was right: Willis.

Conversation and lunch flowed smoothly and, everyone having finished, the Queen rose and led us back to the drawing room where coffee was served. At one point Sir Peter said to me 'come and talk to the Queen' who was engaged with yachtsman Rodney Patisson, so we made a trio. During our conversation she referred to 'your organ at the Minster' and the upheaval of the restoration and I mentioned the removal of the thirty-two foot reed and the ominous cracks in the vaulting. At this point John Edwards, Editor of the Yorkshire Post, joined us and we talked of the cleaning and restoration of old buildings including Leeds Town Hall and the controversial opinions about this. Sir Peter joined us and said to me 'go and talk to the Duke' and I moved on.

In a short time the Queen began to shake hands with us in turn, followed by the Duke, and the guests and staff moved towards the door. It was very nice to be handed copies of the menu, the guest list and seating plan as we left; reminders of a privileged and happy occasion which left one marvelling at the immense amount of care and thought shown by all those participating in the memorable and wonderful occasion. After farewells to staff we left the Palace, the whole event having taken two hours. I had a lift with some other guests in Hugh Scanlon's car to the end of the Mall. A call at the British Council and Valerie Emery's bookshop left me plenty of time to catch my four o'clock train home and to go to the last rehearsal of the Duruflé *Requiem* for the following Saturday's concert by the Musical Society.

||O||

It was suggested that I should pay a visit to Australia in 1978. The idea came from Cyril Cobley, who lived with his wife Audrey on the outskirts of York and taught in Australia. He worked hard out there, promoting interest in the possibility of my going. For me this was a big adventure, not least the flight there on 19 April (take-off 22.15), by way of Bahrain (6.00am breakfast), Madras (11.15 lunch), Sydney (6.00), Adelaide (2.25) – according to my diary.

My first recital was in Adelaide Cathedral where David Swale was organist. David had been a chorister and pupil with Sir Edward at York. He had been a firm and valued friend from his chorister days onwards, sharing the tandem holiday and being my best man at our wedding. He was also on the musical faculty of the University of Adelaide (later becoming dean) and arranged a lecture in which I dealt with Bairstow. By way of Melbourne I flew to Burnie on the north coast of Tasmania for a recital in Saint George's church; another in Launceston, plus a civic reception, and one more at Hobart. This was all overseen by Herbert Woodhouse, well-known as a York organist and now president of the organist fraternity in Tasmania.

Next, to Melbourne University where the recent two-manual organ in Ormond College was not easy. Ron Sharp had built it (as well as the organ in the Sydney Opera House) and it was supplied with a much-vaunted type of action to the keys known as 'suspended tracker' that I had not experienced before. I had, however, heard it praised (though probably not by an organ player) for its lightness of touch. It was more likely to have been an organ maker's achievement, his pride and joy. Having been used to an average key weight of not less than about four-and-a-half ounces as a pretty general rule, I had very great difficulty in being able to play cleanly on a much easier action. I was glad to have three days in which to get used to the new situation, working very hard and, as I thought, becoming equal to it. It was therefore more than a surprise to be confronted with a chapel overflowing with young and enthusiastic humanity who were occupying every square inch of seating and standing space; a severe test for my nerves. Seldom if ever have I been in a position like this. I had imagined I was now immune from mistakes anyway, and especially having made such careful preparations here in the university chapel at Melbourne, but at times it seemed that my labours had been in vain. After it was all finished I do not remember being aware of comment of any sort. I cannot help but bear in mind that one's performance can appear very much worse to oneself than to the listener. I hope that this was the case at Ormond: one day I might meet someone who was there and has a remembrance of it.

Before this I had given a recital in Saint Paul's Cathedral, Melbourne, where June Nixon was doing a great work with the choir and with whom, and her husband Neville, I struck up a delightful and lasting friendship. The splendid Lewis organ did good work on the Wedge, Franck's first *Chorale*, my *Toccata Chorale and Fugue*, and the two Dupré *Sketches*. A recording, which included Bach's *Toccata* BWV 564, was also made by the ABC. There was a similar programme at Canberra, and Sydney Cathedral was given Statham's *Rhapsody on a Ground*, with my *Sonata Giocosa* among other items. At Saint James, King Street, I played for evensong. The choir was run in fine style by Walter Sutcliffe, from Yorkshire, at whose house I stayed. He played double bass in the Sydney Symphony Orchestra, whose concert I attended in the opera house. I did not meet the organ there, but did a recording for broadcast on the famous Hill organ in the Town Hall – the one with the 64-foot reed. I was driven over the Blue Mountains to Bathurst to direct an RSCM service. Much later I found out that a former Bishop of that Diocese was one of the Camidge family of York Minster organists from 1756 to 1859.

Another organ pleasure was provided by Brisbane City Hall where the five-manual Willis III put me in mind of a fresh, clear and sparkling mountain stream. The Statham *Rhapsody*, however, did not please the music critic: 'song-like' he considered it, in a somewhat deprecating vein. A lecture next day (on what topic I have no record) was followed by a sleeper to Sydney, a religious interview by the ABC, and a Eucharist in the cathedral with RSCM town choirs, which was the first broadcast of the new liturgy. The new prayer book had just been published and a lengthy discussion meeting had been enjoined to decide which of the many liturgical options offered by the book were to be taken. Then by way of Adelaide I flew to Perth to be the guest of Canon Peter Mold on Wednesday 10 June, and was met by him and David O'Neil, the cathedral organist. I am reproducing here a slightly edited account of events, written in odd moments somewhat in the manner of a diary.

Chez Precentor Canon Peter Mold, I found a sixteenth century prayer in one of his books:

Help us this day O God to serve thee devoutly and the world busily.
May we do our work wisely, give succour secretly,
go to our meat appetitely, sit thereat discreetly, arise temperately,
please our friends duly, go to our bed merrily and sleep surely:
for the joy of our Lord Jesus Christ. Amen.

– all constituting a very nice recipe.

Recital yesterday at the University in Winthrop Hall. Good Walker 1964. Short scrappy programme chosen by Professor Frank Callaway. Large audience around three hundred lunchtime. Then lunch with Mr & Mrs Rally and Timothy (originally from York, England) in University restaurant overlooking the wide Swan River.

Evening lecture. 160 present – last year 40. I had not received warning of this – letter to Adelaide never reached me. I told them about York Minster for 50 minutes, and then was asked questions mainly about the new liturgy. A definite feeling against it, and that the new Australian prayer book had been forced on them. So we were much in agreement, though at first I thought I might be speaking out of turn. Even Bishop Macdonald agreed with me (an assistant Bishop, not the Diocesan).

Thursday, 9.30 press conference at the Cathedral: much photography, local telly to record interview. Rest afternoon. Evening dinner with Dean, Mrs Cornish and three boys aged fourteen to seventeen, Philip, Jonathan, Nicholas. Torrential rain. Last night (ie Friday), I took the cathedral choir practice – Me in G for Sunday morning mass and Vittoria and Batten motets. Amateur and devoted; not very competent men but try hard. Boys good but flat especially when singing descending phrases. At the lecture (Wednesday) appeared Jane Neurick, Elsie Suddaby's niece with husband (doctor) and son Jonathan who records for the University FM station. He also recorded my Winthrop Hall recital and broadcast *Diversion for Mixtures* last night on a short 'What's On' programme. They had come some distance (one hundred miles I think) and saw the Suddaby in me as I walked in: no doubt whatever, they said. She is very sweet and calm. Daughter of Mabel and is, I think, my third cousin. She has a family tree and will let me have a copy when it turns up from being lost.

Winthrop Hall organ is Walker, new style, somewhat idiosyncratic as regards the Choir which is divided but has the usually enclosed department unenclosed, resulting in a slightly unsatisfactory situation. The Tutti is good and vital, varied and colourful. I was advised not to bother too much about the recital so arrived only about an hour in advance to rehearse. Very soon people began to sit in the hall and they remained as more came to join them. So I had to retire leaving much undone. I felt jittery, not helped by having had two cups of strong coffee at breakfast. *Diversion* was not a success and made me blush at the broadcast: all right as long as no-one recorded it for closer inspection. Professor Frank Callaway attended, as did John Hind, one of the music lecturers who I knew when he was director of music at Sedbergh. He showed me the new regal organ just arrived, very beautiful to see, not all yet in working order. Lunch by the wide Swan estuary. Visited the new concert hall with very good new Ron Sharp organ. A splendid hall complex. The organ, though quite excellent, is not any better than most modern organs of England (Walker, Mander) and Europe, despite the maker's protestations that no one else is able to produce an organ worth the name but himself… 'I don't build organs for organists but musical instruments for musicians to play.' I understand what he says, though would not see any need to be quite so definite.

Sometimes David O'Neill, who has come to replace the organist who was sacked by the present dean for incompetence, feels up against it very much, but does his best and is really bringing the choir steadily upwards. He knows his job and inspires loyalty. He readily accepted my diagnosis on the boys' intonation, flatness caused by too wide downward leaps, and worked on them and effected some improvement. So it was nice to feel that however incompetent one feels oneself to be, my presence seems to have given them some encouragement. I gave an hour's recital for school children, well organised, and a full church. One master seemed nervous of keeping the return bus waiting and led out his pupils before the end, a disturbance which I found disconcerting. And I did not overrun – perhaps by two minutes – but his bus had not yet arrived when the rest were leaving.

On what was to have been my last day in Perth a dinner was arranged in my honour. I think I might have appeared to them to symbolize music from the outside world, from which one is inclined to suspect that they feel themselves cut off. But I could be wrong. I was decked in a dinner jacket on hire (paid for by the Cathedral) and all the world came, except the Archbishop who had another date but sweetly came for cocktails beforehand. The dinner was in what I think they call the Festival Hall – same centre as the Sharp organ. The dining room, which comfortably held the fifty to sixty participators, was richly upholstered in warm bright red, with much brown wood. The Dean, soon after the meal had begun, got up and let off some jokes, indicating we must be light-hearted. Then at the end I had to do my stuff. I had again been advised not to bother about my speech, but it had of course exercised me. I don't know how good it was but they were exceedingly kind and receptive, far more than they should have been. They were not, I think, exclusively organists, so they were much easier to cope with. Canon Young's wife Barbara had learned art with Betty, Priscilla's sister, at Beverley High School in Yorkshire.

The Cathedral organ has a Walker extension choir as has Launceston (though not so markedly) and others of the period (c. 1960-65), so is not so useful in that department. The whole organ used to be in a rather good chamber (where now only the enclosed choir and the console reside) until it was moved into the south transept against the south wall. Whereas the chamber projects diagonally down the nave, the present position of the main organ stops the sound getting there as the pipes speak northward into the opposite transept. It is all in process of being restored – or cleaned – by a one-man concern, making excuses for not doing the job properly (I had to manage with a permanently open swell box for my recital). The matter of organ maintenance in Australia is a difficult one. Not many organs are spread thinly over a vast area, requiring great expense to encompass.

My homeward plane landed at Heathrow, two hours late (which is minimal considering some delays one hears of). Priscilla met me at 9.30am and we took the short journey to Radlett to see my cousin Elsie Suddaby, the singer, then in a nursing home and faithfully befriended by her neighbour Margaret Polhill. The organist of the church there was Robert Crowley, who soon afterwards commissioned a piece from me called *Legend* for a recital he was giving in Saint Paul's Cathedral. Another call was made at Buckden where Stanley Griffiths and his wife (my sister Angela) had recently moved to look after the parish: he was soon to be made a Canon of Ely.

We then moved to Harrogate for a few days on to the site of the Yorkshire Showground where from our caravan we had the viaduct well in our sights and the fascination of trains passing over it. This was a welcome chance to unwind in calm surroundings before setting off together for an extended stay in Switzerland. My absence from duty at the Minster from mid-April to the end of July had come about through my realisation that there were things known as sabbaticals.

They were beginning to gain ground and it occurred to me one day that the principle might apply to me. One was somewhat amazed to find that there were cases of grants for such leave to some who had been in office as little as five years; and the length could have extended to a whole year, though this may have been only in rare instances. There was I labouring intensively for thirty-two years with nothing but the statutory holidays and from 1961 a triennial tour of the United States lasting four or six weeks. My plea was listened to, UK work was halted, and the Minster carried on without me.

We arranged a house exchange with Doktor and Frau Weiss, who came to our Minster house and in turn lent us theirs high up on the mountain above Lake Maggiore where we spent six idyllic weeks exploring the delights of the area. Our excursions included such places as Brissago (for shopping and very expensive supplies); Pallanza (for the botanical gardens at Villa Taranto, put there by an Englishman); Isola Bella, then across the lake to Ranzo and the fine church of S. Abbondos. From our lovely dwelling we could clearly see the hydrofoil as it conveyed its passengers to the various stations along the lakeside. So far below us it looked for all the world like a toy. On our side of the lake was a spectacular yellow chapel standing all on its own half way up the hillside. It was called the chapel of Sacro Monte and was being restored. We returned more than once to make sketches and water-colours of it. As to plant life, Spanish chestnuts clothed the hillsides in unending profusion, and Saint John's Wort was very much in evidence.

Cannobio, a short distance across the border into Italy, held a market (*mercato*) on Sunday morning. It was very popular, well patronized, and the boat was well filled and arrived safely. We found a cheese, Taleggio, which we took a fancy to (and which we came across again to our delight some years later in Rome). It is, as I remember, something like Brie, but does not seem to be a good export commodity. Around two o'clock the whole gathering melted away leaving a vast harvest for the salvage executives, whereupon we set out to explore the town, attractive and cool with its narrow streets. It was noticeable that organs thereabouts had classical cases and bright, new looking pipes, most likely made of tin.

We enjoyed reading; I found *Lark Rise to Candleford* attractive (more so, I think, than the television production many years later). I was also able to work uninterruptedly on Sir Edward Bairstow's biography *Blessed City* which was published in 1996, the fiftieth anniversary of his death. The book you are now reading also received some attention.

Of course this lovely memorable spell must come to an end, and on 30 July we were awake at 5.30 am. The 9.10 bus was to take us back to Stresa; we carried our luggage down the nine hundred and forty-four – and more – (granite) steps to go by steamer to Isola Pescatori. Here we found a hotel for the night preceding Priscilla's sixtieth birthday, on which we took a bus to Orta along what the diary terms a 'hairy narrow road [with] much two-tone hooting'. A ring was bought; and after a peaceful night there was thunder before we boarded the 12.46 train to Paris by way of the happily named Domodossola.

This was not all. On 21 August I was playing a recital in Toronto on the fine Casavant in Yorkminster Baptist Church at last (it was banned by Healey Willan as a venue for me in 1954), with the Willan *IPF* and my (second) *Sonata Giocosa*, the one concerned with York's Minster, perhaps purposely. Back home once more, rehearsals for the YSO began with the Rossini *Petite Messe Solennel*, Mozart's Symphony 40, Vaughan Williams *Viola Suite* and Dvorak *Legends*. The distinguished soloists for *Messiah* were Honor Sheppard, Norma Procter, Neil Jenkins and Henry Herford; and the Minster music went on as it had always done.

||O||

In February 1979 the report came from Rockport of the death aged 75 of Philip Noble, son of T Tertius Noble. He had lived in America from the age of ten when his father left York Minster for Saint Thomas New York. He was a fairly frequent visitor to York, keeping up a tenuous connexion with the city of his birth. The clock he presented in memory of his father, who died in 1953, is a welcome addition to the décor of the Camera Cantorum. I used to meet him occasionally on visiting New York, and once in his Rockport home which steadfastly retained its English atmosphere.

Back in England, 26 February was a significant day not only for me but for the Secretary of what was then called the Old Boys' Association, Sydney Skinner. It was the fiftieth anniversary of our 'Reading In' to the Minster Choir. He had been a constant friend for the whole of his life; a keen organist and preacher in the Methodist church, he was the father of one of my cherished choristers, who later became a counter tenor of exceptional quality and took for the middle of his professional names that of his native city, becoming a well-known soloist and teacher as John York Skinner.

A totally unexpected surprise conveying its best wishes on this fiftieth anniversary came from the choir of Blackburn cathedral in a beautiful card portraying the fourteenth century Swan Inn at Lavenham (where harpsichords came from). It was a mystery how knowledge of this minor jubilee had reached so far westward, but the card was signed by every member of the choir, and I suspect that the whole operation was masterminded by John Bertalot in the midst of his great work with the cathedral music there.

In the concert hall of the Royal Northern College of Music there was a commemoration concert for the distinguished oboist Sylvia Spencer who had died the previous year, to which I contributed Bach's D major *Prelude and Fugue*. Two other renowned oboe players took part – Evelyn Rothwell (Barbirolli) and Janet Craxton – and several other artists. Sylvia had been a permanent fixture in our Bach Passions; her characteristic obbligato to the tenor aria 'I would beside my Lord' was looked forward to from year to year and has left a lasting impression.

The last day of March was one that bore my thanks to the YSO not only for its accompanying Erika Klemperer in the Beethoven violin concerto, but for its brave tackling of the symphony I had written more than twenty years earlier for an academic purpose and which previously I had not made any attempt to have performed. Two of its movements had appeared, however, the last of them in the concert when Cyril Smith and Phyllis Sellick came to play Poulenc with the orchestra, but now my arm was twisted somewhat to do the complete piece and I succumbed to the temptation... At that time it was as much as the orchestral players could manage, although it was by no means a virtuoso showpiece and, despite some inevitable imperfections which did not noticeably injure the total effect, an excellent account was given.

A brief trip to Ireland was made to play on Low Sunday in Maynooth, some twenty miles west of Dublin. The flight there in bright sunlight above the cloud cover ended in the descent to Dublin airport. A continuous flow of conversation between two ladies on the seat in front of mine had been conducted in their delightful native brogue. Landing having been achieved, one was heard to observe 'Did you notice that the moment we landed at Dublin the sun went in?' The recital was in Saint Patrick's College, the seminary for the training of priests and a University College with 1200 students. The huge, long building is joined on to a chapel of impressive proportions containing a fine organ rebuilt by Kenneth Jones. A notable feature was the extensive garden with flowerbeds, bushes and immaculate lawns stretching in front of the complex, with walkways for meditative strolls, all kept in the best of order, engendering peace of mind in the fortunate students.

Not far from York, north-easterly, is the church of Saint Botolph in the village of Bossall, an unusually fine cruciform building on a small scale. It was making an eight hundredth anniversary appeal, and on a June evening, with a Minster chorister, I went there to play the one manual organ (which has pedals) built by Harrison and Harrison in 1906. The said chorister was Andrew, son of Ramsay Silver of Banks Music Publications and Margaret his wife. The organ coped very adequately with Nares, both Wesleys, Sweelinck and Vierne: Andrew contributed two attractive and ingenuous songs composed by Ernest Bullock in his younger days: *Brittany* and *I love my God and he loves me, merrily*. His other group was two of Dvorak's *Biblical Songs*, equally appealing.

An enjoyable co-operation happened in Reading Town Hall that autumn with the Youth Orchestra conducted by Robert Roscoe. The *Adagio* said to be by Albinoni (but is mostly the work of somebody else) stood with the Guilmant *First Symphony*, employing the famous Father Willis organ. It was here also some time previously that Fernando Germani was engaged for a recital but was prevented by illness. It became my happy part to stand in for him at short notice, with different pieces for the first part of the programme and adhering to the Liszt *Ad Nos* for the final half hour or so. These events were organized by the Berkshire Organists' Association who later kindly enrolled me as one of their number.

The significance of a recital in Saint Peter's church, Belper (just north of Derby) was revealed some years later. This September its organ was being inaugurated after restoration, in the presence of what the newspaper described as an Enthusiastic Audience. Little did I think that the time would come when I would be the possessor of an organ from a church nearby. Saint Mark's Church is in Openwoodgate, a mile or so from Belper. This name was immediately of interest in view of the pedal stop that was a favourite feature of Harrison organs (sometimes disrespectfully referred to as 'Big Boom') called Open Wood. It was intriguing to encounter such an organistic association so unexpectedly, with no common relationship, especially as the nature of the weighty organ stop is alien to that of the modestly-toned instrument of chamber proportions which had for a century been housed there. I was fortunate to be able to purchase this organ with its two manuals, tracker action, ten stops and elegant mahogany case in the classical style with its familiar eighteenth-century pattern of three towers and two flats between them. Built in 1794 or 95 by Stephen White, originally with one manual only, it was at first in Bridge Hill House (since demolished) and then in 1905, presented (as the solid silver plate indicates) by GH Strutt Esq DL to Saint Mark's mission church that had recently been erected. Placed high in the rear gallery, it eventually suffered from over-heating and ceased to be useable. An electronic organ took its place, and it was transplanted by Martin Renshaw to the room we had built in our East Acklam garden. Here it has been a treasured and invaluable facility with its swell organ and pedal stop, added when it took up its ecclesiastical duties, and the Fifteenth added to the Great manual on its settling on our premises.

PERFORMANCE

As to performance, I cannot refrain as a start from declaring my allegiance to and expressing my thanks for Sir Edward Bairstow and his influence since my eleventh year of age. He it was who taught me what music was about, its purpose, and how it was communicated. I can never be grateful enough, realizing that he has directed my path in the way that brings music to life and which I have been led to believe has been appreciated by those I have been privileged to count among my listeners. After a long life of interpreting both choral and organ music, it becomes clear, come what may, that a certain spirit is at work: an attitude, a disposition that is personal, and thus unique. We are trusted with the enviable task of recreating the thoughts, the visions, of others; and the responsibility is by no means minimal. Moreover, we do it in our own way, which cannot be reproduced by others, such is the marvellous diversity of the human psyche – our interpretation is ours alone. We know, of course, that attempts can be made to reproduce other interpretations and this is vastly facilitated by mechanically reproduced performances. This can be the starting point of many a new venture and of help; nevertheless sooner or later differences will creep in as one's own style asserts itself.

Then comes the matter of what is right and permissible. One has heard the rejoinder, on the question of why a certain move was made. 'That is my interpretation: that's how I see it', and that can be a position that is hard to deal with, for who is to say which is the right course? There are however certain standards to go by, and undoubtedly they will have been gone into countless times before now – things like *notes inégales*, mordents and such details which are all accepted and employed without question: and the vexed question of authenticity will inevitably raise its head.

There are the more subtle things though, vulnerable things which are subject to the innate musicianship of the performer; things requiring acuteness of perception which are incapable of being indicated in copy or score. There are all the notes, with various directions, of speed, dynamic, touch, as a starting point. These can of course be disregarded at will, and indeed often are. The matter of tempo is a case in point: composers have been known to have second thoughts, so that too much blame cannot be put on the player for choosing something different. And by the same token the varying of the speed within a movement, such as acceleration towards an exciting finish, unasked, can be a violation of the composer's concept. An example of where this occurs too often is the ending of Ravel's *La Valse* where the speeding up is overdone, resulting in chaos. Admittedly something like that was in the composer's mind but not to such an overdone extent. A dramatic effect results, but with what harm to the music: those last five notes need to be clear and emphatic, but can often be a muddle. Certainly, subtle nuances are acceptable, such as appear naturally and without the exaggerated veneer that can sometimes disfigure a phrase and which might have been copied from some other interpretation (I have heard this described somewhat cynically as 'giving *meaning*' to the music).

Quick tempo can be a sore temptation when making an impression is thought to be necessary. *The Magic Flute* overture can be a victim, likewise the Rachmaninoff second suite for two pianos, and Ravel's *Bolero.* We have enjoyed the confrontation of the composer and Toscanini over a too-rapid account of that latter piece, where should reside a lesson for any who wish to handle it. Nevertheless, it has been a matter of wonderment and of admiration that to play every note of the Rachmaninoff in the right place has been possible at such an excessive speed. Time has certainly been saved, but is that the object of the exercise? Changing the speed without the instruction of the composer, accelerating or suddenly going off at an inordinate pace is, to say the least, a pity. Might it even deserve a word such as 'arrogant'? Take time, don't rush, and let the music work its will.

One final matter of objection is a little one, but one that has become a mannerism that has now reached the stage of being an annoyance to the listener. It appears chiefly in eighteenth-century music and comes before the final chord of a movement; I call it a hiccup. It is of no musical use, but seems to be regarded as a necessity and appears to be copied widely because 'that is what *they* do'. I wish *they* would not.

These disruptions are less likely to happen where the discerning performer is in complete possession of the music's message. Whatever the player's idiosyncrasies, playing with understanding of the music will convince the listener of its validity, no matter how different it may be from the interpretation he favours and is accustomed to. It is then, a matter of awareness – of having the facility to know what the composer was driving at, how he felt as he wrote, why he or she chose those particular notes to express it all. How often has one witnessed an account of a composition which has been perfect in technique every note or syllable in place, not a blemish to be heard, eliciting profound admiration for the sheer expertise and perfection of technical accomplishment, but giving nothing of the inner soul of the music?

It seems a pity that this can happen and that the super-brilliant virtuoso can claim greater plaudits than those granted to the less facile but more percipient player – or conductor – or singer. To some the presence of a wrong note can condemn an otherwise worthwhile account. I continually recall with pleasure and satisfaction a dictum of one of the Minster clergy at York, John McMullen, himself a pianist and musician of discernment. He had come across a pianist he had not heard before and was delighted by the superb way he played; and, he added, 'thank God there were some wrong notes'. Not that he advocated their insertion for their own sake: he was glad that their presence was of secondary importance. The odd blot was of no consequence. The primary consideration was the ability to convey what lay under the surface.

A memory from more than eight decades ago that is still vivid concerns interpretation in a minor but significant way. In our market town parish church the choir had been learning Stanford's *Hymn after*

Song of Wisdom, a gentle arrangement of 'O for a closer walk with God' and had sung it at an evening service. There is an introduction in an easy *andante* mood and, as an ending, a few bars in the same vein. The time came when the choir went to York to join several others in a Diocesan Choirs Festival evensong in the Minster, to be rehearsed by Doctor Bairstow, where the Stanford was one of the anthems. What stays with me is the contrast between the accounts of that lovely epilogue. It was played on an exquisite flute with a gentle tremulant as if it had all the time in the world, and we stood there, motionless, holding our breath hoping it would go on and on in its 'calm and heavenly frame' as Cowper's words have it. How different from what we were used to in Malton, with those few final bars got through as if they were of no consequence, and dispatched with all speed and without ceremony. I wondered why it should be like that; could it have been the modesty of the organist who felt, perhaps, that the important component was the choir and that the organ's minor contribution would be of no interest? Or did he not appreciate the value of those few, simple, affectionate chords, looking so innocent on the page but potentially holding so much meaning?

Too often there is a tendency to hurry also in other places: the three-beat note at the end of the line of a four-in-a-bar hymn, or the shortening of a chord, which is not filled with shorter notes that can help keep the timing accurate. The result is a feeling of instability and unnecessary haste that is alien to the right true conception, resulting only in a lack of repose and satisfaction for the listener. Perhaps it is not too fanciful to equate the beat of musical tempo with that of the human heart, which varies naturally to the situation of the moment. If it were to miss a beat or in some way to become unsteady or irregular, something would be amiss and cause for concern – which is probably not what is required for most performances.

Hymns as well as other types of music are often taken at an excessive speed and dotted notes are shortened, giving rise to a breathless feeling and a doing away with dignity. To what purpose? Why all the hurry?

||O||

In the early 1980s I had played in Bonn at the invitation of Johannes Geffert whose complimentary remarks on my playing of Bach were encouraging – in Bach's homeland where presumably the right way of playing his works was to be found – and did a good deal to counter the adverse criticism I had previously had to face, including some from Walter Emery, the supreme Bach scholar.

In my student days Bairstow's method was still that of Sir Walter Parratt where, for instance, any fugue had to begin with nothing but eight-foot stops with the Principal added for the Answer, and similar changes made at frequent intervals; and always with the romantic sound, noticeably unison-orientated. The notion of a Bach fugue begun with a *tutti* combination and continued unaltered to the end was looked upon as impossible. Furthermore, fugue subjects, whatever their character, had to be legato, although this was not taught by Bairstow. Similarly, the way one dealt with the Bach sonatas now seems somewhat odd. I picked up the idea, and Bairstow went along with it, of using three manual combinations (they in themselves looking unsuitable nowadays): they had to be as contrasting as possible, apparently without regard to their quality of tone, and at every rest the hand changed to the vacant manual. In the quiet central movements, the all-important contrast of tone took precedence over the concept of a duet between two equal instruments. The realisation came to me much later that this must have been Bach's intention for the most part, rather than a laudable wish to ensure that the listener was able to follow the progress of each voice. It was not an easy thing to make such a major change in one's thinking; it had to happen gradually. To have had a spell as a student being made aware of this – as well as of Couperin and other styles – would have been of immense value. As things were, it was a matter of finding out for oneself. Of course, radio and recordings have now made it easy to find out what the authentic sounds may be, so they can be imitated as well as possible on the instrument at one's disposal.

Then came about the revival of the classical organ with its somewhat violent disagreements and arguments involving the merits of tracker action, and mixtures described as 'broken glass'. With time our ears have become used to the difference. Nevertheless I have to confess, albeit *sotto voce*, to an occasional reversion to former practice where changing the registration, adding the full swell or doing other tasteless things, underlines the music's progress. Did we not always seek to justify such behaviour with the phrase 'Bach would have approved'? Three hundred years have inevitably made *some* difference.

I possess some written advices from Walter Emery concerning manual changes in the B minor *Prelude* and the big G minor *Fugue*, the latter including dynamic 'steps' to the Great (while you are on the Choir); 'the last can be a biggish one' he says, at bar 110. He also admits (in a letter of 4 March 1960) to not knowing whether he is talking sense about Bach playing or 'just airing a performer's prejudices'. He continues 'I didn't take to scholarly studies out of any abstract love of knowledge; but because I was a performer and there was no other way of finding out what notes I ought to play'. He certainly appears to be sensitive to the emotional content in Bach's works, and not averse to procedures that help to make it plain.

The works of the great composers would not have lasted as they have done had they not been imbued with some human element that reaches out to touch and engage the listener. It entered their compositions naturally, as a matter of course, leaving the work of their less inspired colleagues to be neglected in favour of the more expressive kind. Attempts to resurrect the neglected work in later years, a kindly and hopeful intent, were not always a success, leaving their colleagues in possession of the field, probably quite unaware of the reason why.

In this connexion one thinks of the wisdom of unearthing forgotten music, miles of Vivaldi and mediaeval music indiscriminately revived and foisted – by the *week* – on unsuspecting places. Good for the lungs and pleasant socially as well as interesting historically and knowing how the actual instruments really sounded. But musically, at any rate, a good deal of it doesn't touch me. It is very good in small doses, which is why I try to vary the periods and styles in recital programmes. After a gruelling piece of Hindemith or Dupré, a set of Sweelinck variations comes excellently as a relaxation and will be more to the taste of some listeners. Whole recitals of Bach are of course quite possible, but those of his predecessors and other inferior composers are somewhat of a bore normally to me. They can be mitigated a good deal by a really colourful organ in a resonant enough acoustic, but they need a skilful and understanding interpreter as well. Nevertheless one feels a mixture is preferable.

Mentioning emotion causes me, often, to wonder, parenthetically, why it is that I fail to find it in some composers' works, for instance Vivaldi the expert repeater, the fixation with whose music by the BBC I find puzzling. His vast quantity of compositions must be hard put to contain much human feeling; this is the reverse of other composers, who must include Bach and Ravel who is a favourite of mine. The latter's far smaller output – due to his long periods of inactivity – bespeaks great care, and results in music of an expressive nature, meaningful and significant. Compositions vary immensely in their impact on the listener: I understand that Stravinsky preferred writing unemotional music; Chopin, as reported by Ravel, considered as hateful 'music without a hidden message'. This, I am sorry to say, is the kind of music of which I find there is a great deal produced nowadays, music which seems meant more for the satisfaction of the composer than for the pleasure of the listener.

ORGANS ABROAD

Occasionally there was an event out of the usual run. Early in 1980 I was asked by John Rowntree to play the 1851 organ in Saint Anne's, Limehouse, for the benefit of delegates to an international conference of the British Institute of Organ Studies and the *Gesellschaft der Orgelfreunde*, to be based in Oxford in August. I was to contribute not one recital but two of thirty minutes each, both with the same programme, to demonstrate the character of the organ. It was a great opportunity to find out what a 129-year-old survival by one of the best Victorian builders was like, in its original state, and I relished playing SS Wesley and Smart, nearly contemporary with the organ, as well as a Handel fugue, a quiet Stanford piece and another fugue (by Mendelssohn) in E minor, as an acknowledgement of our guests' native products. Having spent seven years with an organ only slightly younger (in Saint Michael's church at Malton, built by Thomas Harrison in 1867) I was familiar with the period, and indeed have had reason to be grateful for schooling in the hard way rather than having to wrestle with and keep in order all modern conveniences. Here was a very fine instrument, about which Donald Findlay wrote to me afterwards with the opinion he had gathered from some of the German delegates to the effect that we had no need to be importing organs into this country when we possessed our own fine tradition.

That same year saw me in three overseas locations. In February the centenary of Healey Willan's birth was commemorated, and my contribution was a clutch of three recitals in his church of Saint Mary Magdalene, Toronto, where his many years of providing music for the Anglo-Catholic service brought him much fulfilment. The recitals, on three successive evenings, had the same programme and, though I rehearsed assiduously each morning, I was interested to note how the recitals all turned out differently, in a subtle way, the one in the middle being less well played than the other two. Whether this would be noticeable to anyone who underwent all three – of which there would not be many – is a moot point. Those few days in Toronto were a welcome opportunity to meet old friends: John Bradley, Robert Bell, the current organist of Saint Mary Magdalene, and Mary Willan Mason, the composer's daughter. Some years previously she had brought a grandson of hers to see us at Minster Court and to be shown something of old York, they being inhabitants of a city which once bore that name, before it attained its Native American one. For my entire stay in Toronto I was provided with wonderful hospitality by Joan and Len Speed.

Italy and Germany were the other overseas destinations I visited that same year. The erstwhile Master of the Song School at York, the Reverend Bevan Wardrobe had given up that office and had gone to Rome to take charge of the English church there. While being his house guests in his flat high up in *Via del Babuino* (Baboon Street) we were the recipients of many treats such as lunch with the Ambassador – for which Priscilla found she must purchase a pair of respectable shoes, having not anticipated any formal assignations during what was expected to be holiday. As well as the wonders and magic of the Eternal City, a very popular aspect was the *gelati* – ice cream – of which we availed ourselves whenever there was an opportunity. We were also very pleased with the cheese called *Taleggio* whose acquaintance we had made earlier in our Swiss holiday, and looked out for whenever we returned to Rome (which was not at all often).

I was booked for recitals on two adjacent evenings, Sunday night in All Saints and Monday in Saint Paul within the Walls, where George Sharman was the organist. At All Saints the organist was Wijnand van de Pol. His organ had been having a major refit and was being reinaugurated – with the sonata I had provided for the Minster at its rejuvenation in 1972, together with help from Marcel Dupré and his *Deux Esquisses*, but not leaving out the excellent home product by Marco Enrico Bossi, his *Scherzo*.

To come to Rome without a papal audience was perhaps to be expected. But through the good offices of George Sharman we were furnished with tickets and felt very privileged to be there. Its vast scale, enormous crowd and the presence of the Holy Father are a recollection that remains with us. We then went on to Siena for a recital in the spectacular Cathedral (with its black and white stonework) which was at 9.30pm – with people coming in at 10pm – during which I was pleased with myself for making some kind of an announcement in Italian, of which I had picked up some bits during my time as a soldier in that country. It had retained my interest; in fact I would have liked to become proficient in several languages, having a particular liking for French.

Opposite the cathedral, and as I remember it, across a cobbled road or one with stone setts, is the *Ospedale Santa Maria della scala* with its elaborate chapel (as we would call it), the *Chiesa della SS. Annunziata*, which possesses an ancient organ attached to the south wall. Not only has it unbelievably profuse decoration, but its tone is such as I have rarely been privileged to hear. Unfortunately I know nothing of its history or provenance, but can still recall its extreme beauty, and especially that of a flute, of four – or two – feet pitch, which I had great difficulty in ceasing to play. There was one manual only, and I am fairly certain there were no pedals. This was an experience of very great moment, one that can happen only desperately rarely in the course of a lifetime.

While in Rome we very much wanted to visit Priscilla's catacombs, having had our interest aroused by a postcard from a friend depicting a dove with an olive branch in its beak. This is an emblem of the eternal peace of the life beyond, and is among the ancient mural paintings from the second century in one of the underground chapels. It was a fascinating and awesome visit and very cold so deep underground. The nun who was our guide found it necessary to wrap up warmly, having to go down so frequently. We were amazed by the extent of the catacombs with the many galleries, the sizeable Greek Chapel, the *hypogaeum* of the *Acilli*, the *Criptoporticus*, the many sepulchral niches as well as the Greek inscriptions and the many Christian paintings on both the walls and ceiling. One mural showing Virgin and Child is believed to be the earliest known portrayal of this subject. We have commemorated our visit with a painted copy of the dove, taken from the postcard, on a tile above the fireplace of our parlour in East Acklam.

On an earlier visit to Rome I had thought it a friendly act to give Fernando Germani a ring, who had been good company in York on a recital visit. This I did, managing a brief few words and gaining the distinct impression of someone rather struggling to keep abreast of commitments and with little time to spare. This reflected exactly one's own feelings that were inclined to surface at times and under similar circumstances.

It was mandatory that we pay a visit to the home of the saint whose name is borne by me and earlier members of my family. So, on Saturday 19 April 'to Assisi in faith' says the diary, the train being two and a quarter hours late leaving Siena, and two changes to make. 'Cherry trees in full bloom, wheat well on, wisteria, irises, pinky-mauve Judas trees. Later train from Chiusi brought us to the convent in time for supper. A walk in the gathering dusk up the hillside and down to Saint Francis' Basilica (closed). Too many cars in narrow streets: no footpaths: much pottery and commercial business which was quite surprising considering the nature of the town (or city) and imparting a kind of seaside atmosphere.' We went to the Basilica, which was crowded and noisy so we did not stay but walked the four kilometres to the Hermitage all uphill and found the bed of stone on which the Saint is said to have slept.

On our return to Rome we were fascinated by the names of the places the train took us through – *Cannero Spello Foligno Trevi* was a 'mediaeval hill town very spectacular', *Campbello sul Clitrinno, S. Giacomo di Spoleto, Baiano di S. Gillncano*, 'spectacular ride through mountains' to *Terni Narni-Amelia*; we changed trains at *Orte* and stood the last fifty minutes to Rome. And so back to Heathrow.

Three months later I was off abroad again, alone. My pocket diary for Saint Swithin's day has the laconic remark 'Bonn 15.35' and two days later 'Bonn 15.05 LHR. (London Heathrow) 15.30', which is, alas, all the information I can unearth on the subject. I regret this, and do not wish it to be a slight to my host and his fellows. It is quite likely that the filing system has suffered a malfunction of some kind. What is certain is that I would have enjoyed the episode and was grateful for the invitation and for the care that was taken – as always – over the generous hospitality.

◖◍◗

In May 1981 there was the inauguration to be done in the Roman Catholic Church of Saint Christophorus at Schagen (Netherlands) of the 1882 Nicholson organ moved from Saint Mary Magdalene in Worcester, then aged ninety-nine years. John Budgen did the transplant, having valiantly learned the Dutch language especially for his stay. He had also added a Hill pedal trombone. The tone of the instrument, now rescued from a somewhat throttling chamber situation for almost a century, was declared to be 'sounding splendid … in the ideal acoustics of Schagen'. My programme was a showcase of English products (probably inevitably) from Bairstow, Nares, Parry, Smart, Stanford, SS Wesley, myself and one maverick – Mendelssohn, with his rather beautiful, calm F minor fugue. No Bach though, alas. In *Bios Reporter*, July 1981, Vol. V, No. 3, JG van Daal wrote:

> 'It must have been a little tiring for Dr Jackson to play this instrument without a registrant (John Budgen turned the pages), as the organ is completely mechanical, no pistons of any kind, so all stop changes had to be made while playing, no mean feat. The old-time swell foot lever was also left intact. But Dr Jackson was undaunted and played more than an hour non-stop, and for his efforts was rewarded with a bouquet of flowers and enthusiastic applause. It was altogether an unforgettable experience.'

I wondered what indignities Hr. van Daal thought the swell foot lever had undergone. I had done my best to treat it with all due respect.

Here was the beginning of a valued friendship with the Beemster family. Gerard was the organist of S. Christophorus at Schagen, and his wife Nynke a singer and violinist. They came sometimes to Acklam and once brought all three children. Gerard later became organist of Utrecht Cathedral.

Within our own family the first of the next generation arrived in July, when William's daughter Emily made us proud grandparents.

In October that year a second visit to Australia had the two-fold purpose of the Organ and Harpsichord Festival centred on Perth cathedral, and the sesquicentenary of York, Western Australia. York is a town sixty miles inland; Peter Mold was the Vicar who I had visited three years before.

Priscilla and I left Heathrow at 6.45pm and stopped at Damascus and then Bahrain. We were allowed into the air terminal in the latter and it was good to stretch the legs. The sun was rising – a wonderful sight behind the great moth-like, almost phantom appearance of the huge planes drawn up awaiting their passengers. The next lap, Bahrain to Singapore, is around seven hours over the Indian Ocean. Landing at Singapore it was good to have daylight on our arrival and clearly to see the islands, sampans in the sea, vast tracts of forest and very red earth as we began to descend to the airport. Arriving in Perth at 12.20am, we were met by Peter Mold and were driven by him to York. We saw two kangaroos by the roadside. Apparently this was very unusual in that particular place and Peter drove with care, explaining how much damage can be done to both car and kangaroo. We arrived at York around three in the morning.

Typical of the unexpectedness of things that can happen on tour was the race meeting to which we were taken later on the day of our arrival – York Races take place there too. We had hoped to sleep late, having not reached the vicarage from the airport until the small hours, not forgetting the considerable jet-lag. But no harm was done. We rose about 3.30 in the afternoon and were whisked away. The races were still in progress and the last one was the York Cup. We not only survived this unusual (to us) pastime but were much interested in its workings and enjoyed it.

A new organ had been installed at York, Western Australia, and was in need of dedication. Priscilla and I were most kindly treated, meeting the town council and being given a set of beautiful drinking glasses engraved with a commemoration of York's 150 years. This can cause confusion in York, England, so an explanation has to accompany the handsome present in its static, glass-fronted home.

Geraldton on the north coast was a recital venue, achieved by a lengthy car drive along the almost empty road with little or no vegetation on either side for miles in all directions. The Perth Festival included several concerts and recitals. That which exercised us most was the one for which our son Edward had composed a concerto for organ, harpsichord and strings. I had suggested this to him – and the idea was welcomed by the organisers. It was courageous of him to undertake it; he should have been given much longer. But he produced a very nice piece and it was well received, but part of it did not satisfy the composer. He has not however given up hope of doing something about it. I played the organ part and David Swale the harpsichord. Afterwards we made a recording, a private one of whose ultimate fate I am ignorant. Most of the twenty-plus flying hours to Australia had been taken up in the copying of parts.

Our stay in Australia lasted four weeks and we were bound to be missing things of interest at home as well as the ordinary routine. The Archbishop of Malines came to the Minster. There was a close bond there proceeding from Viscount Halifax's Conversations on the matter of church unity in 1921-27. A visit to York, England, was made by makers of famous French wines; when I was given an account of the visit of the *Jurade de S. Emilion* I could only regret having missed it. Not content with prosaic forms of transport they apparently sailed up the River Ouse (from where I never learned) all in their special habiliments, then processing to the Minster for a special weekday service of Matins at eleven o'clock. They were given Stanford in C, Fauré's *Cantique de Jean Racine* and a piece by Jean Langlais for voluntary. In due course there arrived a crate of their best produce for the precentor, Canon Hockley, who had organised the York end of it.

‖◉‖

The years that had flown by since 8 October 1946 with all their multifarious activity may appear from the foregoing to have had organ playing as the chief concern. This is not the case: the feeling may have arisen from my dubious hankering to count up how many recitals I played – a mere sop to my vanity, of no importance to anybody else, and by no means a record. Nevertheless, as a sideline it is not an inconsiderable number and, pursued alongside one's main appointment, appears to oneself late in life to be in the nature of a minor achievement. But it was possible only with youthful energy, and not forgetting the help that was always so readily at one's disposal and so willingly given.

At the top of the list comes the assistant organist who must be ready to hold whatever reins are passed to him. Following Allan Wicks, my first helpmeet freshly down from Oxford in 1947, a succession of loyal enthusiasts did an immense amount towards the continuing well-being of the Minster choir and its efforts. Allan was the breath of fresh air that the choir members all fully appreciated. His first habitat was the erstwhile servants' attic quarters above me in Minster Court, joining with me for feeding purposes. He moved to Manchester Cathedral in 1954 and then to Canterbury after seven years where he stayed for twenty-seven years.

He was followed at York by Eric Parsons, also from Oxford. He held firm views and was always a stimulating companion with interesting philosophies which enlivened our Sunday teatime after evensong. Novellos published something I wrote called *Diversion for Mixtures* in a collection called 'Colours of the Organ' which bears my dedication to him. He went on to follow Doctor Robert Head at Saint Mary's Cathedral in Edinburgh (the Anglican or Scottish Episcopal one) that I knew well from my frequent visits before the war.

Following him came Ronald Perrin who in 1966 after twelve years took over the post of organist at Ripon Cathedral where his contribution to its life was as distinguished as at York, especially with his particular facility in improvisation, and his popularity with the choir members and his cathedral colleagues. And after him, in 1967 Peter Williams came from Windsor where in Saint George's Chapel he had been Sidney Campbell's valued helper.

Then for a while I had what was a new scheme, one that later became the trend widely, of an organ scholar in the person of John Marsh who was reading music at York University. He was shortly to be joined by another organ scholar in the same position, Andrew Wilson-Dickson, one of whose attributes was that of a composer. I had reason to be grateful for his help when writing an organ piece that had run into the buffers, as these things are inclined to do. His wise advice got me out of the quandary.

Geoffrey Coffin came next, at his interview telling us that he liked making things, going no further in his modesty. Only later the full purport became revealed: the 'things' were organs, no less. The eventual outcome was his founding of the firm Principal Pipe Organs in York, which in 1993 rebuilt the Minster organ, as well as making and restoring many more with complete and noteworthy success. But immediately – and after serving as a very valued administrator with the National Youth Orchestra under the formidable Dame Ruth Railton – his energetic assistance was as much appreciated in an ecclesiastical setting for its thoroughness and attention to detail.

Success in another field attended the television series of Bach's works given by Geoffrey's successor John Scott Whiteley who came to York from Bury Saint Edmunds in 1975. He held the post for twenty-five years during which he produced the standard work on the Belgian organist-composer Joseph Jongen, in whose *Symphonie Concertante* for organ and orchestra he played the solo part in a notable Minster concert. In 2001 he was given the title of Organist and Director of the Girl Choristers and in 2008 his title was changed to Organist. John was there in the post of Assistant when I ceased being Master of the Music the day after my sixty-fifth birthday, shouldering the totality of what were no longer my duties in the interregnum from early October 1982 until the arrival of Philip Moore to follow in my tracks at the start of the next year. My birthday was on Saturday, but because the climax to our choir week was always Sunday I stayed on for an extra day (gratis...) after my retirement, for the pleasure of having Bairstow's music all day – the double choir version of the *Te Deum* and *Benedictus* in D, the great communion setting and the evening canticles in the same key.

Avoiding now the yearly enumeration of recitals in my last Minster decade (1972-82), I give the score of all ten years together: three hundred and fifty-seven. That for the entire retirement period will come in due course, to be followed probably by a grand total. All this will raise differing thoughts in the minds of any who care to consider the matter. My own reaction is one of disbelief, as it is with the welter of other activity one has encompassed in a lifetime, particularly a long one. Not all of it, by any means, can be recounted here, though an attempt has been made.

As I was leaving the Minster, going through the tiresome but necessary and unavoidable process of changing habitats with its stresses and strains, parting with furniture that was too much and too large for our future needs, a letter was found among debris in our evacuated Minster

Court home. It was from our university, offering me the honorary degree of Doctor of the University. It had been dispatched several days previously and the envelope was begrimed with dust from the decorating operations that had already begun: it was by the merest lucky chance that we had gone back to the house for some reason and had discovered it. All was well, though, and a happy conferring took place, a fellow honorand, to my great delight, being Dame Judi Dench. We were decked out in our red robes and were each given a hood, red lined with grey silk, to come away with as a pleasant memento. Mine can be used on jolly holiday Sundays for services at the harmonium in Acklam church (the 'Clarabella Organ') as an alternative to the handsome and more sombre purple and cream brocade Durham one, such as I was used to seeing worn always by Sir Edward during my Minster choristership, and one of which I was proud to possess for my own use when the time came.

It was fascinating, as a chorister, to see the infinite variety of hoods on the backs of the crowds of clerics who joined in the big Minster services, and it became a kind of hobby, like collecting stamps or railway engine numbers, with the hope of possessing one of my own one day. I collected eventually five for current use and, though I would have liked to possess that of the Guild of Church Musicians of which I was made an honorary Fellow at Salisbury in 2005, it seemed that I could not make a good enough case to purchase one, there being few opportunities to make use of it in my retirement situation, however handsome a piece of adornment it undoubtedly is. And there was yet another still to come – a significant one, to be related in due course.

The Durham and York doctorates, Fellowships of the Royal School of Church Music and the Royal Northern College of Music, and an updated FRCO, formed my repertoire of plumes, only one of which can be in use at any one time, of course. The latter, which I received in the concert hall of the RNCM at the hands of the Duchess of Kent exists also in duplicate, one having been made by my old friend Philip Lowe and given to me when I did a recital in All Saints, Langley, Greater Manchester where a trumpet sonata I had written for Malcolm Tyner received its first performance on 25 June 2004. Philip was concerned with gowns and hoods from an early age and later with other church soft furnishings. He provided Dean Jasper as well as myself with what was needed (FRCO for me), and three of our grandchildren with their Cambridge and Durham BAs and Sheffield BSc.

I came to possess the Royal College of Organists' original brown hood lined with blue, on gaining the Fellowship in 1937 and never being greatly enamoured of its colour scheme I persuaded the council to try something else, and they agreed to a new design thought up by Priscilla and me which has, I am glad to say, seemed to find favour generally. The repertory of gowns and hoods that the college now operates for its increased number of diplomas is the work of Doctor John Birch who was knowledgeable on academic dress. Incidentally, during his time as organist of Chichester Cathedral he asked me to write an Amen – one of the slightly extended variety – for a purpose I cannot now recall, such as can be used at the end of a service. The one I produced was in G. When I concocted a set of responses for Banks Publications (which includes those for the sovereign's accession), this amen became part of them, but a tone higher. It has the practical advantage of being started by the basses with a beat on their own, which avoids the problem of finding a chord for the full choir to start on.

||O||

I went to Lyons in June 1983 at the behest of Patrice Caire to help in the judging of the eleventh Concours d'Improvisation, held in no less a forum than the Auditorium Maurice Ravel. Donald Wilkins, Randy Westone (USA) and André Fleuri completed the adjudication panel, which was under the dynamic chairmanship of Pierre Cochereau, the organist of Notre Dame, who ran the affair with tremendous efficiency and punctuality, employing his excellent English. The three competition sections of organ, piano and piano jazz enticed an interesting group of competitors, including Naji Hakim (my scribbled notes state: 'Musical. Full of urgent vitality, great facility, formidable musician'), and Olivier Rogg ('musical person, resourceful harmony, technically very proficient'), son of a well-known Swiss organist.

My second venture into Germany took place in July 1985, the tercentenary year of the birth of both Bach and Handel as well as the four hundredth anniversary of Heinrich Schütz. This time it was a jaunt without any responsibility – an instructive holiday in fact. The tour in the German Democratic Republic was organised by Andrew

Armstrong, the well-known Scottish organist of Dunfermline Abbey, and was centred on the organs of Gottfried Silbermann, of which we saw, heard, and played a number. Most of them were small, with two manuals but with ample power and the most beautiful voicing. My notes at Rötha make the point that 'The Silbermann is nothing if not bold, even assertive': it had gained an enviable reputation as the *Klingenden Wunder von Rötha* – Rötha's wonder sound. The cemetery chapel organ, also at Rötha had but one manual and ten manual stops with one for the pedal. 'Superlative beauty of tone in both organs' was my assessment, 'unforced, singing. Principals, flutes cool; upperwork sprightly and extremely colourful. Much power. Mendelssohn played the two-manual often and wrote *Sonata* 6 for it, we were told'. Other organs by Silbermann we heard at Ponitz, Reichardsgrimma, Pfaffrode, Grosshartmansdorf and his last, in the Frauenkirche in Dresden, much larger with its three manuals, some forty-six stops and a substantial pedal with a wood 32-foot and 16-, 8- and 4-foot pedal reeds. It was completed in 1754, the year after his death. The pipes were all original having been removed for safety during the war, but the console and elegant case, in white and gold, were copies due to their having been destroyed. We also heard the similar instrument in Freiburg Cathedral.

It was fascinating to visit the Bach places: Arnstadt where he went aged eighteen, Muhlhausen, Eisenach, Weimar, Cöthen and lastly Leipzig. Here the Tomaskirche, with all its associations and his tomb, was of special significance. We heard a recital on both organs, the romantic one on the west gallery and the north one placed there at Schweitzer's instigation – of a kind to make the playing of Bach's compositions authentic and suitable. The fugue in the *Toccata* in C BWV564 was effectively played throughout on a sprightly *rückpositif* combination. My notes continue: 'The Tomaskirche is large with slender pillars, cream colour-washed, but is distinctly drab, the galleries, on three sides of the nave, having khaki-coloured paint covering all the classical carving. The whole church has a gloom and a dusty, unloved feel. Bach's tomb is in the middle of the chancel floor: his remains were brought there in 1954 from Johanniskirche (which was destroyed or demolished), having been in a cemetery previously.'

Remembering that in August 1931 WH Harris had composed a prelude as he sat in the church – a tribute to the great master and bearing traces of his style – the idea of doing likewise occurred to me. Three others of the party joined in: Philip Sawyer, Iain Galbraith, and John Kitchen. We made our way to the church armed with the necessary materials and resolve, to find that the organ was being played, putting paid to any hopes of composition. We therefore repaired to a seat outside, on the south side of the church, near Bach's statue. At once rain began. Refuge was sought across the square in a *Kaffee* shop where we were beset by determined wallpaper music. My account continues: 'so we had to give it up; but we continued elsewhere later. My efforts came to naught, but early next morning (around 5 o'clock) I had the idea of doing a *cantilena* with reference to the Saint Anne prelude, in E, which became a *tierce en taille* later on. I finished it during the day, missing morning (Lutheran) service for the purpose, and we played them to each other when back at the hotel on a fabulous white Blüthner concert grand. Four completely different pieces'. Mine, under the title *Praeludium*, saw the light of day in the Banks publication (1988) of *Seven Pieces*. Of the others I heard no more, I'm sorry to say.

At Halle, in the Kathedral we saw the huge font, of bronze, where Handel was baptized, and the house where he was born: 'A big one, very well presented, with an English voice on tape and musical examples, fetching up with – guess what – HALLE – lujah chorus'. At Eisenach our young guide with his excellent grasp of English delighted us with his explanation of a fresco, in which somebody managed to quell a lion with a black look: the lion 'bowded or dropped a curtsy'. In one of our hotels the morning greeting from our guide Gerta (whose English was similar) consisted of 'Good morning Altogether'. And Janeiko Fabricius from Holland, who speaks excellent English and German, and is irrepressible and very funny, commented when we pulled up in some town hoping for refreshment, and referring to the posters extolling the system: 'They say that socialism ensures peace, but it doesn't ensure coffee'.

In Berlin we saw the memorial organised by Mendelssohn to the memory of Bach. From our hotel close by the cathedral we could only view the exterior of this classical building undergoing extensive restoration. We had a recital on the 1975-77 tracker, three-manual sixty-seven-stop Klais organ in Saint Hedwig's Cathedral, whose hole in the roof takes its cue from that in the Pantheon in Rome. This was built by

Frederik the Great; whereas the Pantheon is open to the elements (to allow prayers to rise to the heavens) here it is filled with glass causing, one hopes, not too much of an obstruction and perhaps is a little help to the acoustics. The organ was 'modern in every way, light in looks and sprightly in tone. The young organist was very accommodating, and played Dupré's *Noel Variations*, Bach 564 and Liszt BACH, all too fast...' – a situation quite often encountered and of which one was capable of being guilty oneself, especially when younger.

In that area we saw several legendary places. We spent two hours in the Pergamon museum with its astonishing collection of marbles, carvings, gateways from Syria, Turkey, Greece, all quite mind-boggling, Islamic ceramic and tiles *and* walls from Babylon, believe it or not, from the time of Nebuchadnezzar II in a strong blue with animals depicted, some very beautiful. In Wittenberg we saw the door, albeit a later one, on to which Luther pinned his thesis; and to Potsdam to Frederik the Great's *Sans Souci* palace where he lived in the summer time, alone (his arranged marriage having failed), all on its single ground floor. Decoration is very rich, some floors are of marble, in varied designs, for which we were all provided with huge soft slippers (*partoffeln* or *hausschuhen*) for their protection. We welcomed the beer at the end despite its warmth on this hot day (even among the many shading trees) and having to wait for it to be served, its plentiful froth needing to be allowed to settle.

||○||

I had been asked if I would like to write a piece for the 1987 meeting of the International Congress of Organists held at Cambridge, the theme of which gathering was to be the organ in combination with other instruments. This was a golden opportunity to indulge my fancy and resulted in *Eclogue*, my seventy-first opus. It was played, with Philip Ledger's sympathetic pianism, in the chapel of Sidney Sussex College. Nine years later Philip Moore played the piano in a recording at York Minster using the resident Schiedmayer that had been bought with money left over from the rebuilding of the Minster organ in 1930. Bairstow had a liking for this make of piano, having learned that it was as good as Steinway's but cost less to buy. At about the same time he had the old Broadwood grand in the choir practice room replaced by another Schiedmayer. Both have given excellent service. The piano however did not receive appreciation from one reviewer (Paul Hale) who referred to its tone, quite truthfully as rather second-rate, and noting that it is 'too closely recorded to balance with the organ' which is given a back seat. For the occasions when we had the Vaughan Williams *Antiphon* for the anthem, I arranged the orchestral accompaniment for organ and piano. It was always enjoyed and came to be referred to among us as 'The Piano Concerto'. But the role of the piano in Sir Edward's gentle and much loved *Blessed Virgin's Cradle Song* was more modest, less spectacular, and added a quiet piquancy to the sustained organ tones. For many years it was a favourite at the Christmas Eve carol service, with David Swale's *This endris Night* similarly treated.

||○||

It was in August 1989, on the twenty-sixth, that Priscilla and I were returning from Hexham where I had been playing on Laurence Phelps' fine-sounding instrument in the abbey; included in the programme was my only performance of Boëly's *Prelude and Fugue* in B flat, as well as obtaining for myself a fairly determined knock on the head from a splendidly fashioned piece of carving protruding from the organ case. The sixteenth Rheinberger sonata also received one of its occasional airings with its attractive *Skandinavisch* slow movement.

We had just reached York and were held up at traffic lights when I was suddenly taken with a vice-like grip in chest and arms – a new experience to be sure. Was I grateful to have Priscilla driving … she knew exactly the course to take, making straight for the hospital that, providentially, was not far away. Intensive care was applied to my heart attack, and in due time I was restored to the former state of good health that was my wont.

A few years later, one New Year's Day I was visited by a violent pain in the abdomen, the like of which I had never experienced and was hard put to tolerate for the period in which the ambulance was summoned from seven miles away to convey me the fifteen miles to York. Here, after the New Year festivities were completed, I was eventually deprived of the requisite innards necessary to save my life, the internal blockage was cleared, and I was fortunate to have had the expert treatment and the superb care to fit me once more for normal life after some weeks of recovery.

RETIREMENT IN EARNEST?

There are other things to anticipate as one grows old, that there will be time to think, to be leisurely, to enjoy seeing people, to help others, to learn how to make a success of the garden. Such prognostications did not always prove to be right. The leisure one had anticipated was not always present, with recitals still on the schedule, the odd composing commission coming along and other oddments more to be classed as Work than Leisure. Composing can be a very time-consuming process that can push gardening (which is undoubted leisure) into the background. I came to realise, too, that being daily at a keyboard for choir practice, service, voluntary or learning new pieces, one was always 'in practice'. Without all this, strict discipline was found necessary; even well known, oft-played pieces had to be kept in condition whereas previously this had all happened in the ordinary course of events. But it was always pleasure: I was always aware of my great good fortune in having so very many good things to make life so agreeable. Life is so wonderful: it is a pity one must relinquish it at last, but a mercy that one won't be here to regret it.

It so happened that my beginnings as an organist in my early teens had coincided with the emergence of a composer who became very popular, producing a succession of appealing works starting with *Five Short Pieces* in 1930. One of these, the *Folk Tune*, captured my youthful imagination as played by his fellow Rochesterian HA Bennett, organist of Rochester Cathedral and formerly Bairstow's assistant, who had returned to York to play in the Victorian church of Saint Maurice just outside Monk Bar (long since demolished). This composer was Percy Whitlock whose life was cut short at the age of forty-three, but not before he had provided, in addition to many solo pieces and a large-scale sonata, an organ concerto. This latter work, which employs a big orchestra including a saxophone, he chose to call a symphony. After a few initial performances it was neglected until May 1998 in Dulwich when Ian le Grice was the soloist with the Lambeth Orchestra conducted by Christopher Fifield.

It was through the enthusiasm of Robert Gower and Malcolm Riley that the Whitlock Trust came into being. They had each independently set out to study this composer but then collaborated. The exhaustive biography and critical analysis of his output they produced did an invaluable service to the music. I joined the Trust along with Graham Barber, Paul Hale, Julian Elloway, Christopher Moore, William Whitehead, Roy Massey, David Sanger, Denny Lister, Chairman Robert Gower, Secretary Malcolm Riley, Treasurer Ronald Hendey and Gerco Schaap, editor of the magazine *De Orgelvriend* in Holland. Meetings took place at the Sand Hutton premises of Banks Music Publications, run by Ramsay Silver, who was also one of the Trust members. Included as a matter of course was a sumptuous lunch provided by Margaret, Ramsay's wife, and the gathering was always enjoyable and rewarding.

At the 1993 meeting it was a complete surprise to me to be informed by Robert Gower that I was to become Patron of the Trust in succession to Edna Whitlock, Percy's widow, who had died. This is indeed an honour, and one that I am proud to hold, more or less of a sinecure though it may be. What was not a sinecure, though, was the organ part of the Whitlock symphony that I undertook for a performance in the Minster on 16 June 1999. This performance awakened a good deal of interest, and a recording was carried out later in the year by the same forces, the University orchestra under the direction of Doctor Jonathan Wainright.

A different kind of concerto, requiring a smaller orchestra, was undertaken by the same forces. It was one I had written for the sesquicentenary of Andrew Carnegie and which managed something like a dozen performances in that year. For the recording it profited from the cleaner acoustic of the Lyons Concert Hall of the university with its modern organ, and received superb treatment from the students who formed the orchestra, as did the Whitlock symphony at its Minster recording.

John Birch and I took part in the ninetieth birthday commemoration of the celebrated architect Stephen Dykes Bower, brother of John, who I had come to know on the committee of the Council for the Care of Churches. John and I shared the organ-playing at Matins on a May day of 1993 in the parish church of Quendon, Essex, where Stephen was the regular organist. This is a few miles south of Saffron Walden where I had played a recital and was taken by the organist of the Church, Andrew Malcolm, to pay a call on Stephen in his beautiful house, Quendon Court, which his family had owned since the 1930s. I remember on that occasion, as well as its elegant architectural merit, along one side of the garden a hedge of solid wisteria in full bloom which could have been some twenty or thirty yards long, a sight such as I do not remember ever seeing anywhere else and which was a special delight as one of my most cherished horticultural pleasures.

On one occasion in the early 1990s I attended a concert in the little theatre attached to Alan Titchmarsh's house at Alton, Hampshire, a return to the scene of my initial sojourn in the army. It was a programme of Christmas music involving a choral group and was being recorded for broadcast. Unfortunately it was not possible to visit his garden of which we saw glimpses on his regular television appearances. He autographed his book on rock gardens for me.

A loss we could ill afford was suffered through the death in 1995 of Gordon Reynolds, whose presence was everywhere in the church music and organ world. His very special style of writing was always a delight and frequently available to be enjoyed. His last appointment as Organist and Master of the Choristers at the Chapel Royal, Hampton Court Palace lasted for nearly thirty years and was his great pleasure and interest, as was his time previously at Saint Bride's, Fleet Street. At the age of fifteen he had been appointed Assistant Organist at Beverley Minster, then under HK Andrews. Gordon's funeral in May was at Brantingham, his native part of the East Riding of Yorkshire, just north of the River Humber.

An October date – that of Saint Luke, the eighteenth – was an unusual one in 1996. It was fifty years, five months and eighteen days since Sir Edward Bairstow had died, and we were in Saint William's College by the east end of the Minster on that evening, launching a book about his life and works.

The history of its provenance will be familiar to those who know the book, but for others a few brief details may be helpful. It is based on Sir Edward's own writing covering his early life but only until his move to York in 1913, and was written only in his last three years of life and left unfinished. A document of great interest, it was also a problem. After a while its completion was begun by H Percy Dixon, sub-editor of the Yorkshire Post, and a poet as well as a musician who had taken tuition with Sir Edward. Alas, he had not gone far before he died, an unexpected tragedy not only for the book but also for the loss of his wise counselling and delightful company. It seemed then that there was no other course than that I should attempt to take on the onerous task in addition to so much else, a responsibility I found somewhat daunting not least for its novelty. It took some time to formulate a method of procedure, and indeed progress was slow until it was suddenly realized that the last chance of a significant date for its publication was on the horizon, one that was simply not to be missed.

I sought help from those who had known him, notably Sir Ernest Bullock, who had been like a son to ECB from his early days, and from his daughter Nancy. I was utterly fortunate to receive from each a wonderful account of their recollections and intimate accounts of his family life that could not have been done by anyone else. Gordon Pullin and Donald Webster supplied commentary on the songs and hymns, and Alice Knight, a pupil of whom Sir Edward was proud, wrote of her tuition with him and her constant and varied help to him. She was employed by the Yorkshire Insurance Company but was encouraged by ECB to work for the Mus.Bac. degree at Durham, and was a pillar of the York Musical Society and all its doings for many years. David Hird, who was his pupil contemporary with me, provided a fascinating glimpse of the relationship with the teacher, describing a whole day's work in all its variety beginning with the boys' 8.45am practice, tuition in paperwork and organ playing, as well as assisting with the regular weekly broadcast of evensong from the Minster.

So all was achieved satisfactorily with the launch of the book in the fiftieth year since his death. I was grateful to Philip Lowe, organist of Rochdale parish church, who earlier had organised a Bairstow concert there with a title using the first two words taken from what is without doubt his finest anthem *Blessed City, heavenly Salem*, and he kindly let me have it for the biography. One of the items in that concert was the Evening Service in E flat, but in an arrangement filled out for four-part choir with strings and organ. Written for unison voices it contains music of a higher quality than might be expected for such slender forces. This quality was fully brought out in the performance. The arrangement was the joint effort of Philip and me.

A chamber organ with one manual and without pedals had been rescued in pieces from a water-logged cellar in Skipton by John Brown, and lovingly and patiently restored to playing condition. For some years it had stood in our big dining room at York where it had provided the perfect piece of furniture for the scale of the space. I have to admit that in filling this visual role it was more useful than the purpose it was made for – by Elliot and Hill in the 1820s, incidentally quite near the time when they were attending to the Minster organ. Bernard and Molly Rose had become our good friends: several times we visited them at their beautiful house at Bampton, some twelve miles west of Oxford, with its large garden. When the time had come for Priscilla and me to move out of Minster Court it was their previous church in the village of Appleton that provided a home for the organ. Its beautifully voiced stops inevitably were not called upon very often to give of their essence until set up in Appleton church where the style of architecture suits the organ to perfection, as do the acoustics. Bernard joined me in a duet 'for two to play' by Tomkins during the recital that fixed it (it is to be hoped) in its right final resting place. It was then a matter of not a little pleasure and satisfaction – not to say surprise – that in June 2012 when involved in the activities surrounding the completion of Rochdale parish church organ's restoration I was to meet Doctor Diane Clarke who is a part-time organist on this very organ in Appleton church. I was delighted to have up-to-date news of its performance.

An earlier organ expedition concerned that in Bampton village church. The organ had suffered a serious accident requiring a major restoration for which Bernard organised an appeal. My recital (27 July

The apparent abrupt end of the road in East Acklam,
with Nether Garth as the terminus. Alice's beautiful photography
(Page 195)

Alice gives flowers to the Duchess of Kent who holds the copy of the Hovingham Sketches presented to her at the 1974 dinner of the RCO.

Being made an honorary fellow of the Royal Northern College of Music at the hands of the President, the Duchess of Kent.

*Priscilla joined me in 'Montfort'
in our East Acklam garden when
Gerco Schaap brought his camera
from the Netherlands.
(The organ from Openwoodgate.
Page 315)*

*With Dame Judi Dench in July 1996: two Yorkists after having given their
names each to a room in Saint Peter's School, she doing Shakespeare from
memory and me Ravel by the same means.*

The entire family at East Acklam church after recording the tune of that name with Fred Pratt Green's words, which appears on my 80th birthday disk. Photograph masterminded by William.

Aet 80, an affectionate greeting with John McMullen, minor canon and long-time Minster colleague, fifteen years after my retirement.

Saint Gregorius sheds a blessing on my Utrecht Cathedral efforts, caught by Gerco Schaap.

After the thanksgiving service at Manchester Cathedral with the Dean and Sir Tom Courtenay, 24 July 2002.

The brilliant depiction by Martin Cottam of my Desert Island Disc selection for
the Norwich Organists' Association, listening to
L'Enfant et les Sortilèges. (Page 393)

With Archbishop Stuart Blanch who had presented me with the Order of Saint William of York in 1983. Dean Jasper is between us.

After the 2011 Lincoln recital, two or three days before Priscilla's meningitis attack.

March 2012: the recently instituted RCO medal came to Sir David Willcocks and me, seen here, and James Macmillan, who unfortunately is not.

The brand new Lambeth Doctor of Music with Archbishop Rowan Williams who conferred it on 16 October 2012.

1991) contained four of the *Hovingham Sketches*, one of which was Bernard's *Chimes*, a delightful and original impression in which the music faces in opposite directions. Having reached the halfway mark it goes into reverse, unreeling itself back to the beginning. At the head is quoted *'Ma fin est ma commencement et ma commencement est ma fin'*. The piece makes use of the chimes of Magdalen College where the greater part of his life had been spent.

In November 1996 we heard the sad news of Bernard's death and so we came to his funeral at which I played the same organ in the presence of a large congregation. The choir consisted of singers who had served Magdalen chapel under his direction for a good span of years, bearing the stamp of that fine tradition. It is a happy fact that his Responses are used so frequently and so widely, betokening their high quality and acceptability amid the great number of sets that are available.

||O||

09 Feb 1997. Leaving Dallas, 1815 local time, 33,000 feet. Darkness falls quite quickly as we fly eastwards. I came there last Tuesday, a week ago tomorrow, for a conference of church musicians to whom I was required to give a master class in organ playing and to talk about choral repertoire. I was also to play a recital at a Presbyterian Church close by, an annual one provided by the late donor of the organ. The fee was generous and made up for the small amount offered for the lecturing part. This all came about as a result of a visit to Acklam of a party from the University of North Texas in May 1996, a project organised by a Hull resident, Nigel Shepherdson, who was studying organ at the university which is situated in Denton, some thirty miles north of Dallas. His parents run a travel agency in Hull, and his knowledge was useful in setting up a tour of England for some fellow students and one or two of the lecturers. Among other things he wished them to experience a country church service and, as the most convenient of the four churches of our group was Westow, that was the venue decided on. It was rather unfortunate, however, that they were not warned of the distance of the church from the village (a good half mile which they had to walk) causing them to miss all but the final hymn. But they spent quite a while playing the small organ before leaving for lunch at Acklam, where we all arrived in a downpour of rain. It was a

very happy, friendly event, and they were delighted by the countryside, looking good, an aspect they have recalled on this trip. I was unable to tell who were students and who teachers, some of the former appearing mature and one, at any rate, of the latter having a distinctly youthful look. The truth of this dawned when my host was the same Doctor Jesse Eschbach on this latest trip, who put his delightful house at my disposal and made me more than welcome. It was wonderful to see the easy relationship he has with his students – Christian names and all, with no loss of discipline.

Texas is vast, larger than France they say. Certainly one had a preview of this on the flight into Dallas, with mile upon mile of uninhabited (apparently) land and long straight roads with little or no traffic on them, all of it brown at this time of year. It can become green and lush in due season, but can be very hot and dried up in the summer period. This is all rather difficult for an Englander to appreciate; he (or she) who is used to the orderly progress of the seasons and who rarely experiences the droughts of a dry, hot summer, or the excessively hard winter. My visit in this year of grace 1997 has been, like many previous visits to the North American continent, full of interest and friendly intercourse. There is a genuine-ness in the welcome extended. Yesterday, Sunday, began by my being collected at 7.45am by Nigel Shepherdson and driven to his church some 40 minutes distant for the morning Eucharist. After this I was driven by Layton Clark (in his surplice) to Saint Anne's for what remained of their Eucharist. Nothing was too much trouble. Whereas Nigel's choir was depleted by a retreat project, Debbie Clark's was in full spate and gave an excellent account of itself, as did the children's choir in their offertory contribution.

Our next port of call was Holy Trinity, at Port Worth, where at last I was to see the Walker organ for which I had been commissioned to write a piece (which turned out to be *Exultet*) in 1993. This is a most beautiful instrument, exceeding most of those I had experienced in the U.S. It was, also, well placed at the east end with no pipes visible but covered by a splendid oak screen which forms a suitable background for the altar and does not appear to restrict the egress of tone. This was at the rector's insistence, and very right and proper since an organ case can sometimes be a dominating influence, out of keeping with the feeling of worship. Debora Clark played *Exultet* excellently well, and it was a great moment for me to hear my piece in the situation for which it was written. The rector kindly entertained us to lunch – at 'Le Chardonnay' including some delectable white wine.

We next arrived, rather late, at Nigel's house, where scones had been specially baked for tea, with a fig conserve and superb blackberry brandy as a starter. This was cut somewhat short by our departure for 6pm evensong at the church of the Incarnation, where the English tradition is maintained – against odds I think. One cannot but applaud the devotion and dedication of those who strive continually to uphold the great work when all or most of the world appears to be opposed to it, or is simply uninterested. We had Stanford in C and Wood's *O Thou the central orb* – a piece I wish we had done at York – suitable for less competent choirs certainly, but nonetheless worthy of attempts by the more proficient. It may have been the descending semitones at 'and let Thy glory shine' that put me off, in my more particular days, encouraged by ECB who would have branded that gradual descent 'slithery'. A shame; it is a beautiful piece. Afterwards we were invited to view the organ. It had been an Aeolian-Skinner, with an exposed interior but had been rebuilt by Noack and clothed in a comely dark wood case and pipes of burnished tin. With tubas at both east and west ends of the church and four manuals, it made some splendid sounds and was pleasurable to play. I essayed Bairstow's *Prelude* in C after working through the whole spectrum, including a CC celeste which is a lovely feature – that is to say, that it had a full range of pipes whereas most stops of this (undulating) type have no bottom octave.

‖O‖

I visited Utrecht in 1997 where I enjoyed giving a recital on 17 August beneath the benign presence of Saint Gregorius, posed in the attitude of a blessing. This was where the famous composer Hendrik Andriessen (1892-1981) was organist for the last years of his life. I was also given a taste of a more youthful enterprise when, to effect a rapid transference across the streets of the old city I stood on the back step of Gerard Beemster's cycle, accomplishing the journey in practically no time, with perfect safety and at no cost.

Gerco Schaap had also arranged a recital for me (14 August) on the fine four-manual Walcker organ in the Martinikerk of Doesburg. The stops were controlled not by knobs in the age-old manner but by tilting tablets, a modern development, somewhat daunting to a visiting player. I was thus unbelievably fortunate to have all the working of what is quite a formidable array of these registers taken over completely by Dave Lazoe who did it with the greatest of ease and never put a foot wrong. Gerco had made suggestions towards the programmes which included Bairstow's *Sonata*, one or two pieces of mine, four of Whitlock's *Five Short Pieces* and 'the middle parts of his *Sonata* in C minor' as his account runs, adding 'The audience in Doesburg was never quieter… and in Utrecht a collective sigh could be heard after Whitlock's cunning *Scherzetto*'. An informal visit to the Domkerk of Utrecht to play the lovely 1831 organ with its beautiful case was very rewarding. I did my best with *Toccata, Chorale and Fugue*, off the cuff as it were, and it was observed that 'it was as if the former Dome organist Stoffel van Viegen (1916-1988) had returned to the console, because of their resemblance and similar style of organ playing'.

A knowledgeable and discerning appreciator of music, Gerco comes frequently to England, and often to East Acklam. He was present for the Minster concert set up by Philip Moore for my eightieth birthday and wrote a delightful account of it for the Percy Whitlock Trust Newsletter (24 November 1997) in his impeccable English. He noted the works that composed the programme, an interesting and varied collection with new works written especially: *Prayer before the Crucifix* by Philip Moore, Richard Shephard's setting of John Mason's *How shall I sing that majesty* and *Fantasia Espansiva* by John Scott Whiteley for organ solo. I was handed the responsibility of Bairstow's *Lord, thou hast been our refuge*; a more suitable choice I could not have made to conduct in tribute to my revered mentor, an exceptionally fine piece with infinite scope for imagination. Gerco also expresses the point that 'It must have been a treat for the hero of the feast to see two of his grandchildren in the choir' – Sam and Grace, Edward's two elder children, Tom not yet being old enough.

ON COMPOSING

August 2001. One day I had a definite idea that I had come a fraction nearer to realizing how composition, so far as I am concerned, works. It is a mysterious process, capricious and difficult to understand. For something like two years I laboured in my mind how to cope with writing a mass, the stumbling-block being the inclusion of a congregational part, the very idea of which I found not very motivating. On the other hand, the commission for a mass with the addition of a brass quintet elbowed everything else aside and had itself sketched out in a matter of days.

A distinctly retarding element in addition has been the numerous distractions diverting one's attention and occupying the mind to the exclusion of the set purpose: getting down to the business of thinking out the composing process. However, it has to be stated that had the urge been strong enough, all distractions would have been swept aside, which is indeed what happened with the Salisbury mass. In the case of the other mass, the urge not being there, doubt and bewilderment prevailed. Much later I took out what sketches I had made and saw encouraging signs which, in conjunction with the protracted period of the considering of it, gave me a marked confidence and the will to get on with the job.

It helps of course, enormously, to have a free mind. Midsummer is a good time to find business at a low ebb: tiresome matters of planning arrangements, programmes, practising, are less urgent and the pleasant weather brings its own kind of refreshment. Today is taken up with a luncheon party here at home and a business meeting in York this evening: but tomorrow, and for some days, there is nothing to deflect me from the set purpose. I think the urge is strong enough to bid all clamours for attention begone, and I have a strong hope and expectation that it will carry me along in a flood tide.

But you can never be sure. This is a tantalising thing. Sometimes I have set to work with all the good intentions and been unable to make any headway. At other times I have begun writing on the spur of a moment without much hope and proceeded with the greatest of ease. It can be of the greatest help to have something all ready to start on. Healey Willan said in my hearing, 'Get *something* written down'. What at the time of writing might appear of no use can later present a more encouraging prospect and can be the seed from which a whole composition can burgeon, a seed that when looked on more objectively than at its first emergence, contains the confidence that it is the right foundation on which to build.

I think I have always known these facts, but now on this summer day all is very clear. I'm sure there is nothing original in what I've written – it will all have been known long ago and by any creative artist; but it may be of interest to someone.

Did Bach and Mozart have all these misgivings? I would like to know, since they can't have had much time to think out what they were going to compose. Did they have to force themselves? That is something that has never worked with me. Bairstow once wrote, in some sort of testimonial for me: 'You have never forced the composition' which he had been clever enough to see, great teacher that he was.

A marked contrast to an unforced approach to composition appears in the dramatic change instituted by Schönberg (the band wagon he created on which so many composers felt the need to jump). He wanted to be released, as he said, from writing other composers' music. Without commenting on the success or otherwise of his revolutionary system and the level of appreciation it has been accorded by the musical public, one wonders what the motive was: to provide pleasure of a different kind for the listener? To satisfy a belief in himself, or to find a way out of a method of composition he had found unrewarding and played out? Was it for his own or the listener's benefit? Can such a radical step be of more value than gradual evolution based upon what has been tried and proved over previous centuries? No doubt there are good reasons for either course, catering for the disparate views and preferences of those concerned with the consumption of the product. It is as well to keep in mind the ultimate purpose of music, that it is primarily for pleasure and to lift the spirit.

New Year's Day 2004. It dawned on me quite recently that composing is improvising in slow motion. I ought to have known this but it came in a sudden realisation. If you can improvise you can compose and, provided you have a good idea to start with, all should proceed with ease. I remember being warmly commended once in America for some improvised playing I did when trying out an organ. I thought nothing of it but it evidently impressed someone who heard it. I have wondered whether I had stumbled over something worthwhile, something that, had it been recorded, could have formed the basis of a piece, or was it merely some succulent harmonies that seduced the hearer?

For my last few months at the Minster, John Rothera allowed me to use his Ferrograph recorder to preserve my improvised playings in and out of the choir. As with all recordings, they require a deal of time to be heard – a commodity in short supply. Of the few I have heard, only one seemed fit for some permanency and was made into a short piece for the seventieth birthday of Lloyd Smith, organist of All Saints, Pavement, and a devoted supporter of the York and District Organists' Association. It uses a chant by Goss – in E – which formed a useful starting point and was the process Bairstow often used for the choir's entry and exit.

In the early years I carried on composing as best I was able, and wish that I had been told to do as Holst did – to 'spoil manuscript paper' as he put it – in order to arrive at the desired result. I was told by someone that Stanford used to spend a fixed period each day in composing, and this was considered by my informant to be a bad thing as he was thought to be composing without inspiration. How could he be inspired at the same hour every day? But, of course, most of Stanford's time would be taken up not with inspirational activity but with the more menial jobs of orchestration, editing, and making fair copies. I now realise that the act of composition is like anything else a function that must be developed and encouraged and, most important, regularly undertaken. The wheels might not begin to turn at first and may take a long time, sometimes days, weeks or months before they do. It is a necessary part of the process that one gives one's mind to the subject, and does not give up when ideas fail to come. The beginning is the most difficult part, but once begun it is comparatively easy to keep going provided too much time is not allowed to elapse between sessions. I like at least to look at or play through what I have written most recently (for composing is a very time-consuming occupation: there is nothing like it that I know for making the hands of the clock go round at an inordinate rate) and keeping in touch helps to ensure continuity. But at first I was so convinced that the precious inspiration was something which came or didn't, and to be grasped when it did, rather than something that was much more likely to favour one with a visit if the necessary work of tilling the ground has been put in. Sometimes – and this only served to bear out my 'beautiful' theory – sometimes a good idea flashed across one's mind which led on to a successfully completed piece. The trouble was that such situations were far too infrequent. I could have been far more productive had I followed Holst and Stanford in being workmanlike about it rather than romantic and mystical.

I thought that the requisite ideas would most readily appear in the most happy and beautiful situations. Therefore my pre-war walks taking the dog each day were undertaken in the hope that this would happen. It rarely did. Apart from odd times when I have thought of a good tune away from the piano – like the subject of the fugue in opus 16 which came when I was driving the car on a Sunday afternoon jaunt with Priscilla and the children – I have found that by far the greater number of good ideas have come by worrying at them. Nevertheless, the most satisfactory state of affairs is when there is what I can only describe as a gut feeling that one is on the right track, and the composition takes over and writes itself. I have postponed and procrastinated times without number in my uncertainty, only to be driven in desperation to make some sort of a start (with time's wingéd chariot hurrying near) and finding that all was well, the idea was good and the piece was progressing satisfactorily. Whatever it is, it can be changed, and other ideas can flow from it. But strangely that 'something' can turn out to be perfectly satisfactory. You may as you write it think it poor or worthless, but later in a more objective mood you might discern qualities you were unaware of and which can be of use, bringing uncertainty to an end with an indefinable feeling of confidence. This is probably brought about by the unconscious knowledge that groundwork has been done by dint of constant thought, ready for the sowing of the seed.

I was encouraged to read part of an interview Debussy gave to the New York Times on 26 June 1910. He admitted that:

> There are days and weeks and often months that no ideas come to me. No matter how much I try I cannot produce work that I am satisfied with. They say some composers can write, regularly, so much music a day – I admit I cannot comprehend it. Of course, I can work out the instrumentation of a piece of music at almost any time, but as for getting the theme itself – that I cannot do. I have tried it. I have forced myself to work when I least felt like it, and I have done things which did not seem so bad at the time. I would let those compositions lie for a couple of days. Then I would find that they were only fit for the waste paper basket.

Unlike Bach, or Rheinberger, who shunned the use of a keyboard when composing, I must hear exactly what is going down on the paper and, as I prefer complicated and colourful harmonies which I cannot invent in my head, the only course open is that of using a keyboard. And after all, no less a composer than Ravel declared that, without one, new harmonies would not be invented. It depends what you want. We all work differently. The end result is what matters, and whether you arrive at it in silence, hearing the music only in your mind as you write (one can appreciate that a fugue could be better when conceived in this way) and try it out when it is finished, or whether the trying out and the writing down are simultaneous, is entirely an individual matter and should be of no concern to the listener or anybody else. A special bonus of working at the piano is the unexpected chord upon which one has occasionally stumbled. And why not. However, we don't entirely disregard the strictures placed upon composition at the keyboard by – yes – JS Bach.

An interval of some kind is undoubtedly of value for refreshment and for thinking things out away from the work room, as Ives has proved; or just letting the mind get on with the digesting or maturing process, to say nothing of the delights of a change of scene, especially in the countryside, and the almost physical blowing away of dust in the shape of stale or unproductive ideas. An escape such as this can sometimes produce an idea worth developing, as the untrammelled mind ranges freely and refreshed, away from the wrestling with details, looking at the problem from the outside. Any respite, long or short, can be invaluable. I believe Brahms recommended the composer to take the time to write in the clefs and key signature as he came to a new line. This would provide a valuable breathing space, however brief. Such intervals I have found helpful, especially if one has for the moment run dry and knows not where to go next.

Very few of my early attempts were much good. Most of it seems to have been serious, not to say doleful. I must have been trying to produce beauty and in the process missed any vitality, light-heartedness and enjoyment. It was only much later that I began to appreciate the sheer *joie de vivre* in Mozart and Beethoven, and to prefer it to some of the more serious documents of, say, Mahler. The *Eroica* funeral march is just about as serious as music ought to go. Or is this heresy? I know that great thoughts need to be expressed, in words as in music, but let them normally be without turgidity and too much gravity.

It was a long time before I began to find how to compose something worthwhile. My first success was the hymn tune written by me during a communion service at Saint Leonard's in 1934 and appropriately christened 'Malton', which ECB kindly chose for performance in the 1935 Diocesan Choirs Festival to 'Jesu the Very Thought of Thee'; it was used in the Minster afterwards. It is modal and the second chord is a seventh, albeit prepared but considered 'modern' at the time, and was I am sure regarded as in the 'Beautiful' category by ECB as it certainly was by me. That was the first piece that arrived without any effort and which worked from the word go: a piece of very little value to the world at large, but to me an initial step of some significance.

Many years later the tune was used on the sad occasion of my chorister friend Robert Holtby's funeral. Mary, his wife, had done her best to choose a tune for a hymn that Robert had wished to have sung, and by the merest fluke came upon 'Malton' in an old English Hymnal in their possession where it was pasted over poor Doctor Slater's 'St. Botolph'. So after decades of disuse it saw the light of day once more and was kindly received. Soon afterwards – in fact having achieved age ninety – I wrote a prelude on the tune, having failed in the attempt some sixty years previously, intending it then for my sister Angela's wedding (but it took on the form of a memorial to her since her sad death in December 2006). The prelude then appeared in the book of *Acklam Pieces*. A year later Robin Walker used the tune as a basis for what he entitled a *Postludio Estatico Sulla Melodia del Maestro*, one of the eleven pieces written as a ninetieth birthday present organised by the Whitlock Trust.

I have a soft spot for pieces of mine that have had trouble-free births and fell on to the paper in their final form such as the song 'Tree at my Window', as related earlier. It had had a long gestation, which probably accounts for the speed and certainty with which it finally appeared. Others have arrived easily, though without any preparation, but both the organ concerto and *Eclogue* were very slow in getting going, as was the symphony. The latter's final movement and that of the concerto, however, were written very quickly and with little or no turning back.

In spite of the regard one has for pieces that have come easily, one cannot think of them as being better than ones that have caused a deal of trouble: I cannot always see the situation clearly enough to make a judgement about my own products. They need to be put away and forgotten about in order to be judged objectively after an interval.

A little canon in A minor emerged one day by way of an exercise for ECB sometime during the thirties. At Boufârik (1943/4) I used it as a middle section to a pastoral piece. It worked quite well. Eventually it found its way into the *Trio*, opus 128, for violin, cello and piano commissioned by Erika Klemperer, and first performed at a British Music Society concert in York in 2001, but before this I scored it for flute, viola and piano, encouraged by Debussy's trio with harp.

There was, I am fairly certain, no conscious thought of producing something beautiful in these pieces. The main concern was to produce the goods. But by that time one's directions had been set, and one chose only the themes and chords that presented themselves as appropriate; what beauty was present had arrived on its own. But can a discordant piece be beautiful? What is beauty anyway? Each one of us rates it differently. I can see none in most of the modern music that comes from the wireless [radio], much of it commissioned by the BBC. Not only is beauty, as I see it, lacking, but there appears to be no logic in the music. What we are given is a succession of wrong notes creating a disagreeable result that provides nothing but irritation and bad feeling. What the object is I cannot imagine, try as I will. Does it all originate in Schönberg whose variations I have suffered along with many others in the hope of seeing some sense and purpose to no avail? I can go as far as Bartôk with profit and admiration and to Stravinsky in his less extreme moments; but the experimenting and the unceasing efforts to push out the frontiers of music since then seem to have lost and forgotten the whole purpose of it – to please and to enlighten. It seems that the objective that is pursued is to go one better than the previous composer no matter how nasty a noise ensues. I am well aware of reactions to past progressive music – late Beethoven quartets, for instance – but I find it difficult, if not impossible, to equate that with the present situation. I keep trying to come to terms but never get further than frustration and bewilderment. Is it perhaps the difference between composing music which has something to say, as against writing mere notes? It would be so nice if answers could be found to so many questions and doubts. How does an inspired melody arrive, the one that lasts and remains fresh, never going stale? Not by the latter system but from a deeply human urge. There is a decided difference.

As to the way of assembling your material, I wonder if talk of 'first subject' and 'second subject' has been much of a help. More material than that is needed; a good deal more in fact. That is what the great symphonies have and what is essential for a large-scale work. One of Bairstow's pieces of advice was to bring in plenty of thematic material for development, rather than trying to get by with one first subject and a lone second subject, as he said some of the exercises submitted for degrees were prone to do.

Mozart's two-piano sonata is a wonderful example of plentiful material. I was struck by this when working it up with Tim Tunnard for performance at Nun Appleton near York, with its spontaneous, endearing motifs, ideally contrasted, following one another effortlessly, invention never flagging. This is one of Mozart's compositions that has made a deep impression after regarding him as a mostly facile tinkler, the last three symphonies always excluded, of course. Similarly Brahms' fourth and Dvorak's sixth (and his others) impressed me in the same way; and of course there are countless other examples – Schubert's ninth not least. I am glad to say that my attitude to Mozart became enlightened, allotting him his just measure of appreciation and total admiration.

Bairstow said I should experiment with forms, doing things as Brahms did when he recapitulated the second subject before the first. After all, the way is open for your to do exactly as you wish, not sticking to existing forms. Apart from fugue, it seems that sonata form occupied us mostly, though we certainly looked at Aria, Rondo and others as we worked through the manuscript and typescript of his Counterpoint book. My grounding was thorough, for which I have always been grateful, particularly with regard to strict counterpoint, a subject which fell into disfavour in the 1950s and '60s and, I believe, gradually began again to be recognised once more as a basic essential for good writing, a discipline to be gone through to gain the benefits that can be had no other way.

Bairstow was keen that music should be continuous, without stopping and having to keep starting again. He likened such to someone with a weak heart that needs frequent resting. I do not remember whether he had any adverse opinion of Franck in this regard, but his Symphony and, more so, the *Fantaisie* in A (both of which I have a lot of time for) would surely have merited some criticism of this aspect.

Working somewhat intensively with a deadline to meet on a late opus (164) the truth of what I have been saying here was confirmed: a doubtful start, an increasing confidence, and when nearing completion the hope of a convincing ending. The piece was an anthem for the annual Shakespeare commemoration service at Stratford-upon-Avon (2013) with words specially written by Canon Michael Hampel, Precentor of Saint Paul's Cathedral. I was grateful at 95 still to be able to come up with something, especially remembering someone's opinion that your best work is done when you are young. If this is indeed so, we should not regret so much the loss of many composers long before their time and instead be satisfied with, for instance, the *Jupiter*, The Great C major symphony, Pergolesi, Bizet, Chopin, Mendelssohn, Gershwin, with their indispensible products. (And many more who, had they lived longer, would have laboured to bring forth works we could well be doing without.)

Mercifully there is no answer and, to refute the theory, there is Verdi to consider with his *Falstaff* and *Ortello* at nearly eighty, Tallis, Byrd, the *Sinfonia Antartica* and plenty more examples. What will probably be my swan-song gives me slight cause for satisfaction whatever its qualities. Whatever its fate, whether it is performable, whether it makes musical sense: these are the kind of thoughts that assail you as you await the judgement on it.

After all you are bringing into being out of nowhere a sequence of sounds which never existed before (at least not in that particular order: that is a hope not always realised) and its value cannot always be accurately assessed at once. The results of this phenomenal process may leave one feeling ecstatic or awful after one session, only to be reversed on re-visiting the manuscript at the next. Your most hopeful piece could be rejected and the one that does best (and brings in the most royalties) is the one you never thought anything of. But not always. You never can tell.

NEW CENTURY

22 May 2000: I came here to Norwich on Friday to play in Saint Thomas, Heigham (not far from the cathedral) on an excellent tracker organ with plenty of mutations and mixtures – built by Richard Bower. Matthew Martin the organist runs an adult choir and works hard at promoting recitals. I stayed in a bed and breakfast belonging to a choir lady who fed me on the fat of the land and who keeps her garden in great condition. The church is brick, comely and light, with a good acoustic. A good audience included a critic each from the *Eastern Daily Press* and *The Organ*, the former producing an appreciative review this morning.

Yesterday I was called for by Ron and Isabel Watson and taken to Eucharist at the cathedral, then to spend the night with them at Mattishall. I had played his *Jubiläum* at the recital; a jolly piece he wrote for me to play in the recital I did for the jubilee of the Norfolk Organists Association in July 1997; I played it twice on that occasion, beginning and ending with it. The cathedral choir was good but the Haydn *Little Organ Mass* has left no impression; the *Gloria in Excelsis* is so compressed as to be almost negligible. The fashion for using Viennese masses has grown somewhat out of proportion, and I wonder if they are more worth doing, or more suitable for our English service than Stanford, Ireland, Bairstow, Vaughan Williams, Wood and Byrd.

The Sunday evening service was a diocesan choirs' festival and the launching of the new hymnbook (*Common Praise*) with various commissioned pieces and a setting by Peter Aston, who conducted alongside David Dunnet, the cathedral organist. We were too near the organ though, in the nave aisle, and a sudden start of an acclamation or something made me jump. Allan Wicks did a very good short talk launching the book, he being on the editing panel.

This morning, after a full English breakfast, Ron and I called on Fred Pratt Green in his Methodist home. He was asleep in his chair in the hall but woke and, despite his ninety-six years and failing brain, carried on an enjoyable conversation without much repetition. He managed to sign a copy of *East Acklam* that, by an oversight on my part, did not include the words he wrote for it: 'For the fruits of his creation'. He had done this once before, but the ink appeared to be fading, so I took the chance of a replacement, which I had hardly thought possible. The writing was more shaky than before.

John Gielgud's death was announced – well over ninety; last week Donald Coggan's at ninety; and Barbara Cartland's today at ninety-eight. Whitlock, Walton and Flor Peeters would have been ninety-seven.

Next day, a train to Oxford, where I was met by Douglas Fairhurst at whose house I was staying in order to play at lunchtime tomorrow in the town hall on the four-manual Father Willis – which I have done more than once previously. A good turn-out and a kind and enthusiastic audience, who were seated at tables enjoying coffee and snacks. I was pleased with the organ tuner's comment that he liked the 'flow', something he said Philip Marshall's playing also produced. I think Bairstow must have brought this about: I remember his saying how unrhythmical playing, with unwarranted stops and jerks, upset the listener, just as bad driving with sudden braking spoilt things for the passenger.

||O||

I began to make serious efforts to work on this book. The act of calling up past events and writing was fun and I didn't expect to set down anything weightier than that. I was never anything approaching a thinker, let alone an original one. I don't think I ever had any potential in this direction and if I did it had no chance to be realised. Nor was I a reader at school and after leaving at 15 I was so caught up with music that there was no time for other things academic. Or perhaps I was too interested in gardening, tennis, making things, running wild in my teens and indeed until I joined the army *aetat 23*. Ironically, only then did the opportunity to settle down to bookish pursuits present itself. It has been a regret, for sure, realising what one has missed all one's life. Lacking a broad knowledge of Shakespeare is a particular sadness. For some exam at school, probably matric, I had to study *Julius Caesar* and found it very heavy going. But then one realises how full life has been and how blessed has been one's lot with such a multitude of other interests. Progress on this chronicle has been fitful. The collection of potential autobiographical material was begun with quite some years of strict order and discipline, though eventually it descended into a mass of confusion that in itself reflected the variety and intensity of activity over the years. Nevertheless my fervent hope was to provide out of the muddle a readable and true record that will help me to share some of the things I have undergone.

For our summer holiday of 2001 Priscilla and I were quartered in the area around Rutland Water, which was new to us. In the course of exploring we happened upon the church of Saint Mary the Virgin in the village of Edith Weston inside which we found an organ of the greatest interest – a small, one manual, with no pedals, made in 1787 by Samuel Green, the great organ builder born in 1740. Of course we were anxious to hear the sound of it. The only course open was to attend a service, which we did the following Sunday evening. On arrival we found two people concerned with producing evensong who were discussing ways and means and appeared to be in some difficulty. I am not sure if a priest was to take part, but we overheard a remark about there being a lack of an organist. This was my cue to butt in and offer my services: they were accepted perhaps a little uncertainly, quite naturally, and all proceeded without further hindrance, giving me everything I could have wished for. And more. The way was opened for a summer evening concert the following June when my *Georgian Suite*, Boyce, Arne, Sam Wesley, Sweelinck, Haydn, Vierne and Nares items were interspersed with a Danzi Wind Quintet and Mozart's *Divertimento 14* given by the Beaufort Ensemble. That was not all: soon a recording was made of Samuel Wesley's works by Martin Monkman for his Amphion label. During this enjoyable session Martin and I were given delightful hospitality by Kenneth and Gillian Orrell, enthusiastic supporters of the church.

Early in 2002 we suffered the grievous loss of Donald Webster who had been such a strong support and a most stimulating companion. His fabulous memory produced startling results when the matter of musicians' dates was under review, and his reportage of concerts and recitals was entirely dependable and utterly sound: his books on hymns and Leeds Parish Church are significant and valuable. A memorial service was held at his home village Askham Bryan on 26 May.

In Saint Luke's, Chelsea, where John Ireland was organist from 1904 to 1926, I spoke to the Guild of Musicians and Singers and played the central movement of Bairstow's *Sonata*. The talk's title was 'An Octave of Decades', perhaps because I was eighty. And I came away with one of their distinctive neckties, enrolled as a member of the illustrious body, receiving regularly thereafter the excellent periodical booklet.

On 25 June John Barry was granted the freedom of his native city, York. He had taken lessons with me in the 1950s and now was considered one of the best composers of film music in the world. The ceremony took place in the Assembly Rooms amid a host of admirers and supporters. There had been a very splendid concert of his music in the Albert Hall at which I was a guest and where I was able to learn something of his skills and inspirations, which was all very revealing. Not being a follower of the cinema I had, I regret to say, heard none of his music so was more than glad to have my eyes and ears opened to its special qualities and originality. He was always experimenting. During an interview on one of his visits to York we discussed orchestration, and a remark I made about the cor anglais brought forth the surprising idea that six of them all playing the same thing was worth hearing. It caused me to wonder whether such a thing had ever happened in the entire history of music; in fact whether he had actually done it himself. I neglected to ask him, but he spoke with sufficient assurance to convince me that he had tried it and found it worthwhile. This interview took place in the Minster Organist's house kindly lent for the purpose by Philip Moore because it was the room in which Barry had come for his tuition sessions. Barry was also given an honorary doctorate by York University at one of the usual kind of colourful academic graduation ceremonies when he gave an address; and at lunch we enjoyed his company and that of his wife Laurie, his young son Jonpatrick, and June his sister, still living in York.

The name of Richard Hickox became well known as a conductor, particularly of English music of which he made many recordings, music that might never have otherwise been heard. So it was a tragedy that he died in 2008 at far too young an age. I met him only twice, for the second time at an RCO meeting when he had attended his first and probably only Council meeting. On that occasion we reminded each other (if that were necessary) that on 25 January 1967 he had helped me by turning the pages for the recital I played in the parish church of High Wycombe. He was then still at school, only a few years older than my own children. Little did either of us foresee his brilliant success that came so soon.

In the Temple Church in London I played one of the June lunchtime recitals. When the time came for a Minster recital at York in August I took the bull by the horns and followed the trend towards transcriptions, selecting something which I am fairly certain had not been heard before within those hallowed walls – Ravel's *Valses Nobles et Sentimentales*. No harm was done, in fact the scene was notably unruffled; I did not receive a single comment on a work which is as replete with attraction as any. In 1998 I had played Debussy's nocturne *Nuages* in an arrangement I had made in March 1940 with the same result. But the *Pavane pour une Infante defunte* in 2008 brought forth a most kindly letter enquiring about the possibility of a recording. There was no opportunity to make one, and though the sympathetic expression was much appreciated, I cannot honestly say that I would consider one fit to stand beside Ravel's own orchestration of which many recorded versions are available.

A joyful happening, as a visit to the great city of Paris always is, was the IAO Congress in July. We had an evening in Notre Dame, one in César Franck's Sainte Clothilde under the direction of the late organist's widow Marie-Louise Jaquet-Langlais, and others in Saint Sulpice, once Widor's patch and then Marcel Dupré's, La Madeleine, Saint Etienne-du-Mont, Saint Eustache, and more. It was interesting and instructive to be reacquainted with the sound of French organs, particularly the reeds with their very characteristic sound. These were given full play, especially by candidates who were able to 'try' the organs (as one does), giving more attention perhaps to them than to other sounds which are the preserve of organs of this nationality such as the *fond de huit pieds* or the *célestes* of generous scale. There was a feeling, in the Madelaine, that an encore other then 'the Widor' would have suited us better, a softer one to follow a rather loud, reedy programme. There was a particularly beautiful Cavaillé-Coll in the church of Notre Dame d'Auteuil that gave great pleasure and earned the distinction of being my favourite among a line-up of several great instruments. Or was it the player Frédéric Blanc working the magic?

On 24 July 2002 I was presented to the Queen after the service of thanksgiving for the restoration of the centre of Manchester following its devastation by the IRA bomb. I had been commissioned to write an anthem to the very appropriate words from Psalm 31: 'Thanks be to the Lord for he hath shown me marvellous great kindness in a strong city'. Christopher Stokes conducted the choir in an excellent performance, which her Majesty told me she had enjoyed.

As November came to an end I spoke to the British Institute of Organ Studies (BIOS) in London, an interesting body concerned with the technicalities of organ building. It is always fascinating to meet and to pick the brains of those present. I doubt if my speech would be of very much use to people with such a high standard of knowledge of the subject, but I was interested to note the effect of my recounting my meeting with the great organ builder of Durham, Arthur Harrison, who came to inspect the two organs I was then playing at Malton from 1933 when I was 16. I have always felt privileged to spend time with him, and remember his pleasure on hearing the Great Diapason again which he certainly voiced himself in 1907, and his enthusiastic response on hearing the sound: 'What a glorious diapason'. And there it is in Malton still, all newly restored to its finest condition in the last year or two.

‖O‖

By 2003 we were clearly reaching the time when we must bid farewell to friends, many of them life-long. We had known Lionel Dakers since student days, organist at Saint Mary at Finchley, assistant to Sir William Harris at Windsor, then for a time at Ripon and Exeter Cathedrals, and lastly at the Royal School of Church Music. I was unable to attend his funeral, in Salisbury Cathedral on 21 March, but Priscilla was. I wrote a short anthem to the words of John Donne, arranged by Eric

Milner-White, *Bring us O Lord God at our last awakening*. The anthem's dedication reads 'For my god-daughter Juliet Dessain in memory of her father Lionel Dakers, and in gratitude for almost six decades of his friendship'.

Then but three days later a funeral I *was* able to attend was that of my school friend Robert Tinsley Holtby who had suffered a long illness here in retirement at Malton and at Huttons Ambo close by. One of the hymns at the funeral had led to the rediscovery of my hymntune 'Malton'. As fellow choristers in the Minster Choir in the 1930s, we would go by train together between York and Malton. He was my junior by some three years, and latterly was stricken with a grievous illness of long duration. His last post had been the deanery of Chichester where Priscilla and I had visited him and Mary his wife, and where we met the Prime Minister Edward Heath at the time of the Southern Cathedrals Festival with the Chichester, Winchester and Salisbury choirs.

The poetry written by Mary is of a very high order. Not only did I have a poem, *The Word* especially written for a commission, but her lovely metrical version of the Magnificat was there to inspire a composition; it begins 'My Lord and Saviour is my song'. The eightieth birthday acrostic poem is a marvel of craft, and the pair of Limericks for my ninetieth is too good to be allowed to perish without trace and appears below. She once sent Priscilla a postcard with words using no vowel but 'a', beginning naturally 'Madam'.

On the centenary of the birth of Percy Whitlock I had the good fortune to play the commemorative recital during the annual musical festival in Bournemouth. This is always a happy event lasting for a long weekend under the enthusiastic direction of Ian Harrison who provides an interesting and varied programme that includes a visiting choir as well as that which he runs; also chamber concerts and recitals. I wrote a sonata in four movements, my fifth, dedicated 'To the honour of Percy Whitlock in the centenary of his birth, and first performed by the composer … on 5 May 2003'. I took my cue from Percy's own monumental sonata of 1937. It is in the same key of C minor and uses the same titles for the inner movements but in reverse order.

An unusual request came from the Reverend Doctor Peter Mullen. It was to 'complete' Mozart's C minor mass by adding an *Agnus Dei*. I did not realise that more sections would be needed for its full completion, and set to work using Mozart's forces. I had been asked if I would be writing in the style of Mozart, and I really could not decide what that would be. All I could do then was to use a plain straightforward manner, which is what I imagined Mozart was doing anyway, and to hope it would pass muster. The piece was duly performed, and it might have been gratifying when an enthusiastic couple came afterwards assuring me that it was the best piece of the lot, had I been remotely prepared to believe it. However, it was proposed to me in quite definite terms on another occasion that the nineteenth century style I had employed was wide of the mark and a mistake. I find this difficult to agree to. There is such a thing as a timeless style belonging to no period which was the kind of thing to aim at: but it is not at all easy to copy a composer's style utterly and exactly. Perhaps it was only worth attempting for a less than serious purpose.

I have played more than once in Oxford Town Hall, most recently on 8 July 2003, in a programme consisting entirely of my compositions, including the fifth sonata which was written only a short time before, and ending with *Toccata, Chorale and Fugue*. This piece seems to be liked somewhat; people are playing it and there are several recordings. One of the pieces, called *Fantasia Campanulatica*, or *Campaniculata*, was written for the seventieth birthday of Douglas Bell of Huddersfield who had been a pupil of mine some fifty years earlier. It is founded on *Ding Dong Bell, Pussy's in the Well*. I mention it because for some reason it turned out very discordant – I cannot explain why – and difficult to learn to play. I am not disowning it yet, but for the moment it remains unpublished. On this visit to Oxford I was put up in Queen's College through the kindness of Christopher Rowland, one of the professors. Years ago he came and sang his excellent alto in the Minster choir when he lived with his family in Doncaster; this was effected by Magnus Black, organist of Doncaster parish church at the time. During my stay at the college I had the enormous treat of playing the wonderful Frobenius organ in the Queen's College chapel. It must be one of the most beautiful organs to be found anywhere.

Oddly enough, on the very next evening, in a programme for the Huddersfield Organists' Association I played only my own works again, including the fifth sonata. One of those present said it was a magical evening – it is usually the case that you are unaware of the effect you are having on your audience; but if there is an absence of coughing and shuffling and they are lively at the end, that is a sign they have enjoyed themselves.

That summer the *Salisbury Mass* with accompaniment for brass quintet and organ fared well in the cathedral on 18 July, though there was some slight difficulty with pitch due to the organ's sharpness. The composing had been more than ordinarily pleasurable; it came easily, and the performance under the direction of David Halls was successful. Priscilla and I then drove to Harrogate for a speech I was to make to those attending the annual dinner of the congress of the Incorporated Association of Organists. The Minster recital in August had my Sixth Sonata and Vierne's *Première Symphonie* as well as a Dvorak *Legend* in C that begins like 'Land of hope and glory'. This last was one of Sir Edward's pieces and has all that composer's inevitable charm.

October brought another sad event in Edinburgh with the funeral of Andrew Armstrong who only as recently as June had organised the restoration of his organ at Pilrig and had me to play the opening recital. Priscilla and I had so much enjoyed the Pilrig event with his elaborate, meticulous organisation and with the delightful companionship of his wife Antje. It was he who had arranged the splendid 1985 tour of East Germany.

Also in the same month the Tyndale lyric drama *A Time of Fire* was produced in Leeds Parish Church with John Stuart Anderson and the Saint Peter's Singers under their conductor Doctor Simon Lindley. And there was another production of it in Ely Cathedral the following July, again with the Saint Peter's Singers of Leeds, Richard Rastall taking the author's place in the role of Tyndale, and the organ played by Jonathan Lilley.

A brief visit to Boston, Massachusetts, involving choir work, a workshop, question and answer session, a Eucharist and a recital filled 8-15 March 2004. The famous Armley organ in Leeds was heard again on 28 May after extensive restoration and through the enthusiasm of. Professor Graham Barber. His recital had three new works, one being my sixth *Sonata* in three movements, the others being by Philip Wilby and Wolfgang Stockmeier. I had previously written a third sonata for the centenary of the organ, heard there in 1979, that I dedicated to my cousin Elsie Suddaby, the well-known soprano who was native to those parts in the 1890s. A sonata for trumpet and organ requested by Philip Lowe was played at the church of Langley, Middleton, in Greater Manchester by Malcolm Tyner during a recital I gave there. And not far away, in Saint Anne's church also in Manchester, not two months later it was a huge pleasure to be joined by Ronald Frost to play the *Eclogue* I had written for piano and organ. I played my sixth *Sonata* in the Minster on 21 August.

On the last day of April 2005 I became an Honorary Fellow of the Guild of Church Musicians in Salisbury Cathedral at the hands of their President, Doctor Mary Archer, to join the formidable number of persons so honoured. There was dinner and a speech to make the previous evening in the White Hart. Their enjoyable magazine 'Laudate' has come regularly ever since to keep us abreast of events in the realm of church music.

On 13 July in Norwich Cathedral there was a commemoration of what would have been Brian Runnett's seventieth year. Graham Barber, who had been his assistant during the short time Brian was organist before his tragic premature death aged thirty-seven, played a memorable recital of Krebs, of which Brian had made a notable recording; three of Arthur Wills's *Christmas Meditations* dedicated to him; one of Jehan Alain's *Trois Danses*; a *Toccata* I wrote dedicated to his memory; and the *Variations* opus 73 by Max Reger.

A Time of Fire was again done by the loyal Leeds forces, this time in Derby Cathedral late in July, and immediately afterwards I went to Tavistock for the annual festival run by Matthew Owens and the Exon Singers. This is on a similar scale to that at Bournemouth with a varied programme centred on the parish church. Here I had my first experience of that fashionable modern dish, the Curry, accompanied by quite some leg-pulling on account of my innocence. It occurred to me afterwards that I could have been put through a certain amount of torment by being prescribed one of the stronger-flavoured examples of the genre; I was completely in the hands of the choir, being in the privileged position of Composer in Residence for the duration of the festival. They could have taken their revenge for the trouble there must have been when coping with compositions of mine they so willingly and doughtily dealt with, but they were merciful in prescribing me the mildest korma of the considerable choice available for my initiation. It did not end there, for a few days later this incident of which I was the innocent cause was referred to by Canon Stephen Shipley while taking the daily service of the BBC ('daily' but not Saturday) though I heard about it only second-hand. I wonder whether my curry escapade was of any help to the souls of that morning's listeners as proposed by Canon Shipley; if so I am pleased to have had a part in it.

During the Festival the evening office of Compline was sung daily in Tavistock church, and Matthew wanted to know if I had composed a *'Te Lucis'*, one of the items needed to be sung as part of the service. Regretfully I had to admit that I hadn't. The magnificent setting by Balfour Gardiner had since chorister days more than satisfied my needs, so it had not entered my head that any other was necessary. But at once the obvious thought occurred – I could write one, for next year. Brave, or foolhardy, it could not compete with the Gardiner and would have to be quite different. It was soon written, and in due course I was treated to an audition of it at home, relayed through a mobile phone in Tavistock church. Its later history belongs to the year of the Queen's Diamond Jubilee. A collection of some forty choral items was planned, entitled 'Choir Book for the Queen'. Matthew's suggestion of *Te Lucis* was accepted in preference to the one I had originally submitted. It is pleasant to see from print-outs of future church service music I have been sent from the ever-present Internet that the existence of *Te Lucis* has not been ignored; it is rather easier and more traditional than some of the others. It has been interesting to hear them so competently performed by our cathedral choirs week by week during the Jubilee Year on Wednesday's Radio Three. The turn of *Te Lucis* came on 8 August 2012 when the Exon Singers broadcast a service of Evening Prayer from Buckfast Abbey with their new conductor Richard Wilberforce.

The year 2005 ended sadly in December with a memorial service for Philip Marshall at Lincoln Cathedral, during which I gave an address. He was a special and valued friend who had put his trust in me for advice concerning his Durham doctorate submission many years before. It was during practice in the organ loft of this cathedral that one of those uncanny coincidences happened. Having not been anything like a habitual user of the mobile telephone, I happened to have one in my pocket that suddenly came to life, something I had not experienced before. It had switched itself on and had responded to a call our son Edward was making in a desperate attempt to let us know that my sister Angela had died. (This was unexpected although her health had not been of the best.) With some difficulty I managed to do what was necessary to receive the call, and was grateful to Providence for making it possible. This was 17 December, and eleven days had to pass until her funeral in Saint Michael's Church in Malton. We had her favourite hymn 'Angel voices ever singing' and I thought it would be appropriate to play the prelude I had recently written for that tune. Later I used the hymn tune *Malton* for another chorale prelude in her memory, which appears as one of the *Acklam Pieces* alongside *Sarabande*, my brother Paul's commemorative piece. Angela had almost reached her eighty-second birthday and Paul, three years later, ninety-three.

There was a second visit to that splendidly designated Norfolk village Tittleshall some sixteen miles east of Kings Lynn on 7 June 2006, this time starting the new life of the restored Binns organ, a splendid one of two manuals which cheerfully rejoiced in the Boellmann *Suite Gothique*, a Smart *Andante*, Wolstenholme, Bossi (*Scherzo*), Bach's *Gig Fugue* and my recently composed three *Hymn Tune Preludes*. The organs (there was another one on the opposite side of the church) were the particular care of the Vicar, the Reverend Jonathan Boston, whose father the Reverend Noel Boston had been a regular and respected writer and adviser on organ matters for many years.

Yet one more recital on the splendid Gateshead Father Willis in 2006 had an item in the programme perhaps worth a mention: the second of Ravel's unaccompanied part songs *Trois beaux oiseaux du Paradis* which seemed to lose nothing with the words omitted. The melody is beautiful, equally so with the Fauré song *Après un rêve* which is perhaps as often played on a melody instrument as it is sung, and probably receiving the composer's approval when done thus. It was worth risking this with the Ravel, especially since the melody is shared between the four solo voices, providing the opportunity to vary the tone, as well as the pitch, of the tune.

There came a period when the playing of transcriptions of orchestral – and other – works on the organ reached almost epidemic proportions; this was a practice regarded as legitimate long before my student days for very good reasons. But with the advance in radio and recording bringing performances into the home in their authentic form, transcriptions were thought unnecessary. After some time, perhaps around 1990, they began to appear once more, some very much more ambitious than before. Eventually it occurred to me that to subject my symphony to this treatment might be a way of putting it into use, and this is what happened in the Minster in my August recital of 2006. I cannot maintain that it proved a startling world-beater, though there were appreciative comments. The one I liked best was from my great friend Leslie Matthews who felt at one point that the organ was going to explode. I was playing from my pencil-written copy (pages turned, as often, by grandson Sam) which then became totally superseded by a printed version made at his own suggestion by Ronald Watson – a gargantuan operation as I saw it but made light of by him with his computer experience, earning once more my thanks for one of the many acts of kindness that have come my way from so many quarters.

In 2007, when the BBC celebrated Elgar's sesquicentenary, I was tremendously taken with *The Dream of Gerontius*, revising my opinion of the work as with many other Elgar pieces (symphonies, *Sea Pictures*, *Enigma*, which I knew well), and realised what a great composer he is and what a fascinating character. In addition to his known output, the completion of his third symphony came about (first performed in 1998). This was a very significant event, somewhat controversial, but for me most welcome. It was a remarkable achievement on the part of Anthony Payne to complete the work, deserving of much commendation and acclaim. This was added to by my reading again the superb *Portrait of Elgar* by Michael Kennedy; we had the great pleasure of meeting him while we lunched with Robin Walker in Manchester art gallery in May 2007. This was when John Joubert was eighty years old, and Priscilla and I went to the Barbirolli Room in the Bridgewater Hall for the concert in celebration. I had written a setting of *Ode to a Pill* (for soprano, recorder and piano) at the request of John Turner who played the recorder part. This, incidentally, was my second setting of these words, which were found in a local publication and were anonymous; all attempts to trace the author proving fruitless. The first setting is for SATB, and was produced for John Scarfe's choir in Exeter. I was apprehensive about the acceptability of the solo version at the Joubert concert, but it was received with quite some amusement and pleasure, though it was not always possible to hear clearly the trend of events. Certainly it introduced a momentary lifting of the spirits amongst some rather serious items. John Turner kindly provided a copy of my piece to sign and send to John Joubert. He replied with a lovely picture postcard of Albrecht Durer's portrait of a young man – fantastic (as they *will* say nowadays) for an artist who lived from 1471 to 1528. It reminded us of our discovery of *The Apostle Saint Thomas* by Valasquez in the art gallery at Orleans during our September summer holiday of 1998 – a staggering achievement of 1620-22 when the artist was in his early twenties, though it has been said that your best work is done in your younger days.

Howden le Wear offered an intriguing and unique escapade on 9 June 2007. Priscilla and I drove northwards some forty or fifty miles to find a former chapel housing the cinema organ (a thoroughly genuine one) on which I had contracted to play. Having no experience of this genre of instrument, time was needed to ferret out its *modus operandi*. This was not a problem, and it was a delight to have the freedom of a different kind of organ. It answered willingly and cheerfully to the needs of my usual repertoire pieces: Bairstow, Bach (542), my fifth *Sonata*, Statham's *Ground*, Saint-Saëns, Whitlock, and sounding very happy with Guilmant's First Sonata for the last item. Actually, and strictly speaking, this was not my first experience of a cinema organ. That had taken place briefly in London in the Dominion Theatre, Tottenham Court Road, some time in the late 1940s at the hands of its resident organist Bobby Pagan. He let me 'try' the organ (as we organists so frequently and insistently had the habit of doing) with, I may add, no great success in the short time available.

On 24 June we were in Sutton Coldfield for a recital on the Willis organ in Emmanuel Church where Richard Mason works hard on the music to splendid effect. This was a happy visit, enabling us to meet again our erstwhile next-door neighbour of Minster Court, Canon Raymond Hockley who had served as precentor at York and had left us some time before. The weather was beginning to show its temperaments as we made our way home. The diary notes that, of premature birthday greetings, there were 'Ten today on returning by the skin of our teeth from Sutton Coldfield. Torrential rain caused flooding all over the country and a journey of three hours or so took us eleven. Starting from Tamworth our train was cancelled, so we boarded one to Derby and a tardy bus to Sheffield. All trains from here were cancelled except one to Manchester which we took, to Piccadilly. But no trains to York. A taxi (£6) to Victoria where there was some doubt about trains to York, and eventually one at 7.15 which took an hour to arrive – twice its usual time'.

Not long before retiring from his memorable term of office at Wakefield Cathedral, Jonathan Bielby was kind enough to arrange a recital for me one July Saturday morning on the famous five-manual Compton organ there. The programme contained no pieces except some I had once 'perpetrated' (as Mr Wybergh once said) – a treat for a composer that happens rarely, but that followed the model of the Oxford and Huddersfield recitals in this my ninetieth year.

Soon after which Priscilla and I took a train to Exeter, met by Paul Goodman who took us to his lovely home at North Tawton, preparatory to a recital at Great Torrington. The organ there is a fine transplanted Willis with a strong personality, rewarding to play. In his house (with its fine view of countryside from its elevated position) is a similar characterful instrument, to be joined in a short time by another.

◖◗

Greetings began arriving in June, in ample time for the October event. The eve of my birthday brought forty cards, among them Mary Holtby's pair of brilliant limericks that have continued to give so much pleasure, amusement, not to say admiration:

'Dear Francis, famed anniversarian   But happy that lexical chance is:
The task I address is a scary'un: Since youthfulness scorns the advances
 While far from the Stone Age,   Of calendar dating,
 You're not in your NONAGE   Your fans are awaiting
And yet you're a NONAGENARIAN...   CENTENARY junkets, Dear Francis.'

And next day, necessitating a fairly capacious container for the postman to deliver them, seventy-four greetings, followed by forty the day after and then eleven, and the occasional laggards for a day or two afterwards. My nine decades were achieved on the second of October. There were twenty telephone greetings on the day, and an average of ten each day during the following week, which was lovely, if time-consuming. It was never expected that I should be able to clock up (OR be able to record) anything like ninety years of age. In our youth three score and ten were considered a generous and satisfactory allowance, but such are the marvels of modern medical matters that so many of us have been granted the extension in which to enjoy the world and its wonders for longer. Given good health, as I have been, life is wonderful. For the moment it went on as before, and my four score years and ten could not be ignored; it was almost overwhelming to have so much affectionate attention. But there was more birthday activity. The Doncaster Minster Munchers under the organisation of Raymond Chapman invited us to one of their lunches, a thoroughly friendly and enjoyable undertaking. Our friends here at East Acklam, Colonel and Mrs Sackville-Hamilton, put on a wonderful dinner party for a substantial number of guests in their house.

On the actual birthday was a family gathering with lunch in Acklam village hall, the cottage being too small to contain all twenty-one of us. William's speech proposing my health was a matter for fatherly pride; the same having happened ten years before when Alice did the same for my eightieth celebration with such grace and affection. My seventieth and eightieth had already been celebrated more than adequately so I was bound to expect something; but this year's events turned out to be more than I could ever have imagined. Priscilla warned me that on the previous day there was to be some kind of Minster concert or recital in which the Whitlock Trust was to be involved, followed by a reception. This I thought was to be a modest affair and within one's capacity to cope but, on being taken into the north quire aisle through what we usually referred to as the Stokehole door (from Chapter House yard) and then into the Quire, Priscilla and I were staggered to be greeted by applause from the assembled company who seemed to be filling every seat, and very nearly were. (The Quire when full holds something like five hundred.)

Greetings were done by Robert Gower and Paul Hale and I was presented with a book of pieces especially written by eleven composers with the title *Fanfare for Francis*; the same number as the *Hovingham Sketches* for the Duchess of Kent – a coincidence surely. My copy was specially bound in stiff black boards. Many had been bought beforehand; each contained a compact disc with all the pieces, plus my *Impromptu*, played in consummate fashion by John Scott Whiteley. Such a complete surprise was impossible to comprehend, the more so when John began to play the whole lot from start to finish. To accomplish that, having spent so much energy and expertise in learning the notes for recording, was a prodigious feat: and at the end, when I had stumbled out my inadequate thanks to all those who had done so much, sparing no effort, we repaired to the Chapter House for refreshment and what our American cousins call 'visiting'.

The annual reunion of old Minster choristers was usually, and quite coincidentally, held on a day close to my birthday. This year's was a bumper attendance giving me the chance to catch up with the doings of many of those who long ago had borne the burden and heat of the treble line, and to recall the pleasure and profit of their chorister days. There were speeches at the dinner and many kind things were said. It was now Edward's turn to do the honours, and in a rather more public situation; he succeeded brilliantly with a wonderful speech over which he had taken a great deal of trouble.

An exhibition of photographs was mounted in the Minster's North Transept to do with my efforts in the building over the years, and with the choristers at the Song School. This was done single-handedly by the Reverend John Roden, retired vicar of Appleton Roebuck, who had taught in the school before his ordination and who continued to take a close interest thereafter. The exhibition was entirely his own idea, a great success and greatly appreciated, as were the albums he had put together and presented to me, full of photographs of my time as organist at the Minster. There was yet one more illustration of the regard held by the former choristers for the Minster. Having learned that my doctoral gown (obtained in 1957, and previously owned by CS Lang) had sustained a tear, and the beautiful cream silk brocade become frail and seriously damaged, their immediate thought was to take the business of repair into their hands. The garment was placed in the care of the most expert of restorers, seeing to the entire operation and its expense, and furnishing me with the rejuvenated raiment in its pristine state once more. A more kindly, generous act I could not have imagined, particularly coming as it did from so many of the choristers I had so much happiness with during that short period when their voices were at my disposal.

There were presented to me four compositions: a nativity carol to words by Eleanor Thompson especially composed for me by Eve Barsham which only now, to my shame after some years I am acknowledging; a delightful *Francis's Fandango* from Jonathan Bielby that I have played in a holy place, Mill Hill Chapel near Leeds Railway Station; *A Fugal Offering* containing all the devices necessary for that musical form by Leslie Bresnen, long-time colleague prominent on the York musical scene; and another intriguing piece with the title *Ninety Bars* characteristic of its composer Ronald Watson's whimsical turn of mind, one bar or measure for each year of my existence and craftily managing to bring in the 'York Tune' to fix the piece in a homely latitude. After all of this I retained a definite feeling that it had been well worth living so long (which I knew already, of course).

For my part I wanted to do something as a memento and as a gesture of thanks for a long life full of wonders. The idea of some new lighting in the church at East Acklam was suggested and was readily received. To have an alternative to the strip lights fastened alongside the beams on the ceiling was a happy prospect. Simple wooden chandeliers, cross-shaped with four upright lights on each were designed and made by Kit Hamar, our son-in-law, providing light for us with unaffected modesty befitting a small uncomplicated building. The faculty had been obtained without any hindrance, and the workmanship of the chandeliers – all five – is, as with all Kit's work, of the finest. The lights were switched on at a Sunday evening service by Rachel and Christopher, the young children of Mr and Mrs Inman of our neighbouring farm.

||◉||

In February 2008 I was suddenly motivated to produce a mass for Timothy Storey's choir at Saint Botolph-without-Bishopgate in London. What gave me the idea was that this particular choir then consisted of two soprano parts, and no doubt it would be less trouble to write. At all events, on receiving it Tim immediately telephoned and the *Missa Sancti Botolfi* was duly made use of. I had put it in E major to join up with the evening canticles that I had written for Saint David's

Cathedral in 1999 which I presumed to call *Canticula Decima*, no doubt with a reason.

Later in the month a visit to Birmingham of great interest brought me to the Oratory, well-known for its connexion with Cardinal Newman, to play the fine four-manual organ, this through the good offices of my old friend John Pryer, the organist there. (He had also been closely involved with London's Alexandra Palace where I was to play twice during the next two years.) The occasion I took part in was the annual celebration of the birth of Cardinal Newman, his two hundred and seventh. There were readings and addresses, philosophical and eulogistical, and items by the choir as well as organ pieces. For their wonderful solemnity suitable for the occasion I chose the Franck *Fantaisie* in A and Statham's *Rhapsody on a Ground*; for lighter contrast the *Fantaisie* written at the age of twenty-two by Camille Saint-Saëns; and Parry's *Fantasia and Fugue* in G for the concluding voluntary.

It was not long afterwards that it was proposed to move the cardinal's tomb to a different location in the Oratory, arousing much expectation. To me, having been there so recently, it was a matter of no little interest. It was therefore more than a disappointment when no remains were to be found, and completely and utterly unexpectedly causing much grief to those concerned in the planning. The countless devotees of Elgar's masterpiece also would be taking a sympathetic interest since it was the cardinal who wrote the poem *The Dream of Gerontius*, the catalyst that brought forth one of the world's greatest choral works.

On that particular day of my Oratory recital, another natal happening was being attended to eight thousand miles underneath us (although by that time of our evening, down there the next day had been entered into). It was that of the former cathedral organist in Adelaide, my friend of long standing David Swale, having attained eighty years of age. The programme planners at the Oratory welcomed the recognition of this very personal celebration by the inclusion of a piece I dedicated to him, and I was very happy that it could be included on such an occasion. It was based on a carol and, with the title *Susanni Scherzo* became one of the collection of *Acklam Pieces*.

‖◯‖

Occasionally there has happened a recital unlike any other and will happen no more than once in a lifetime. However there were two I particularly remember, quite different from each other and some years apart. In Saint Martin's church in York's main (Coney) street, or in what was left of it – the walls of the south aisle – after the fire following the wartime air-raid, in 2008 a somewhat select audience attended 'A celebration of the fortieth anniversary of the rehallowing of the church on 28 April 1968'. The organ was a gift from the German government and the German Evangelical Church. It has no pedals but its single manual is the proud possessor of three stops, all the work of JW Walker whose superb voicing is quite equal to the intimate acoustic. It was an interesting problem finding what to play since little of one's usual stock of pieces could be of use, and with not a great variety of tone to choose from. Perhaps it was in the same category as a piano recital where so much depends upon the quality of the music and the performance rather than on tone colour. The eighteenth century came in useful, with Nares (of York), Arne, two Soler sonatas, and two of Bach's *Forty-Eight*, of which the ninth of the second book seemed made for the lovely stopped Diapason. Four present-day composers followed, three of whom were present. A few years earlier Richard Shephard had been good enough to supply me with *Tempo di Valse* for the other 'unique' recital and Andrew Carter's contribution was specially composed for the occasion, with the title *Three pieces for Three stops* with the names *1. A Cipher, 2. Tuning Slides* and *3. Gremlins on the Great*, all of which were appropriately illustrated in sound. Philip Moore, my successor at the Minster, was represented by what he had once written for his mother to play: *Three Pieces for Withycomb – Prelude, Sarabande* and *Postlude*. Lastly came my *Georgian Suite*, which can be played with or without pedals: so I chose the latter course, perforce.

The other occasion, some years earlier, was quite different: after the meagre but exquisite resources just related I was offered an almost limitless supply of harmoniums for my pleasure, of every conceivable design and size, the varied, ornate appearance of the majority suitably matched by their names – Kelly, Gregorian, Apollo, Beecham, Boudoir, Conway, Piano Harp and of course Mustel, each with its own subtle variety of reed tone. I used thirteen of them from among the considerable total number that are housed there. Again it was a matter of unusual pieces, although the familiar names of Vierne and Guilmant appeared (the latter represented by his *Communion* in G which can be managed without pedals) along with Adams, one Hunt, Richard Shephard's commission *Tempo di Valse*, and my *Georgian Suite*. Three of Vierne's *24 Pièces en Style Libre* of 1914 were companionable, being in my normal repertoire, providing a touch of reality in the somewhat exceptional but highly enjoyable situation offered by the Harmonium Museum in the unique town of Saltaire near Bradford on that September day of 1995.

It was there that I saw Charles Macdonald for the last time. He had been organ scholar at the Minster and, after various college and school appointments, finally set up a music business in Steyning, Sussex, from where he had brought music to sell at Saltaire. By those means, Vierne's *Messe Basse* came into my possession. Charles was an unusual, interesting character, good company and a fine musician; his premature loss was a shock, affecting his many friends deeply, as the large attendance at his funeral testified. This I learned afterwards, having not been present.

My third medical misdemeanour was in late spring 2008 when my foot became caught in long grass on a bank forming the verge of the road in Acklam. Thus I was caused to take a fall on to the hard road, which successfully produced some hip damage and the postponement of a recital. It necessitated a spell of wonderful hospital treatment that after a mere couple of months enabled me to play in the Minster. Also as a consequence of the hip, five months late appeared the composition I was asked to write in memory of Michael Gillingham. It was specially requested that it should contain a fugue, which automatically would include some sort of introductory movement. Some time before this Michael had asked for a tune for Charles Wesley's hymn 'God is gone up on high' for use in his London church of Saint James. As this was in the district of Clerkenwell, that is the name it could not avoid being given, and which adhered to the *Fantasy and Fugue* for which I used the tune as a basis. The fugue subject is an inversion of the first few notes of the tune. Michael had had a long and close connexion with the church and with Noel Mander had organised an imaginative rebuilding of the organ upon which I eventually played the finished piece – in November rather than June – in the presence of his brother Colin and other members of his family, with my pages expertly turned by Gerard Brooks.

Simon Lindley celebrated his sixtieth birthday with an event in Leeds Parish Church on 10 October 2008 where he had been organist for nigh on thirty-four years. In the course of an absorbing sequence of events a book containing expressions of goodwill, admiration and affection, such as are universally felt towards Simon, was presented to him. The following week there was a notable concert in York Minster involving Simon's Saint Peter's Singers who he conducted in three of his anthems, *Ave Maria, Now the green blade riseth*, and *Lord I have loved the habitation of thine house*. Three other conductors presented their own works: Simon's Leeds predecessor Donald Hunt, then in office at Worcester Cathedral, conducted his *Hymnus Pascalis*; I took my turn with *Benedicite* and *Stabat Mater*, the latter having Quentin Brown's distinguished account of the baritone solo part; and Philip Moore's *Prayers of Dietrich Bonhöeffer* were heard in ideal conditions. All the organ playing was in the skilled hands of David Houlder, Simon's helpmeet in what has since become known as Leeds Minster.

The next year saw three minor new organ pieces and the first performance of an anthem *Most glorious Lord of Life* commissioned for the Edington Festival in the summer of 2009. It was begun on the first of April, setting Spencer's Sonnet LXVIII. It begins sturdily, and ends gently with the words: 'Love is the lesson that the Lord us taught'. It was broadcast on a Wednesday afternoon on Radio Three but has not been published.

The new organ pieces were, first, *Cantilena*, published in a collection of fourteen works celebrating the centenary of the Oldham, Rochdale and Tameside Organists' Association; second, a *Fanfare* for a recital at Hallam organised by ex-Yorkist Drummond Gillespie which took the venue's name for its title; and third, *Reverie*. This last came about by reason of my receipt of a theme, originally requested of Ravel by Marcel Dupré for an improvisation in the Trocadero in Paris on 30 April 1925. Six themes had been asked of that number of France's leading composers. Now the themes had been re-discovered and Roger Nichols, the writer and biographer with special reference to French music, knowing of my interest in Ravel, was kind enough to send me his. It was an event of major importance after my lifetime's admiration and love of this composer and his music, a wonderful thing to have, raising thoughts on what Dupré could have made of it all. Then the possibilities that the theme offered for development all too soon made themselves felt. But who was I that I should dare to handle such a precious thing, and what opinions would *le maître* have expressed on learning of my arrogant intentions. Nevertheless it was impossible to restrain the urge, and *Reverie* emerged, with the fervent hope that I had done no harm, and speculation on what might have happened had I been able to take it to *Le Belvedère* for the Master's comments. The piece, whatever its worth, is a grateful tribute to Ravel whose music with its unique enduring qualities has meant so much: as have accounts of his fascinating personality, his interesting life and his opinions, which he expressed without fear of any consequences.

The book *Acklam Pieces* was at that time in the late stage of production, and *Reverie* was just in time to become one of them. My very real gratitude was with Roger Nichols, whose monumental biography of Ravel appeared very soon, containing much new material that is of absorbing interest. He was kind enough to send me a copy which I had soon read from cover to cover twice: it arrived when we were out, so the resourceful postman had left the parcel on the lawn mower in the shed which joins the music room we call 'Montfort' at the top end of the garden. This in its turn is some eight yards from the cherry tree that has grown from the seedling I brought from Montfort l'Amaury in 1972 and which I have relished every springtime when it is hung with snow, as Housman has it.

TENTH DECADE

Christmas Day 2009: Having now reached not three but *four* score years and ten, it was certainly *unbelievable* that such an august and enviable position would, or could ever, be attained. I will not employ that much overworked favourite word 'incredible', used so often on the wireless when 'very' is quite adequate – though it would not be at all out of place here. After all, what is the real meaning of that word? Were we not taught it at school? Or are we in too much of a hurry to think?

That privileged state, then, from where looking back can be instructive, amusing, nostalgic, regretful, and other things besides (yes, 'unbelievable' certainly), is something to treasure; it provides perhaps a final opportunity to survey the ground that has been covered. For many years now, the prevailing cry has been for change, in the belief that changing something will improve it: a fond hope not always realised. Why, for instance, do our diaries now have to begin the week with Monday? Can Sunday's feelings be imagined; and what has it done to deserve such cavalier treatment? How much better are we all as a result? But there are other and more serious examples: the abolition of matrons has not been helpful to the hygienic running of our hospitals; has indeed contributed to some dire happenings. Currency probably needed to be changed, though decimalisation had its untoward effects. One wonders what advantages were brought by the seemingly drastic changes of county boundaries. Changes in the workings of the police force appear only to have taken officers away from their watching over of the public. A policeman is a rare sight; and is law and order (NOT Laura Nawda) as much maintained as it should be, and once was? Guards had to follow the trend and become Train Managers. In the same way it has been a kind of sadness to see my title – and that of so many of my York forerunners – of Master of the Music needlessly altered to that of a director, as of something more prosaic of which I will not trouble to give examples.

For many of those in the service of the church, changes in the liturgies have been unnecessary as well as distressing and hurtful, depriving us of the matchless language of the Book of Common Prayer, replacing it with inferior phraseology, doing away with the poetical aspect and the essential mystical element. There seemed to be no good reason. The Prayer Book liturgies were perfectly intelligible and it is less than likely that they had constituted a problem in all the four centuries of their use. Has church attendance increased as a result? If not, could it be that it has worked in the opposite direction and turned away those who hold the Prayer Book dear in their affections. No account evidently was taken of the susceptibilities of the congregation of a certain church near York who came to service one morning to find the new liturgy in their places and the Book of Common Prayer removed. This was done without any notice or warning. Neither was thought given, it would seem, to the effect of rocking the very foundations of the whole edifice and doing away with the stability that is such a crucial element in a religious milieu – and of many another. The only reason that came my way (and that from a high-up person in the movement) was what was described as the 'wordiness' of the services and the repetitiousness. But is this not an essential characteristic of the style, seen frequently in the psalms; and is it not found as a fundamental axiom similarly in musical composition where phrase lengths are balanced against each other and repeated as necessary and with variation, as Cranmer and his team so expertly and sensitively handled them? There is a sureness, an inevitability, an eternal feeling to those timeless words which is right for its purpose, creating the appropriate feeling and atmosphere, as it has stood there magisterially and unchallenged for so long.

But one does not lose sight of the fact that there have been changes for good – perhaps in greater number – which are I am sure always in the minds of those who look after our welfare; and I shall refrain from trying to enumerate them (if that were possible) for the sake of space, and almost certain boredom for the reader.

Most of us who were brought up on the Book of Common Prayer have a great affection and a profound respect for it. I for one have had no problem with it at any time of my life and have seen no necessity for far-reaching changes to it. As a chorister at Malton and York Minster, and as organist in both places, one regarded it as an essential part of life. It was, then, a great sadness to have it largely swept away and replaced by something of an inferior quality, whose effect was to lower the tone and the level of inspiration one expected to find in a Eucharistic service.

On leaving my Minster post it was a joy to find the prayer book in use in the village where we were to spend our retirement. The troubled subject of revised liturgies was always liable to be raising its head. When, during our long interregnum at Acklam we were trying to find a vicar, among our requirements was adherence to the Prayer Book, clearly indicating that the East Acklam congregation was solid on this point as on every other. So the appearance of an ASB Eucharist one day (whether by accident or design) raised the question of the necessity to make any such change, and produced anxiety as to what future policy might bring forth. I did not relish the prospect of losing the Prayer Book service and having to put up with one I was not in sympathy with. I was therefore prepared to cede the position of organist for the Eucharist and, subject to agreement, to continue accompanying evensong and other services. But this turned out not to be necessary. My fears were allayed and it is a joy to continue with the familiar words, heard, now, for close on ninety years. Evensong has fared even less well than the Eucharist at the hands of the revisers and does not seem to have been widely accepted, leaving the Prayer Book version as the preferred one in most places.

Matins, which during my Minster choristership was an important service, filling the quire to capacity has, alas, fallen from popularity. Before the 1939 war and for a few years after 1945 it took place on four weekday mornings, also every Sunday when it was followed immediately by the *Sung* Eucharist, as it was then known. It had a sermon, usually by a notable preacher, a visitor or one of the home team. There was no anthem, but as well as psalms, and the Venite, there were two hymns and a setting of the Te Deum with either Benedictus or Jubilate. These were – are – fine compositions: one remembers with nostalgic pleasure Bairstow in D, Ireland in F, Wesley in E (spacious and colourful), four splendid Stanfords and a good many more. Matins was always an occasion with best Sunday clothes, providing a perfect prelude to the Eucharist which had its own splendid settings, always with the singing of the Creed, which is seldom if ever to be heard nowadays. Is there a really good reason for this? Cannot the choir do for the congregation what it does for them in the other parts of the service that it enunciates and affirms on their behalf? Matins is a fine conception and deserves its place in the canon of religious observances. Broadcast services, apart from the Communion Service, have appeared, with few exceptions, to ignore the use of Matins. Instead have been substituted programmes consisting of various commentaries interspersed with musical items which can be of any type and not, as a rule, using material from the Prayer Book orders.

A new service has thus come into being, which is rather a type of recital containing readings, poetry and music; a free and informal pattern which can be tailored to one's particular requirements and be either sacred or secular, the kind sometimes rudely dubbed a 'hymn sandwich'. Opinions will differ as to what advantage may accrue therefrom. The quality will inevitably be variable: it will probably be more interesting to some who may feel themselves bored by the weekly or daily repetition of the noble, familiar phrases. There is a matter, however, of how much it is possible for one to take in of new, unfamiliar, information and whether the 'ordinary' parts of the service are of use in demanding, as they do, less concentration such as is required for a deep theological sermon or something equally unfamiliar. These great poems and epics can fulfil a need by the grandeur of their thought and expression however often they have been heard and used.

||O||

In London's Alexandra Palace I played in both 2009 and 2010, in a *room* of enormous proportions. In the first programme my third Sonata rubbed shoulders with Bach (543), Schumann, Parry, Wolstenholme, Vierne (*Naïades*) and the Franck *Final*. In its day the Willis organ had been acclaimed the finest concert organ in Europe. Later it suffered many vicissitudes and was only kept alive by the enthusiasm of many devoted volunteers of which Felix Aprahamian, the distinguished writer on music and organs, French especially, was a notable chairman. Its remarkable qualities may still be heard in the gripping recordings made in the 1930s by such players as GD Cunningham, Marcel Dupré, George Thalben-Ball and Sir Walter Alcock, recordings which have since been reproduced on compact discs. Though not as complete as it was, the organ still retains a great deal of its splendour as work goes on gradually towards total restoration.

Saint Michael's Church in Malton, where my first permanent organistship (with Saint Leonard's) began in 1933, had its 1907 Harrison organ restored in 2010, which would set it up for another century of service. Seventy-seven years after my appointment I was playing the restored instrument at the start of its second spell of duty which there is little doubt of its fulfilling – the organ that was built so strongly of the best materials, and was always grateful to play within the limitation of its fifteen speaking stops.

At home the University orchestra provided the rare treat of a chance to hear my symphony, in a sight-read run-through in the Sir Jack Lyons Concert Hall. This was a great achievement on the part of the students, earning my gratitude for the splendid job they made of it under John Stringer's direction. It was a happy circumstance to note the pleasure it afforded the students, who made no secret of their feelings.

Yet another loss befell us late in June with the death of Leslie Matthews. I had come to know him when he was in charge of the music at Saint Gregory's Minster near Kirbymoorside and did wonderful work sustaining a constant choral programme week by week with a fully surpliced choir of mixed voices. All this in the diminutive country church standing alone with its imposing title, in its very desirable situation in the valley among the luxurious outlay of trees. I would occasionally play for a service, as I did for Leslie's funeral service. This was carefully planned with the choir in full force, and among the chosen pieces played on the organ was one that was surprisingly effective and appropriate, sounding well on another medium: the second movement of Elgar's *Serenade for Strings*.

It was an unusual and interesting diversion regaling the Norwich Organists' Association in November with my choice of Desert Island Discs, with Ronald Watson eliciting my comments and keeping me on track. It is not easy to single out eight pieces from such a wealth of treasures, and no doubt several other series of that number could be found. However, if it is of interest: Dvorak began with the *In der Natur* overture, which I had learnt as an organ piece with Bairstow; Heathcote Statham's *Rhapsody on a Ground*, he having been Norwich Cathedral organist; Mozart's *Kegelstatt* Trio; Bairstow's anthem 'Lord thou hast been our refuge'; *Edelma*, an attractive piece of light music by an Argentinian, Terig Tucci, in a luxurious orchestral arrangement; part of Ravel's opera *L'Enfant et les Sortilèges*; one of Debussy's *Nocturnes* and, for a decisive finish, the Saint Anne *Fugue*, one of Bach's supreme moments when the pedals bring in the subject for the last time not on the dominant but the subdominant, a stroke of sheer genius. As ill luck would have it, my recording of the fugue was found not to be in its case, so we all repaired to the church to which the hall we were in was attached. Here I did my best to fill the void from memory.

A few days later, there arrived at home an astonishing gift in the shape of a framed portrait in watercolour of me on my mythical desert island, listening to Ravel. It is a work of consummate artistry by a pillar of the Association, Martin Cottam, soon to become its President. A more welcome souvenir of the occasion could not have been thought of, causing much admiration, continuous pleasure and amusement.

Two London recitals followed next year, the second of those at the Alexandra Palace on Saint Swithin's day, almost a year to the day after the last one. This time my sixth sonata kept company with Vierne (*Impromptu, Carillon de Westminster*), with Smart, the 'Big G minor' and Statham's wonderful *Rhapsody on a Ground*, one of the greatest passacaglias for the organ, a very powerful and most eloquent conception. After many years' admiration of it and many performances I have a strong conviction that the composer's speed is too fast and can prevent the full import and depth of the music from showing.

Saint Michael's, Cornhill, had a major rebuild of its organ and ran a series of recitals in celebration. Mine carried the Bairstow *Sonata*, on Saint Luke's day, and was attended by a great many of my friends who were bound to be curious about how the organ was comporting itself as a result of the going-over it had had. This restoration had been planned, worked at very hard and brought to its triumphant conclusion by Jonathan Rennert, friend of long standing. Some years before (April 1993) at his wedding in Saint Michael's I played them out with the first movement of Elgar's *Sonata*. Very soon afterwards an IRA bomb was exploded in Bishopsgate, which almost demolished Saint Ethelburga's church and threw Liverpool Street station into utter confusion, but thankfully did no harm to the wedding festivities taking place not far away.

On 25 September 2010 a fond grandfather experienced an especial delight in having his twenty-three-year-old pianist grandson Sam, Edward's elder son, join him with the piano part of *Eclogue*. This made use of the electronic piano which had been introduced into the church of Saint Michael in Malton not long before and was a proud possession: *Eclogue* was then twenty-three years old too, having been produced for the annual Congress of Organists at Cambridge in the year of Sam's birth. Now, some years later it was at Cambridge that he was pursuing his music studies at Selwyn College, to be brought to fruition in due course with the expected degree.

||O||

Very soon it was All Saints Day, the first of November, and this was our sixtieth wedding anniversary, something we could not have banked on being able to celebrate, particularly as Priscilla and I were into our fourth decade when we married. So plans were laid, and cards came including one from Her Majesty which was heart-warming. Sixteen of the family sat down to lunch in the Old Lodge in Malton, some hundred yards from the house in East Mount where my family lived from the late 1920s. We then took ourselves home in a body to Nether Garth for tea.

There seemed to be rather frequent celebrations happening around this time, and looking back it is not always easy to keep them in their own separate memory compartments. As they have come along they have brought such a wonderful assurance of regard and affection from so many people. We have been very blessed with our friends – and relations – and, in the midst of a busy life, have enjoyed the fairly infrequent jaunts and visits of various kinds we undertook. These included a decent summer holiday, usually lasting something like four weeks, at first inclined to be adventurous but later quieter and less ambitious. And as time went on the ambition was to be at home tending the garden, taking life in a leisurely fashion. But this did not seem to work out in quite this way; there was always something needing attention and there was often a backlog to be tackled. Then it gradually began to come clear that life must slow down on its way to a final full stop. What was needed was the ability to accept the situation without any regrets and to be glad and grateful for the way one's life had turned out; and this is what happened.

Completion of the fourth decade of my retirement from the Minster in 2011 was still to come. There were still spills and thrills and fourteen recitals, but a tragedy came early in the year: the death of David Sanger, unexpected and much mourned. I went to his memorial service at Cambridge in Great Saint Mary's church and Selwyn College, which was a remarkable tribute by many of his friends.

On the day in April when Prince William married Catherine Middleton, Priscilla and I took the 11.27 train from York and duly landed at Bournemouth, effectively and unfortunately cancelling out any chances of witnessing the ceremony on television. Our purpose was the annual festival held in Saint Stephen's church where Percy Whitlock was once organist. His music is featured there frequently and the whole event is organised by his present-day successor Ian Harrison, whose energy and inspiration provides an interesting and pleasantly enjoyable three days. For companions we had Roy and Ruth Massey (retired from Hereford Cathedral) and Canon Stephen Shipley (of the BBC) and Mrs Shipley. From him we had a fascinating talk on the history of broadcast evensong; a beautiful sermon by Canon Neil Heavisides, Precentor of Gloucester, and the Whitlock Recital by Andrew Lumsden, organist of Winchester Cathedral. At the high mass on the first day I conducted my setting 'Me in G'. The next day, the first of May, was the sixty-fifth anniversary of the one on which Whitlock died, and not only him but Sir Edward Bairstow as well. At Mass I conducted his introit *Jesu the very thought of thee* which was sung beautifully. The choir joined me in a recital next day, they singing my *O Salutaris* and *Gloria in Excelsis*. My fifth sonata composed for Whitlock's centenary in 2003 was included, with the *Intermezzo* and *Canzona* from his Sonata, and *Sortie* from his *Seven Sketches*.

The following week I was in Worcester Cathedral with the conference of cathedral organists. Sir David Willcocks spoke at the dinner reminiscently, and I was given the welcome opportunity to meet the new organ on which I was booked to play on the eve of my next birthday in October. A very fine instrument it is and a source of much pleasure when the time came.

In late May Priscilla and I drove to Lincoln for me to play the cathedral organ, one of my most favourite ones. We spent time enjoyably with Colin Walsh and ate his delicious cooking in his interesting cathedral organist's dwelling. On our way home we called in for lunch near Worksop with Reg Elson who had had some lessons with me and I had not seen for many years. Though principally a medico he was also a skilled organist, so much so that he made recordings of Mendelssohn and Liszt, including *Ad Nos*, on his resident electronic organ of fine quality.

And so we reached home once more, and settling in the following day Priscilla was beginning to show disturbing signs that developed into meningitis. This was diagnosed when York hospital was reached, and was a condition beyond the experience of any of our family, and of the utmost seriousness. For three days there was doubt about her survival until the danger passed and a very gradual recovery was begun. There was what could be called a miracle, and that was the preservation of the brain, hardly affected – if at all – and leaving her, in her own words 'most fortunate'. So much was owed to so many who supported us with their thoughts and prayers when it seemed that medical care had reached its limit. A change in our lives was brought about – more to Priscilla's than mine. No more car driving, medical matters high on the agenda, serious loss of hearing, short walking-distances not easy even with a walking frame. But appetite and food matters were unaffected, and domestic activities if slightly curtailed carried on as ever, at a slower pace. We were very comfortably placed in the modest cottage with its generous garden, and we had all the medical attention we could need seven miles away in Malton, all administered with thoughtful kindliness. It was still possible for me to take engagements as Priscilla was soon able to be on her own at home. But not long afterwards a restriction fell on me, driving after dark becoming difficult and unsafe. This caused problems, but none were insurmountable given the thoughtfulness of so many friends. Driving in daylight was unaffected and indeed a necessity in our rural situation.

There were two recitals that I could not carry out at the time of Priscilla's illness – at Glasgow University at the invitation of Kevin Bowyer, and at Lancaster Cathedral. The latter, however, was postponed from 3 June to 11 November and was a happy and very interesting episode at the hands of Damian Howard the cathedral organist. To him I had dedicated yet another fanfare, this one motivated by Doctor Reginald Dixon, organist of the cathedral for a long time, the centenary of whose birth was being recognised. Incidentally at the same time his biography was being written by Joan Johnson – faithful supporter of organ doings over a wide area of the county – for which I supplied a preface.

In June it was a keen delight to discover the unaltered Hill organ in Brighton; not the one I had often played in the extraordinary and dramatic Saint Bartholomew church, but Saint Martin. High up on the north side of the chancel, it was doing its work as well as ever, albeit on the stiff side, but superbly voiced and a pleasure to play. I cannot help claiming a rather special and unusual connexion with the organ: I like to think of its being installed in 1888 simultaneously with the birth of my father William Altham Jackson on 8 April.

Another visit to North Tawton in Devon to the house of Paul and Muriel Goodman was made to play the imposing electronic organ for the benefit of the London Organ Club that was touring the West Country. Two more interesting organs also came my way around this time: the first in Trinity College, Cambridge, where the Stanford and Howells Societies were meeting. To represent the former composer his delightful *Prelude in the form of a Toccata* was chosen and *De La Mare's Pavane*, intended by Howells for the clavichord; it sounds well on the organ, especially one so beautifully voiced as this. In this instance it was probably a more appropriate choice for an organ designed in a bygone and less convenient style, and less trouble than some of his organ works might have been. Just as interesting (and challenging, with its generous acoustic) was the second recital on the Walker organ in the Roman Catholic Cathedral in Liverpool. Here I was able to begin the programme with the *Fanfare* written for my ninetieth birthday by Noel Rawsthorne, my very good friend of long standing and the doyen of

Liverpool musicians, with whom I had spent many happy and profitable times. More than once during his tenure at the Anglican cathedral I played that astonishing instrument, as well as the Lady Chapel organ that in its way is just as exciting as the main organ. Once Noel impressed me by rescuing my car with jump leads, things that up till then I was quite ignorant of but was glad to learn about from him.

‖○‖

As 2011 came to an end a complete surprise fell through the letterbox, utterly unexpected and so very welcome. It was a letter from James O'Donnell, President of the Royal College of Organists, telling me of a new award that was being introduced – a medal – and offering one to me among the first recipients. The reason given was 'for organ playing, organ and choral composition, and choral conducting'. This was more than I could ever have hoped for, causing me to muse on the substantial number of my College predecessors (since its founding in 1863) – not least Sir Edward Bairstow whose presidency started forty-four years before mine – who would all have been obligatory recipients. I recalled those anxious student days of 1937 in preparation for the diploma examinations, not so much learning the pieces (that was no trouble, pure pleasure in fact) but conditioning oneself for the 'Tests at the Organ', not to mention coping with a broiling hot London pre-war July day and the long stair-climb to the testing place. I quote part of an interview for the Yorkshire Evening Press to do with my twenty-fifth year as organist at the Minster: 'I arrived late and ran all the way there. I staggered up the steps and went straight in to the examination, still sweating and panting. It's a way of taking examinations I recommend': I got the highest marks for those tests. My fellow recipients of this honour on 10 March 2012 were the composer James MacMillan and my long-standing friend of approaching seventy years, David Willcocks.

Thoughts have also been directed towards kindly gestures from other sources which have come one's way deserved or otherwise, but greatly prized and appreciated. I mention for the record the Fellowship of the Royal School of Church Music in 1963, which was followed seven years later by that of Westminster Choir College at Princeton, New Jersey, America, when it had as president Doctor Lee Hastings Bristol. Then, the OBE in 1977, and the next grade, 'Commander of the Civil Division of Our said Most Excellent Order of the British Empire', this on the 'Sixteenth day of June 2007 in the Fifty-sixth year of Our Reign'. During his archbishopric the Most Reverend Stuart Blanch conferred the Order of Saint William of York: this was in 1983, shortly after my retirement from the Minster the previous year. It was heralded in a letter from the Archbishop that began: 'I am proposing, whether you like it or not, to invest you with the Order of Saint William – in recognition of your outstanding services to both the Minster and Church Music in general … I would like to be involved personally in any little ceremony which might be arranged'. At that ceremony I was given a beautiful hand-made silver cross for wearing on a ribbon round the neck.

From time to time it has been suggested to me that, because Sir Edward became a Knight, why not the same for me: a kindly notion and a question I couldn't possibly answer. I can truthfully say that it does not in any way bother, displease or disappoint me, but it does give me the opportunity of expressing to those who took the trouble, my warmest thanks for their kindly thought which is as valuable and cherished as the initial aim.

It was a sad day in May 2012, when the sudden death of John Birch at the age of eighty-two became known. He was a friend of long standing, from his days at All Saints, Margaret Street, then Chichester Cathedral and the Temple Church. His cheerful presence was always something to enjoy, which usually included a string of inconsequential jokey quotes involving hymns and holy writ, such as the deaf man's psalm … 'before the morning watch: I SAY BEFORE THE MORNING WATCH'; or the footballer's hymn (Through the night of doubt and sorrow) which has the line, 'One the earnest looking forward'.

The final year of recitalling arrived. The constructing of programmes was always an exacting business. The logistical arrangements too, which were very often protracted, had been carried out with comparative ease until latterly when, like other aspects of life, they became more trouble. In addition, one's performance could not be wholly relied on despite careful preparation; unaccustomed errors would sometimes appear unannounced, to one's frustration, which inclined to raise thoughts of taking a less responsible course in life. Memories of the late 1950s and early 1960s when it was possible to spend whole days working in the garden kept occurring and also, after all, the almost unbelievable unceasing procession of activity of which half or even a quarter would have been quite adequate. I had had more than my share. The garden that I enjoyed so much came gradually to be more neglected though it managed to keep a respectable aspect until bindweed took control, engulfing large sections, necessitating stern action to restore its former orderly state. There was this book to finish, and it was clear that an end was the course to take.

Early in the year I had a request from Oxford University Press and Robert Gower for a chorale prelude on John Ireland's tune *Love Unknown* to go in a book of pieces for use at Passiontide and Easter. This was unexpected and somewhat of a challenge, one's first reaction being (bearing in mind the great Bach legacy alongside the Lutheran chorale) that it would be an awkward association. But on starting work such doubts were soon dispelled, and though a completely authentic Bachian product did not emerge there may be some likeness. The result was accepted and even welcomed; I can even hope that it will fill a need and perhaps give a little pleasure to any organists who make use of it.

Seven was the total of recitals for this last episode and, by the way, only twice did I ever *ask* to give a recital; for the rest I was always asked. Beginning the recitals of 2012 at Lincoln in May the supreme Father Willis cathedral organ was an intense pleasure, and most of the notes I played on it were the right ones… The same could not have been said of Saint-Saëns' delightful youthful *Fantaisie* with its hopping about between manuals, a piece I know well and had always got right. But it went wrong in the Central Methodist church in York. It could be said that I 'got out of sync' [-ronisation] but had to keep going. It was not easy or even possible to set things straight without stopping and beginning again. It was a signal not to be disregarded – and actually to be welcomed. After so long a stretch of time doing something so enjoyable, now was the chance for a quieter life and a return to those happy early days which were (or seem in retrospect to have been) more leisurely. After Lincoln there was a programme to play in York at Saint Helen's church opposite the Mansion House on the organ I had a hand in designing some sixty-plus years before. Rochdale Parish Church organ followed, rebuilt by Geoffrey Coffin, then the Victoria Hall, Hanley (or Stoke-on-Trent) for a Saturday midday event called an Organ Prom. This was as enjoyable as previous visits there with Michael Rhodes, friend of long standing.

The August Minster recital at York was not to be taken for granted as a success or as a foregone conclusion. Much serious investment in the way of practising was therefore undertaken, and this took care of the situation. My successor-but-one Robert Sharpe caused the series of concerts in the Queen's Diamond Jubilee year to have a royal flavour. I was able to celebrate the Duchess of Kent, born not far from York, for whose wedding I had produced music and played the organ. The piece which stole the limelight at the wedding was Widor's *Toccata*. However, in view of its ubiquity, for this Minster recital it seemed preferable to use something else, so two pieces which preceded the ceremony were used – the Bach G major *Prelude and Fugue* and César Franck's *First Choral*, a piece with amorous overtones. (Indeed at the time of the wedding the Franck had very much caught the fancy of an aristocratic lady guest who was able afterwards to be furnished with Sydney Campbell's recording made in Saint George's Chapel at Windsor, appropriately, as her husband was a Knight of the Garter.) Four other short pieces included in my recital were from the set of *Hovingham Sketches*, written for the Duchess by council members of the Royal College of Organists, William Lloyd Webber, Richard Popplewell, Bernard Rose and myself.

For the last two items in the programme (first Bernard Rose's *Chimes*) the audience left their stalls, chairs and pews in the quire for the nave, in order to obtain the full benefit of the Tuba Miribilis which, from the parapet of the choir screen, unleashes its magnificent golden rich tones horizontally in a westerly direction. An additional reason for the change of location – necessitating an upright standing position for most of the witnesses – was said to enable a view of the organist in the throes of his activities at the nave console. The final scheduled piece was Norman Cocker's *Tuba Tune*, which provides ample opportunity to display a tuba stop, of which few if any are finer than this inspiration of Doctor Bairstow's, brilliantly carried out by the organ builder Arthur Harrison in 1916. The reason for the piece's presence in this royal programme was the choice by the Duchess of Kent of its York recording as one of her 'Desert Island Discs' on the wireless some years earlier. A piece I cannot help but admire greatly, it came to my notice first when I finished my course as chorister in the Minster Choir in 1933. Having received my wages then amounting to something over nineteen pounds for my four-year employment, I bought a gramophone and a dozen records, one of which was this piece played by Doctor (later Sir) Stanley Marchant on the organ of Saint Paul's Cathedral. Then, determined to play it myself (without a tuba) and having bought the necessary score, I was interested to see that he introduces a suspended note D into the last chord of the third page which is I think an improvement. I wonder if the composer's sanction was sought. Knowing him quite well I could have found out. Ever since, I have found myself unable to play what is printed at that point, and must follow Doctor Marchant's example, allowing him to take the responsibility. Such was the warm reception awarded for that Minster performance – my last there – something contrasting, gentle, thoughtful and of course by Bach seemed the right encore for my ultimate play after eighty-odd years' association with one of the world's superb organs: '*Liebster Jesu wir sind hier*'. And the choir Tierce combination with Tremulant was lovely …

When Colin Walsh rang inviting me to play in Lincoln Cathedral for a third successive year in 2013, it had become plain to me that what had been achieved so often with perfect ease and without anxiety was beginning to present problems. Signals had been showing and I would be foolish to disregard them. The sensible course was to call a halt. I had so tremendously enjoyed the Lincoln Father Willis for two years running, but to imagine that I could make yet another success in almost a year's time was rather tempting providence. Therefore without any misgivings I was able for probably the only time in my life to decline a mission that would have brought immense joy. This was accompanied by feelings of gratitude to Colin for putting his trust in somebody well beyond the normal age of retirement, and I knew it was right to decline his invitation. Indeed it seemed to bring a measure of relief; some seventy years of playing recitals had reached an end, and how wonderful it had been; something that came about of its own accord without my planning it, and in addition to the privileged appointment to the Minster as well as so many other things of interest.

The daily postal delivery is something one cannot help looking forward to, inevitably with a mixture of pleasurable anticipation and a touch of apprehension. There can be a pleasant surprise, a shock, or nothing but advertisements, consuming our paper supplies, which find their way into the salvage sack without delay. On the morning of 29 August a letter came with a hand-written address. At a first glance the contents seemed to bear the signature 'Rowan Cantuar'– unlikely. An appeal or some church matter of minor interest? But no, typewritten, topped and tailed by the Archbishop of Canterbury himself, was His Grace's expressed wish to confer on me the degree of Doctor of Music; a complete surprise, there having been no whisper, nor any thought of such a possibility. The Lambeth Doctorate of Music is a well-known award formerly made mostly to cathedral organists who did not possess the degree, and was much cherished as one of those characteristically typical English phenomena from centuries ago that give our country and nation its very individual character. Indeed, as the Archbishop explained, it is by an Act of Parliament of 1533 that he has the authority to award full degrees.

Having had a hand in obtaining a Lambeth doctorate for Healey Willan, and being present at the conferment as well as being aware how highly he regarded the honour as a recognition of service to church music, it did not occur to me that I could be in the same category. It was a heart-warming thing to come into one's life, all of a sudden, unannounced, causing grateful feelings to His Grace and to anyone who may have made the suggestion. This further visit to Lambeth Palace was not only a full-circle turning of the wheel which is liable to happen in the course of a long lifetime, but a rare and valuable opportunity to meet once more the head of the Church of England as well as my fellow graduands. There were several Doctors of Divinity, an MPhil, and Martin Neary my companion DMus and old friend of long standing who had been organist of Westminster Abbey.

Now I was to wear the full dress Oxford gown just as Sir Edward Bairstow had done late in life on receiving his honorary doctorate from Oxford University. The Lambeth degrees take the robes of the Archbishop's university, and those with which I was provided for the ceremony on 16 October 2012 had been worn by John Birch for his Lambeth degree, just as they had been in the service of John Dykes

Bower for his Oxford University conferment. And it was wonderful to have the support of half a dozen family members including three grandchildren. The only sadness was Priscilla's inability to travel, a disappointment which she bore with her usual stoicism and concern for the happiness of others. The last happy aspect was the gift to me of the appropriate hood by Acklam church: a gesture much appreciated and providing Philip Lowe with the chance to supply yet another academic symbol to the family, his fifth.

Two non-organic pleasures were promised in the interim: the first a rare chance to see the two Ravel stage works, *L'Heure Espagnole* and *L'Enfant et Les Sortilèges*, which I know well and have a fondness for. This was one of those technological miracles that have proliferated in recent years. We were actually in a cinema in one of York's main streets witnessing a performance going on at Glyndebourne simultaneously, complete with all the advantages enjoyed by the audience there: clear vision, immaculate singing and (French) diction, with subtitles, and Ravel's wonderful music and incomparable orchestration given full brilliant attention.

Secondly, a birthday present from the York Symphony Orchestra under Alasdair Jamison's direction, came in the shape of a performance of my symphony to see me safely into my ninety-sixth year at their autumn concert; a most generous gesture. It was a treat to anticipate and one such as is not often to be enjoyed by a writer of notes who is neither Elgar nor Beethoven. It involved a good deal more than the performance, with many rehearsals, much application and patient concentration by many people. Some legible copies of the orchestral parts were needed, to replace the parts used for its previous performance. These had been written out laboriously by hand over thirty years previously and were not easy to play from. Huge strides have been made in the technique of music copying since those days. Now it was possible to print out the complete score of the entire work and, by technological miracles, to produce the parts for the different instruments separately in clear, tidy print. All this had been undertaken entirely voluntarily by Robert and Liz Thorlby for which there is no possibility of being able to express adequate thanks. And when all is accomplished it is to be hoped that it has all been worthwhile and that the music has given some measure of satisfaction and pleasure. I can here and now express my deep appreciation of this opportunity to hear one's figments come to life more than half a century after their initial glimmerings. I can think of no better finish for a musical career than this.

There were two more recitals to come: Saint Martin on the Hill (Scarborough) and Bradford Cathedral, bringing the grand total to 1,621. Both in their own way had their attractions. The Father Willis at Scarborough I know well, and the Bradford one I had played before on more than one occasion during the tenure (1963-81) of Keith Rhodes as organist, whose premature death was a very great loss to the church music scene.

The final one of all at Bradford Cathedral was to be ten days before the performance of my symphony and for me a special event. I knew the organ, having had a hand in its restoration, and a very splendid and satisfying instrument it is. The pieces forming a valedictory programme should be significant. To establish a positive feel at the start, what better than Karg-Elert's Opus 65, *Lobe den Herren, O meine Seele*, with its majestic final chords. Bach's 'Little' G minor prelude and fugue is so nice and handy at lunchtime when one of the big monumental ones could be rather weighty for the office-worker. I learned it long after my student days and was delighted to come across it with its interesting features. A quiet piece for contrast was Henry Smart's *Andante* in F, a Victorian piece of much beauty, followed by *Variations on a Hymn Tune* by William Mathias. I had lately brought this out again having let it lapse; it was a coincidence that having chosen it for this occasion I found I had also included it in a previous recital on this very same organ for a broadcast on 29 October 1970. I had played it in a Festival Hall recital with the composer there to hear it, and had been rewarded with a long generous letter from him as a result.

The last three pieces were nearer home, my *Reverie* on Ravel's theme being one. I thought my first published piece whatever its merits surely deserved a place, an *Impromptu* written in 1944 for Sir Edward's seventieth birthday, the generous applause for which surprised me. And I wanted the last offering of my career to be Bairstow's, recognising the incalculable amount I had learned from him; and what better than a *Prelude* as a finish, especially one containing a theme so memorable, with its Neapolitan fanfare and final upward flourish.

And now I was free: I could ply the secateurs, spade, hedge cutters and all, as much as I liked without guilty feelings about ducking organ practice, while still working away at this document. This however was nearing completion watched over by our daughter Alice without whom pretty certainly it would never have been finished. She for her part, coming close to the time of her own retirement, employed her youthful energy and editorial expertise as well as knowledge of the helpful electronic aids that so facilitate such exercises, over which I languish in total abysmal ignorance. Moreover it was all done with no other motive than a wish to help and to see the project's completion, always with evident relish and enjoyment. Nothing was ever too much trouble, the merest detail receiving its due attention, order being restored out of a somewhat chaotic mass of material. All this would have been quite beyond me to do. It is thus impossible to thank her at all adequately. But I can here record my heartfelt appreciation in fullest measure.

Looking back over all those years, it has been a good innings, and far better than I could possibly have imagined.

|O| |O| |O|

ACKNOWLEDGEMENTS

O ver the years a great deal of help towards this book has come from many sources, for which acknowledgement is now made and my warmest thanks offered:

To the Duchess of Kent for her willing and prompt Preface recalling earlier Yorkshire days.

To Anne Bell who did the lion's share of the typing with unfailing reliability and punctuality.

The list of my compositions is based on one originally produced by Patricia Robottom from my own record. David Rogers, Martin Monkman and Brian Culverhouse aided the completion of the discography. The inclusion of several photographs by Gerco Schaap is gratefully acknowledged, also John Roden helped with some historic photographs.

To Martin Cottam for his brilliant depiction of my desert island sojourn.

For the many details requiring accuracy, thanks go to a number of patient and willing friends. Also to any I may have overlooked.

Eric Addy, Albert Ainsworth, Andrew Carter, John Durham, Roger Fisher, Brian Hibbins, Beverley Jones, Stephen Oxley,

Michael Phipps, John Pryer, Malcolm Riley, John Roden, Philip Rushworth, John Scarfe, George Sharman, Richard Shephard, Robert Shrubsall, Margaret Silver, Tim Storey, Ian Tracey, Robin Walker, Irvine Watson and the late Stuart Gray.

To Lambeth Palace for permission to reproduce the photograph of 16th October 2012.

To York Publishing Services for their helpful and courteous guidance.

Most of my family – half-a-dozen strong and, notably, Priscilla – lent a hand with different aspects, some wading through the entire script and offering invaluable comment.

FURTHER READING

Hollis, Howard   *The Best of Both Worlds*
Sir Wm. McKie Memorial Trust (1991)

Jackson, Francis   *Blessed City, the life and works of Edward C Bairstow*
Sessions of York (1996)

Nichols, Roger   *Ravel: A Life*
Yale University Press (2012)

Roden, John   *The Minster School, York. A Centenary History*
1903-2004
Sacram Publishing, York (2005)

COMPOSITIONS

COMPOSITIONS

Key:

A	Anthem/carol
C	Choral work
CH	Chamber music
HT	Hymn tune
MD	Monodrama
L	Liturgical settings
O	Organ
OD	Organ duet
ORC	Orchestral
O+	Organ and other instrument
PD	Piano duet
PS	Part song
S	Song
U	Unnumbered

Opus	Type	Title	Date	Other details	Publisher
U	HT	Malton	1935	Diocesan Choirs Festival in York Minster	
1	CH	String quartet in B	1937	For BMus Durham	
2	ORC	Overture *In winter*	1938	MS	
3	CH	Poem for cello and piano	1939-40	MS	
4-1	S	Song cycle: *Echoes and laughter* for high voice:		*The Owl, Widow Bird, St Mary's Bells, Carillon, From a Railway Carriage* (see Opus 23), *Tree at my Window*	Banks
-2	S	Four songs	1939-49	*Stopping by the woods on a snowy evening, Windy day in August, In Romney Marsh, Western Wind*	
4a	CH	Pastorale for flute, viola and piano	1944	One movement. Incorporated in opus 128	
5	O	Impromptu	1944	For Sir Edward Bairstow on his 70th birthday	OUP, Novello (York Album), Banks 2007 (Fanfare for Francis)
6	PS	The owl	1945	For SSA, also Opus 4-1 as solo song	OUP/Banks
7	ORC	Invocation	1948	MS	
8	A	How bright these glorious spirits shine	1948	Anthem for SATB unaccompanied	Yearbook Press/Banks
9-1	L	Te deum in C	1948	Boys' voices	
-2	L	Magnificat and Nunc Dimittis in C	1946	Boys' voices	RSCM
-3	L	Benedictus	1993	Boys' voices	
10	A	St Patrick's Even Song	1949	SATB unaccompanied, organ added 28 September 1964	Banks
11	PS	St Mary's Bells	1949	SSA (also Opus 4-1 as solo song)	OUP/Banks
12	A	Ave Maria, blessed maid	1950	Based on the tune *St Alban*	Faith Press
13	L	Communion Service in G	1950	Creed separate	OUP
13a	L	Benedicite in G	1951	Manuscript with York Minster Old Choristers Association	Banks
14	A	Audi filia (Hearken, O daughter)	1950	SATB (Version for SSA in MS)	OUP/Banks
15	L	Magnificat and Nunc Dimittis in G	1952		OUP
16	O	Toccata, chorale and fugue	1955	*Toccata* first broadcast 8 January 1956 by Hugh MacLean, King's College Cambridge	Novello
17	O	Three pieces: Procession, Arabesque, Pageant	1955	For Priscilla, Alice and William respectively	Novello (Organ Music Club No. 4)

No.	Cat.	Title	Year	Notes	Publisher
18	O	Fanfare in B flat	1956	To John Bradley	OUP (Festive Album)
19-1	O	Toccata prelude on Wachet Auf	1956	Chorale prelude	Novello (Festal Voluntaries)
-2	O	Division on Nun Danket	1956	Chorale prelude	Novello (Festal Voluntaries)
20	O	Scherzetto Pastorale	1955	Broadcast by Sydney Campbell from Canterbury 2 September 1956	OUP (Christmas Album)
20a	A	Remember for good, O Father	1956	SATB and organ, dedication of astomonical clock	Novello
21	ORC	Symphony in D minor	1957	For DMus Durham	Banks
U	HT	East Acklam	1957	Old Choristers' Service in York Minster	
22	L	Magnificat and Nunc Dimittis in G minor	1958	For St John the Baptist, Leytonstone	Novello
23	PS	From a Railway Carriage	1956	Unison (Opus 4-1 as solo song)	Novello
U	O+	Two Edinburgh fanfares for brass and organ	c1957	For a festival service in Saint Giles' Cathedral. The second arranged for organ solo 1985, included in Opus 84	
24	O	Prelude for a solemn occasion	1958	First British broadcast 13 November 1958	Banks (The Modern Organist)
25	O	Diversion for mixtures	1960	1st performance Llandaff Cathedral 16 June 1959	Novello (Colours of the Organ)
26	ORC	Variations on *Mantegna*: Homage to Vaughan Williams	1961	Commissioned by Iris Lemare (MS)	
27	O	The Archbishop's Fanfare	1961	For Archbishop Coggan's enthronement	OUP (Ceremonial Music 1971)
28	L	Magnificat and Nunc Dimittis in F# minor	1961	For Hereford Cathedral (2 voice parts) Re-written for SATB 1979 (unpublished)	Novello
29	MD	Daniel in Babylon	1962	Monodrama for speaker, chorus and organ, for the dedication ceremonies of Coventry Cathedral. Libretto: John Stuart Anderson	
30	A	Blow ye the trumpet in Zion	1963	For the St Cecilia Festival, St Sepulchre, 19 November	Banks
31	L	Te Deum and Jubilate in G	1964	For the Leeds Festival	OUP/Banks
32	O	Recessional	1963	For Edward	OUP/Banks
U	ORC	Hornpipe and Pavane	1966	For small orchestra (unfinished suite) (*Pavane* is in Opus 84)	OUP (An Album of Postludes)
33	MD	A Time of Fire	1967	Monodrama for speaker, chorus, soloists and organ, former title *Tyndale*. Libretto: John Stuart Anderson	
34	A	Daughters of Zion	1969	Anthem for Exeter Cathedral Voluntary Choir, 15 July 1969	Banks
35	O	Sonata in G minor (Sonata 1)	1969-70	For the opening of Blackburn Cathedral's new organ, 10 January 1970	OUP
36-1	A	Laetentur coeli	1958-70		OUP
-2	A	Evening hymn (Sir Thomas Browne)	1970		Banks
-3	A	O most merciful	1970	For West Riding Cathedrals Fesitval	Banks
-4	A	Sing a new song to the Lord (Ps 98)	1970	For Leeds Philharmonic Centenary	Banks 1986
-5	A	Lo, God is here	1971	Anthem for Dedication Festival	Novello
37	O	Festival Toccata	1970	For Bradford Cathedral, West Riding Cathedral Festival in memory of Brian Runnett	OUP (Anthems for Choirs)
38	ORC	Overture 'Brigantia'	1971	Commissioned by York Symphony Orchestra	Banks 2005
39	ORC	Music for York Pageant	1971	MS	Banks (Hire Library)
40-1	A	Alleluia laudate pueri	1971	Anthem for double choir, for the Chapter House Choir	Banks

No.	Type	Title	Year	Notes	Publisher
-2	A	Can I not sing but Hoy?	1972	Carol	Banks
41	L	Communion Service in E (Series 3)	1972	Commissioned by the Church Music Society	Banks (revised version)
42	O	Sonata Giocosa per la Renascita di una Cathedrale (Sonata 2)	1972	Commissioned by Bernard Fielden for the Builders' Festival on 28 April 1972, at the completion of York Minster's repairs	OUP
43-1	O	Heraldic flourish	1973	For the RCO grant of arms, January 1973, played by George Thalben-Ball, dedicated to Ralph Covell	Banks 'Two Flourishes' 1978
-2	O	Prelude on an American folk hymn: Lonesome Valley	1973	For Lee Bristol's Collection of Pieces based on More Hymns and Spiritual Songs	Harold Flammer
-3	O	Prelude and Fugue in C: The Brook	1972	for the re-opening of St Neot's Parish Church organ in May 1972, revised 1995	
U	O	The sweet rivelet	1974	In Hovingham Sketches	Banks
44-1	A	Blessing and glory	1974	Anthem for RSCM book	Banks
-2	A	Lift up your heads, great gates	1974	Anthem for St Alban's Choirs Festival	OUP/Banks
-3	A	A 'solempne' Nunc Dimittis (sic)	1952	For ATB for Caius College, Cambridge (see Opus 75)	Banks 2007
-4	A	O people of Zion	1975	Advent anthem for ATB (alternative accompaniment for strings and organ)	Banks
45	A	Psalm 134	1975	Introit for SATB and organ, for St Mary's Parish Church, St Neots	Banks
45-1	A	Psalm 139 (Mary Herbert)	1975	SSAA, organ and piano, for Harrogate College Choir	Banks 1982
45a	O	Partita on a Somerset tune	1975	For a Chapter House Christmas concert	
46	A	Henry VI prayer	1975-6	Anthem for SATB unaccompanied for Richard Darke and the choir of St Edmund's Church, Roundhay	
47	L	Preces and Responses, including those for the Sovereign's Accession	1976	Commissioned by the West Riding Cathedrals' Festival	Banks
47a	A	Rejoice in the Lord	1976	For Barry Bruton's Choir	Banks
48	A	Praise God in his sanctuary (Ps 150)	1978	For Macclesfield Parish Church 700th anniversary	Banks
49	L	Te Deum in D	1979	For St Mary's Cathedral, Edinburgh, first sung 4 November	
50	O	Organ Sonata 3	1979	For St Bartholomew's, Armley, organ centenary	
51	L	Missa Brevis	1980	Unaccompanied, for St Mary Magdalene, Toronto	
52-1	L	Ave Verum	1980	Unaccompanied, motet for St Margaret's, Ilkley	Paraclete Press
-2	L	O Salutaris Hostia	1989	Unaccompanied motet	Paraclete Press 1989
-3	L	Missa Ave Verum	1981	Unaccompanied, for St Margaret's, Ilkley	
-4	L	Tantum Ergo	1986	Unaccompanied motet	
53	O	Centenary Flourish	1980	For Arnold Pugh, Rugby Parish Church	Banks (Seven Pieces for Organ)
54	L	Evening Service in D	1980	For Birmingham Cathedral	Banks
55	A	Sing praise to God who reigns above	1981	For Exeter Cathedral Voluntary Choir	
56	O	Fantasia Argenti	1981	Commissioned by Dr Harold Smart for his wife Margaret on their silver wedding	Novello (York Album)
57	A	Song of Caedmon (incl. Ps 148:1-12)	1981	Anthem for the RSCM Newcastle Centenary, Dec 1982	
U	A	There came three kings	1981	Arrangement Köln Gesängbuch 1623	
58	PS	Song on May morning (John Milton)	1983	For London Cantata Choir and Peter Moorse (see Opus 131)	Banks
59	A	Psalm 117 (118) (Latin)	1983	For Gerard Beemster and St Christoph, Schagen	Banks

No.	Code	Title	Year	Description	Publisher
60		Five Preludes on English Hymn Tunes:	1984	For Cyril Baker and Kirkwall celebrations	Banks
-1	O	St Magnus	1984	Suggested by and dedicated to The Revd James Holdroyd	
-2	O	Veni Sancte Spiritus	1984	For Fr James Holdroyd, Brighton	
-3	O	St Bartholomew	1984	For Margaret and Ramsay Silver	
-4	O	East Acklam	1983-4	For All Saints, Winnipeg, and Donald Hadfield	
-5	O	Sine Nomine	1984	Trebles, mostly solo/unison and organ.	
61	A	Prayer of St Francis (Italian, Latin, English)	1984	For George Sharman and Dover College Junior Choir; first performance Assisi, Holy Week 1984 (alternative accompaniment for strings and organ)	Banks
62	A	Up to those bright and gladsome hills	1976	Anthem for St Bride's, Fleet Street, revised 1984, first performed 21 October 1984	
63	A	Tu es Petrus	1984	Unaccompanied anthem for Peterborough Cathedral, first performed 29 June 1985	Paraclete Press
64	ORC	Concerto for organ, strings, timpani and celesta	1984-5	Commissioned by Carnegie UK Trust for the Sesqui-Centenary of the birth of Andrew Carnegie, first performance 23 June 1984	Banks
65	C	The genius of the Thames	1984	Cantata for Jonathan Rennert and St Michael's Singers, Cornhill Festival, first performance Drapers' Hall 16 May 1985	Banks
66	S	Cantio exsequialis	1985	Tenor and organ. Text: Ps 84, Milton and Office of the Dead 'In Paradisum'. First performance Bradford Grammar School, James Griffett (tenor), Stephen Cleobury (organ) 17 June	
67-1	A	Rejoice in the Lord, all ye saints	1985	For Ronald Stalford and the Choir of Worcester, Massachusetts	Paraclete Press
-2	A	Eternal power	1986		Roger Dean, Heritage Music Press, Dayton, Ohio
68	O	Organ Sonata 4	1985	For Doncaster Parish Church commissioned by the Friends of the Music, first performance 5 October	Banks
69	L	The Mass of St Mary	1984-7	No creed, for Blackburn Cathedral	
70	O	Festal prelude (on Praxis Pietatis)	1987	For Graham Matthews	Banks
71	O+	Ecologue for piano and organ	1987	For the International Congress of Organists, Cambridge	Paraclete Press
72	L	Missa Matris Dei	1988	For Farm Street Church, London (creed for St Bartholomew's, Brighton and Peter Ellifsen)	Paraclete Press
U	PS	The Blackbird (Drinkwater)	1988	For Thomas (Tim) Tunnard aet 70, 30 July	
73	A	Three Advent carols	1987	1. Gabriel's message (two versions) 2. I know a flower 3. While the careless world is sleeping	Paraclete Press
74	A	Gaudeamus	1989	For Harry Bramma on his retirement from Southwark Cathedral	RSCM 1994
75	L	Magnificat in D minor	1988	ATB, for Guildford Cathedral, to go with Opus 44-3	Banks 2007
76	O+	Recitative and allegro for trombone and organ	1989	For Eton College Trombone Concourse	
77	PS	If I should ever by chance grow rich (Edward Thomas)	1989	For David Lang	

No.	Type	Title	Year	Description	Publisher
78	L	Te Deum and Benedictus in A	1989	For John Birch's 60th birthday	OUP
		The Temple Service			
79	O	Legend	1989	For Robert Crowley	Banks 1998
80	L	Mass of St Giles (Rite A)	1989	No creed, for Anne Gelston, Durham	Paraclete Press
81	O	Georgian suite	1990	Organ with optional pedals. For Donald Findlay	OUP
82-1	A	Te Deum V in B flat	1990	For Colin Tipple and St Cuthbert's Church, Edinburgh	
-2	A	How awesome is this place	1990	Introit for St Cuthbert's Church, Edinburgh	
-3	A	For all thy saints O Lord	1990	For Derby Cathedral	
-4	A	For the fruits of his creation	1989	Anthem based on *East Acklam*	RSCM (Crown of the Year)
83	O	Worcester Procession	1990	For the Church of St Mary of the Angels, Worcester, Massachusetts	Banks
84	O	Seven Pieces for Organ	1988	*Edinburgh Fanfare, Improvisation, Centenary Flourish, Pavane, Flourish on the tune Warrington, Praeludium, Intrada* from *Daniel in Babylon* (Opus 29)	Banks
85	A	Come thou holy Paraclete	1991	SATB and organ for Richard Hobson, Grosvenor Chapel	Paraclete Press
86	A	Carmen festiale 'When in our music God is glorified' (F Pratt Green)	1992	SATB double choir, unaccompanied; for Dennis Townhill on his retirement from St Mary's Cathedral, Edinburgh, May 1991	
U	A	The Lamb's high banquet we await	1992	Arrangement of tune *Deus Tuorum Militum*	Banks
U	A	Cherry Tree Carol (unaccompanied)	1992	Arrangement of traditional tune for SATB	Banks
87	L	Missa Sancti Petri (BCP)	1991	SATB and organ, for Simon Lindley and Leeds Parish Church	Paraclete Press
88	O+	Goss-Radley Fanfare	?	Two trumpets and organ, to precede 'Praise my soul, the king of heaven'	
89	L	Magnificat and Nunc Dimittis in E flat	1991	Trebles plus optional ATB, for Clayesmore School	
90	A	At the name of Jesus (based on hymn tune *Evelyns*)	1990-2	For Anthony Burns-Cox	
91	A	Christ is our cornerstone	1993	Anthem for Ronald Stalford and All Saints, Worcester, Massachusetts	Banks (in Homage to Whitlock)
92	O	Scherzo Amabile	1993		
93	OD	Suite Montrealaise - Five Dances (organ duets)	1993	*Rigaudon, Habanera, Forlane, Mazurka, Polonaise* for Philip Crozier and Sylvie Poirier. First performance Montreal, 12 July	
94	A	Except the Lord build the house	1993	Anthem for the 75th anniversary of Guild of Mace Bearers, Leeds Parish Church, 15 June	
95	A	Order our days in thy peace	1993	For Leslie Matthews and the choir of St Gregory's Minster, Kirkdale	
96	O	Exultet	1993	Postlude. For Fort Worth, Texas	Banks
97	OD	Ballade (prelude and allegro)	1993	For McVicker/Barsham duo first performance St Paul's Church, Huddersfield, 10 November	Banks
98	L	Magnificat and Nunc Dimittis in E flat (St Bride's)	1994	For St Bride's, Fleet Street, 6 February	

No.	Code	Title	Year	Notes	Publisher
99	A	Praise the Lord and call upon his name	1994	St George's, Belfast	
U	L	Responses set 2	1994	For Sir Peter Newson-Smith (SSAA)	Banks
U	L	Responses set 3	1994	For St Bride's, February	Banks
100	A	Christ is the morning star	1994	Latin words on tomb of the Venerable Bede, Durham Cathedral	
101	O	Interlude	1998	For Kenneth Leighton Memorial Album	Banks
102	L	Magnificat and Nunc Dimittis (Fauxbourdons)	1994	For St Margaret's Church, Ilkley	
103	O	Capriccio	1994	For Peter Blackhouse's 40th birthday	Banks
104	S	At break of day (Traherne)	1994	Tenor, recorder and piano	
105	A	On Christmas Day (Traherne)	1995	Choir and organ, for Ampleforth Schola Cantorum	Banks
106	OD	Colloquy	1996	For the Chenault Duo	
107	A	I will extol thee	1996	For Southern Cathedrals Festival, Winchester Cathedral	
108	PS	The west wind (Masefield)	1996	TTBB, for Dore Male Voice Choir and their conductor John Kenyon, first performance 15 November 1997	Banks
109	O	March in C	1996	For Ceremonial Music for Organ edited by Robert Gower	OUP
109a	A	Judge eternal	1997	For RSCM Area Festival, St Paul's, London	
110	A	Introit: Verbum caro	1996	Communion motet, collection entitled Draw near with faith	Kirklees Cathedral Music
111	C	Stabat Mater	1997	Baritone, choir and organ for St Peter's Singers and their conductor Simon Lindley	Banks
112	A	Christ is made the sure foundation	1997	For St Barnabas Dulwich, first performance 19 September	
U	HT	Clerkenwell	?	For Michael Gillingham and St James, Clerkenwell	Kirklees Cathedral Music 1998
113-1	A	Come Holy Ghost	1997	Compilation of ten anthems	Kirklees Cathedral Music 1998
-2	A	God is gone up on high	1997	To Michael Gillingham; founded on Clerkenwell. In a second compilation of ten anthems.	
U	A	Spirit of joyfulness	1998	Hymn anthem on the tune Stradsett in Love Divine	Church Music Society 1999
U	A	Jesu child of Mary	1997	Carol in The Promised Messiah (Philip Ledger)	Roger Dean Publishing Co. Dayton, Ohio 1998
114	A	Incarnation's promise	1998	Anthem for the Church of the Incarnation, Dallas	
115	A	O salutaris hostia No.2	1998	For St Stephen's Bournemouth, Whitlock Festival, 2 May	Banks
116	L	Mass of the Holy Family	1998	Choir and congregation, for the Church of the Holy Family, New York, 27 December	
117	L	Evening Service in E Canticula Decima	1999	Two sopranos/trebles, for St David's Cathedral, June	
118	A	Tantum Ergo 2 (uaccompanied)	1999	For Caterham Parish Church	Banks
119	A	Come let us anew our journey pursue	1999	A Millennium Anthem for Bradford Choristers at Evensong in York Minster on the last Sunday of 1999	
120	A	Thee will I love (Wesley and Scheffler)	1999	Anthem for an Age Concern service in St Ann's Cathedral, Belfast, 26 September	
121	A	O thou not made with hands	2000	Anthem for the Old Choristers' Federation, York Minster	Banks
122	L	Missa Decima	2000	For St Stephen's Bournemouth, Latin, no creed	Paraclete Press
123	CH	Sonatina pastorale (recorder and piano)	1999	For John Turner. Middle movement 'Moonrise' scored for strings by Robin Walker, recorded 2006: DUTTON CDLX 7191	Forsyth Recorder Music 2000

No.	Code	Title	Year	Notes	Publisher
124	A	May the grace of Christ our Saviour	2000	Commissioned by Miss CM Wren in memory of Miss Bedson	Paraclete Press
125	L	Jubilate Deo in A flat	2000	For the Bingley Myrtle Singers in Liverpool Cathedral, 6 August	Banks
126	A	The spacious firmament on high	2000	Anthem for John Scarfe, Holy Island choir holiday	
127	A	Father eternal (Housman)	2000	Introit for St Mary's Cathedral, Edinburgh, 15 June	
128	CH	Trio for volin, cello and piano in three movements	2001	For performance by the Klemperer Trio, York, 11 October 2001 (including Opus 4a)	
U	CH	Romance for Oboe and Piano	2001	For Grace Jackson, granddaughter	
U	PD	Variations on Coe Fen (piano duet)	2001	For Elizabeth Dakers – in memoriam	
129	L	Mass of St Francis (no creed)	2001	For Ampleforth	
130	L	Mass for Salisbury	2001	With brass quintet and organ	
131	PS	Song on May morning (second setting)	2002	For the Easingwold Singers, see also Opus 58	
132	O	Fantasia Campanulatica/ Campaniculata	2002	For Douglas Bell aet 70	
133	A	Thanks be to the Lord	2002	Introit for the Thanksgiving Service after the restoration of the city centre, Manchester Cathedral, 24 July attended by the Queen	
134	A	Song of Mary (Mary Holtby)	2002	For John Scarfe, aet 65 (Buckfast Abbey 17 May 2003)	
135	PS	Ode to a Pill	2002	For John Scarfe, aet 65	
136	A	Adam lay y bounden	2002	Sewanee University	
137	O+	Cavatina for bassoon and organ	2002	For Benedict Coffin (including tune in Opus 1)	
138	L	Eight Latin motets	2002	For Ampleforth Abbey	
139	PS	The shell (James Stephens)	2003	For the Cantoris Chamber Choir	
140	O	Organ Sonata 5	2003	'To the honour of Percy Whitlock. First performed by the composer in St Stephen's Church, Bournemouth, 5 May 2003'	Banks
141	O	Acklam Pieces:	2010		Banks
-1	O	Fanfare Dixoniana	2009		
-2	O	Improvisation on Irish	2003	For the centenary of Pilrig Church organ, Edinburgh	
-3	O	Prelude on Kettlebaston	2003	For Gordon Pullin's recording Favourite Hymns	
-4	O	Susanni scherzetto	1994	For David Swale aet 80, 21st February 2008 (revised 2008)	
-5	O	Aria Celtica (Slane)	2005	For John Scarfe at St James, Teignmouth, 17 March 2007	
-6	O	Prelude on Malton	2007	AB(J)G - for Angela (sister)	
-7	O	Sarabande	2008	For Paul (brother)	
-8	O	Reverie on a theme of Ravel	2009	Dedicated to Roger Nichols	
142	C	Agnus Dei for Mass in C minor (Mozart) K427	2003	For the St Sepulchre Festival, May	
143	A	There comes a galley laden	2003	Carol for the NHS annual carol service in York Minster 25th anniversary: December 2003	Banks
144	A	What sweeter music (Herrick)	2003	Carol for Richard Darke and the choir of Knaresborough Parish Church, October	
145	O+	Sonata for trumpet and organ	2003	For Philip Lowe and Langley Parish Church, Lancs	
146	A	Tune me, O Lord (Christina Rosetti)	2004	Anthem for All Saints Church, Worcester Mass.	

No.		Title	Year	Notes	Publisher
147-1	A	Prayer of John Donne (Bring us, O Lord God - E Milner-White)	2003	Written for the funeral of Lionel Dakers	Banks
-2	A	Hymn to God the Father (Wilt thou forgive that sin - John Donne)	2004	For the Exon Singers, Tavistock Festival, July 2005	
U	A	'Twas in the year that King Uziah died	?	SATB and organ	
148	O	Organ Sonata 6	2004	For the restored Schulze organ at Armley, played by Graham Barber 28 May 2004	Banks
149	L	Magnificat and Nunc Dimittis in B flat (Homage to Thomas Weelkes)	2005	For five voices, for the Exon Singers at the Tavistock Festival, July 2005	Banks
150	O	Three hymn preludes: Laudate Dominum, Repton, Angel Voices	2005	For David S Johnson	Banks
151	O	Festivo	2005	For Douglas Fairhurst, Oxford Town Hall, 16 August	Banks
152	A	Hymn for the martyrs	2006	For St Laurence Day, Derby Singers, Ludlow First performance: St Laurence, Ludlow, August 2006	
153	S	Serenade to a Pill (second setting) (soprano, recorder and piano)	2007	For John Joubert aet 80, Manchester, 28 February	
154	O	The February March	2007	For David Johnson, 2 March 2007	
155	O	Fantasy and Fugue (Clerkenwell)	2007	Remembering Michael Gillingham	Banks
156	A	Te Lucis	2007	For Exon Singers, Tavistock July 2008, requested by Matthew Owens. In Choir Book for the Queen.	
157	L	Missa Sancti Botolfi	2008	For SA, December/January 2008 for Tim and Cynthia Storey (St Botolph, Bishopgate)	
158	S	The Word (Mary Holtby)	2008	Commissioned by John Scarfe, Christmas	
159	O	Cantilena (three sopranos and accompaniment)	2009	For Philip Lowe and the Rochdale Organists' Association, 11 February 2009	Rochdale Organists' Association
160-1	A	Most glorious Lord of life	2009	For Edington Festival	
-2	O	Arioso	2009	For Tim Griffiths (nephew), 19 May	
-3	O	Tritune	2009	For David Titterington, July 2004 (in *Organ Works*)	UMP 2009
U	O	The Hallam Fanfare	2009	For the Reverend Drummond Gillespie, Hallam Methodist Church, 22 October	
161	O	Jubilee sounds (Pezza Cambiata)	2010	Stoke-on-Trent, Golden Jubilee of North Staffordshire Organ Society, 11 June	
U	C	Grace (words: Adam Fox)	2011	For the Guild of Corpus Christi (TTBB)	
162	A	Risen Again (Canon David Adam 2011)	2012	For John Bradley's memorial service, Toronto (20 January)	
163	A	God of time (For a new day) (Canon David Adam)	2012	For the Rev Peter Mullen's retirement service, St Sepulchre, Holborn, 20 January	
U	O	Meditation: Love Unknown (John Ireland)	2012	Lent and Easter organ music	OUP
164	A	The Mind of the Maker	2013	For the Shakespeare Service, Stratford, 21 April Words by Canon Michael Hampel	
13+	L	Gospel Ascriptions and Fanfare in G	2013	For Blackburn Cathedral, Eucharist broadcast Pentecost Sunday, 19 May	

DISCOGRAPHY

Played and directed by Francis Jackson

Discography   Played and directed by Francis Jackson

As it has not been possible to keep track of all re-issued recordings, this list should not be considered exhaustive.

Title	Details	Date	Recording Company	Code
78rpm records				
	Bach BWV 542	1948	BBC	
	Bairstow (*Prelude in C*)	1948	BBC	
	Rheinberger (*Concerto in G minor*) Conductor: Charles Groves. Manchester Town Hall	1949	BBC	
	FJ (*Fanfare*), Whitlock (*Scherzo*), Schumann (*Sketch in D flat*)	c.1950	Radio Relay, York [Eboracum Record Society]	E108
	Vierne (*Divertissement, Scherzetto*)	c.1950		E109
	FJ (*Impromptu*)	c.1950		E102
	Stanley R Dearlove, chorister 1946-51, with FJ, piano: Boyce (*Tell me, lovely shepherd*)	c.1950		E501
	Mendelssohn (*Sonata 3*)	c.1950		E503
	Franck (*Final*)	c.1950		E504
	Beverley Jones, chorister 1950-54, with FJ, organ: Handel (*I know that my Redeemer liveth*)	c.1950		E505
	Roy Bean, chorister 1949-52: Greene (*The Gentiles shall come; The sun shall be no more*), Boyce (*Tell me, lovely shepherd*)	?	HMV [special recording] 2EB 7699	
	S Wesley (*Voluntary in E*)	1954	BBC	

7-inch EP records

Title	Details	Year	Label	Catalogue
York Minster Choir (English Church Music)	Conducted by FJ, Allan Wicks (organ): Ley, Bullock, Ouseley, Walford Davies, Wood (Recorded under the auspices of the British Council)		EMI	SEG 8039
Francis Jackson at the Organ of York Minster	Widor, Guilmant	1964	Alpha	AVME 016
Cathedral Music York Minster Choir	FJ, Ronald Perrin (organ): Bairstow and Wood	1966	(In aid of York Minster Appeal Fund)	
Organ Music at York Minster	JS Bach and FJ	1965	Ryemuse	RP 7018
Choral and Organ Music from York Minster	The Choristers with FJ (organ) and Peter Williams (assistant organist): JS Bach, Stanford	1967	Abbey	E7619
Choral and Organ Music from York Minster	The Choristers with FJ (organ) and Peter Williams (assistant organist): Widor *Toccata*, Lassus, Ireland	1967	Abbey	E7620
Carols from York Minster	The Choristers with Peter Williams (organ) and FJ (piano)	1967	Abbey	E7626

Long-playing records

Title	Details	Year	Label	Catalogue
	With Gordon Thorne and BBC Northern Singers: Liszt (*Via Crucis*)	1961	Saga	STM 6040
	Liszt (*Missa Choralis*)	1961	Saga	XID 5105
	With Leeds Parish Church Choir, Simon Lindley, Tom Corfield: Liszt, Elgar, Psalm 48,	?	Abbey	LPB 813
20th Century British Organ Music	Parry, Bairstow, Howells, Statham, Whitlock, Fricker, FJ	1964	Alpha	AVS 014
Great Cathedral Organ Series 2	Nares, S. Wesley, Bossi, FJ, Willan	1964	CSD	1550

Title	Contents	Date	Label	Catalogue
Selected Organ works of Healey Willan	Including *Passacaglia 2, Prelude & Fugue* in C minor	1965		MS 6798
An Organ for an Organ Scholar [with P Hurford]	Mendelssohn, Brahms, Hindemith 2, Bach BWV 649, 538, *Toccata*	1966	Abbey	601
The Organ in Sanity and Madness [with M Neary]	Soler: *Concerto for Two Organs*	1966	Abbey	APR 606
19th Century Organ Music	Camidge, Stanford, Liszt, Franck	1967	Abbey	621
Historic Organ of Down Cathedral	Stanford, SS Wesley, S Wesley, Mendelssohn, Wood	1970	Guild	GRS 7003
Organ Music fom York Minster	FJ, Guilmant, Dupré (*Deux Esquisses*)	1973	Counterpoint	CPT 3974
The Organ of the York Minster Golden Treasury of Organ Music, Vol 1	Parry, Bairstow, Howells, Statham, Whitlock, Fricker, FJ	1973	Saga	5326
Bairstow Choral and Organ Works	Including *Sonata* in E flat	1974	Canon	CNN 4977
Organ Music fom York Minster	Boëllmann, Franck, Vierne, Alain, Widor	1974	Polydor Select	2460 225
In Quires and Places (York)	Byrd, Walford Davies, Gray, FJ, Leighton, Tallis, Vaughan Williams	1975	Abbey (re-issued on CD Priory 2007)	721
Sounds of York Minster (includes Minster bells)	The Minster Choir, with JS Whiteley: Bairstow, Balfour Gardiner, Attwood, Talbot, Bach	1977	HMR	7711
Music from York Minster	With BBC Northern Singers: Nares, Bairstow, FJ - choral and organ works	1977	Abbey	LPB 737
York Minster Organ Music by Guilmant	Including *Sonata 1*	1978	Abbey	LPB 794
Music for Easter	York Minster Choir, directed by FJ: Bach, S Wesley, Gauntlett, Bairstow, Wood, Ley, Middleton, Brockless	1978	Abbey	LPB 793

Title	Contents	Year	Label	Catalogue
The Organ at York Minster [with JS Whiteley]	Smart, Bairstow, Peeters, Dupré	1979	Music from York	HAR 791
The Organ at York Minster French Music	Boëllmann, Franck, Vierne, Alain, Widor	1979	Chalfont (USA release of Polydor 2460 225)	77018
The Hovingham Sketches	11 Sketches, Willan *IPF*	1982	Gamut	UT 7504
The Choir of York Minster sings music by FJ	Conducted by FJ, JS Whiteley (organ): Communion Service in G, Magnificat and Nunc Dimittis in G, six anthems.	1982	Ambisonic	HAR 821
The King of Instruments [with nine other players]	Cocker	?	EMI (Australia)	

Compact Discs

Title	Contents	Year	Label	Catalogue
Edward Cuthbert Bairstow, The Complete Organ Works	Recorded April 1990	1990	Mirabilis (Re-issued on Amphion PHI CD 143)	MRCD 902
The Bairstow Tradition: organ works by the teachers and pupils of Sir Edward	Bridge, Alcock, Bullock, Bairstow, Finzi, FJ, Slater Hull City Hall organ	1993	Amphion	PHI CD 124
Stanford Organ Works at Sledmere House, Yorkshire	Including the Complete Set of *Preludes* and *Postludes*, Opus 101 & 105.	1993	Amphion	PHI CD 126
The Organ at Castle Howard	Handel, Guilmant, Wolstenholme, Macdowell, Jongen, Smart, Vaughan Williams, FJ, Bach, Mendelssohn	1994	Amphion	PHI CD 130
Francis Jackson plays Organ Music from York Minster	Nares, Wesley, Bossi, Cocker, Willan, FJ, Guilmant, Dupré (*Deux Esquisses*)	1996	Amphion (Re-issue of EMI Great Cathedral Organ Series 1964 & Counterpoint Stereo Recordings 1973)	PHI CD 142

No.	Cat.	Title	Year	Notes	Publisher
124	A	May the grace of Christ our Saviour	2000	Commissioned by Miss CM Wren in memory of Miss Bedson	Paraclete Press
125	L	Jubilate Deo in A flat	2000	For the Bingley Myrtle Singers in Liverpool Cathedral, 6 August	Banks
126	A	The spacious firmament on high	2000	Anthem for John Scarfe, Holy Island choir holiday	
127	A	Father eternal (Housman)	2000	Introit for St Mary's Cathedral, Edinburgh, 15 June	
128	CH	Trio for violin, cello and piano in three movements	2001	For performance by the Klemperer Trio, York, 11 October 2001 (including Opus 4a)	
U	CH	Romance for Oboe and Piano	2001	For Grace Jackson, granddaughter	
U	PD	Variations on Coe Fen (piano duet)	2001	For Elizabeth Dakers – in memoriam	
129	L	Mass of St Francis (no creed)	2001	For Ampleforth	
130	L	Mass for Salisbury	2001	With brass quintet and organ	
131	PS	Song on May morning (second setting)	2002	For the Easingwold Singers, see also Opus 58	
132	O	Fantasia Campanulatica/ Campaniculata	2002	For Douglas Bell aet 70	
133	A	Thanks be to the Lord	2002	Introit for the Thanksgiving Service after the restoration of the city centre, Manchester Cathedral, 24 July attended by the Queen	
134	A	Song of Mary (Mary Holtby)	2002	For John Scarfe, aet 65 (Buckfast Abbey 17 May 2003)	
135	PS	Ode to a Pill	2002	For John Scarfe, aet 65	
136	A	Adam lay y bounden	2002	Sewanee University	
137	O+	Cavatina for bassoon and organ	2002	For Benedict Coffin (including tune in Opus 1)	
138	L	Eight Latin motets	2002	For Ampleforth Abbey	
139	PS	The shell (James Stephens)	2003	For the Cantoris Chamber Choir	
140	O	Organ Sonata 5	2003	'To the honour of Percy Whitlock. First performed by the composer in St Stephen's Church, Bournemouth, 5 May 2003'	Banks
141	O	Acklam Pieces:	2010		Banks
-1	O	Fanfare *Dixoniana*	2009		
-2	O	Improvisation on *Irish*	2003	For the centenary of Pilrig Church organ, Edinburgh	
-3	O	Prelude on Kettlebaston	2003	For Gordon Pullin's recording *Favourite Hymns*	
-4	O	Susanni scherzetto	1994	For David Swale aet 80, 21st February 2008 (revised 2008)	
-5	O	Aria Celtica (Slane)	2005	For John Scarfe at St James, Teignmouth, 17 March 2007	
-6	O	Prelude on *Malton*	2007	AB(J)G - for Angela (sister)	
-7	O	Sarabande	2008	For Paul (brother)	
-8	O	Reverie on a theme of Ravel	2009	Dedicated to Roger Nichols	
142	C	Agnus Dei for Mass in C minor (Mozart) K427	2003	For the St Sepulchre Festival, May	
143	A	There comes a galley laden	2003	Carol for the NHS annual carol service in York Minster 25th anniversary: December 2003	Banks
144	A	What sweeter music (Herrick)	2003	Carol for Richard Darke and the choir of Knaresborough Parish Church, October	
145	O+	Sonata for trumpet and organ	2003	For Philip Lowe and Langley Parish Church, Lancs	
146	A	Tune me, O Lord (Christina Rosetti)	2004	Anthem for All Saints Church, Worcester Mass.	

Title	Contents	Year	Label	Cat. No.
The Father Willis at St George's Church, Gateshead	Vierne, Bach, Nardini, Statham, FJ, Mozart, Guilmant, Sowerby	2004	Amphion	PHI CD 194
Organists of the 1950s (Vol. 1) [with six other players]	From the 1952 radio series 'Organ Music from British Cathedrals and Abbeys'. FJ spoken introduction (Whitlock, Franck)	2004	Amphion	PHI CD 200
Organists of the 1950s (Vol. 2) [with three other players]	From the 1957 International Congress. FJ (Westminster Abbey - S Wesley, Peeters, Sowerby)	2004	Amphion	PHI CD 201
Organ Music from the Isle of Purbeck	Silas, Smart, Nicholson, Willan, FJ, M Camidge, Festing, Widor, Salomé, Guilmant	2004	Amphion	PHI CD 213
Choral Music from York Minster (The Alpha Collection No.6)	Directed by FJ, Geoffrey Coffin (organ): Byrd, Gray, Walford Davies, FJ, Leighton, Tallis, Vaughan Williams	2007	Priory (re-issue of Abbey 721)	PRAB 105
Great Cathedral Organs of England	Cocker, Dubois, Gigout, Mulet	2008	Regis	RRC 1304
Organ Classics from York Minster	Cocker, Purcell, FJ, Leighton, Dubois, Guilmant, Gigout, Mulet, Boëllmann, Franck, Vierne, Widor	2008	Griffin	
Music from Castle Howard [with other artists]	Ravel, Boëllmann, Mayerl (organ and piano)	2009	Amphion	PHI CD 225
Francis Jackson Live	York Minster, recorded 1947-2012: JS Bach, Vierne, Stanford, FJ [Fantasy & Fugue Clerkenwell, Sonatas 5/6, Fanfare, Impromptu, Improvisation], Nares, Bairstow, Noble, Moore, Statham, Thalben-Ball	2012	Amphion	PHI CD 227